VULNERABILITY IN RESISTANCE

VULNERABILITY
IN RESISTANCE

....

Judith Butler, Zeynep Gambetti,

and Leticia Sabsay, editors

....

DUKE UNIVERSITY PRESS

Durham and London

2016

Typeset in Minion Pro by Westchester Publishing Services

Library of Congress Cataloging-in-Publication Data
Names: Butler, Judith, [date] editor. | Gambetti, Zeynep, editor. |
Sabsay, Leticia, editor.
Title: Vulnerability in resistance / Judith Butler, Zeynep
Gambetti, and Leticia Sabsay, editors.
Description: Durham : Duke University Press, 2016. |
Includes bibliographical references and index.
Identifiers: LCCN 2016021707 (print)
LCCN 2016023798 (ebook)
ISBN 9780822362791 (hardcover : alk. paper)
ISBN 9780822362906 (pbk. : alk. paper)
ISBN 9780822373490 (e-book)
Subjects: LCSH: Feminist theory. | Social movements—
Philosophy. | Identity politics. | Sex role—Political aspects. |
Vulnerability (Personality trait) | Power (Social sciences)
Classification: LCC HQ1190.V86 2016 (print) |
LCC HQ1190 (ebook) | DDC 305.4201—dc23
LC record available at https://lccn.loc.gov/2016021707

Cover art: Graffiti by Ghadeer Wagdy and Fagr Soliman.
Photo credit: Mia Gröndahl (from the Women on Walls
project).

CONTENTS

ILLUSTRATIONS

ACKNOWLEDGMENTS

The "Rethinking Vulnerability and Resistance: Feminism and Social Change" workshop took place at Columbia University's Global Center in Istanbul, Turkey, September 16–20, 2013. We would like to thank Marianne Hirsch and the Women Creating Change initiative at Columbia University's Center for the Study of Social Difference for organizing that workshop, which made this book possible. We are also indebted to the Mellon Foundation award to Judith Butler for Distinguished Scholarship in the Humanities that helped to support the event. Our enduring appreciation goes to Ipek Cem-Taha, Rana Zincir, Verda Özer, and Neslihan Berkman of the Istanbul Global Center for accommodating us and coordinating the venue's heavy schedule. We thank Vina Tran from the Center for the Study of Social Difference for coordinating the event and for all her assistance during that week. We also thank Amanda Armstrong for her invaluable assistance in preparing the manuscript. We would like to acknowledge Nacira Guénif-Souilimas of Paris XIII University, who was an invaluable interlocutor at the workshop. The production staff at Duke University Press has also been enormously helpful throughout this process, and we thank them for all their support. We are most thankful to Ayelet Even-Nur and Saniya Taher for their help with copy-editing, and to Eileen Quam, whose index is invaluable.

This project was assisted through various highly appreciated forms of social and intellectual conversations: we thank Banu Karaca from Sabancı University and the anticensorship organization Siyah Bant, Dilan Okçuoğlu from Queens University, Bade Okçuoğlu from the LGBTQI organization Lambda Istanbul, Özlem Aslan from *Feminist Approaches in Culture and Politics*, Zelal Yalçın from Mor Çatı Women's Shelter, Özlem Yasak from the Diyarbakır Democratic Independent Women's Movement, Müge Sökmen from Metis Publishers and PEN Turkey, Sezen Yalçın from the Socialist Feminist Collective, Volkan Yılmaz from the Social Policy, Sexual Identity and Orientations Research Association, and Nazan Üstündağ from Boğaziçi University, for sharing their views and political struggles with us. We are also thankful to

Vuslat Doğan Sabancı of Sabancı Holding for generously inviting us to meet other feminist activists and academics in Istanbul during our stay there.

The workshop took place a few months after the Occupy Gezi movement in Turkey, when the spirit of the uprising was still alive. We were trying to make sense of those events, registering both the exhilaration and the sorrow. So we would like to conclude by extending our gratitude to those bodies on the streets who embodied the promise of an alternative society where vulnerability would cease to be a curse and would instead constitute the very ground for modes of solidarity from below.

Introduction

JUDITH BUTLER, ZEYNEP GAMBETTI,

AND LETICIA SABSAY

This volume takes up the challenge to reformulate two fundamental concepts—vulnerability and resistance—beyond two assumptions pervasive in several popular and theoretical discourses. The first holds that vulnerability is the opposite of resistance and cannot be conceived as part of that practice; the second supposes that vulnerability requires and implies the need for protection and the strengthening of paternalistic forms of power at the expense of collective forms of resistance and social transformation.

Our point of departure is to call into question through the analysis of concrete contexts the basic assumption that vulnerability and resistance are mutually oppositional, even as the opposition is found throughout in mainstream politics as well as prominent strands of feminist theory. Dominant conceptions of vulnerability and of action presuppose (and support) the idea that paternalism is the site of agency, and vulnerability, understood only as victimization and passivity, invariably the site of inaction. In order to provide an alternative to such frameworks, we ask what in our analytic and political frameworks would change if vulnerability were imagined as one of the conditions of the very possibility of resistance. What follows when we conceive of resistance as drawing from vulnerability as a resource of vulnerability, or as part of the very meaning or action of resistance itself? What implications does this perspective have for thinking about the subject of political agency? What ideas of the political subject, and political subjectivity, emerge outside, or against, this binary? These preliminary questions lead us to others, where our initial conceptions must be rethought: How are vulnerability and bodily exposure related, especially when we think about the exposure of the body to power? Is that exposure both perilous and enabling? What is the relation between resistance and agency? In what ways is vulnerability bound up with the problem of precarity?

As we know, there is always something both risky and true in claiming that women or other socially disadvantaged groups are especially vulnerable. On the one hand, we very much want to point it out where it exists. Yet one might conclude that women are in a powerless position and, by implication, that men are always in a powerful one. As a result, feminist activism may turn to paternalistic political and social institutions, investing them with the power to realize feminist goals.[1] In other instances, women struggle to establish practices and institutions that seek to provide protection, or to rescue (always already othered) women, which, albeit not necessarily linked to paternalistic powers, do still enforce paternalistic logics, or rely on figures of victimhood that assume that those who are vulnerable are therefore without agency, or can be summarized by categories that figure them as essentially without agency.[2] Yet there are other initiatives that, while refusing these forms of politics that amount to the stigmatization and the further disempowerment of the women they are said to protect or save, do not dismiss the induced vulnerability to which many women are exposed and try to offer alternative resources for self-empowerment, collective agency, and protection. These can include feminist forms of self-defense, networks and shelters for battered women, and grass-roots modes of organizing within civil society or outside its established terms.

By itself, the discourse on vulnerability can support any version of politics and has no special claim to supporting a politics on the Left, or a politics for feminism. It can describe the vulnerability of those in power against the forces of resistance by those who are seeking a new political order. Moreover, the discourse on vulnerability can lead to objectionable ontological claims about the constitutive vulnerability of women's bodies, claims we would doubtless want to reject in favor of a social and political account about how vulnerability is produced and distributed. That latter view would be compelled to point out that women—and here we seek to rely on a gender category at once inclusive and open-ended—are the ones who suffer most from poverty and illiteracy, two defining global features of the oppression of women. So the question that emerged for this group, and formed one of our areas of contention, has been this: How do we think about feminist modes of agency, and how can we re-think them in light of global conditions and emerging possibilities of global alliance? And though we concur on this as a task that feminism must take up, we are in different ways engaged in queer, trans, antiracist, anti-authoritarian, and anti-austerity struggles. The terms we examine take on very specific meanings under neoliberal and austerity conditions when the state structures of social democracy and institutions of social welfare are losing their own resources and standing, thus exposing more populations to homelessness, unemployment, illiteracy, and inadequate health care. How, then, is the political demand to address these issues to be directed toward those institutions that should be responding to these conditions, at the same time that we seek to resist the models of power represented by those institutions? Are we stuck in the situation in which there are two opposing alternatives, paternalism and victimization? And in accepting those alternatives, do we not reinstate a gendered opposition?

In some forms of feminism, vulnerability has been regarded as a value in feminist theory and politics. Feminists of different strands have long argued for a relational subject as a way to contest liberal forms of individualism primarily, implicated as they are in capitalist concepts of self-interest and masculinist fantasies of sovereign mastery. Whereas some feminists have sought to establish vulnerability and care as values which are specific to women and to which women have special access, we are making no claims about the capacities or dispositions of women as a group. Indeed, what follows is a wide-ranging feminist approach to questions of power and agency that prove to be quite central to some forms of resistance today.

Our common point of departure is derived from critical feminist social theory that seeks to overcome uncritically accepted versions of the mind/body distinction and its reliance on associations of activity with masculinity and passivity with femininity, in order to show that the received definitions of vulnerability as passive (in need of active protection) and agency as active (based on a disavowal of the human creature as "affected") requires a thorough going critique. In our view, the focus on vulnerability is not intended to validate conventional ways of distinguishing between men and women (or even to validate that binary as a mode of framing an analysis), so the conclusion is, once again, not to make ontological claims about women, nor to underscore their singular ethical dispositions. Those modes of stabilizing gender division through generalized forms of differentiation do not further the task of rethinking modes of resistance. Whatever differential distribution of attributes we may find in some locations depends in part on the lens through which we see, the epistemic grid laid into that lens, and the operative norms of gender operating in the description.

As much as we can, and do, track the way that power operates to establish the disenfranchised as "vulnerable populations," it remains imperative to critically examine the logic of disavowal by which vulnerability becomes projected and distanced from prevailing ideas of agency and mastery. Psychoanalytic feminists have remarked that the masculine positions are effectively built through a denial of their own vulnerability. This denial or disavowal requires one to forget one's own vulnerability and project, displace, and localize it elsewhere. Such a mechanism of disavowal operates within the scene of power. In fact, it can work to exacerbate vulnerability (as a way of achieving power) or to disavow it (also as a way of achieving power). For instance, when nations advertise their hypervulnerability to new immigrants, or men openly fear that they are now the victims of feminism, the recourse to "vulnerability" in such instances can become the basis for a policy that seeks to exclude or contain women and minorities, as when the vulnerability of "white people" constructs black people as a threat to their existence.

The argument about disavowal has to be attended to carefully. On the one hand, if we are interested in how vulnerability is socially produced and managed, then we may seem to be saying that vulnerability is the effect of social power. On the other hand, if we claim that vulnerability has a purely ontological status, it seems that we accept a presocial account of vulnerability, and that opens up a new set of theoretical and political problems. So if we argue instead that vulnerability emerges as part of social relations, even as a feature of social relations, then we make (a) a general claim according to which vulnerability ought to be understood as relational and social, and (b) a very specific claim according to which it always appears in the context of specific social and historical relations that call to be analyzed concretely.

The language that we use to describe vulnerability and its disavowal presumes that there is "an already there-ness" to the vulnerability, or that denial is secondary, a cover-up, and so always somewhat false and frail. We can speak of individuals who deny their own vulnerability, or whole nations. Though individuals and groups are different, the logics that condition and reproduce disavowal cut across that difference. When vulnerability is projected onto another, it seems as if the first subject is fully divested of vulnerability, having expelled it externally onto the other. When vulnerability is owned as an exclusive predicate of one subject and invulnerability attributed to another, a different kind of disavowal takes place. Indeed, asymmetry and disavowal work together. Such strategies can work either way: "others" may be exposed to vulnerability as a way of shoring up power, but vulnerability can also be claimed by those who seek to rationalize the subjugation of minorities. Such strategies of claiming vulnerability on the part of the powerful become all the more complicated, and paradoxical, when norms of white heterosexuality are considered "under attack" by LGBTQ communities, or when feminism is figured as a castrating "threat" to ostensibly vulnerable men. If the concept of vulnerability always operates within a tactical field, how do theoretical affirmations of vulnerability enter into that field? Can such affirmations ever avert the risk of being appropriated by paternalism? At stake is whether this dialectical inversion—which can, at one time, assert the hypervulnerability of those in dominant positions of power and, at another, rely on the presumptive invulnerability of those with power—can be refuted. Further, can that refutation give way to a notion of bodily vulnerability linked with practices of resistance in the service of social and political justice?

In Marxist analysis, the politics of redistribution pertains to goods, and we see water and land rights activism asking for equal distribution of such resources. It may sound odd to refer to an unequal distribution of vulnerability, but perhaps there is no other way to understand the condition of contemporary precarity. That unequal distribution often works in tandem with the management of "vulnerable populations" within discourse and policy. Often social movements, human rights advocates, and institutions refer to precarious or vulnerable populations, for whom political strategies are accordingly devised to ameliorate conditions of exposure and precarity. Does that way of naming a population extend or ameliorate conditions of precarity? Do we lose the sense of those operations of power that differentially assign vulnerability when we take such assignments for granted in launching the analyses that we do? Do we need to understand through what mode of power vulnerable populations are formed as such? While we could think of those forms of institutionalized violence that render certain populations disposable as a form of necropolitics,[3] those humanitarian governmental practices that designate them "in need of protection" not only negate the capacity of those declared vulnerable to act politically, but also expand biopolitical forms of regulation and control.[4]

When such redistributive strategies abound, then other populations, usually the ones helping to orchestrate or effect the processes of redistribution, posit themselves as invulnerable, if not impermeable, and without any such needs of protection. In order to counter this untenable framework, vulnerability and invulnerability have to be understood as politically produced, unequally distributed through and by a differential operation of power. In following this path, our discussion moves beyond the human rights framework in which the positing of "vulnerable populations" can become a way of foreclosing or devaluing modes of collective resistance among those designated as vulnerable.[5] The significance of human rights would not be negated within such a framework, but human rights would not operate as the presumptive framework for such discussions.

We would like to recontextualize the discussion of vulnerability in such a way that its links with paternalism or even with discourses of victimization are critically ameliorated, precisely to make room for an analysis of the role of vulnerability in strategies of resistance. In thinking vulnerability and resistance together, we hope to develop a different conception of embodiment and sociality within fields of contemporary power, one that engages object worlds, including both built and destroyed environments, as well as social forms of interdependency and individual or collective agency. The strategies of resistance on which we propose to focus involve a rethinking of human acts and infrastructural mobilizations, including barricades, hunger strikes, the improvised character of informal groups at the checkpoint, modes of deliberate exposure, and forms of art and artistic intervention in public space that involve "laying bare" and opposing forms of power. The wager of this volume is that one of the main reasons why there is opposition to (if not an outright denial of) vulnerability is that vulnerability has not been adequately related to the existing practices of resistance. Such a formulation involves thinking as well the psychoanalytic and political dimensions of resistance, taking into account its different registers, from the practices of the self, to collective, individual, subjective, or social practices.

Further, we propose to consider resistance in a new light in order to differentiate its strategies from notions of neoliberal resilience that cover over the structural conditions of accelerated precarity, inequality, statelessness, and occupation. Our task is to resist the neutralization of practices of social transformation that follows when the discourse of protection becomes hegemonic, undermining and effacing varied forms of popular resistance or political agency. Our aim is to expand our political vocabulary to meet the challenge to think about modes of vulnerability that inform modes of resistance, and to "resist" those frameworks that seek to underplay or refuse forms of political agency developed under conditions of duress, without presuming, as some accounts of resilience tend to do, that they always prove effective.

Drawing from recent demonstrations that mobilize important forms of embodied resistance as ways of calling attention to the unjust effects or austerity, precarity, neoliberalism, authoritarian control, and securitarian politics, we track the emergence of a vocabulary that breaks with masculinist models of autonomy without essentializing the feminine or idealizing vulnerability as an ultimate value. The point is to show that vulnerability is part of resistance, made manifest by new forms of embodied political interventions and modes of alliance that are characterized by interdependency and public action. These hold the promise of developing new modes of collective agency that do not deny vulnerability as a resource and that aspire to equality, freedom, and justice as their political aims.

Although dedicated to thinking about these common problems, each of the authors represented in this volume undertook different tasks of cultural translation—we came at the issue from very different geopolitical locations and through different modes of theoretical reflection.[6] Whereas each contributor has a distinct view, each of us also made an effort to participate in what Zeynep Gambetti called "plural and collective thinking." Our collaborative work on this topic required a practice of translation that sought to traverse, without denying, the distances among languages, disciplines, theoretical and political genealogies, and areas of research, among academic work, the arts and art criticism, and activism. Not least of our tasks was to mediate among different political and academic tonalities, logics, and lexicons, striving to find a polyphonic mode of making sense of the shifting problematic before us. If we were able finally to move beyond the conventional binary that governs the relationship between vulnerability and resistance, that effort was made possible by our commitment to attend to these different modalities of thought, the different political space-times with which they engage, and the formulations of the political field within which they operate and intervene. Although in some ways the contributors to this volume take these precepts as a common point of departure, their chapters resonate with one another not because they came to adhere to any one language or theory. On the contrary: questions of self-determination, hegemony, mourning, violence, memory, occupation, public demonstrations, representation, the visual field and the visual arts, or freedom pose different challenges to the task of political thinking within a framework that does not oppose vulnerability to resistance. The exchanges among the authors here are reflected in their finished essays, showing how these concepts work or vary when reflected in different registers, moving from the individual scholarship to collaborative forms of making knowledge, all refracted by varying geopolitical conditions and concerns.

The essays in this volume draw from recent events in Turkey and Greece, but also focus on ongoing political struggles of women and minorities in the face of state violence, antiwar and antioccupation activists, struggles at the level of cultural representation and aesthetic practice, and oppositional dilemmas emerging within anti-austerity politics. They do not claim to represent a full global field; rather, they represent the partial and perspectival offerings of politically engaged scholars working in various regions. Judith Butler's contribution seeks to establish the important ways that vulnerability, reconceived as bodily exposure, is part of the very meaning and practice of resistance. Construing bodily vulnerability as induced by social and material relations of dependency, she shows how popular gatherings in public spaces enact the demand to end precarity by exposing these bodies' vulnerability to failing infrastructural conditions. Zeynep Gambetti revisits the notions of exposure and popular protest, but this time through an Arendtian theory of agonistic individuation. She evokes the Occupy Gezi protests of 2013 to illustrate the intricate connection between acting and suffering, as a result of which social identities and political alignments are destabilized through pluralistic encounters with others. In her critical consideration of a different set of concepts and practices, Sarah Bracke foregrounds how the neoliberal category of "resilience" functions as a governmental tactic aimed at managing resistance and concealing destitution. She argues that "resilience" constitutes a new moral code that works through gendered notions of subjectivity and agency to produce the idea of a subject willing to cope with conditions of increasing precarization. One other major theoretical dilemma is addressed by Marianne Hirsch's chapter. Hirsch brings notions of vulnerability and resistance to bear on theories of trauma and memory that often falter on the question of how it is possible to identify with the pain of others without appropriating that pain. She focuses on the work of several artists and writers who mobilize vulnerability as a way to respond to and take responsibility for traumatic and violent histories. The Occupy Gezi protests and the theme of memory reappear in Başak Ertür's contribution on barricades as a resource of resistance. Ertür understands forms of barricading with human and nonhuman resources as forms of countermonumentalization and bricolage whose strength might be found precisely in their transient and vulnerable structure. She argues that the barricades simultaneously operate as repertoires of collective action and as forms of reattunement to vulnerability.

Elena Loizidou's chapter on dreams and the political subject offers an alternative consideration of involuntary forms of longing as crucial to the understanding of political action, and thus revises our understanding of the political actor as one who exercises wakeful mastery in the course of acting. Can we understand resistance without the sensual domain in which

mastery no longer controls love, dreams, and the arts so essential to civil disobedience or other forms of resistance? Considering the artwork of Mona
Hatoum, Elena Tzelepis in turn asks what grammar of vulnerable belonging
is produced in the wake of forcible expulsion and diasporic existence for Palestinians. Is there a potential for resistance opened up by art that focuses on
questions of loss and finitude? Provoked by such questions, Tzelepis reflects
on how Hatoum's feminist aesthetics bring forth a bodily representation of
vulnerability. Turning to the occupied West Bank, Rema Hammami's chapter
focuses on the struggle and strategy of Palestinian activism that happens within
the daily labor of sustaining existence. In contrast to the concept of "protective
accompaniment" popularized by human rights discourse, it underscores those
forms of connection and alliance that are based less on the need for protection
or, indeed, philanthropy than on informal networks of solidarity. The question
of the differential visibility of violence in occupied zones foregrounds Hammami's exploration of forms of resistance under conditions of hyperprecarity.
In her contribution, Nükhet Sirman focuses on another precaritized population, the Kurds in Turkey. By engaging with the Kurdish struggle for political
freedom, she considers the salience of the figure of Antigone for thinking about
Kurdish women's vulnerability to Turkish state violence. She highlights the dis-
similarities between Turkish and Kurdish feminist discourses and shows how
the latter produce a new form of knowledge that accounts simultaneously for
the victimization of Kurdish women and their achievements as guerrilla fighters. Meltem Ahıska's critical consideration of the "Violence against Women"
campaign in Turkey also questions the language of victimization. Ahıska argues
that the efforts to "humanize" battered women establish their substitutabil-
ity and anonymity, such that "women" come to represent death and victimhood anonymously. She argues for a mode of resistance against this form of
"humanization" that would counter the conflation of women's sexuality with
injurability and death. In a quite different geographical context, Elsa Dorlin
visits a similar yet different problem. Dorlin's essay offers a critical analysis of
how the "face" as an ethical category undergoes a political transvaluation in
France. Situating "unveiling" as a requirement of French civility, Dorlin shows
how mandatory hypervisibility informs the debates on the *niqab* and contemporary surveillance. She explores how the figure of the "mask" connects
with forms of resistance that are prefigured in vigilante feminist writings. The
double valence of vulnerability is also examined in Athena Athanasiou's considering of agonism as a nonsovereign form of power. The Serbian Women in
Black movement is the focus of her analysis of a form of resistance that relies

on what she calls agonistic mourning. She shows how the not-being-at-home-with-itself of mourning poses a challenge to the ordinances of the "affirmation versus mourning" structural opposition. Finally, using a different conception of agonism and antagonism, Leticia Sabsay's contribution poses a set of critical questions to theories of vulnerability and the contemporary discourse on affect to see how far they are compatible with the theory of hegemony and a broader concept of the political. She suggests permeability as the marker of subjectivity as a transindividual way of being in the world and, drawing on Bakhtin, offers a way to think about the relational subject in conjunction with hegemonic articulation.

As these chapter descriptions suggest, we differ on issues such as agonism and antagonism, how best to think about vulnerability, and which versions of resistance ought to be foregrounded. What strikes us as most important, however, is that vulnerability and resistance enter the picture differently depending on the context and the political question we pose. Our regions vary (Greece, Turkey, Palestine, France, Europe, the United States) and so, too, do our theories (hegemony, agonism, performativity, Marxism, feminism). The terms, vulnerability and resistance, are implicated not only in one another, but also in the settings that activate their relations. This multiplicity does not undo our common aim; rather, it facilitates and furthers the aliveness of this exchange. We are aware of the many sites we could not touch on within the framework of this volume, including the prison industry, refugees, epidemics, and various forms of violence, including state-sponsored racism. We trust that this volume will continue in a perpetual state of becoming, so that what we offer here is not a "result" of our collaboration, but a series of provocations for further thought. We were ourselves provoked by the events in Turkey in 2013, but our questions changed in the course of the journey. One of the principles of collaboration is that each member is affected by the other, becoming transformed in the process, and constituting now a provisional yet promising form of textual belonging in which all the rough edges matter.

Notes

1 Nancy Fraser's "Feminism, Capitalism and the Cunning of History" makes an appeal to women's movements to reconsider calling the state back in. But many feminists are highly critical of state institutions that perpetrate white heterosexual middle-class supremacy in dealing with domestic violence, gender inequality, or

legal justice. Among the most powerful of these critiques are Beth Richie's *Arrested Justice* and Angela Davis's *Abolition Democracy*. Martha Nussbaum's capabilities approach has also been criticized for implicitly requiring paternalistic intervention and regulation. Cf. Claassen, "Capability Paternalism," and S. Charusheela, "Social Analysis and the Capabilities Approach," for a review of charges of institutional and cultural paternalism inherent in Nussbaum's framework. Martha Fineman's ontological approach to vulnerability as a universal and constant characteristic of all human beings, and therefore the ground of a reconceived subject of rights, may lead to forms of state paternalism as well (see Fineman, "The Vulnerable Subject"). Inspired by Fineman's perspective, the "Vulnerability and the Human Condition" Initiative, hosted at Emory University, is dedicated to envisioning models of state support and legal protection on the grounds of subjects' vulnerability conceived as a human feature.

2 For a critical review of these trends, see D'Cruze and Rao, "Violence and the Vulnerabilities of Gender."

3 Mbembe, "Necropolitics."

4 Didier Fassin offers a complex and nuanced understanding of the relationship between the Foucauldian notion of biopolitical regulation and humanitarianism. Fassin highlights that while the notion of biopolitics refers to the technologies of government and normalization of populations, humanitarianism also contributes to the production of differentiated meanings and values of human lives (see Fassin, *Humanitarian Reason*).

5 Cf. the seminal text by Pithouse, "Producing the Poor," and a more recent critique of the "fight against poverty" by Cornwall and Fujita, "Ventriloquising 'the Poor'?"

6 This volume is the collaborative result of a week-long seminar, "Rethinking Vulnerability and Resistance: Feminism and Social Change," organized by Judith Butler and Zeynep Gambetti at the Columbia University Global Center in Istanbul in 2013. The seminar was sponsored by the "Women Creating Change" initiative housed in the Center for the Study of Social Difference at Columbia University.

CHAPTER I

Rethinking Vulnerability and Resistance

JUDITH BUTLER

We know that those who gather on the street or in public domains where police are present are always at risk of detention and arrest, but also forcible handling, even death. So when we consider police violence against protestors—the killing of forty-three students assembled for a protest in Ayotzinapa, Mexico, in September 2014 is a flagrant example—it is already more than clear that those who gather to resist various forms of state and economic power are taking a risk with their own bodies, exposing themselves to possible harm.

That formulation seems true enough: vulnerability is enhanced by assembling. But perhaps we need to rethink this sequence that gives narrative structure to our understanding of the relationship between vulnerability and resistance. First you resist, and then you are confronted with your vulnerability either in relation to police power or to those who show up to oppose your political stance. Yet vulnerability emerges earlier, prior to any gathering, and this becomes especially true when people demonstrate to oppose the precarious conditions in which they live. That condition of precarity indexes a vulnerability that precedes the one that people encounter quite graphically on the street. If we also say that the vulnerability to dispossession, poverty, insecurity, and harm that constitutes a precarious position in the world itself leads to resistance, then it seems we reverse the sequence: we are first vulnerable and then overcome that vulnerability, at least provisionally, through acts of resistance.

Of course, it will be important to establish a more precise relationship between vulnerability and precarity (they are not the same), but let us consider as a clear example modes of resistance that emerge in opposition to failing infrastructure. The dependency on infrastructure for a livable life seems clear, but when infrastructure fails, and fails consistently, how do we understand that condition of life? We have found that that on which we are dependent is, in fact, not there for us, which means we are left without support. Without shelter, we are vulnerable to weather, cold, heat, and disease, perhaps also to assault, hunger, and violence. It was not as if we were, as creatures, not vulnerable before when infrastructure was working, and then when infrastructure fails, our vulnerability comes to the fore. When movements against homelessness emerge, the unacceptable character of that vulnerability (in the sense of exposure to harm) is made clear. But a question still remains: does vulnerability still remain an important part of that mode of resistance? Does resistance require overcoming vulnerability? Or do we mobilize our vulnerability?

Consider that a movement may be galvanized for the very purpose of establishing adequate infrastructure, or keeping adequate infrastructure from being destroyed. We can think about mobilizations in the shantytowns or townships of South Africa, Kenya, Pakistan, the temporary shelters constructed along the borders of Europe, but also the *barrios* of Venezuela, the *favelas* of Brazil, or the *barracas* of Portugal. Such spaces are populated by groups of people, including immigrants, squatters, and/or Roma, who are struggling precisely for running and clean water, working toilets, sometimes a closed door on public toilets, paved streets, paid work, and necessary provisions.[1] The street, for instance, is not just the basis or platform for a political demand, but an infrastructural good. And so when assemblies gather in public spaces in order to fight against the decimation of infrastructural goods—for instance, to protest austerity measures that would undercut public education, libraries, transit systems, and roads—we find that the very platform for such a politics is one of the items on the political agenda. Sometimes a mobilization happens precisely in order to create, keep, or open the platform for political expression itself. The material conditions for speech and assembly are part of what we are speaking and assembling about. We have to assume the infrastructural goods for which we are fighting, but if the infrastructural conditions for politics are themselves decimated, so too are the assemblies that depend on them. At such a point, the condition of the political is one of the goods for which political assembly takes place—this might be the double meaning of "the infrastructural" under conditions in which public goods are increasingly dismantled by privatization, neoliberalism (the United States), accelerating forms of economic inequality (Greece), the antidemocratic tactics of authoritarian rule (Turkey), or the violent combination of government and cartel interests (Mexico).[2]

I wish to point out that even as public resistance leads to vulnerability, and vulnerability (the sense of "exposure" implied by precarity) leads to resistance, vulnerability is not exactly overcome by resistance, but becomes a potentially effective mobilizing force in political mobilizations. In effect, the demand for infrastructure is a demand for a certain kind of inhabitable ground, and its meaning and force arise precisely when that ground gives way. So the street cannot be taken for granted as the space of appearance, to use Hannah Arendt's phrase—the space of politics—since there is, as we know, a struggle to establish that very ground. And Arendt is at least partially right when she claims that the space of appearance comes into being at the moment of political action. That is a romantic notion of an embodied performative speech act, to be sure, since in any time or place that we act, the space of appearance for the political comes into being. It is not always true, of course—we can try to act collectively, and no space of appearance is established, and that usually has to do with the absence of media, or particular ways that the public sphere is structured to keep such actions from appearing (e.g., zoning, permits, rules against congregating). Arendt clearly presumes that the material conditions for gathering are separate from any particular space of appearance. But if politics is oriented toward the making and preserving of such conditions, then it seems that the space of appearance is not ever fully separable from questions of infrastructure and architecture, as Arendt herself clearly acknowledged.[3] Although Arendt could not have formulated the relationship between contemporary media and the public sphere, for us, infrastructure now includes not only public media, but all forms of media through which, and within which, the space of appearance is constituted. This would include forms of media that constitute, mediate, and monitor the public. Media can function as part of "infrastructural support" when it facilitates modes of solidarity and establishes new spatio-temporal dimensions of the public sphere, including not only those who can appear within the visual images of the public, but those who are, through coercion, fear, or necessity, living outside the reach of the visual frame.

What implications does this notion of supported political action have for thinking about vulnerability and resistance? We are already familiar with the idea that freedom can be exercised only if there is enough support for the exercise of freedom, a material condition that enters into the act that it makes possible. Indeed, when we think about the embodied subject who exercises speech or moves through public space, across borders, it is usually presumed to be one who is already free to speak and move without threat of imprisonment or deportation or loss of life. Either that subject is endowed with that freedom as in inherent power, or that subject is presumed to live in a public space where open and supported movement is possible. The very term "mobilization" depends on an operative sense of mobility, itself a right, one that many people cannot take for granted. For the body to move, it must usually have a surface of some kind, and it must have at its disposal whatever technical supports allow for movement to take place. So the pavement and the street are already to be understood as requirements of the body as it exercises its rights of mobility. No one moves without a supportive environment and set of technologies. And when those environments start to fall apart or are emphatically unsupportive, we are left to "fall" in some ways, and our very capacity to exercise most basic rights is imperiled.

And we could certainly make a list of how this idea of a body, supported yet acting, supported *and* acting, is at work implicitly or explicitly in any number of political movements: struggles for food and shelter, protection from injury and destruction, the right to work, affordable health care, protection from police violence and imprisonment, from war, or illness, mobilizations against austerity and precarity, authoritarianism and inequality. So, on one level, we are asking about the implicit idea of the body at work in certain kinds of political demands and mobilizations; on another level, we are trying to find out how mobilizations presuppose a body that requires support. In many of the public assemblies that draw people who understand themselves to be in precarious positions, the demand to end precarity is enacted publically by those who expose their vulnerability to failing infrastructural conditions; there is plural and performative bodily resistance at work that shows how bodies are being acted on by social and economic policies that are decimating livelihoods. But these bodies, in showing this precarity, are also resisting these very powers; they enact a form of resistance that presupposes vulnerability of a specific kind, and opposes precarity. What is the conception of the body here, and how do we understand this form of resistance?

If we make the matter individual, we can say that every single body has a certain right to food and shelter, freedom to move and breathe protected from violence. Although we universalize in such a statement ("every" body has this right), we also particularize, understanding the body as discrete, as an individual matter, and that individual body is significantly shaped by a norm of what the body is, and how it ought to be conceptualized. Of course that seems quite obviously right, but consider that this idea of the individual bodily subject of rights might fail to capture the sense of vulnerability, exposure, even dependency, that is presupposed by the right itself and corresponds, I would suggest, with an alternative view of the body. In other words, if we accept that part of what a body is (and this is for the moment an ontological claim) is its dependency on other bodies and networks of support, then we are suggesting that it is not altogether right to conceive of individual bodies as completely distinct from one another. Of course, neither are they blended into some amorphous social body, but if we conceptualize the political meaning of the human body without understanding those relations in which it lives and thrives, we fail to make the best possible case for the various political ends we seek to achieve. What I am suggesting is that it is not just that this or that body is bound up in a network of relations, but that the body, despite its clear boundaries, or perhaps precisely by virtue of those very boundaries, is defined by the relations that make its own life and action possible. As I will hope to show, we cannot understand bodily vulnerability outside this conception of social and material relations.

But we also undergo linguistic vulnerability, and in this sense who we are, even our ability to survive, depends on the language that sustains us.[4] One clear dimension of our vulnerability has to do with our exposure to name-calling and discursive categories in infancy and childhood—indeed, throughout the course of life. All of us are called names, and this kind of name-calling demonstrates an important dimension of the speech act. We do not only act through the speech act; speech acts also act on us. There is a distinct performative effect of having been named as this gender or another gender, as part of one nationality or a minority, or to find out that how you are regarded in any of these respects is summed up by a name that you yourself did not know and never chose. We can, and do, ask with the great nineteenth-century black feminist Sojourner Truth, "Am I that Name?"[5] How do we think about the force and effect of those names we are called before any of us emerge into language as speaking beings, prior to any capacity for a speech act of our own? Does speech act on us prior to our speaking, and if it did not act on us, if it were not actively working on us, could we speak at all? And perhaps it is not simply a matter of sequence: does speech continue to act on us at the very moment in which we speak, so that we may well think we are acting, but we are also acted on at that very same time?

Eve Sedgwick wrote about the relationship between performance and performativity in consequential ways, showing that speech acts deviated from their aims, very often producing consequences that were altogether unintended, and oftentimes quite felicitous.[6] For instance, one could take a marriage vow, and this act could then establish a public recognition of marriage which then allows, or opens up, a zone of possible sexuality that takes place quite under the radar, taking advantage precisely of its nonrecognizability. The marriage vow provides public cover for forms of sexual life that remain unrecognized, and happily so. In such cases, marriage organizes sexuality as we might expect, in conjugal and monogamous forms, but it also produces another zone of sexuality defined precisely by its lack of overt recognition in the public sphere. Sedgwick underscored the sense of how a speech act could veer away from its apparent aims, and this "deviation" was one sense of the word "queer," understood less as an identity than as a movement of thought and language contrary to accepted forms of authority, always deviating, and so opening up spaces for desire that would not always be openly recognized within established norms.

Discourses on gender seemed to create and circulate certain ideals of gender, generating those ideals. What we sometimes take to be natural essences or internal truths are ideals, phantasms, or norms that have taken hold of us in a deep and abiding way. So the ideals produced by a discourse—in this case, a set of gender ideals—can be inhabited in one's gestures and actions, even come to be understood to be essential to who we are. Indeed, we cannot cast off abiding and governing images, norms, and ideals such as these without losing a sense of who we are. That essential sense of who we are is to some extent the workings of a set of social norms. Having a sense of who we are "essentially" is not for that reason an argument for innate differences; arguments from innate-ness constitute only one form of essentialism, and one can have a sense of what is essential for one's life without exactly being an essentialist.

My early formulation that "gender is performative" became the basis for two quite contrary interpretations: the first is that we radically choose our genders; the second was that we are utterly determined by gender norms. Those wildly divergent responses meant that something had not quite been articulated and grasped about the dual dimensions of any account of performativity. For if language acts on us before we act, and continues acting in every instant in which we act, then we have to think about gender performativity first as "gender assignment"—all those ways in which we are, as it were, called a name, and gendered prior to understanding anything about how gender norms act on and shape us, and prior to our capacity to reproduce those norms in ways that we might choose. Choice, in fact, comes late in this process of performativity. And then second, following Sedgwick, we have to understand how deviations from those norms can and do take place, suggesting that something "queer" is at work at the heart of gender performativity, a queerness that is not so very different from the swerves taken by iterability in Derrida's account of the speech act as citational, but that takes on specific embodied and social meanings in Sedgwick's view.

So let us assume, then, that performativity describes both the processes of being acted on and the conditions and possibilities for acting, and that we cannot understand its operation without both of these dimensions. That norms act on us implies that we are susceptible to their action, vulnerable to a certain name-calling from the start. And this registers at a level that is prior to any possibility of volition. An understanding of gender assignment has to take up this field of an unwilled receptivity, susceptibility, and vulnerability, a way of being exposed to language prior to any possibility of forming or enacting a speech act. Norms such as these both require and institute certain forms of corporeal vulnerability without which their operation would not be thinkable. That is why we can, and do, describe the powerful citational force of gender norms as they are instituted and applied by medical, legal, and psychiatric institutions, and object to the effect they have on the formation and understanding of gender in pathological or criminal terms. Yet this very domain of susceptibility, this condition of being affected, is also where something queer can happen, where the norm is refused or revised, or where new formulations of gender begin. Although gender norms precede us and act on us (that is one sense of its enactment), we are obligated to reproduce them (and that is a second sense of its enactment). Precisely because something inadvertent and unexpected can happen in this realm of "being affected," we find forms of gender that break with mechanical patterns of repetition, deviating from, resignifying, and sometimes quite emphatically breaking those citational chains of gender normativity, making room for new forms of gendered life. The theory of gender performativity, as I understood it, never prescribed which gender performances were right, or more subversive, and which were wrong, and reactionary. The point was precisely to relax the coercive hold of norms on gendered life—which is not the same as transcending all norms—for the purposes of living a more livable life.

It seems important to distinguish here between two different actions of the norm. In the first case, the norm is interpellated, and it could be understood most easily in this context as the interpellating action of gender assignment. We are treated, hailed, and formed by social norms that precede us and that form the constraining context for whatever forms of agency we ourselves take on in time. We do not precisely overcome our formations, but we do veer from the apparent aims at times, and this means that finding a queer way and becoming an agent are somehow linked. But there is a second sense of norms, and those are not precisely counter to our sense of agency: they constitute the intersubjective and infrastructural conditions of a livable life. We hardly seek to overcome those social and material conditions of our lives, but we do seek to make them more just, more equal, and more enabling. In relation to both interpellating and infrastructural norms, we are embodied creatures who are to some extent exposed to what we are called and dependent on the structures that let us live. So whatever performative agency might mean, it cannot overcome these prior and constituting dimensions of social normativity. It is here, then, that I would identify both dependency and vulnerability as part of the performative account of agency. Indeed, the embodiment presupposed by both gender and performance is one that is dependent on institutional structures and broader social worlds. We cannot talk about a body without knowing what supports that body and what its relation to that support—or lack of support—might be. In this way, the body is less an entity than a relation, and it cannot be fully dissociated from the infrastructural and environmental conditions of its living. Thus, the dependency of human and other creatures on infrastructural support exposes a specific vulnerability that we have when we are unsupported, when those infrastructural conditions characterizing our social, political, and economic lives start to decompose, or when we find ourselves radically unsupported under conditions of precarity or under explicit conditions of threat.

Both performance studies and disability studies have offered the crucial insight that all action requires support and that even the most punctual and seemingly spontaneous act implicitly depends on an infrastructural condition that quite literally supports the acting body. This idea of "support" is quite important not only for the retheorization of the acting body, but for the broader politics of mobility: what architectural supports have to be in place for each of us to exercise a certain freedom of movement, one that is necessary in order to exercise the right to public assembly? In the same way we claim that the speech act depends on its social conditions and conventions, we can also say that the performance of gender more generally depends on its infrastructural and social conditions of support. This bears implications for a general account of embodied and social action, and also for understanding the bodily risks that women take walking on certain streets at night, assembling in public squares (the sexual assault would be a clear example), and trans people risk in walking on the street or gathering in public assemblies.

As I have argued elsewhere,[7] all public assembly is haunted by the police and the prison. And every public square is defined in part by the population that could not possibly arrive there; either they are detained at the border, or they have no freedom of movement and assembly, or they are detained or imprisoned. In other words, the freedom to gather as a people is always haunted by the imprisonment of those who exercised that freedom and were taken to prison. And when one arrives in public or common spaces with radical and critical views, there is always an anxious or certain anticipation that imprisonment may well follow. Sometimes we walk, or run, knowingly in the direction of prison because it is the only way to expose illegitimate constraints on public assembly and political expression. The deliberate exposure to harm was crucial to Gandhi's notion of nonviolent civil disobedience.[8]

In Gezi Park, some who were assembled were detained, and others were hurt. The lawyers who came to help those who were detained were themselves detained; and sometimes the medical workers who came to help the injured were themselves subject to injury. And yet a new group of activists or journalists, health professionals or lawyers, would arrive, replenishing the network of support. With the imprisonment of some Pussy Riot members after their Cathedral performance in Moscow, demonstrations broke out in major cities all across the globe, and Internet forms of solidarity emerged to put pressure on governments and human rights agencies to press for the release of those imprisoned and to object to the conditions of political imprisonment. Both of these examples, and the growing movement against the death penalty, compel us to turn our attention to political imprisonment, and to the institution of the prison industry as a global mechanism for the regulation of the rights of citizenship, for the administration of violence. In the United States, two-thirds of prisoners are black men, and nearly every person on death row is a person of color. Angela Davis has argued that the prison in the United States continues the work of slavery by suspending the very rights of citizenship for people of color; in this way, it becomes the continuation of slavery by other means.[9]

Feminism is a crucial part of these networks of solidarity and resistance precisely because feminist critique destabilizes those institutions that depend on the reproduction of inequality and injustice, and it criticizes those institutions and practices that inflict violence on women and gender minorities, and, in fact, all minorities subject to police power for showing up and speaking out as they do. We are now witnessing popular movements against the notion of "gender" in France and in several Eastern European countries, such as

Poland, Hungary, and Slovakia, and these are allied with movements against reproductive freedom and gay marriage, against lifting constraints imposed on women's literacy, employment, and expressive freedoms. Time and again we hear from government authorities in several parts of the world that what women and minority populations regard as basics of equality and freedom go against the "common norms" of a national culture, or that their goals are unrealistic or ungrateful, or that what they call equality and freedom are actually dangerous, posing grave security risks to the nation or to Europe or, indeed, to civilization itself. The Russian government accused Pussy Riot of "attacking the soul of man." Few struggles are more important than those that call into question so-called common norms by asking whose lives were *never* included in those norms. Whose lives are, in fact, explicitly excluded from those norms? What norm of the human constrains those common norms? And to what extent is that a masculinist norm, or a norm of racial privilege?

I have suggested that we rethink the relationship between the human body and infrastructure so that we might call into question the body as discrete, singular, and self-sufficient, and I have proposed instead to understand embodiment as both performative and relational, where relationality includes dependency on infrastructural conditions and legacies of discourse and institutional power that precede and condition our existence. I am also suggesting that certain ideals of independence are masculinist and that a feminist account exposes the disavowed dependency at the heart of the masculinist idea of the body. This is different from saying what women's bodies are or what men's bodies are. I am not making those claims; I am only showing what I take to be a masculinist conception of bodily action that should be actively criticized. My reference to dependency may well include dependency on the mother or the primary caretaker, but that is not the form of primary dependency that concerns me here. By theorizing the human body as a certain kind of *dependency* on infrastructure, understood complexly as environment, social relations, and networks of support and sustenance by which the human itself proves not to be divided from the animal or from the technical world, we foreground the ways in which we are vulnerable to decimated or disappearing infrastructures, economic supports, and predictable and well-compensated labor. Not only are we then vulnerable to one another—an invariable feature of social relations—but, in addition, this very vulnerability indicates a broader condition of dependency and interdependency that challenges the dominant ontological understanding of the embodied subject.

Of course, there are many reasons *not* to like vulnerability. Most of us wish we were less vulnerable under conditions in which we are impinged on in ways we do not choose, and "vulnerability" names this very condition. But that alone is no reason to reject a theoretical consideration of its uses, especially when it turns out that vulnerability cannot rightly be reduced to what we cannot willingly want. In the final set of my remarks, I want to argue against the notion that vulnerability is the opposite of resistance. Indeed, I want to argue affirmatively that vulnerability, understood as a deliberate exposure to power, is part of the very meaning of political resistance as an embodied enactment. I know that speaking about vulnerability produces resistance of various kinds for the reasons I have just mentioned. There are those who worry that vulnerability, even if it becomes a theme or a problem for thinking, will be asserted as a primary existential condition, ontological and constitutive, and that this sort of foundationalism will founder on the same rocky shores as have others, such as the ethics of care or maternal thinking. Or some people worry that if feminism in any way becomes associated with vulnerability, no matter which version, it will become captured by the term and women will end up being portrayed in ways that rob them of their agency. Does a turn to vulnerability seek to reintroduce those foundationalist or essentialist modalities of thinking and valuing back into public discourse?—is it smuggling in discounted paradigms for reconsideration? Does the idea of vulnerability work to the detriment of women? Or does that very question presuppose that any concession made to vulnerability will lead to vulnerability as (a) a foundational premise for politics (which it is not), (b) an essential identity (which it is not), or (c) an identification of women with injurability (which is not necessary)? All of these concerns assume that vulnerability is disjoined from resistance, mobilization, and other forms of deliberate and agentic politics. Such an assumption is at the basis of many of our political misunderstandings about the importance of the term.

Yet the resistance to vulnerability is often based on political anxieties such as these. After all, if women or minorities seek to establish themselves as vulnerable, do they unwittingly or wittingly seek to establish a protected status subject to a paternalistic set of powers that must safeguard the vulnerable, those presumed to be weak and in need of protection? Does the discourse of vulnerability discount the political agency of the subjugated? So one political problem that emerges from any such discussion is whether the discourse on vulnerability shores up paternalistic power, relegating the condition of vulnerability to those who suffer discrimination, exploitation, or violence. What about the power of those who are oppressed? And what about the vulnerability of paternalistic institutions themselves? After all, if they can be contested, brought down, or rebuilt on egalitarian grounds, then paternalism itself is *vulnerable to* a dismantling that would undo its very form of power. And when this dismantling is undertaken by subjugated peoples, do they not establish themselves as something other than, or more than, vulnerable? Indeed, do we want to say that they overcome their vulnerability at such moments, which is to assume that vulnerability is negated when it is converted[10] into agency? Or is vulnerability still there, but only now assuming a different form?

Finally, there are justified political objections to the fact that dominant groups can use the discourse of "vulnerability" to shore up their own privilege. In California, when white people were losing their status as a majority, some of them claimed that they were a "vulnerable" population. Vulnerable to what? A multinational and multiracial state? Such a claim was clearly racist. Indeed, colonial states have lamented their "vulnerability" to attack by those they colonize and have sought general sympathy on the basis of that claim. Some men have complained that feminism has made them into a "vulnerable population" and that they are now "targeted" for discrimination. Various European national identities now claim to be "under attack" by new and established migrant communities. We can see that the term has a way of shifting, and since we may not like some, or even many, of the shifts it makes, we may find ourselves somewhat awkwardly opposed to vulnerability. Of course, that is a rather funny thing to say, since we might conjecture that any amount of opposition to vulnerability does not exactly defeat its operation in our bodily and social lives. Indeed, vehement opposition to vulnerability may prove to be the very sign of its continuing operation. That seems to be a minimal truth that we can accept from psychoanalysis. Yet do our political objections to vulnerability make us into psychoanalytic fools? And do our psychoanalytic affirmations of vulnerability make us complicit with political positions we do not condone?

When we oppose "vulnerability" as a political term, it is usually because we would like to see ourselves as agentic, or we think that better political consequences will follow if we see ourselves that way. If we oppose vulnerability in the name of agency, does that imply that we prefer to see ourselves as those who are only acting, but not acted on? And how might we then describe those regions of both aesthetics and ethics that presume that our receptivity is bound up with our responsiveness, a zone in which we are acted on by the world, by what is said and shown, by what we hear, and by what touches us? If we take this domain of impressionability as primary, then can we ask what aspects of the world impress on us at the very moment we form an impression of that world? What we find is at the same time that we act on it in certain ways. Does the opposition to vulnerability also imperil a host of related terms of responsiveness, including impressionability, susceptibility, injurability, openness, indignation, outrage, and even resistance? If nothing acts on me against my will or without my advanced knowledge, then there is only sovereignty, the posture of control over the property that I have and that I am, a seemingly sturdy and self-centered form of the thinking "I" that seeks to cloak those fault lines in the self that cannot be overcome. What form of politics is supported by this adamant mode of disavowal? Is this not the masculinist account of sovereignty that, as feminists, we are called on to dismantle?[11]

As I have tried to suggest by calling attention to the dual dimension of performativity, we are invariably acted on and acting, and this is one reason performativity cannot be reduced to the idea of free, individual performance. We are called names and find ourselves living in a world of categories and descriptions way before we start to sort them critically and endeavor to change or make them on our own. In this way we are, quite in spite of ourselves, vulnerable to, and affected by, discourses that we never chose. In a parallel way, I want to suggest that there is a dual relationship to resistance that helps us understand what we mean by vulnerability. On the one hand, there is a resistance to vulnerability that takes both psychic and political dimensions; the psychic resistance to vulnerability wishes that it were never the case that discourse and power were imposed on us in ways that we never chose, and so seeks to shore up a notion of individual sovereignty against the shaping forces of history on our embodied lives. On the other hand, the very meaning of vulnerability changes when it becomes understood as part of the very practice of political resistance. Indeed, one of the important features of public assembly that we recently see confirms that political resistance relies fundamentally on the mobilization of vulnerability, which means that vulnerability can be a way of being exposed and agentic at the same time. Such collective forms of resistance are structured very differently than the idea of a political subject that establishes its agency by vanquishing its vulnerability—this is the masculinist ideal we surely ought to continue to oppose.

A most important criticism emerges from those who argue that vulnerability cannot be the basis for group identification without strengthening paternalistic power. Once groups are marked as "vulnerable" within human rights discourse or legal regimes, those groups become reified as definitionally "vulnerable," fixed in a political position of powerlessness and lack of agency. All the power belongs to the state and international institutions that are now supposed to offer them protection and advocacy. Such moves tend to underestimate, or actively efface, modes of political agency and resistance that emerge within so-called vulnerable populations. To understand those extrajuridical modes of resistance, we would have to think about how resistance and vulnerability work together, something that the paternalistic model cannot do. In my view, as much as "vulnerability" can be affirmed as an existential condition, since we are all subject to accidents, illness, and attacks that can expunge our lives quite quickly, it is also a socially induced condition, which accounts for the disproportionate exposure to suffering, especially among those broadly called the precariat for whom access to shelter, food, and medical care is often quite drastically limited. Even so, it would not be a sufficient politics to embrace vulnerability or to get in touch with our feelings, or bare our fault lines as if that might launch a new mode of authenticity or inaugurate a new order of moral values or a sudden and widespread outbreak of "care." I am not in favor of such moves toward authenticity as a way of doing politics, for they continue to locate vulnerability as the opposite of agency, to identify agency with sovereign modes of defensiveness, and to fail to recognize the ways in which vulnerability can be an incipient and enduring moment of resistance. Once we understand the way vulnerability enters into agency, then our understanding of both terms can change, and the binary opposition between them can become undone. I consider the undoing of this binary a feminist task.

To summarize: vulnerability is not a subjective disposition. Rather, it characterizes a relation to a field of objects, forces, and passions that impinge on or affect us in some way. As a way of being related to what is not me and not fully masterable, vulnerability is a kind of relationship that belongs to that ambiguous region in which receptivity and responsiveness are not clearly separable from one another, and not distinguished as separate moments in a sequence; indeed, where receptivity and responsiveness become the basis for mobilizing vulnerability rather than engaging in its destructive denial.

Of course, I am aware that I have used "resistance" in at least two ways: first, as the *resistance to* vulnerability that characterizes that form of thinking that models itself on mastery; second, *as a social and political form* that is informed by vulnerability, and so not one of its opposites. I have suggested that vulnerability is neither fully passive nor fully active, but operating in a middle region, a constituent feature of a human animal both affected and acting. I am thus led to think about those practices of deliberate exposure to police or military violence in which bodies, put on the line, either receive blows or seek to stop violence as living blockades or barriers. In such practices of nonviolent resistance, we can come to understand bodily vulnerability as something that is actually marshaled or mobilized for the purposes of resistance. Of course, such a claim is controversial, since these practices can seem allied with self-destruction, but what interests me are those forms of nonviolent resistance that mobilize vulnerability for the purposes of asserting existence, claiming the right to public space, equality, and opposing violent police, security, and military actions. We may think that these are isolated moments in which a group decides in advance to produce a blockade or to link arms in order to lay claim to public space or to resist being removed by the police. And that is surely true, as it was in Berkeley in 2011 when a group of students and colleagues were assaulted by police forces on campus at the very moment they were practicing nonviolent protest. But consider as well that for trans people in many places in the world and women who seek to walk the street at night in safety, the moment of actively appearing on the street involves a deliberate risk of exposure to force. Under certain conditions, continuing to exist, to move, and to breathe are forms of resistance, which is why we sometimes see placards in Palestine with the slogan "We still exist!" As we know, this is certainly true of groups who gather without permits and without weapons to oppose privatization and rally for democracy, as we saw in Gezi Park in Istanbul last June. Although such groups are shorn of legal and police protection, they are not for that reason reduced to some sort of "bare life." There is no sovereign power jettisoning the subject outside the domain of the political as such; rather, there is a renewal of popular sovereignty outside, and against, the terms of state sovereignty and police power, one that often involves a concerted and corporeal form of exposure and resistance.

Vulnerability can emerge within resistance and direct democracy actions precisely as a deliberate mobilization of bodily exposure. I suggested earlier that we had to deal with two senses of resistance here: resistance to vulnerability that belongs to certain projects of thought and certain formations of politics organized by sovereign mastery, and a resistance to unjust and violent regimes that mobilizes vulnerability as part of its own exercise of power.

In political life, it surely seems that first some injustice happens and then there is a response, but it may be that the response is happening as the injustice occurs, and this gives us another way to think about historical events, action, passion, and vulnerability in forms of resistance. It would seem that without being able to think about vulnerability, we cannot think about resistance, and that by thinking about resistance, we are already under way, dismantling the resistance to vulnerability in order precisely to resist.

Notes

1 Part of this discussion is adapted from my *Notes toward a Performative Theory of Assembly*.
2 See Wendy Brown's work on the privatization of public goods in *Undoing the Demos*.
3 Arendt, *The Human Condition*, 194–195.
4 See "On Linguistic Vulnerability" in my *Excitable Speech*, 1–42.
5 See Brezina, *Sojourner Truth's "Ain't I a Woman?" Speech*.
6 See Sedgwick, "Around the Performative."
7 See Butler, *Notes toward a Performative Theory of Assembly*, chap. 5.
8 See Gandhi, "Part I. Satyagraha: The Power of Nonviolence."
9 Davis, "Slavery, Civil Rights, and Abolitionist Perspectives toward Prison."
10 For this double sense of resistance, see Jacqueline Rose, *The Last Resistance*, 17–38.
11 White, "Writing in the Middle Voice," 255–262.

....

CHAPTER 2

Risking Oneself and One's Identity

Agonism Revisited

ZEYNEP GAMBETTI

This essay is an attempt to understand and develop an unusual insight by Hannah Arendt, one that seems to fly in the face of (patriarchal, humanitarian, utilitarian) modes of thinking that oppose "greatness" to "suffering." In one of her posthumously published pieces Arendt writes: "[The] common world comprehends and assures survival for everything that men do to, and suffer from, each other, whereby it is understood that human greatness is not restricted to the deed and the doer in the strict sense of the word, but can equally be the share of the endurer and sufferer."[1] This is an enigmatic insight for those of us who have evacuated suffering from our range of "desirables." What does it mean for the sufferer to have a share in greatness? This is obviously not a call for empathy with sufferers. Despite its tricky syntax, the statement possesses ontological certainty: Arendt seems to be convinced that, given a common world, what "men" suffer from each other will effectively survive and that this is reassuring.

To add to the perplexity, Arendt's comment appears in the midst of her analysis of the agonistic spirit of the Greek polis. Those who are familiar with Arendt's political theory know that her construal of agonism has been accused of harboring aristocratic and masculine ideals.[2] She is faulted with disregarding the subjugated, the faint-hearted, or the feeble-bodied. Her agonism is more often associated with heroic understandings of conflict and competition. Could her comment at best be considered as an acknowledgment of the idea that politics comprises both *polemos* (dissociation) and *polis* (association)?[3] Is this what is being meant here? In Greek, *agonia* designates a struggle for victory, but it is an exceptionally equivocal term. The struggle need not be with an adversary; it can also be with impending death, illness, or adversity. To agonize is to undergo extreme mental anguish, to contend with or against a difficulty, to be tormented by a decision that needs to be made. To remember the verses that the chorus sang in *Antigone*: "O passionate heart / Unyielding, tormented still by the same winds!"

Hence, *polemos* fails to convey the sense of suffering implied in *agon*. The French word *épreuve* comes closer, since it signifies "ordeal." An *épreuve* well endured proves, reveals, or manifests the presence of a certain quality as a token of ability and power—not so much a "power over" as a "power to." But *épreuve* also means hardship and adversity.

The aporetic nature of *agon* may appear too hopelessly to fuse agency and fatality, activity, and passivity, to be of any conceptual use, but it is precisely because of this reason that it may actually contain the germs of rethinking the very binaries that construct vulnerability and power as incommensurate terms. In what follows, I propose to reflect on vulnerability through the intricate connection between acting and suffering implied in agonistic politics. Reading Arendt's political thought in the light of the Occupy Gezi movement in Turkey in June 2013 (and vice versa), I ask whether vulnerability has exclusively to do with the violation of rights, of bodily integrity, of sources of livelihood, or whether it can (also) encompass permeability and receptiveness. This question cannot be divested of what it means for (gendered, sexed, racialized) bodies to be vulnerable, or of the topographical features of the manifold and uneven strata on which the drama of doing and suffering is played out. Besides, if *agon* implies activity as well as passivity, then it demands that we inquire not only into the nature of permeability, but also into that of agency. Is there agency in suffering? What forces must concur so that suffering takes its place in the common world as a form of "greatness"?

To engage with such questions, this essay communicates with but also partially disputes feminist constructions of the self as composite, embedded, and embodied, such as those developed by Judith Butler, Bonnie Honig, Rosi Braidotti, and Adriana Cavarero. My dispute concerns the specific place (or rather nonplace) of action within the terms of what can be very crudely summarized as the foundationalist vs. nonfoundationalist controversy. One is caught between reclaiming the purposive subject and dissolving it into multiple lines of flight, between deconstruction and re-membering agency, between materiality and discursivity, between too much and too little. Feminist thinkers such as Seyla Benhabib and Nancy Fraser have argued that nonfoundationalist theory removes the very ground on which an emancipatory ethics can be constructed.[4] Their apprehension is not unwarranted, even more so because the (feminist) preoccupation with inequity and injury is *bel et bien* a matter of ethics—if only for being animated by the desire to transform and overcome patterns of exclusion, subjugation, and humiliation. But couldn't we engage with the triple question of embodied selfhood, ethics, and action without being trapped by the terms of this controversy? My hunch is that Arendt's take on *agon* opens a promising path in this respect—given, of course, that it can be creatively appropriated and bent to serve this purpose. Evidently, this essay will come nowhere near a satisfactory mapping out of this promise, but what it will do, I hope, is to suggestively point to the virtual in the actual.

To this end, I begin by developing and slightly modifying Bonnie Honig's quest for the virtual agonistic feminist in Arendt. I then put what Honig calls "generative performativity" to task to pursue the aporia that I detect in agonism by summoning Arendt's category of "actor." This allows me to distinguish between agonistic (generative) and antagonistic (constative) registers of vulnerability, whereby difference either becomes an affirmative differential or a deformity, an injury. A series of snapshots from Occupy Gezi will serve to gauge the possibility of an agonistic ethics of "ex-posure" and "becoming-other" without falling back on humanist conceptions of subjecthood. Paraphrasing Braidotti, the aim is to suggest a conceptual framework through which to "rethink embodiment in conjunction with *action*; to rethink grounding in relation to nomadic shifts; to rethink a sense of belonging with the paradox of multiple and shifting *positions*."[5]

Agon and Identity

Arendt is not a feminist, nor does she entertain an embodied notion of the self. But what Honig finds valuable in Arendt is the tension between the constative and generative dimensions of identity. While social identities such as gender appear as constative and compelling references to self-evident or natural "truths," the Arendtian self is a "complex site of multiplicity whose identities are always performatively produced."[6] Instead of repeating Arendt's gesture of confining politics to a topographically designated public realm, Honig proposes that we think of "action as an event, an agonistic disruption of the ordinary sequence of things that makes for novelty and distinction, a site of resistance of the irresistible, a challenge to the normalizing rules that seek to constitute, govern, and control various behaviors."[7] This is critical, since it helps to unsettle the frontiers between the social and the political, the private and the public, action and behavior.

From her creative appropriation of Arendt, Honig retrieves the double advantage of politicizing identities *and* lodging them within a dynamic framework. To this end, Honig reformulates Arendt's fundamental categories of labor, work, and action. She notes that the "body, for Arendt, is a site and source of mute inaction, cyclical nature, or senseless violence that ought to be confined to the private realm."[8] It is associated with the activity of laboring, not with that of acting. But the Arendtian distinction between the private and the public would indeed be untenable, Honig claims, if the body and gender are considered as the sediments of actions and norms generated in the public realm. Thus, the seemingly rigid demarcation that confines labor to the private domain and action to the public one is circumvented. Labor and action become performatives at work in *all* selves in a variety of agonistic spaces. The body ceases to be natural, univocal, and closed to contestation, but, rather, becomes a site of contestation. Honig thereby connects performativity and agonism, a theoretical move of much value to the present essay.

Developing Judith Butler's notion of the subversion of reified binaries through reiteration, Honig then explores the possibility of a politics of identity that would eschew closure without having to reject a politics of representation altogether. The impossibility of stabilizing constative identities provides the ontological ground for this endeavor. A feminist politics of performativity would build on communality (for instance gendered identity) while admitting that this communality would always be up for contestation through a dispersed notion of *agon*. Contra Benhabib, Honig argues that "Arendt invites us to think of concerted action as a practice of (re-)founding, augmentation, and amendment that involves us in relations not only 'with' but also always simultaneously 'against' others. In short, . . . we stop thinking of agonism and associationism as mutually exclusive alternatives."[9]

I fully appreciate this perspective, since it allows us to rethink social identities through an Arendtian framework, something Arendt herself cannot do. It is also valuable in that it rejects the either/or binary whereby we are either attendant to others or we shun them. But I am also disconcerted by the way Honig fails to appreciate the sense of "new beginning" implied in Arendt's claim that action "springs up ex nihilo" or "happens to us."[10] In fact, Honig seems to vacillate between: (1) Arendt's quite Nietzschean account of the agent as brought forth by its deed;[11] (2) Butler's theory of performativity as the re-iterative reproduction *and* subversion of social identities; and (3) an account of the self as the principle (*arche*) or cause of action.[12] The significance of Arendt's claim that "who" somebody is cannot be exhausted in "what" she is (a gendered, sexed, racialized, social being) is somewhat lost in translation. But doesn't Honig also admit that Arendt's action-based theory of performativity is both "dramatic and nonreferential"?[13] If so, what conceptual tools do we need so as to construe the performative as nonreferential instead of reiterating or contesting available social scripts?

Honig's construal also misses the following argument in *The Human Condition*: "Whether an activity is performed in private or in public is by no means a matter of indifference. Obviously, the character of the public realm must change in accordance with the activities admitted into it, but to a large extent the activity itself changes its own nature too."[14] This surprisingly structural argument insinuates that the elements constituting the "public realm" stand in a relation of complex interdependence such that any change in one affects a number of others. The public realm functions in different ways depending on the type of activity that takes place in it. And vice versa: action loses its revelatory quality when performed in a space in which plurality has been effaced and the automatism of processes has taken over. Thus, Arendt is able to write of her cherished concept of action as "the most dangerous of all human abilities and possibilities."[15]

If the Arendtian notion of performativity were to be maintained, action must be construed as a type of "generative performativity."[16] Could we not dispense with asking whether "identity" as a constative exhausts the differential positions taken by individuals in agonistic spaces? Are differences *states*, or are they also *performatively* located in the relation *between* actors, in their *ex post facto* discernable capacity to compose with or constrain one another? And what kind of encounter qualifies as agonistic? Under what conditions do differences constitute sites of contestation?

Registers of Vulnerability

We might want to proceed by delineating those tensions inhabiting the performative that cannot be abridged to disagreement only. Consider the following claim by Arendt in *The Human Condition*: "Although nobody knows whom he reveals when he discloses himself in deed and word, he must be willing to risk the disclosure."[17] Why? What is this "risk" that Arendt is alluding to? She tells us that action—the individuating activity—requires exiting "the security of an inward realm in which the self is exposed to nothing but itself."[18] One thereby risks "disclosing and exposing one's self."[19] What we have at our disposal is a set of ominous terms: risk, disclosure, exposure, and derivatively, the lack of security. It is as if the sites of agonistic individuation were plagued with perils.

But a closer reading also reveals that these perils are constitutive of the acting self. The position phrases juxtaposed above seem to be at odds with the modernist vision of a willful and conscious selfhood. Arendt's particular take on individuation or on processes of political identity formation cannot be said to follow the risk-free paths that characterize the deliberative model of democracy.[20] On the contrary, Arendt seems to build on the ambivalence between *poeien* (to do) and *pathein* (to suffer) to develop her notion of selfhood.[21] To paraphrase Arendt, politics is a dis-placement as well as a taking-place. One would need to "dis-close" oneself, move out of one's shelter, step out into an open and unprotected site. There, one is "ex-posed" or re-positioned. One's word and deed *precede* the knowledge of "who" one might be—for the simple reason that the "outside" is populated by others. Others present a dis-locating risk in terms of the identicalness of the self to itself. But should we then be tempted to recite the Sartrean interjection "Hell is other people"? The opposite seems to be the case as far as Arendt is concerned: there can be no "self" without others. How she triangulates the notion of *agon* with the presence of others and the question of "becoming-human" is well revealed in the following claim: "The agon, the strife of *aristeuein*, . . . is . . . the political equation of reality with appearing to others. Only where others were present, could a specifically human life begin. Only where one was noticed by others could he, by distinguishing himself, come into his own humanity."[22]

I interpret the possessive in the phrase "one's own" as a paradoxical one, in that it is predicated on the self's dependence on others. This fundamental "interdependence"[23] has two effects. First, if I am who I am by virtue of my actions that take effect among others, then I am "in act" before being "in identity." To effectuate one's existence among others necessarily implies leaving the solipsistic inner space of subjectivity where one may imagine oneself as identical to oneself. But, second, if appearance to a *plurality* of gazes is the prerequisite for the constitution of a self (notice the use of "others" in the plural, instead of a dialectic or incorporeal "Other"), it is also the condition of possibility of its evasiveness: "Since action acts on beings who are capable of their own actions, reaction, apart from being a response, is always a new action that strikes out on its own and affects others."[24] The risk, then, consists in that others may carry (*prattein*) the initial action (*arkhein*) into completion or carry it into a totally unintended and unforeseen direction, or else refuse to carry it through altogether. My action is not *mine* in the possessive sense, but sets forth waves of attraction, diffraction, revision or variation. This augments and *collectivizes* the deed such that it takes its place in the world as a *common* reality—neither mine, nor yours. This formulation displaces the "I" such that individuation occurs in a web through embodied and situated practices. Individuation is an in-between, a *potentia* that escapes *potestas*.

As opposed to exhibitionist narcissism, this sense of individuation has to do with the ontology of an active and relational self.[25] Nor is it a disguised form of atomistic individualism, since it necessarily implies a collectivity. Individuation is the actualization of the power-to-become of selves who, through their pluralistic encounters, constitute a collective site of power. As a matter of fact, Arendt's highly idiosyncratic notion of power repeats her theoretical gesture of decentering the self, but this time in order to dispossess power of its instrumental and institutional underpinnings. Power is always a *power potential* that "can only be actualized but never fully materialized" and it is only "where men live so close together that the potentialities of action are always present can power remain with them."[26]

Construed in this way, *agon* would relate to the event-character of access to the world. One produces an effect on the *res publica* or "public thing" by becoming an "objective" reality that must be reckoned with, or reacted against, or narrated in the form of a story. Put differently, the positive or active charge (the *agon* involved in acting or doing) does not exclude the negative or passive charge (that of being acted on). On the contrary, agonistic encounters presuppose the effective occurrence of both at the same time: "Because the actor always moves among and in relation to other acting beings, he is never merely a 'doer' but always and at the same time a sufferer. *To do and to suffer are like opposite sides of the same coin,* and the story that an act starts is composed of its consequent deeds and sufferings. These consequences are boundless, because action . . . acts into a medium where every reaction becomes a chain reaction and where every process is the cause of new processes."[27]

My take on the preceding account is that the emphasis is on the *conditionality* of plurality itself. Plurality cannot be reduced to numerical quantity; nor can it consist of the mere copresence of bodies marked by different social attributes. That my neighbors have diverse ethnic origins does not mean that my encounters with them are agonistic. If the liberal term "pluralism" designates the coexistence of defined or definable groups, "plurality" implies a much more radical contingency whereby the actualization of the *potentia* inherent in action turns every single self into a unique being who is never "the same as anyone else who ever lived, lives, or will live."[28] Plurality, then, can be said to imply the egalitarian distribution of the capacity to do and to suffer in such a way that each self tends toward uniqueness.[29]

To come back to my question concerning the kinds of encounter that qualify as agonistic, my presentiment is that we should distinguish between two registers of risk arising from the type of exposure alluded to by Arendt. These registers must be considered as sites or surfaces enabling certain types of encounter to take place at the expense of other forms of relationality. The type of exposure that corresponds to the first level of risk—which I call agonistic—relates to difference as *differential*. The latter does not obtain from any pre-established role, norm, or societal location, since no constative may saturate the contingent positions in a matrix (or web, as Arendt calls it) of encounters. This first register decenters and refigures the "self" who thereby becomes the sufferer of its *own* actions. In other words, the risk of *decomposing* is inherent in agonistic relations, even when the composition and cofoundation of a community is concerned. It can thus be stated that social identities such as ethnicity, gender, and class do not exhaust the tensions arising from the differential positions of individual actors in agonistic spaces. The differential is agonistic not only because of the ever-present possibility of discord, but also because of the prospect of "becoming-other"—of parting with one's (subjective or constative) self. It is only in this sense that it can be called "generative" in such a way as to create something new—a "who" or a new beginning.

The second register of risk—which I call antagonistic[30]—derives from extensive economic, social, and political arrangements that destroy plurality as defined above, not only locally, but also globally. Both the denial and the fixation of differences severely reduce the possibility of contesting established norms or of transgressing assigned places within societal grids of affectability and representation. In the case of social identities, for instance, the hegemonic reduction of spaces of agonistic encounter may result in the exclusion of minorities potentially capable of destabilizing normalizing discourses and practices. Such minorities are thus exposed to physical or symbolic death through invisibility. When boundaries are demarcated and firmly maintained by spatial or temporal *dispositifs* allowing for the denial of differences, the doer is separated from the sufferer, epistemologically as well as practically. This constitutes a world in which "the winners only put their money in line, while the losers risk their bodies."[31] If agonistic politics hinges on the egalitarian distribution of the capacity to act and be acted on by others, by contrast, antagonistic political spaces can be described as those in which some groups in society have become the predominant actors/doers and some are relegated to the place of endurers/sufferers. Hence, antagonism replaces agonistic vulnerability; the risk of exposing one's self is replaced by exposure to loss, injury, or damage.

It must be noted that agonism and antagonism need not qualify mutually exclusive spaces of existence. Spaces and the agents that construct or occupy them can alternate between permeability and aversion. As Veena Das has poignantly shown, the opposite movements of "ascent" toward eventness and "descent" into ordinary life may be the only way of "turning back to inhabit the same space now marked as a space of destruction, in which you must live again."[32]

The distinction that I am proposing between agonism and antagonism echoes the one Butler constructs between precariousness and precarity. There is a difference, however: my central category is action, while hers is life.[33] According to Butler, the differential distribution of states of precarity is brought about by the denial and actual avoidance of our shared condition of precariousness as human beings. I maintain that what is being avoided in antagonism is the suffering implied in agonistic relations. In Butler's formulation, what is being violated under antagonistic circumstances is the likelihood of the "sufferers" to gain access to basic resources or to live a decent "human" life. I suggest that the violence of antagonism consists primarily in impairing the capacity of any living being, human or other, to act on the common world while being acted on by others. For, isn't the act of determining who or what should count as "human" already a form of violence, as Agamben suggests?[34] Or again, isn't it a hierarchizing value judgment to say that violence reduces the "human being" to a "thing," as if things and material assemblages weren't part and parcel of what makes any body "human"? It is by proceeding from such considerations that I propose, with and beyond Arendt, to call antagonistic those forces that act on agon so as to reduce or eradicate the *potentia* inherent in it. I thus hope to eschew predefining the "human" in any constative manner.

It remains to be asked what it means to construe agonistic difference as a differential that is performatively located, not in any of the social attributes purportedly possessed by the actors (gender, ethnicity, class), but in the very relation *between* them. Such a construal would evidently eschew conceptions of determinate individuation that carry masculine charges and would move instead toward a more feminist notion of fluid and mobile individuation. Braidotti, for instance, building on Luce Irigaray as well as Gilles Deleuze, argues that "masculinity is antithetical to the process of becoming and it can only be the site of deconstruction or critique; on the other hand, the becoming-woman is a fundamental step in the process of becoming, for both sexes."[35] In order to move in this direction as well as to relate my theoretical gestures to concrete practices of permeability between social identities, I shall now turn to exploring the various instances of agonistic vulnerability that I detect in Occupy Gezi.[36]

The Agonistic Unfolding of Occupy Gezi

At first glance, Occupy Gezi appeared as an antagonistic moment. On the one hand, the police used excessive force (tear gas, water cannons, and real bullets) against protestors, taking away eyes, limbs, and lives. On the other hand, symbolic violence made the events invisible *as such* for a portion of the Turkish public. This took the form of outright lying; the flagrant censuring of the event by the quasi-totality of the media; the stigmatization of the protestors as "marginals," "thugs," "illegal groups," and agents of Western powers; and the denial of their demands by the prime minister and other officials. The bodies at Gezi thus encountered the risk of physical as well as symbolic death and mutilation. As Rancière compellingly argues, the "partition of the sensible" divides bodies into two categories: "those that one sees and those that one does not see, those who have a logos—memorial speech, an account to be kept up—and those who have no logos."[37] What was at stake in the Gezi resistance was the becoming-visible not only of those whose lives are ungrievable, but also of the "event-ness" of the event itself. The management of visibility by the government controlled the signification of the event in the eyes of a large portion of Turkish society, pinning it to available structures without allowing for new meanings to emerge.

But if these were the antagonistic conditions under which the protests took place, Occupy Gezi was also fraught with another kind of tension: it brought together an unexpected variety of people, most of whom had not physically encountered each other until then. The predictability of the *antagonism* (state violence in its physical as well as symbolic forms) stood in striking contrast with the *agonism* that characterized relations among the protestors. I can illustrate this only through a number of short stories or snapshots.

Appearing to Others

The first story runs like this: LGBT individuals were present with their flags and drag outfits at a barricade in the Istanbul neighborhood of Beşiktaş one day when the police started taking over. Leftists and soccer fans were taken aback. Some of them went to the LGBT protestors to say: "You're the most organized group here. You must go up front to halt the police while we gather our forces." As recounted by a friend who was there, this took the LGBT block by surprise: "It's probably because we stood so close together and had the colorful flag waving above our heads. Most of us had high heels; some of us were in skirts. We weren't that many in number, actually. We must've looked numerous because of all that color and flurry." So a bunch of LGBT activists found themselves facing the armor-clad riot police all alone while the boisterous soccer enthusiasts took a retreat. When they caught their breath and came back a while later, the LGBT block was still standing out on its own, swallowing the tear gas and protecting the barricade. The fans seemed also to fully appreciate that "the boy in the skirt has a first-aid kit" and were spreading the word.[38]

What's so unusual about this story? In the words of Mehmet Tarhan, conscientious objector and gay rights activist, "LGBT individuals who distributed food and drinks, or who ran to the barricades in high-heel shoes that nobody would desire to wear in the midst of combat, certainly weren't rebelling only against the government, but also against their comrades-in-arms at the barricades, and were aiming at a transformation."[39] Soccer fans, their comrades-in-arms, are the most outspokenly homophobic of all social groups—and not only because of their slogans.[40] Homosexuality is dreaded across the board in Turkey, much more than atheism or alcoholism.[41] The hegemonic heterosexual norm stigmatizes lesbian, gay, bisexual, and trans identities as perversions of human nature, sicknesses that need to be cured or, at best, sins. Especially under the Justice and Development Party government, homosexuality became "the constitutive 'Other' of conservative democracy."[42]

It goes without saying, therefore, that LGBT individuals are particularly vulnerable in Turkish society. The anecdote above is unusual in the sense that LGBT protestors were making a claim on the collective shaping of the "we" at Gezi. Their presence at the barricades was not only the embodiment of the constative "We exist!"[43] This being-there was the performative actualization of their claim to be an actor. They were thus short-circuiting the impractical-ity of addressing a demand for recognition to soccer fans. In turn, the soccer fans were already responding positively to a nonvocalized demand by asking the LGBTs to go up front. The unforeseeable presence of a "boy in a skirt" fighting alongside a homophobic soccer fan was a disruption straining the bounds of convention. This was what Arendt would identify as a truly politi-cal moment, I think, since it was nonnegotiable through available norms. I would also call it a performative moment: it "happened" to the actors; it took them by surprise and hence beckoned the exercise of virtuosity and judg-ment instead of rule following.

Occupy Gezi was fraught with numerous moments that may qualify as ordeals or *épreuves*. The following account by a trans woman is revelatory in this regard:

> On the first day, June 1, I was very close to the police barricade and found myself in the midst of a group of people with red masks. I lost track of my friends . . . There were four or five people with red flags. They signaled at me as if to say "Come, come, we'll climb on top of the barricade." But the police appeared all of a sudden and shot tear gas all around me . . . I had to pass through the gas to get out of there . . . I swallowed a couple of full breaths of gas. Then my eyes closed. I couldn't open them; they kept clos-ing involuntarily. I figured "My friends would probably be over there" and sprinted without opening my eyes. I'm a trans woman, so I'm not confident in public like everyone else. For the first time ever, I was running with my eyes shut that day. I knew someone would hold me . . . Just imagine, you're running with your eyes shut . . . Sure enough, someone did hold me by the arm. It was wonderful.[44]

In a society where trans are scorned, harassed, beaten, and murdered,[45] the space of coappearance opened up by the Gezi protests had allowed this woman to experience "publicness" in unforeseen ways. But the hand that held her steady as she was blindly running was probably undergoing an *épreuve* as well. We may only speculate, but it is highly likely that that hand would not have touched a trans body under "normal" circumstances.

What needs to be underlined here is how the differential positioning of various identities involved several levels of contingency. The soccer fan / LGBT differential was repeated in other forms. Feminists, for instance, defied soc-cer fans by intervening to prohibit sexist curses whenever possible. Women armed with paintbrushes also patrolled the streets to obliterate sexist slogans on the walls. Whether this line of action was initially planned by feminists is second in importance to the fact that feminism at Gezi was performatively actualized and acquired effective visibility through the correction of patriarchal language. The emergence of differential positions *with and against others,* as depicted in Tarhan's observation, is one of the reasons Occupy Gezi could not be represented: no political party or identity group could practically or discursively subsume it under an available label or sign. Nor could anyone speak in the name of Gezi or fully claim to represent its interests. It was as if the event was taking place at such a level of immanence that it refused to yield to available discursive denominations. It seemed to unfold on a shifting ground that "ex-posed" social identities to each other, but also shifted the markers of vulnerability and suffering in complex ways.

The Whos and the Becomings

This having been said, Occupy Gezi cannot be recounted as a juxtaposition of social identities, and the following second short story will help show why. A young woman in a black mini dress was among protestors confronting a police vehicle armed with a water cannon (TOMA) in a street near Gezi Park on June 1. She suddenly jumped ahead with her arms wide open and was hit frontally by the spray of pressurized water. Journalists nearby shot several pictures of this drenched woman, standing with a bright smile on her face in a pool of water. The image immediately went viral, and in a very short time it was reproduced en masse, stylized, turned into artwork and stencil. Had that woman (a gendered identity, a "what") expected to become iconized as "the woman in black" (a "who")? An interview near the end of the month revealed that she obviously hadn't: "I felt that I owed something to this movement in solidarity with the protesters . . . We all knew that the Turkish media was not broadcasting any of these protests and how important it was to spread the incidents through the media. I realized that there was a group of photographers near the TOMA and I decided to stand in front of it and open my arms in order to emphasize the peacefulness of the protests despite the violence."[46]

The woman in black actually turned out to be Kate Mullen, an Australian exchange student in Turkey. Or, rather, Kate Mullen turned out to be the woman in black. As she herself also states: "The photograph is not about me anymore. If we think on a general scale, my action is nothing. . . . It's not more courageous than protesters who did the same things or more. The woman in black is not me anymore."[47] This is undoubtedly true, but is it solely because her icononization is a patriarchal sign, a projection of the republican desire of marking women's bodies as symbols of the modern nation, as some scholars have forcefully argued?[48] Is it because the indefinite potential in her act was captured and tied to a citational practice or Master Signifier? This cannot be so, since the uptake of the deed—how others responded to it, or, in Arendt's words, the *prattein*—was manifold. At one of the entrances of Gezi, the woman in black stood photocopied on a sign that read "Everything is free of charge in the park." It must be conceded that the articulation of the open arms of a (courageous? sexy? happy?) woman with the banishment of money (the becoming-commune of Gezi) cannot unproblematically be subsumed under the sign of republican patriarchy. The "meaning" of the act, as Arendt would say, could not be foreclosed either by "what" Kate intended or by her being a "woman," "Australian," "student," "modern," "appealing to republicans," "sexy," and so forth. This, I believe, is the appeal of the Arendtian perspective: the actor (willingly or unwillingly) inscribes herself into the course of events in such a way as to modify the initial circumstances under which she acts without, however, becoming the author of the whole story. The actor exerts herself into a "now" that inflects preordained future paths, including her own; she *exposes* herself to the "risks of new experiences" to which she doesn't yet know how either she or others shall respond.[49]

Thus one line moves out of the act toward the emergence of a self. Kate is now what she has performed, an actor in a drama. She is a differential, not a difference: her position within the "event" Gezi does not arise from any preestablished role or societal location. Her relation to others is a position within an indefinite set of movements without Cartesian coordinates. Within the mesh of events that subsequently unfolded, some lines condensed into the republican appropriation of the woman in black that had all the potential of being a dead end, an antagonistic capture, a usurpation. But infinite others moved into other directions. Kate's act and its image (the icon) become part of the "world" erected at Gezi. She became a "public thing" (*res publica*) that was commented on, reproduced, and appropriated by many others whom she did not—and probably will not—know. But she had also acquired a face, a public persona, an individual status as a "who," probably beyond her own expectations. She was part of the acting-in-concert that constituted Gezi, one that inspired a multitude, but also a unique being who can never be exactly reproduced or imitated by any other.

The face, the proper name, and the sheer unrepresentability of an act or a life story made their way into Gezi, either as physical signs (photos and names of victims of state violence attached to trees in the park, barriers turned into sites of memory),[50] or as viral messages, pictures, artwork, and comments. The double vulnerability of the trees and the protestors defending them at Gezi opened up a conduit through which those who had suffered in the past could be remembered.

The indefinite contours of what appeared as a collective uprising condensed into the figural without any set pattern. For instance, could it have been predicted, through probabilistic calculation or sociological generalization, that Sırrı Süreyya Önder, the MP of the pro-Kurdish Peace and Democracy Party (BDP), would become one of the first heroes of a resistance to which the BDP itself was initially reluctant to support?[51] Other unpredictable actors also emerged in the heat of the action: the Standing Man, the Woman-in-Red, Cheerleader Vedat . . . One would thus need to underline that "what" went into Gezi, came out altered. The way the identity was symbolized *before* acting and *after* having acted was not the same, since the proliferation of sites of encounter reduced the chances of remaining immune to the effect of others. On the one hand, social identities were altered by acquiring "individuality" (an LGBT protestor who went to the barricade came out as the boy in the skirt). This appellation was produced in action by the encounter between LGBT protestors and the soccer fans. It was therefore an in-between—a *nom de combattant*, if you will. On the other hand, new designations had to be created to name the differential. For instance, fans continued calling the police *ibne* (faggot), but then turned to LGBT protestors to excuse themselves, saying, "They are the *real* faggots; you're one of us!" For how else does a (previously? still?) homophobic soccer fan identify the boy in the skirt struggling against the police right next to him? Fans eventually started calling the transsexuals *abla* (elder sister), signaling that the becoming-sister of transsexuals was at the same time the becoming-br/other of soccer fans.[52]

This is to say that at Gezi, difference consisted of multiple and fleeting positions within a common project, a collective moment of acting, of moving in and out of selfhood and social identities. The theoretical path sketched above allows us to conceive of these identities as *performative positions* emerging in the midst of the action.[53] The resistance did not offer sources of identification, but merely interpellated practices of negotiation, differentiation, and composition within its structure of appearance and encounter. These practices were generatively performative; they gave rise to a new vocabulary, novel claims and repertoires, and a new mode of relating. In the words of an LGBT activist at Gezi: "If someone had written a script like this, nobody would have been able to act it out."[54]

Agonistic Suffering

But how credible is it to narrate the uprising as the story of a blissful composition of multiple identities, of a happy multicultural rave party? There is also the story of agonistic suffering to tell. The LGBT protestors, for instance, did not "become sister" without paying the price of swallowing tear gas. They thereby earned the rather macho qualification of *delikanlı ibne* (red-blooded faggot), whether they liked it or not.

I therefore find valuable how Athena Athanasiou productively shifts the Arendtian notion of the space of appearance toward the idea of "spacing appearance," implying a "performative plane of 'taking place'" irreducible to surface phenomenality in that "it opens up to concern what is performed in ways that avow the unperformable."[55] I interpret this as underlining the uncontainability of the lines of flight crisscrossing the multiple exposures enacted, as when an uncanny stranger's appearance faces an assembly with "the disjunctive performative force of sheer socio-historical specificity."[56]

Nearly verbatim, the uncanny stranger faced Mete, a young man sitting in a public forum taking place at Abbasağa Park in Beşiktaş shortly after Gezi was evacuated.[57] He was seriously offended by a speaker addressing the auditorium. Mete then broke the ad hoc code established at Gezi forums, which required that those wishing to speak should sign up and wait for their turn to come to the middle of the crowd. The code forbade interrupting a speaker. The first speaker that evening turned out to be a retired army officer who likened resistance to fulfilling one's patriotic duty. Pure chance had it that the second person to speak was a conscientious objector. A few minutes into the speech, someone in the audience interrupted him. The voice was claiming that no one had the right to question the sacredness of military service. The moderator attached a name to the voice: "Mete," he said, "If you have something to say, you must sign up." The voice (having now become Mete) stomped up front to write his name on the speakers' list. He then sat down to endure not only the conscientious objector's speech, but also that of a speaker reading out a letter sent by his brother, a conscript admitting that he would have disobeyed had his commanders ordered him to shoot at Kurdish villagers protesting the erection of an army post in Diyarbakır's Lice district. The audience had all but forgotten about Mete when, several speakers later, someone stepped up to plead for conscientious objection yet again. This time, the speaker interpellated Mete directly before beginning his speech: "Didn't we struggle at the same barricades together?" he asked Mete. "Didn't we risk our lives when facing the same police? Well, then, you must listen. I don't have to like the army and I want to express this here." His was an attempt to establish the bond between bodies at Gezi as the more genuine ground of engagement. The divisiveness of speech had to be bridged by recalling the immediacy of collective action. It was as if learning to listen to each other was a sort of unsolicited pedagogy, a price to be paid for solidarity. Obviously, Mete was not "at home" in this forum, but no one wished to ban him. After his long wait, he spoke very briefly, in a somewhat bitter tone, but having shed his initial aggressiveness. "My father is an army officer," he said, "and I have respect for people who are willing to face death in order to fulfill their duty to the country. You must also respect them, that's all I ask." Hands were waved to show him that the audience approved (clapping was unwelcome in the forums). And here I am, narrating his story because he had the power to endure the uncanny and formulated a commendable response to a very upsetting *épreuve*.

The uncanny emerged in countless other sites and instances at Gezi. Nationalists singing "We are all Mustafa Kemal's soldiers" (alluding to Mustafa Kemal Atatürk, the founder of the Republic) were haunted by the sporadic chants of antimilitarist groups: "We won't kill, we won't die; we won't become anyone's soldier!" The dissonance of not being able to readily resonate with others, and the distress of finding one's firmest convictions incommunicable or unacceptable, were decentering experiences. No identity or ideological standpoint was "at home" in the streets and parks that the resistance transformed into public spaces they all shared, irrespective of whether they would have chosen to do so with this assortment of "others." The streets were spaces that no one could domesticate despite or at the expense of others. Rather, one had to find his or her own (ethical) response to these unfamiliar others so as to continue acting in concert with them.

This having been said, Occupy Gezi cannot be recounted without noting that the Kurdish movement was a case apart. Their positioning in the collective action could not be detached from the stigmatized place assigned to Kurds by authoritarian nationalistic discourses, which is why the Kurdish party initially hesitated in participating in the resistance despite its battle-seasoned youth being already at the barricades. Furthermore, the BDP was interpellated to join a struggle that required it to efface its ethnic demands. This caused much resentment among the Kurds, an extremely vulnerable population.

Ethnic Turks seemed much more avid to jump in front of armed vehicles to protect trees than to shield Kurds from state violence. As soon as the BDP set up its tent and banners in the park, it was physically attacked. Nevertheless, the experience of Gezi did have a huge impact on the Kurdish movement. Fusing both the doer and the sufferer, it became the only institutional actor to disband itself and subsequently reunite a myriad of oppositional groups into a new party. This was—and continues to be—an enormous political risk that could affect not only the Kurdish movement, but also the whole institutional set-up in Turkey.[58]

Thus, for many, Gezi was an unexpected "initiation" into pain, suffering, and decomposition, as well as into collective euphoria and solidarity. As Zeynel Gül eloquently writes, participating in Gezi was like acquiring the scar that marks the body in the rites of initiation of the Guayaki.[59] I would need to add that these rites were inscribed nowhere but had to be invented.

Reconstituting a "Home"

In an interview during the resistance, M. Efe Fırat stated, "They say that LGBT individuals are being othered, but even more than that, they are totally alienated. Theirs is a condition, steered by the media, of not being taken into account, of being intimidated, turned a blind eye on, made invisible, of heterosexuals not being allowed to hear them. And maybe this resonated with social practice as such: the desperate attempts of the LGBT movement were not being taken in, that is, a heterosexual did not feel the same agony and humiliation to which an LGBT was being subjected. *All this was equalized during the Gezi resistance.*"[60]

What sort of equalization is being alluded to here? The stories narrated so far show how equal vulnerability to state violence (antagonism) was complemented by differential vulnerabilities to the internal components of the resistance. One needs to beware of romanticizing the subaltern and the precarious: certain groups that engage in agonistic relations with other groups in one context, may themselves contribute to the antagonistic distribution of vulnerability, either in that same context or in others. On the antagonistic plane, exposure to tear gas and police brutality was shared across the board by all of the bodies taking to the streets for one reason or another. To be sure, Occupy Gezi was a "negative community"[61] formed by resisting a complex range of politically induced conditions of precarity. This did not exclude the differential distribution of affectability among its vulnerable agents. Ethnic Turks came to acknowledge with great astonishment that the media could spin an entirely calumnious representation of the resistance; ethnic Kurds could barely hide their satisfaction at Turks being smothered with tear gas, retorting: "Do you now see what we were going through?"[62] It might well be that some identities would need to affirm themselves as dialectic differences before being expected to "become other." Paraphrasing Braidotti again, both the hegemonic "majority (the 'same') and the minorities (the others) . . . [had] to relinquish their ties, but they [did] so in dissymmetrical ways."[63]

But while the antagonistic frontier was more clearly traced, the porosity of the agonistic folds owed to the absence of a permanent power position—that is, of any permanent *doer*—within Gezi Park. The chances of doing and suffering were rather transient. Hence, the following tentative suggestions must be made as to what distinguishes the Gezi movement from other "negative communities" (such as xenophobic groups or lynch mobs) that are also founded on shared perceptions of vulnerability. On the one hand, we must take into consideration what action does to the *actors themselves* in addition to what it does to others. The theoretical perspective outlined earlier differs from other-directed forms of inquiry that paradoxically reproduce the centrality of the "I" as the agent of the ethical act. Isn't ethics *political* precisely because dilemmas that cannot be resolved, either through Kantian morality or any altruistic social code, present themselves in the form of an event, as irreproducible singular instances that happen to us, that encroach on us by surprise? Doesn't the "I" then become a differential—and not merely a dialectical difference with respect to an other? This would entail construing ethics as situated and action as the ultimate testing ground of the ethical self.

This, I believe, is the most radical sense of plurality emanating from Arendt's theorization of action. The ethical self would have to be considered as an *effect*, the outcome of a set of unpredictable responses to differential positions opening up as one acts. Hence, determining what kind of encounter or act can qualify as agonistic as opposed to antagonistic would require gauging the various types of responses to "ex-posure." Do the actors open themselves up to mutual affectability, or do they act so as to freeze differentials and thereby produce practices of exclusion and segregation? Is permeability between agonistic positions possible, or are the latter effaced under univocal categorizations or stigmas? Is the emphasis placed on difference or on sameness, on the "unlikely" or on the "likely"? Obviously, the first options would qualify as agonistic—and therefore ethical—while the second wouldn't.

On the other hand, however, it can be objected that the sheer indeterminacy of the event-character of situational ethics makes it an unsuitable ground for exploring "ordinary" as opposed to "extra-ordinary" ethics. Is ethics never "at home"? Do ethical dilemmas arise only in rare moments in collective life? While being cautious of the pitfalls that such a question entails, I would nevertheless suggest that Gezi was a spatial, situational, and relational reconfiguration that territorialized ethics in a *site* structured in such a way as to enable multiple encounters. What came to be called the "Gezi spirit" seems to have contained the contours of a situated ethics inseparable from the praxis of setting up an alternative mode of being in the park while at the same time defending it against the forces of the state. The *hexis,* or disposition—emerging from cohabiting the park, procuring staple products, cooking food, setting up a vegetable garden, or sharing tea or cigarettes—was not dictated by any established order or law. But both the Gezi resistance and the forums taking place during and after it appear to have worked on "sensibilities" in such a way that certain "ethical obligations imposed themselves" on participants.[64] As Goulimari convincingly argues: "Any given territoriality is analyzed as a process with two tendencies: one towards exclusive encounters with other territorialities, the other towards inclusive encounters and their lines of flight or escape. This is then the ethics of inclusion that underlies the concept of 'becoming minoritarian'—to invent, within a particular territoriality, the practical procedures that will enhance or accelerate the second tendency."[65] It might very well be that Gezi enacted the latter: it was a radically ethical site populated by the becoming-other of its agents, a micro-polis producing singularities even as bodies went about accomplishing everyday chores of sustenance. One might even venture to say that such sites as Gezi might not have to be invented *ex nihilo,* since they might already be actualizing in diverse collective struggles around the world.

Notes

1 Arendt, "The Great Tradition II," 948.
2 Cf. particularly criticisms of Arendt's citizens as "posturing little boys" in Pitkin, "Justice," 338; of Arendt's "rhetoric of greatness and men trying to be men" in Cornell, "Gender Hierarchy, Equality, and the Possibility of Democracy," 259; and of her "female mind nourished on male ideologies," in Rich, *On Lies, Secrets and Silence,* 212.
3 Mouffe, "For a Politics of Nomadic Identity," 105. My perspective is rather different from Mouffe's, however, as she emphasizes the conflictual potential of democratic pluralism and construes agonistic politics as one between adversaries, albeit sharing a common ground. Cf. Mouffe's "Deliberative Democracy or

Agonistic Pluralism?," 745–758, and *Democratic Paradox*, for a fuller account of Mouffe's version of agonism.

4 For a "correction" of Arendt's "halfway plausible theory of ethics," see Benhabib, "Judgment and Moral Foundations of Politics in Arendt's Thought"; for a critique of a nonfoundational ethics, see Benhabib, "Toward a Deliberative Model of Democratic Legitimacy"; and Fraser, "Michel Foucault."

5 Braidotti, "Becoming Woman," 55. The emphasis is mine.

6 Honig, "Toward an Agonistic Feminism," 149. This is a revised and augmented version of her 1992 paper with the same title, published in *Feminists Theorize the Political*, ed. J. Butler and J. Scott, *Feminist Theorize the Political*.

7 Honig, "Toward an Agonistic Feminism," 146.

8 Honig, "The Arendtian Question in Feminism," 7.

9 Honig, "Toward an Agonistic Feminism," 160.

10 Honig, "Toward an Agonistic Feminism," 140, 145.

11 Honig, "Toward an Agonistic Feminism," 138, and note 6. Cf. also Villa, *Arendt and Heidegger*, esp. 80–109, for the tense but close relationship between Arendt and Nietzsche.

12 Honig, "Toward an Agonistic Feminism," 159. The problem becomes more acute in Honig's afterword to her 1995 text, when she writes that "the process of individuation is not *for* an audience, though any set of actions or performances may be witnessed by one" (160). While Arendt's notion of action precludes a means/ends type of instrumentalization, it can never be divorced from the question of appearance. Cf. Tassin, "La question de l'apparence."

13 Honig, "Toward an Agonistic Feminism," 137.

14 Arendt, *The Human Condition*, 47.

15 Arendt, "What Is Freedom?," *Between Past and Future*, 63.

16 Honig, "Toward an Agonistic Feminism," 143.

17 Arendt, *The Human Condition*, 180.

18 Arendt, *The Human Condition*, 301.

19 Arendt, *The Human Condition*, 186. The term "risk" is meant to connote this Arendtian meaning throughout the chapter and is not related to any of the meanings associated with what Beck, *Risk Society*, calls "risk society," i.e., neoliberal cosmopolitan modernization.

20 For a paradigmatic example, cf. Benhabib, "Toward a Deliberative Model of Democratic Legitimacy."

21 Arendt, "Ruling and Being Ruled," 948; *The Human Condition*, 190.

22 Arendt, "Ruling and Being Ruled," 946. Needless to say, there are traces of a Hegelian construct in this agonistic construal of the "self," although, as I hope to show further on, Arendt eschews both the antagonistic dialectics inherent in the Hegelian formation of subjecthood and the politics of recognition that derives from it.

23 Arendt, *The Human Condition*, 189.

24 Arendt, *The Human Condition*, 190.

25 I explore this more explicitly in Gambetti, "The Agent Is the Void!," 425–437.

26 Arendt, *The Human Condition*, 200–201.

27 Arendt, *The Human Condition*, 190, emphasis added.

28 Arendt, *The Human Condition*, 8.

29 I find in Arendt's underdeveloped theory of "uniqueness" the promise of overcoming the metaphysics of the signifier or machine without falling back on a metaphysics of the subject. What Arendt refers to as the "who" is irreducible to any of the "whats" in circulation, as hybrid or multiple as can be. Adriana Cavarero's account of the profundity of Arendt's notion of uniqueness captures this very well. Cf. Cavarero, *Relating Narratives*, esp. 20.

30 Obviously, the sense in which I use "antagonism" differs from the conceptualization developed by Laclau and Mouffe in *Hegemony and Socialist Strategy*, according to which antagonism is a "constitutive outside" indicating the limit of all objectivity and universality. As such, Laclau and Mouffe remain committed to a Hegelian notion of difference that can be expressed as the distance between "a" and "not-a." I employ antagonism to designate the opposition of conflicting or hostile forces, especially underpinning the will to vanquish, conquer, and subjugate the other. My dual construal of distance as "difference" and "differential" disallows me to accept the notion of a "constitutive outside."

31 Braidotti, *Transpositions*, 58.

32 Das, *Life and Words*, 62.

33 Butler, *Frames of War*, 25–26. I would also like to note the similar yet counterpunctual ways in which Leticia Sabsay appropriates this distinction in her contribution to the present volume.

34 Agamben, *Homo Sacer*.

35 Braidotti, "Becoming Woman," 49.

36 As shall be remembered, the Gezi Park in Istanbul was to be demolished, and a shopping mall and luxury residence was erected in its place. This was part of the conservative Justice and Development Party (AKP) government's gigantic urban transformation and gentrification projects. After several trees were pulled down, peaceful protestors squatted the park in tents but were brutally evicted on May 30, 2013. This sparked anger, and massive support for the protestors flowed to the park. The occupation lasted seventeen days, but the protests continued well into July.

37 Rancière, *Dis-agreement*, 22.

38 This event was related in a slightly different manner in a published interview: Yazıcı, "Velev ki ibneyiz, alışın her yerdeyiz," 61.

39 Tarhan, "Barikatın LGBT Tarafı."

40 Cf. Erhart, "Ladies of Besiktas," 83–98; Bora, "Erkeklik ve Futbol."

41 "Farklılıklara Kapalı Toplum," *Cumhuriyet*, May 31, 2009.

42 Birdal, "Queering Conservative Democracy," 123. Cf. Ataman, "Less than Citizens"; and Burcu Baba, "The Construction of Heteropatriarchal Family and Dissident Sexualities in Turkey."

43 This was conveyed by a banner held up in the Gay Pride march in Istanbul: "Gays exist! Kurds exist!"

44 Uluğ and Acar, *Bir Olmadan Biz Olmak*, 168.

45 Cf. Öktem, "Another Struggle."

46 "Woman in Black, One of the Gezi Park Heroes, Wanted to Show Protests' Peacefulness," *Hürriyet Dailiy News*, June 25, 2013.

47 "Woman in Black, One of the Gezi Park Heroes, Wanted to Show Protests' Peacefulness."

48 Cf. particularly Tekay and Ustun, "A Short History of Feminism in Turkey and Feminist Resistance in Gezi."

49 Dunne, "Beyond Sovereignty and Deconstruction," 146.

50 Cf. Başak Ertür's contribution to this volume and also Athena Athanasiou's questions on spectral memory, enforced effacements, and the problematics of visibility. The ways in which Athanasiou interpellates us to complicate the notions of (dis)appearing and (dis)appearing under conditions of physical presence is a challenge that I cannot fully address here. I can but be grateful that she has done so.

51 Cf. Yetkin, "Occupy Taksim."

52 This is also revealed in the fact that fan groups from outside Istanbul invited LGBTs to watch matches together and want to participate in LGBT meetings. Cf. Kandok, "Spor eşcinsellerin varolmaları için bir fırsattır."

53 The socialist Left's position vis-à-vis the LGBT block seemed to have changed, for example, as expressed by Altunpolat, "Gezi Vesilesiyle LGBT Hareketi ve Sosyalistler": "As one of the components of the resistance, the LGBT movement's vitality, endurance, and creativity seem to have attracted the attention of the Socialist Left. Let's express this openly: the LGBT movement—irrespective of whether it had such an aim—has in a way proved to the Socialist Left that it has 'come of age.'"

54 Belgin Çelik, interviewed by Çağlar, "LGBT'lerin Gözünden Gezi Direnişi."

55 Butler and Athanasiou, *Dispossession*, 194.

56 Butler and Athanasiou, *Dispossession*, 195.

57 Numerous public forums took place during and after Occupy Gezi in cities around Turkey throughout the summer of 2013. These were generally organized by self-appointed conveners in neighborhoods where parks allowed all those who wished to participate to sit in circles and take turns to bring up issues of concern for all. The crowds were largely heterogeneous, although some forums were more republican than others.

58 Cf. Celep, "Can the Kurdish Left Contribute to Turkey's Democratization," 165–180, and Küçük, "Between Two Rationalities."

59 Gül, "Gezi, Temsiliyet, Ütopya." Gül is referring to the rites narrated by Clastres, *Society against the State*, particularly 185–186.

60 Fırat, interviewed by Çağlar, "LGBT'lerin Gözünden Gezi Direnişi," emphasis added.

61 Balibar, "Historical Dilemmas of Democracy and Their Contemporary Relevance for Citizenship," 536.

62 Şirin, "Gezi'de Kürt Olmak."

63 Braidotti, "Becoming Woman," 55.

64 Butler, "Precarious Life, Vulnerability and the Ethics of Cohabitation," 137.

65 Goulimari, "A Minoritarian Feminism?," 111.

···

CHAPTER 3

Bouncing Back

Vulnerability and Resistance in Times of Resilience

SARAH BRACKE

The Power of Resilience

Resilience has friends in high places. Resilience has become a protagonist in recent visions, programs, and policy interventions designed by global economic institutions. The World Bank initiated a working group on "Social Resilience and Climate Change," which takes "social resilience" as a means of fighting poverty and overcoming the weakness of fragile states. In conjunction with the UN, the World Bank increasingly promotes resilience as the means for "growing the wealth of the poor."[1] The IMF turns to resilience most prominently in its strategies to deal with disaster and its aftermath (so-called disaster resilience) and in its programs that focus on the capacity building of financial systems and national economies as well as the development of human capital. In the United States, resilience figures among the terms the Department of Homeland Security (DHS) deems "fundamental to the practice of homeland security risk management and analysis" and is hence included in the DHS Risk Lexicon, where it is defined as "the ability to adapt to changing conditions and prepare for, withstand, and rapidly recover from disruption."[2] This post-9/11 "strategy of risk management" is a key organizing principle for all homeland security strategies, programs, and activities.[3]

Resilience, in short, is a powerful idea whose deployment spans the macro-level of ecological and economic systems to the micro level of selves, and the complex circuits of power that connect and constitute these different levels of social reality. In this essay, I am interested in the power that resilience exercises on subjects and the ways such subjects come into being and are maintained. I understand this power to operate in complex manners, not merely as programs imposed on unsuspecting individuals, although that is surely one of the ways in which the impact of resilience in our world is felt, but also as a desired good, or the prize that many of us have come to set our eyes on as we seek to navigate the constraints and possibilities of our daily lives. The way in which resilience permeates popular culture is truly striking, finding a notable expression in the popularization of psychological theories that revolve around the notion of the "resilient self": *Build Your Resilience: Teach Yourself How to Survive and Thrive in any Situation*; *Resilience: Bounce Back from Whatever Life Throws at You*, or *The Power of Resilience: Achieving Balance, Confidence, and Personal Strength in Your Life* are just a few titles of literally thousands of recent books that offer visions on becoming resilient as well as exercises and techniques to do so.[4] Such visions belong to a particular political economy: the prevalence of resilience as a term knew a spectacular rise at a moment in time that is generally recognized as a shift in political economy and cultural hegemony, that is, the 1980s or the beginning of the hegemony of neoliberalism.[5] In his seminal work on the connections between expertise, subjectivity, and political power, Nikolas Rose reminds us of how psychological expertise, and particularly in its popularized guise of self-help books, became a technology of neoliberal government, actively constructing truths about the self and encouraging their readers to regulate their conduct according to specific liberal virtues.[6] That many of the aforementioned books are best sellers indicates that the notion of a resilient self resonates with a broader public, yet the idea of resilience as a personal virtue now reaches far beyond the readership of such self-help books. Resilience, we could argue, has become a force to be reckoned with in the realm of hegemonic ethics of and truths about the self.

What does an ethics of self that privileges resilience look like? Which subjects does it shape under its auspices? What modalities of agency does such a process of subjectivication produce and foreclose? This essay takes resilience as a point of departure to tell yet another tale of neoliberal governmentality. I explore the notion of resilience in relation to two critical terms that are the primary subjects of inquiry of this volume—vulnerability and resistance—as well as in relation to social relations of gender, and ask what a gendered understanding of resilience might tell us about vulnerability and resistance. I also raise the question of what a politics of resistance to resilience might look like.

Resilience as a Keyword

The ubiquity of resilience in contemporary political and psychological discourses is striking.[7] If Raymond Williams were writing *Keywords: A Vocabulary of Culture and Society* today, resilience, I believe, would figure among his selection of terms that hold particular salience in contemporary culture.[8] Williams took keywords to be critical for the purpose of understanding contemporary culture and society; they provide a privileged entry, as it were, into the cultural significations that shape a given time and place.[9] Keywords have been described as "socially prominent word[s] that [are] capable of bearing interlocking, yet sometimes contradictory and commonly contested contemporary meanings," and as such they are characterized by polysemous as well as contested qualities.[10]

Resilience emerges as a keyword from the 1980s onward.[11] While the term is brought to bear on a strikingly wide array of thematic areas (such as ecology, economy, psyches, or political regimes) as well as on distinct levels of analysis (from the macro level of systems to the micro level of selves), the concept retains its coherence by commonly relying on the ability of a substance or object to bounce back and spring into prior shape. The *Oxford English Dictionary* defines resilience as "Rebounding; recoiling; returning to the original position" and "Tending to recover quickly or easily from misfortune, shock, illness, or the like; buoyant, irrepressible; adaptable, robust, hardy." Resilience is indeed frequently characterized as the ability of something or someone to return to its original shape after it has been pulled, stretched, pressed, or bent. It is understood as the capability of a strained body to recover its size and shape after deformation caused by compressive stress.[12] Resilience, in sum, revolves around shock absorption.

Williams understood keywords to be polysemous, which he recognized not as a potential source of undermining the operation of the term, but as contributing to its social force. Resilience's travels through different thematic fields and disciplinary contexts have generated various shifts in meaning. Some of these semantic shifts are a mere effect of its usage in different contexts, and most often these transpositions remain unthought. The origins of the term bring us back to nineteenth-century physical sciences, where "resilience" sought to capture a physical property of certain materials, which can be understood as elasticity, or the capacity to absorb energy. Its more contemporary usage is largely attributed to ecological thought in the second half of the twentieth century, when it was conceptualized as a measure of an ecological system to recover. The first articulations of resilience in ecological thought signified persistence, that is, the capacity to absorb or buffer shocks while maintaining structure and function.[13] In academic literature, the term subsequently traveled to studies about disaster and its aftermath, including climate and other hazards, and eventually was used in relation to people, communities, institutions, cities, economies, and political regimes.[14] The scope of thematic areas as well as levels of analysis that the concept seemingly effortlessly encompasses is rather dizzying, not in the least because it remains questionable whether the resilience of an ecosystem is identical to that of an economic system, or whether the elasticity of latex rubber is comparable to that of highly resilient individuals. Yet most often the necessary work of reconceptualization that such a conceptual transposition would require is lacking, a reservation that seems all the more pertinent in the shift from thinking resilience as a property of a system to a property of an individual. Lest my point be misunderstood: I do not wish to make a principled argument against the transposition of a concept from one level of analysis, and from one field of study, to another; rather, I seek to draw attention to the fact that such transpositions might require a fair amount of conceptual work—work that seems largely absent in the case of the "traveling concept" of resilience.

This original sense of resilience, moreover, has also been deliberately elaborated and modified throughout its current usage in a neoliberal context, as merely bouncing back or returning to a prior state has often been considered not enough. In ecological thought, Carl Folke argues, the meaning of transformability—in other words, the potential of the system to recombine structure and processes and to reorganize and renovate itself—as well as the meaning of adaptability—that is, the capacity of an ecosystem to adapt and learn—joined the concept's original emphasis on persistence.[15] Within sociology, Gérard Bouchard distinguishes three ways in which the capacity to recover after shock can be achieved: by resisting stress and returning to a prior state as the original meaning of resilience intended, but also by adapting to a new situation through adjustment, negotiation, and compromise, and finally by seizing on the occasion by "creatively" responding to the challenge of the shock or trauma.[16] Bouchard calls these different modes (respectively) conservative, adaptive, and progressive forms of resilience. Peter Hall and Michèle Lamont, moreover, intently use the term "social resilience" in order to "refer to the capacity of groups of people bound together in an organization, class, racial group, community, or nation to sustain and advance their well-being in the face of challenges to it."[17] The adjective "social" thus shifts the emphasis away from the individual and toward the institutional, social, and cultural resources that groups as well as individuals mobilize for their well-being. Here resilience includes the social networks the individual finds herself in, as well as the cultural repertoires that are available to her when responding to crises. Such rearticulations, and the creative and social dimensions that they engage, matter, yet given how resilience operates as a keyword in the way that Williams understood keywords to operate, the primary sense of resilience is all but severed from these elaborations or rearticulations. Rather, resilience as a keyword mobilizes all of those meanings at once, and shifts between them, oftentimes unaccountably.

This sketch of the operation of resilience as a keyword would not be complete without attending to the particular connection of resilience to the question of security. It is not so much that security is yet another thematic area under the spell of the rise of resilience; rather, the sensibilities of resilience and security have become intimately intertwined in contemporary biopolitics driven by the "threats from terrorism, natural disasters, health pandemics and other disruptive challenges."[18] Resilience, Mark Neocleous argues, has subsumed and surpassed the logic of security, understood both as a structure of individual subjectivity and as a principle of national policy. Hence, the contemporary emphasis on resilience might be considered as part of a new security apparatus, as resilience "connects the emotional management of personal problems with the wider security agenda and the logic of accumulation during a period of crisis."[19] We might begin understanding this dense connection in the following manner. As the idea of a society, as well as a self, that can be protected and defended in such a way that it remains unshakable, untouchable, and sheltered from any kind of undoing increasingly falters, security is reconfigured through the prism of resilience. This opens a new horizon, indexed by the increasingly common expression "security and resilience,"[20] in which security is understood not (only) as effective protection against the possible impact of something that threatens or injures, but (also) in terms of fostering the capacity to reverse such impact or undoing, as another way to preserve the integrity of a society, system, or self. In other words, if security cannot (solely) be understood as effective shelter from hazards of various kinds, it can be rearticulated as finding ways not only to prevent and control damage, but also to reverse it. This new understanding of strength does not revolve around preventing dreadful things from happening to oneself; rather, it lies in being prepared to face all challenges and threats. Resilience arguably recalibrates security, as it complements security as prevention as well as detention with an understanding of security as minimizing impact and erasing traces. In precarious times, resilience is the new security.

Security and Resilience

This reconfiguration of security can be situated in relation to what sociologists, and notably sociologists situated in Europe, began framing as "risk society" in the 1980s. In Ulrich Beck's influential account, risk society is understood as "a systematic way of dealing with hazards and insecurities induced and introduced by modernization itself." This reflexivity—this "second moment" in the life of modernity, as Beck understands it—engages with the dystopian outcomes of processes of rationalization that Beck situates at the very heart of modernity, and envisions the possibility of its own destruction. Risk society thus refers to complexity and interdependency, as well as skepticism about human ability to control these processes.[21] It notoriously condemns its inhabitants to live in uncertainty. Beck's understanding of risk society emerged in the context of the ecological crisis as it became tangible in the West in the 1980s, and a corresponding consciousness that environmental risks had become the predominant product, rather than just an unpleasant yet manageable by-product, of (post)industrial society. Beck's very first formulation of risk society was published shortly before the explosion and fire in the Chernobyl nuclear power plant in the Ukrainian Soviet Socialist Republic in 1986, yet much of the theory's subsequent elaboration was thought in relation to that nuclear disaster. The trope of ecological disaster was critical in the early development of contemporary understandings of risk as well as resilience; meanwhile, terrorism has prominently joined the ranks of tropes. The attack on the World Trade Center in New York City in 2001, one of the most critical events in the rise of "security and resilience," arguably recasts terrorism from a manageable by-product of the contemporary globalizing world to one of its central products, fixated through a permanent War on Terror. Dominant US accounts of those attacks combine a narrative of shock, marked by an inability or refusal to understand one's individual as well as collective body as so susceptible to undoing, with a narrative reconfiguration of injurability and untouchability. Until the attacks, the narrative goes, it was unimaginable that the national body might be injured on its domestic grounds by a foreign attack in a way that shakes and undoes the nation to the core. Then the events of 9/11 exposed the belief that such a breach could never happen to be a naive illusion. As a way of holding fast to this extinguished illusion, resilience emerged as the appropriate response, one of bouncing back and returning to business, and one might add the market, as usual.[22]

This entanglement of resilience in the security apparatus reveals something of the profound situatedness of the question of secure selves and societies, as well as how this situatedness informs the concept of resilience. To begin understanding what the dominant US account of the 2001 attacks produces, and what it forecloses, it is fruitful to turn to *Precarious Life*, Judith Butler's moving account of the psychosocial dynamics involved in the aftermath of the attack, in which a national sense of having been undone in the United States was met by the solidification and securitization of boundaries, both in terms of national boundaries and national identity.[23] Writing against these hegemonic constructions of identity and security in order to interrupt them and carve out the space to imagine and do otherwise, Butler draws attention to the self's primary vulnerability to others, as well as its fundamental dependency on others. National sovereignty tries to overcome these facts of life, and thus misrecognizes or denies the fundamental relationality that holds that we are constituted, as well as dispossessed, by others.[24] Grief, in Butler's account, is permeated by the possibility of apprehending a mode of dispossession that is fundamental to the self,[25] and in this apprehension Butler situates the transformative power at the heart of grief and mourning, one that might turn grief and mourning into a ground of politics. Perhaps mourning, Butler suggests, has to do with agreeing to undergo a transformation in the sense of self and ties to others, the full result of which one cannot know in advance.[26] This contrasts sharply with what occurred in the dominant responses to 9/11, as sovereignty, from a sense of self-mastery and mastery over the environment, was asserted at the price of denying vulnerability and dependency.

Here a first contemporary figure of a resilient subject emerges—that of a First World subject who feels threatened by terrorism and other looming disasters and whose longing for security aligns, to a significant extent, with securitarian politics as they are developed in the global North. This figure renders something of the relation between resilience and vulnerability tangible: the resilience it is committed to entails precisely the erasure of the transformation that is central to Butler's account of vulnerability, dependency, and grief. Or perhaps more adequately, here resilience absorbs potential transformation for the purpose of going back to the same, to a ground zero where the hazard or impact ultimately leaves no imprint, no traces. Thus resilience resurrects a form of self-sufficiency, and hence a fantasy of mastery, and it does so when climate change, the War on Terror, and economic crises (to name but a few systemic "risks" and hazards of our times) increasingly affect livelihoods around the world, and disproportionally those of the poorest. Resilience turns away from vulnerability, and the way it does so can be seen as symptomatic for contemporary subject formation, if we follow Lynne Layton's argument that neoliberal subjectivity is built on a denial of vulnerability, which is deemed shameful, and on a disidentification with dependence, need, and other kinds of vulnerability. The defense against these states of being, Layton suggests, takes the form of manic activity punctuated with the meditative and restorative services that people can afford to purchase.[27] Resilience is the terrain of restoration par excellence.

Thinking through the intimate connection between this First World resilience and security might yield further insights into how resilience is structurally linked with the threats against which it is supposed to give shelter. From the very outset, resilience depends on disaster or threat, without which it cannot exist. Indeed, it is dialectically bound to such disaster: without disaster, or at least a threat of it, there is no (need for) resilience. The insistence on resilience, in other words, keeps on mobilizing and animating disaster or at least its threat.[28] The recognition of this dialectical bond holds the suggestion that, in order for resilience to be sustainable, it is possible that disaster, or at least its threat, might need to be permanent. Moreover, if at the outset resilience is the desirable good that post-9/11 risk management strategies seek to pursue and cultivate, it also becomes part of the problem that such strategies target. If that which is considered to be the threat turns out to be resilient and continues to bounce back, possibly becoming stronger than before, then resilience is a significant risk. If environmental disasters, deadly viruses, or terrorist groups turn out to be resilient, then resilience becomes undistinguishable from the very threat or disaster that resilience first sought to overcome, and ultimately the distinction between threat and resilience collapses.

An Army of the Resilient

For most inhabiting this world, however, security understood as the protection of integrity and boundaries, whether those of individual or collective bodies, is virtually nonexistent. This lack of security is socially differentiated in terms of social relations of class, gender, ethnicity, and race, and those of the international division of labor. Secure selves and secure societies, sovereignty and mastery, are not fantasies to which most populations are entitled.

Yet these populations are often precisely the ones who are so readily labeled as "resilient," which in this context aligns not with security but with survival.

Here a second contemporary figure of a resilient subject emerges: the subject of the global South who has survived colonization, exploitation, and wars and has been subjected to austerity programs, most often conceptualized in the global North, and other forms of exploitation. We might call this a subject of *subaltern resilience*, or the resilience of the wretched of the earth, which is born out of the practice of getting up in the morning and making it through the day in conditions of often unbearable symbolic and material violence. Practices of survival under conditions of destitution—practices of picking up life time and again, wherever and in whatever state it is to be found—have a much longer history than the current use of resilience, and I would like to suggest that the price for calling this wrestling with the conditions one finds oneself in "resilience" might be too high. It has not escaped global economic institutions such as the IMF and the World Bank that there is an army of resilient people out there who are skilled in bouncing back from all kinds of shocks, including Structural Adjustment Programs and other, more recently invented, austerity measures. The resilience of the wretched of the earth is arguably fetishized by the economic and political institutions that bear great responsibility for the contemporary conditions of precarity that are (designed to be) met with resilience, if that is what we want to call it. As Neocleous argues in his critique of the centrality of resilience in poverty alleviation programs: "The beauty of the idea that resilience is what the world's poor need is that it turns out to be something that the world's poor already possess; all they require is a little training in how to realize it. Hence the motif of building, nurturing, and developing that runs through so much of the IMF literature."[29]

Here resilience, we might argue, is approached as a "raw material" that is available in abundance in this neoliberal world that came into being, if we follow Naomi Klein's argument, through the systematic exploitation of disaster-shocked peoples and countries.[30] Raw material invokes long-standing processes of colonization and international division of labor in which materials in the political and economic margins of the world are extracted for the manufacturing and other uses in the economic centers. Crucially, subaltern resilience and its legion of strained bodies and affluence of "nimble fingers"[31] provide the infrastructure for global processes of economic production and consumption. Raw material also invokes the late capitalist keyword of human capital, as the stock of knowledge and skills, including personality traits, which are embodied in the ability to produce value through performing labor. When it comes to the production process and the labor market, laborers' resilience is a valuable good, perhaps akin to raw materials that are, in the eyes of the global centers of power, too valuable not be extracted and processed. Global institutions such as the IMF and the World Bank are currently investing in training programs to build and enhance resilience of individuals, notably those in the global South, an investment that might be understood as a way to ensure that long-standing and ever-creative strategies of survival are safely molded into the needs of the greedy global economy: a resilient subject is one who can absorb the impact of austerity measures and continue to be productive.

Technologies of the Resilient Self

Thus far we have encountered two figures of resilient subjects, and they are positioned very differently in relation to contemporary geopolitical and economic power relations. Yet resilience as a mode of subjectification affects and shapes many others: Who are the many subjects that come with this way of worlding, who are equipped to live in this resilient new world? And do processes of resilient subjectification imply they have something in common beyond vast structural differences? In a classical psychological approach, resilience refers to individual characteristics that are associated with coping with stress situations and mitigating the negative effects of risk factors. While material conditions can be objectively hard, the reasoning goes, there are subjective differences in how people cope with such stress, shock, and trauma. A psychological approach to resilience is interested in finding those subjective differences and characteristics that account for why some individuals are more resilient than others. What does it take for an individual, hit by disaster and subsequent conditions of hardship, to absorb the shock, bounce back, and overcome those conditions?[32]

Such an approach, however, takes for granted that selves do not get shattered, and thus posits a continuity and coherence of the self prior to, during, and after the shock. What falls out of its purview are the operations of power involved in the very constitution of the subject, and the possibility that such a shock might profoundly reconstitute a subject. My interest here lies not in how personal traits might account for the fact that some people cope better with shock or trauma but, rather, in how various resilient subjects of our times come into being. I take resilience, in other words, not as a term to describe the ways in which individuals might deal well with the challenges of contemporary society, but as a key to investigate contemporary operations of power and notably to further explore processes of subjectification that belong to the realm of neoliberal governmentality and biopower. This point of departure understands neoliberalism not only in terms of political economy, but also as a cultural project bent on reshaping the structure of social relationships and subjectivities, as scholars such as Lauren Berlant or Wendy Brown have argued so eloquently.[33]

In a neoliberal political economy, resilience has become part of the "moral code": the "good subjects" of neoliberal times are the ones who are able to act, to exercise their agency, in resilient ways. Good subjects, Neocleous writes, "will 'survive and thrive in any situation,' they will 'achieve balance' across the several insecure and part-time jobs they have, 'overcome life's hurdles' such as facing retirement without a pension to speak of, and just 'bounce back' from whatever life throws, whether it be cuts to benefits, wage freezes or global economic meltdown. Neoliberal citizenship is nothing if not a training in resilience as the new technology of the self: a training to withstand whatever crisis capital undergoes and whatever political measures the state carries out to save it."[34]

There is, one could argue, an ethical imperative at work here, which holds that one ought to overcome the hazards and shocks of our times and that moral good is to be found in this overcoming. Moreover, as the keyword "resilience" also encompasses the meaning of bouncing back stronger than before, of adapting to the new shock-shaped world, the resilient subject ought to be able to cash in, so to speak, on whatever life throws at her.[35] Robin James characterizes this imperative as a sort of transformation of Nietzsche's "What doesn't kill me makes me stronger" into a universalizable maxim: "You ought to be stronger."[36]

In order to appreciate how moral codes relate to the subject, it is rewarding to turn to Foucault, who argues that a moral code calls for the formation of oneself as an ethical subject, and becoming an ethical subject takes place through modes of subjectivation that are supported by practices of the self.[37] Ethical formation is understood as the work an individual does on herself, work that includes subjecting herself to moral rules and guidelines for conduct. Thus a resilient subject comes into being when an individual, directly or indirectly, feels or is made to feel that the moral code of resilience applies to her, and acts accordingly. As she increasingly accepts she ought to conduct herself in resilient manners, she might, for instance, turn to resources that advise her on building a resilient self. In this approach, the modality of power through which individuals transform themselves into the willing subjects of a moral discourse is the subject's agency. Agency thus refers to the capacities and skills required to undertake particular kinds of actions, and these capacities and skills are acquired precisely through submitting to particular disciplines. In the case of resilience, the training and discipline is elaborated, and readily available, through the blooming business of self-help books and resilience courses. Thus the specific biopolitical power at work in and through resilience as a keyword produces a new regime of subjectivity, that is to say, new resilient subjects.

If every kind of subjectivation enables particular capacities and skills to act, while foreclosing others, what kind of agency is proper to resilient subjects, and what kind of agency is hindered or rendered almost impossible through disciplines of resilience? To state that subjecting the self to an ethos of resilience produces modes of agency that are skillful in flexibility, persistence, and adaptability is to state the obvious. Crucial to these skills is the capacity of losing much or perhaps almost everything—losing one's belongings, as well as one's place and sense of belonging, as millions of refugees and displaced persons do—and building up everything all over again. And while this worst-case scenario might not exactly happen in its full horror (although for so many in this world it does), disciplines of resilience cultivate a sense of "preparedness." "One needs to be prepared for all that might happen, and all one might not be prepared for," Neocleous contends, from the next crisis-to-come to the worst-case scenario to the apocalypse itself. The formation of a resilient self occurs in and through a particular temporality: resilience involves an apprehension of the future, but a future projected both as disaster and recovery from disaster.[38]

The skill of apprehending the future as a cycle of disaster and recovery is crucial to resilient self-formation, and this brings me to the kind of agency an ethos of resilience forecloses: it thwarts the developing of skills of imagining otherwise. Resilience, Neocleous argues, implies a colonization of the imagination, given its profound investment in the motto at the heart of neoliberalism: "There is no alternative."[39] A well-known refrain by now holds that it has become easier to imagine the end of the world—by ecological disaster, terrorist inferno, deadly contagious disease wiping out the human race, or a fatal combination of all of these—than the end of capitalism, including neoliberalism, as a political economy. In other words, resilience entertains a significant relationship with dispossession in a twofold way: resilience is not only incited by the dispossession it seeks to overcome, but it also further creates the dispossession of underdeveloping the skills and capacities of imagining other possible worlds, as well as the agential modalities to pursue those imaginations.

The latter kind of dispossession resonates with the "cruel optimism" that Lauren Berlant described so pertinently as an affective response to neoliberal conditions. Berlant understands cruel optimism as the subject's relation of desire to something that is in fact an obstacle to the flourishing she desires so much. She notes that individuals in our societies remain so attached to fantasies of upward mobility, job security, political and social equality, and durable intimacy, despite the evidence suggesting that these fantasies are unachievable.[40] Berlant means to suggest not that optimism is inherently cruel, but that it can become cruel when the object that draws our attention and becomes an object of an optimistic relation in fact impedes the desired transformation that brought us to this object in the first place. If resilience holds a promise of individual survival, its cruelty might be somewhat limited; although it remains all but clear how a resilient individual on her own might survive, just to name but one threat, an ecological disaster that destroys her entire livelihood, and what such survival would look like. Yet if a promise of flourishing and transformation brings us to pursue resilience, which of course is not an object, but a posture, an embodiment, a new self, then the cruelty is extensive. Optimism is cruel, Berlant writes, when the object that ignites a sense of possibility actually makes it impossible to attain the transformation for which we risk striving. Resilience does ignite a sense of possibility, a sense of possibility that might have significant grassroots support,[41] but the material, intellectual, and emotional labor an ethos of resilience requires,[42] as well as the temporality in which it is caught up, I suggest, undermine precisely the possibility of substantial transformation. The cruelty here is double, Berlant points out, as it also resides in how the very pleasures of being inside a relation, regardless of the content of the relation, sustain a person or a world, which then finds itself bound to a situation of profound threat that is, at the same time, profoundly confirming.[43] It is not difficult to sense the pleasure and sustaining force of finding oneself in a resilient relationship to one's surroundings, as well as to intuit how such pleasure desperately binds one to that world and its disasters. The attachment to resilience, which indeed takes cruel forms, might on the one hand be accounted for by the desire to frame the absence of food and shelter, an income or a job, or a safe environment as temporary situations that must and will be overcome. It positions the resilient subject in the process of overcoming. This positioning comes with its own kind of comfort, because what would it take to face the situation that the much-needed shelter, job, or safety might simply not be likely or even possible in the way our current world is organized? Letting go of such hope or belief, and posture of overcoming, clearly holds the potential to undo the subject, yet it is less clear what kind of potentiality such undoing might hold—what kind of new horizons it might open. An attachment to resilience, however, effectively prevents us, as individuals and collectively, from going there. Here resilience becomes a symptom of the loss of the capacity to imagine and do otherwise, and cruelty is one of the more politically cautious names for such a condition.

Gendering Resilience

Neocleous opens his essay *Resisting Resilience* with a letter from a young woman to an advice column in the British newspaper *The Observer*. The letter offers an account of being stuck in a bad relationship with an angry and bullying man. Isolated from her friends and family, and dependent on a job she cannot afford to lose, she feels immobilized, or in her words: "I have no idea how to leave." Crushed by feelings of shame for having gotten herself into this situation, she ends her letter with the lament "If I could only learn resilience, I feel like maybe the practicalities wouldn't be so daunting."[44] While Neocleous does not comment on the gendered character of the anecdote that serves his argument on the connection between resilience and security, I turn to this anecdote to explore the gendered dimensions of resilience. Here enters a third figure of the resilient subject, namely the female subject who continues to survive patriarchy, is increasingly exposed to the neoliberal labor conditions of flexicurity, and is considered individually responsible for her survival. We might call her a subject of *postfeminist resilience*.

What could it mean to suggest that resilience is gendered? There are at least two relevant questions to pursue in this respect. First, does resilience as a keyword rely on gendered understandings of subjectivity and agency, and more particularly those gendered as female? Some suggest that this is the case. Commenting directly on the young woman's letter in Neocleous's essay, James argues that the clearest hinge between the subject and the social experience of resilience manifests itself in experiences that are gendered as feminine. The emotional management by women of problems that have been gendered as feminine, she argues, often turns out to exemplify the logic and practice of resilience most aptly.[45] The feminine, we might infer, informs resilience in specific ways. It is difficult to miss that resilience's core concept of elasticity, in association with notions such as flexibility or pliability, is commonly connoted as feminine. This particular casting of femininity, moreover, has played a significant role in a neoliberal political economy, with neoliberalism co-opting cultural notions of femininity, as well as the language of feminism, as Mary Evans recently noted.[46] María Puig de la Bellacasa captured such intricacies when she mobilized the figure of "flexible girls" to discuss the generational politics of young feminist researchers who find their way through the neoliberal academy at the dawn of the new millennium, in conditions already shaped by the adjunctification of academic labor, which in the meantime has come to represent the academic "business as usual." Flexibility is indeed highly valued within a neoliberal political economy, and crucial in our understanding of late capitalism as a regime of flexible accumulation, with new regimes of flexicurity, which promote the flexible workplace as well as discontinuous work.[47] This flexibility is arguably a response to an untenable tension between formal paid work and informal reproductive work; it is a way of releasing some of the pressure on the gendered division of labor as it was inscribed in a capitalist industrial political economy.[48] Social relations of gender, in other words, are crucial when accounting for the centrality of flexibility in late capitalism, and flexibility has gender as an organizing principle written all over it, as well as a particular connection to experiences and conditions that are gendered as female.[49]

Yet flexibility is not the only meaning that resilience encompasses. Resilience is not merely about endlessly bending without breaking; it is also about bouncing back in shape, possibly stronger than one was before. The resilience the young woman longs for in her letter is not about enduring or adapting to the situation she finds herself in, as a more classic understanding of femininity in terms of pliability might suggest. Rather, she confers upon resilience the power to escape her conditions and to return to life as she knew it before the abusive relationship. Resilience here implies efficient action—that is, the opposite of her current state of being paralyzed. It also captures the toughness and relentlessness that come with bouncing back, which are commonly connotated as masculine. "If I could only learn resilience" expresses her lonely longing for boldness and determination to attack "the practicalities" that keep her stuck in a bad place and to recover her world. This renders the gendered politics of resilience more complex, and beyond the connotation of resilience with (traditional) femininity, we might want to consider the gendered dimension of resilience as a particular reconfiguration of qualities commonly considered as feminine or masculine. Or we could think about gender and resilience as follows: understandings of masculinity as tough and unyielding but without the capacity to bend, as well as understandings of femininity as flexible and pliable but without the capacity to reclaim space, are both somewhat at odds with the "good subject" of a neoliberal, resilient world.[50]

This brings us to a second question. Does the rise of resilience suggest a shift in hegemonic notions of femininity? James suggests that this is the case. Traditional normative femininity requires the performance of fragility and vulnerability; it trains women to be timid, uncertain, lacking confidence, and to be afraid of getting hurt, James argues, relying on Iris Marion Young's classic discussion (in "Throwing Like a Girl") about the connections between feminine body comportment and feminine structures of subjectivity. In a neoliberal "affective economy," in contrast, the fragility of normative femininity is replaced with a new ideal geared towards overcoming this traditional logic of femininity.[51] Women must overcome the fragility and vulnerability they have learned to embody and to believe, James argues, and turn their "gendered damage" into human capital.[52] The question of damage is significant here, as in times of resilience damage is reworked into resource.[53] Indeed, most often postfeminism does not assume that power relations are now equal or that power differences have simply evaporated. Rather, the assumption is that an individual woman, who might have suffered structural disadvantage and has the damage to show for it, now has the means at her disposal to overcome such disadvantage. James calls this resilience the "Look, I Overcame" narrative that is at the very heart of postfeminist rhetoric, and she notes that it always seems to implicitly hold the complementary question "So why did *you* not overcome?," which turns out to be a mark of distinction and possibly an accusation. In a neoliberal postfeminist political economy, frailty as an ideal of femininity has been superseded, James suggests, and "good girls" have become resilient and able to turn damage into opportunity.

Understandings of femininity in terms of fragility and vulnerability are of course deeply shaped by relations of race, sexuality, and class. The figure of the frail woman in need and worthy of protection is decidedly marked as middle-class and straight, and racialized as white. The postfeminist "Look, I Overcame" narrative and its particular ethos of resilience is marked by these same positionalities, and stands in contrast to the post-feminist "bad girls," who continue to suffer from fragility, fail to turn their damage into opportunity, or are in need of rescue or protection. In a West European context, we might think of the figure of the Muslim woman within prevailing civilizational discourses. While some "exceptional" Muslim women might indeed appropriate the "Look, I Overcame!" narrative (think Ayaan Hirsi Ali),[54] the resilience that they embody and rhetorically mobilize is inseparable from contemporary civilizational politics.[55] Here a conjuncture between a neoliberal ethos of resilience and racial politics becomes particularly visible, but I would like to suggest that racial politics are never far from the ethos of resilience. The figure of the "exceptional Muslim" operates in contrast to "ordinary" Muslim women who are often, through the same gendered racial politics, positioned and interpellated as in need of salvation and protection. Yet these interpellations remain remarkably unstable: the "bad" Muslim woman who lacks the necessary resilience to leave her patriarchal religious community is simultaneously the "good" Muslim woman who can be saved, but she can also shift, in a split second, to a "bad" subject—dangerous, not to be trusted, with hidden loyalties and agendas—even if she is a "good" subject of resilience (think Ayaan Hirsi Ali's revocation of her Dutch citizenship). The postfeminist "Look, I Overcame" narrative is a forceful one in our contemporary world and is particularly revelatory of the gendered politics of resilience. It is also a narrative that in various ways is shaped, as well as unsettled, by racial politics, which turns out to be a crucial feature of the gendered dimension of the ethos of resilience.

Moreover, the unstable and sometimes seemingly contradictory character of resilience's gendered politics is related to the complex relationship between frailty and vulnerability on the one hand, and "overcoming" on the other. Recent discussions about "trigger warnings" in US college classrooms are an interesting case in point. Trigger warnings on syllabi and teaching materials are used to signal that the material contains upsetting scenes of violence that might trigger past trauma, thus acknowledging that students might suffer from posttraumatic stress disorder (PTSD) and other mental health conditions. While the debate is often held in gender-neutral terms, thus suggesting that this might be the case for any student in the classroom, the figure of the female survivor of rape strongly informs the discussions. Trigger warnings have been defended as well as criticized for various reasons, which fall beyond the scope of this essay. I merely invoke the debate on trigger warnings here for the sake of pointing to how the figure of the student traumatized by her reading materials resonates with traditional notions of female vulnerability, and the race and class politics that inform such understandings of vulnerability, as some commentators have noted.[56] I am particularly struck by the juxtaposition of the "Look, I Overcame!" narrative and its current prevalence among female college students with sudden eruptions of vulnerability like those expressed in arguments in favor of trigger warnings—instances in which that postfeminist femininity is undone. Or are these eruptions, contained in time and space, perhaps part and parcel of how postfeminist femininity is constituted? If that is the case, trigger warnings might be seen as a form of neoliberal containment of vulnerability that does not deal with the undoing, or rather, that seeks to control, contain, and securitize such undoing, which draws on medicalized strategies to do so.

By Way of Conclusion: *We Are Not Resilient*

Resilience holds various and contradictory meanings, which is part of its social force if we follow Williams's understanding of how keywords operate and exercise power. In this essay, I have looked at resilience as a keyword, an ethos, and a mode of subjectification situated at the heart of neoliberal's cultural project, and I considered different figures of resilient subjects, which by no means exhaust all possible resilient forms of subjectification, and which are related to each other in differentiated and complex ways. To conclude, I turn to the common threads that run through this volume, vulnerability and resistance, and discuss their conceptual relation to resilience.

What does the rise of resilience tell us about vulnerability? It has been argued that resilience forces its subjects to abandon dreams of achieving security and to embrace danger as a condition of possibility for future life.[57] In this view, vulnerability to threat, injury, and loss are relegated to the realm of resilience, and hence contemporary intellectual efforts that seek to think with and through vulnerability are seen as yet another expression of the neoliberal worlding that produced resilience. In such accounts, vulnerability is bound to resilience; it becomes part of the ground on which an ethos of resilience thrives. My discussion, however, suggests otherwise. While the notion of resilience does indeed assume damage and impact, and remains dialectically bound to threat as I have shown, it is also conceptually designed to overcome vulnerability—to contain and evade it, to bounce back from it, to minimize its traces, to domesticate its transformative power. Butler's recent work engaging vulnerability as an ontological characteristic of social relations, as well as a ground for politics and ethics, gives us an account of what such transformative power might look like. It also serves as a ground to critique the ethos of resilience that seeks to overcome vulnerability. The notion of vulnerability that is mobilized in this essay, through the work of Butler but also Layton, seeks to reconstruct an ethical condition of human life, which is domesticated and obscured within contemporary political economies of neoliberalism and the War on Terror. This understanding of vulnerability offers possibilities to think and enact a world beyond neoliberalism, which stands in sharp contrast to how resilience remains bound to the world as we know it and more specifically to its greatest threats, disasters, and apocalyptic visions. This is not to say that such different understandings of vulnerability are entirely unrelated, but rather to draw attention to conceptual differences and the ways in which they matter, as well as to show that the rise of resilience fosters a particular understanding of vulnerability, that is centered in its overcoming. Ignoring such conceptual and political differences, and rejecting vulnerability as such as part of a critique of resilience and a search for more secure selves and livelihoods, fails to acknowledge the ways in which the question of security is situated (who is and has been the subject of security?) and the profound connections between security and resilience that Neocleous and others have laid out. Thus vulnerability and resilience are not precisely semantic opposites, but operate as political opponents: vulnerability here brings us to the question of social transformation, while resilience further separates us from it, even though transformation might be part of its cruel promise.

This begs the question of alternatives to resilience, and prompts the other term that organizes our discussion in this volume—resistance. The concept of resilience, I have argued, has a tendency to dispossess individuals and communities from future visions beyond the future imagined as disaster and overcoming disaster. Neoliberalism as a hegemonic worldview is generally known to colonize imaginaries of alternatives and other worlds possible, and subsequently to deprive practices of resistance of the oxygen they require. It is hard to miss that resistance as a way of relating to social conditions of hardship and injustice has suffered from a loss of purchase in the recent decades, both in theoretical as well as in political terms; resilience has indeed come to occupy, at least partially, that vacant place. If resistance has become futile, as a well-rehearsed contemporary narrative goes, then the shaping of resilient selves and communities easily passes as our best bet of navigating increasingly complex worlds and operations of power. In his sharp and unyielding critique of resilience, Neocleous concludes that resilience effectively undermines the capacity to resist, and therefore should be resisted and rejected. What does resisting resilience look like?

Clearly the gesture of refusing resilience can be powerful, as testified by this poster produced by the Louisiana Justice Institute,[58] which here is seen in the streets of New Orleans, a city that knows about resilience:[59]

3.1 "Stop Calling Me Resilient": poster on lamppost in New Orleans. Courtesy of Candy Chang. This image is created by Taiwanese American artist Candy Chang, who is renowned for her interactive public installations that provoke civic engagement and emotional introspection and whose work examines issues ranging from criminal justice and the future of vacant buildings to personal aspirations and anxieties. For more information, see http://candychang.com/.

"Stop calling me
Resilient.
Because every time you say
'Oh, they're resilient,'
that means you can
do something else to me.
I am not resilient."

Yet it is less clear what refusing resilience might entail. Throughout this essay I have highlighted that resilience means different things in different geopolitical contexts and according to different positionalities. This tells us that one general strategy of resisting resilience could never suffice. It should be noted, moreover, that in sharp contrast to the ubiquity of resilience as a concept and frame to make sense of experiences and politics under a neoliberal regime of biopower, there are few in-depth accounts of situated processes of resilient subjectification and the kinds of embodied agential modalities they foster and foreclose. Effective strategies of resisting current biopower regimes of resilience could do well with such accounts.

I have also suggested that resilience has become tied up with our sense of survival. On a visceral level, resilience is experienced as an attachment to life. The powerful frameworks that shape the concept of resilience, and that I have tried to render visible, suggest that resilience is in fact an attachment to life *as it is*, or *as it was* before disaster hit. In a conflation between the two— life as such, and a particular instance of life—lies the cunning of resilience. At best, resilience brings survival in a world hit by disaster, but here the words of Dorothy Allison come to mind: "I need you to do more than survive . . . The only hope you have, the only hope any of us has, is the remade life."[60] If for many of us an understanding of resilience has become tied up with our sense of survival as well as futurity, the material, intellectual, and emotional labor of undoing such a sense and reeducating our temporal desires is daunting.[61] As a result, the refusal of resilience might often seem "unaffordable"—it might mean the refusal of things that can only be refused at a very high price, such as work, shelter, care, bailout loans, or development aid. Yet a politics of resisting resilience begins with apprehending how high the price might be of continuing a regime of survival and resilience, as well as the necessity of rethinking and redoing of social relations and dependencies. We might begin by becoming increasingly conscious that part of this daunting character stems from a neoliberal social ontology that revolves around the individual, and the paralyzing effect that the complexity of our world has on that individual. If we refuse such ontology, and shift to a social ontology centered in relationality and interdependence, as is the case in the understanding of vulnerability that is fostered throughout this volume, the overall task is not less daunting, but it is perhaps less lonely.

Notes

My heartfelt gratitude goes to Judith Butler and Zeynep Gambetti for organizing our precious workshop in Istanbul and all the workshop participants for their generosity; Judith Butler, Zeynep Gambetti, and Leticia Sabsay for their editorial commitments and valuable input; and Sahar Sadjadi and María Puig de la Bellacasa for their readings and engaging comments. All of these engagements with earlier versions of this essay have become traces in the text.

1 Neocleous, "Resisting Resilience." My search in the database of documents and reports published by the World Bank revealed that almost four thousand documents draw upon the term resilience, including more or less eighty that have "resilience" in their title, and all of those are published after 2007. See the *Open Knowledge Repository* of the World Bank, https://openknowledge.worldbank.org.

2 Risk Steering Committee, *DHS Risk Lexicon*, vii. The DHS Risk Steering Committee compiled its first Risk Lexicon in 2008, including more than seventy terms and definitions, to which fifty more terms were added in the second edition of 2010.

3 Risk Steering Committee, *DHS Risk Lexicon*, 1. See also this DHS statement on resilience: "While DHS is still new to resilience, there has been significant maturation over the past few years. In 2010, it was not uncommon for meetings to be dominated with a discussion of 'What do we mean by resilience?' Now, the principles of adaptability, withstanding and rapidly recovering are generally understood and accepted. The focus of the meetings today is on action." *Resilience*, US Department of Homeland Security, September 10, 2015, http://www.dhs.gov/topic/resilience.

4 As Neocleous notes, these books have largely been published in the last decade. Neocleous, "Resisting Resilience," 5. My quick search in the book section on Amazon.com revealed about five thousand titles when searching on the keyword "resilience," and ordering these publications according to date reveals that more than one thousand of those were published after 2013.

5 For a convincing account of this periodization, see Harvey, *A Brief History of Neoliberalism*. Commentators who have related the prevalence of resilience to the political economy of neoliberalism include Neocleous, "Resisting Resilience," and Hall and Lamont, *Social Resilience*.

6 Nikolas Rose, *Inventing Our Selves*.

7 Neocleous, "Resisting Resilience."

8 Raymond Williams, *Keywords*.

9 In this digital age, algorithmic formulas are able to track down the prevalence of a term within digital cultural webs of signification in a split-second, and simply typing resilience as a keyword in a search engine such as Google generates more than 2.5 billion references.

10 See "What Is a Keyword?," *Keywords Project*, http://keywords.pitt.edu/, accessed March 8, 2016.

11 Google's statistics of the prevalence of the term in digitalized resources shows us that, while in the nineteenth century resilience was hardly used at all, it emerged as a concept around the turn of the twentieth century, knew an increase during the Second World War, and exponentially rose from the 1980s onward.

12 S.v. "resilience," *Merriam-Webster Online*, http://www.merriam-webster.com/dictionary/resilience, accessed March 8, 2016.

13 Folke, "Resilience," 253.

14 McAslan, *Community Resilience*, www.torrensresilience.org/origins-of-the-term, accessed March 8, 2016; Hall and Lamont, *Social Resilience*.

15 Folke, "Resilience," 259.

16 Bouchard, "Neoliberalism in Québec," 267.

17 Hall and Lamont, *Social Resilience*, 2.

18 McAslan, *Community Resilience*, 1.

19 Neocleous, "Resisting Resilience."

20 Examples can be found in the expansion of "Security Studies" to "Security and Resilience Studies" (e.g., at Northeastern University), or the Presidential Policy Directive/PPD-21 "Critical Infrastructure Security and Resilience," February 12, 2013, http://www.whitehouse.gov/.

21 Beck, *Risk Society*, 21.

22 This became quite explicit in President Bush's address to the nation on September 20, 2001, which included the following request: "I ask your continued participation and confidence in the American economy."

23 Butler, *Precarious Life*.

24 Butler, *Precarious Life*, xii.

25 Butler, *Precarious Life*, 28.

26 Butler, *Precarious Life*, 21.

27 Layton, "What Divides the Subject?," 68.

28 This dialectical bond finds a captivating expression in a popular song that reflects the ethos of resilience quite well: toward the end of "What Doesn't Kill You (Makes You Stronger)," by Kelly Clarkson (subsequently adapted by Kanye West), the subject who represents the disaster or undoing (of a relational breakup in this case) is directly addressed with gratitude. "Thanks to you I got a new thing started, Thanks to you I'm not the broken-hearted, Thanks to you I'm finally thinking about me," the lyrics go, thus giving credit to the disaster as the origin of the resilience the song celebrates.

29 Neocleous, "Resisting Resilience," 4–5.

30 Klein, *The Shock Doctrine*.

31 Elson and Pearson, " 'Nimble Fingers Make Cheap Workers.' "

32 Hall and Lamont, *Social Resilience*, 12–13.

33 Berlant, *Cruel Optimism*; Brown, "Neoliberalism and the End of Liberal Democracy," and *Edgework: Critical Essays on Knowledge and Politics*.

34 Neocleous, "Resisting Resilience," 5.

35 A recent popular book on resilience has called this the "resilience dividend," which enables taking advantage of new opportunities that might arise because of disruption, and deploying these for further growth and expansion. See Rodin, *The Resilience Dividend*.

36 James, *Resilience and Melancholy*.

37 Foucault, *The History of Sexuality*, vol. 2; Foucault, *The Use of Pleasure*.

38 Neocleous, "Resisting Resilience," 6.

39 Neocleous, "Resisting Resilience," 4.

40 Berlant, *Cruel Optimism*, 1.

41 See, for instance, the Transition Movement, www.transitionus.org.

42 While their discussion of resilience is focused on the level of national policies, Lentzos and Rose draw attention to the material labor and infrastructure resilience requires: see Lentzos and Rose, "Governing Insecurity." I believe it is important to think a personal ethos of resilience in terms of labor as well.

43 Berlant, *Cruel Optimism*, 2.

44 Neocleous, "Resisting Resilience."

45 James, *Resilience and Melancholy*.

46 Evans, "Feminism and the Implications of Austerity."

47 Harvey, *A Brief History of Neoliberalism*.

48 Weeks, *The Problem with Work*.

49 Puig de la Bellacasa, "Flexible Girls."

50 Many figures spring to mind, such as the laid-off factory worker whose masculinity is tied to a breadwinner model and who fails to "reinvent himself" on the postindustrial labor market, or indeed the female survivor of domestic violence who fails to transform her situation, to name but a few. Welfare state provisions and social services, or what is left of them, are quick to point out that such subjects lack resilience, and increasingly make their aid dependent on the trainings in capacity building and resilience they have on offer.

51 For affective economy, see Ahmed, *The Cultural Politics of Emotion*.

52 James, *Resilience and Melancholy*.

53 James, *Resilience and Melancholy*.

54 On the notion of the "exceptional Muslim," see Haritaworn, Erdem, and Tauqir, "Gay Imperialism."

55 See Bracke, "Subjects of Debate."

56 See, notably, a provocative blog post by Jack Halberstam and the debate it provoked: Bully Bloggers, "You Are Triggering Me! The Neo-Liberal Rhetoric of Harm, Danger and Trauma," July 7, 2014. https://bullybloggers.wordpress.com/2014/07/05/you-are-triggering-me-the-neo-liberal-rhetoric-of-harm-danger-and-trauma/.

57 Evans and Reid, "Dangerously Exposed."

58 The Louisiana Justice Institute is a nonprofit civil rights legal advocacy organization devoted to fostering social justice campaigns across the state of Louisiana for communities of color and for impoverished communities.

59 In the aftermath of the 2005 disaster of Hurricane Katrina, the population and reconstruction of New Orleans were managed through strategies of resilience: with the Federal Emergency Management Agency, part of DHS and the post-9/11 "security and risk management" programs of the DHS. Unsurprisingly, New Orleans figures in the "100 Resilient Cities Challenge" that the Rockefeller's Rockefeller Foundation announced in May 2013.

60 Allison, "Survival Is the Least of My Desires."

61 Weeks, *The Problem with Work*; Tonstad, "Touching across Time."

....

CHAPTER 4

Vulnerable Times

MARIANNE HIRSCH

You don't have a story until you have two stories. At least two stories. That's what I always tell my students.

—GRACE PALEY

The First Story

When I arrived in Providence in the summer of 1962, I didn't know English. I was almost thirteen and due to enter eighth grade, though, as it turned out, I went to ninth, prodded by my father's ambition for me, so typical of immigrant parents. But his ambition now seemed unwarranted as I proceeded to regress into speechlessness and lost my confidence in the unfamiliar surroundings into which I had been misplaced, through no choice of my own. Even my name no longer belonged to me—from Marianne, I became Mary Ann, and, since I was unable to pronounce the English *r*, I had to struggle every time someone asked, responding, inaudibly, head hanging, "Mady Ann." Lonely and out of place, the only child of parents anxiously preoccupied with their own transition, I had to resort to the one constant that I had transported with me and that could transport me to more familiar worlds—reading. But the trunk containing the small number of German books that would become the germ of a new family library had not yet arrived from across the ocean.

It was thus that I found my way into the Rochambeau branch of the Providence Public Library. Why was it pronounced "ro-SHAM-bo," I wondered, and not "ro-sh'm-BO"? I tried out the French pronunciation I'd been working on, practicing that *r*. Small for my age and further infantilized by my broken speech, I surprised the librarian when I asked for books in German. "We have some German books, little girl," she tried to explain, gesturing to me as she

4.1 Mirta Kupferminc, *On the Way*, 2001, metal-plate etching, 15.75 × 25.25 in.
COURTESY OF THE ARTIST.

spoke, "but none for children." I had found some books by writers I recognized in the card catalog, and I pointed to a title by Thomas Mann. "That's an adult book," she said, "you're too young for that." Seeing how close my tears were to welling up, she went to check with someone behind the desk. "Perhaps if your parents give you permission." I came back with my mother the next day and checked out *Buddenbrooks*. And that's how I got through that summer.

What could Thomas Mann's *Buddenbrooks* possibly have offered a thirteen-year-old immigrant girl who had grown up Jewish and German-speaking in postwar communist Romania? I have no recollection of my response to Mann's multifaceted family saga of decline, set in nineteenth-century Lübeck in northern Germany. Surprisingly, perhaps, the world into which *Buddenbrooks* drew me that summer was not entirely unrecognizable. In Romania, I had been an avid reader of another epic German story that was equally remote from my own surroundings. The popular ten-volume *Nesthäkchen* series, by Berlin children's book author Else Ury, follows the lively and rebellious Annemarie Braun from her bourgeois childhood to white-haired grandmotherhood in early twentieth-century Berlin. By the time I read *Buddenbrooks*, I had repeatedly reread all the *Nesthäkchen* books I could acquire in Bucharest's used bookstores. But, sadly, one or two of the volumes were missing, and that left some gaps in Annemarie's life story. As a child growing up in vulnerable circumstances—in a linguistic and religious minority under a politically repressive regime—I longed for the reassuringly stable conservative world of Ury's early twentieth-century Berlin, especially the idealized version of comfortable bourgeois German femininity that she evoked. It's only recently that I found out that Else Ury was in fact Jewish and that she was murdered in Auschwitz in 1943.[1] This was a shock, because nothing in these classic children's books would allow one to guess that their author was in any way marginal to German bourgeois society.

My parents encouraged my reading that summer: my mother, especially, resisted Americanization by maintaining firm links to her past. Thomas Mann was a great favorite of theirs, as was Brecht, both, unlike Ury, exiles from Nazism. German Jewish writers—Werfel, Feuchtwanger, Kafka, Stefan Zweig— were in the trunk, but so were some classics: Goethe, Schiller, and, of course, Heine. Their bookcases were structured by poignant contradictions. My parents had been raised in Czernowitz, the capital of the outlying Austro-Habsburg province of Bukowina, in an assimilated community of Jews who, a generation earlier, had enthusiastically embraced the German language and its lifeways in exchange for secular education, modernization, and political rights.[2] They were educated after the first World War collapse of the Austro-Hungarian empire, in what became greater Romania, but they still stubbornly perpetuated and passed down their allegiance to German—even after it had become the language of the murderers, and after their world and its promises had imploded many times over. German was, after all, their language too, a kind of anchor for them through decades of persecution by fascist and communist dictatorships, and the trials of emigration and refugeehood. I believe that they continued to speak German not so much out of nostalgia for a world of yesterday, but as a complex gesture of resistance to Romanian anti-Semitism and loss of rights and, I would say, also out of a refusal to accept the failures of the cosmopolitanism they had so hopefully adopted with their German. By the time this German came to me, it was inflected by its contiguities with Yiddish, Romanian, and Ukrainian, contaminated by fascism and genocide, and it was also politically reshaped in the German-language elementary school I attended in Bucharest, where we read only bona fide communist German Romanian and German Democratic Republic writers. Ironically, it was in Providence, in my own second displacement—just when I was supposed to be learning English and starting high school—that my readings reconnected me to my so-called native language.

I had become used to shuttling between incongruous worlds. Reading Mann by way of Ury in Rhode Island must have allowed me to develop some flexibility in response to a newly acquired vulnerability. By fall, however, I was further humiliated in ninth-grade English class, where I was supposed to be reading *Julius Caesar,* and in American Civics, where I failed to recognize a single point of reference. Thus, I reluctantly set my mind to studying English and to acclimating, as best I could, to an American teenagehood that was inimical to such disjointed histories. It would be a long time before I could again claim language—any language—as my medium.

The Second Story

I've never had the occasion to write about the ironies that marked the threshold moment of my first American summer, the choice of looking backward, reclaiming worlds I had lost, rather than facing the anxieties and vulnerabilities of my cultural and linguistic displacement. In my writing, this history of emigration and Americanization has been displaced by another history—that of the hybrid cultures that my parents and thousands of others born in places like Czernowitz had bequeathed to me. I have thought a great deal about the flowering of these cultures and their destruction, and about their embrace and their persecution and expulsion of their Jewish populations. And I have thought about my own relationship to these past lives—about how I can listen to these histories and retell them without appropriating them, without allowing them unduly to overtake my own life story, without celebrating or idealizing acts of survival that preceded me, and without shaping them to my own fantasies of the past. I've tried to characterize the peculiar tension between nostalgia and trauma that characterizes my parents' memory and what I have called my postmemory of their native culture, and the oppression they suffered there as Jews. But how has my own history of multiple displacement and acculturation modulated my reception of these inherited memories and the scholarly work that they have occasioned?

Trauma, memory, and postmemory have proven to be generative concepts in works on the archives of violence emerging from the Holocaust and other catastrophic histories. They have offered a lens through which to recognize forgotten or disposable lives and stories, and also to acknowledge injury and injustice and their continuing afterlives for subsequent generations. The concept of trauma in its psychoanalytic, social, and embodied resonances certainly illuminates our present moment and the effects of the multiplying historical catastrophes we have witnessed in the decades since the Second World War. Trauma has offered new conceptions of time, in that it always occurs in the present, as a form of perpetual return. It has offered new epistemologies in the ideas of unknowability, unspeakability, and aporia—ideas hotly contested.[3] The tough debates surrounding these fundamental contributions have enriched our understanding of the aftermath of personal and historical catastrophes. Also debated has been the widespread conception of trauma as a singular, if multifaceted, event—an accident, a war, a genocide. This punctual conception of trauma occludes the insidious, cumulative, and daily experiences of poverty, persecution, enslavement, and abuse suffered by populations across the globe, and also the "slow violence," to use Rob Nixon's term, that humans are perpetrating on the planet and thus also on vulnerable species and populations. Trauma studies have evolved beyond a concentration on the singular event and beyond their foundational European psychoanalytic origins.[4]

If I am bringing the notion of vulnerability and, specifically, *vulnerable times*, to the study of trauma and memory, it is in response to a different concern—a frustration with the unforgiving temporality of trauma and catastrophe, the sense of inexorable repetition of the past in the present and future in which injury cannot be healed or repaired, but lives on, shattering worlds in its wake. I have been trying to think about how the retrospective glance of trauma might be expanded and redirected to open alternate temporalities that might be more porous and future-oriented and that also might galvanize a sense of urgency about the need for change, now, in our contemporary moment.[5] About how memory can be mobilized for a different future.

In her book *Time*, Eva Hoffman writes: "It is tempting to say that finitude is the intrinsic cost of life and that vulnerability is a necessary correlative of vitality."[6] As embodied species, we share a common vulnerability emerging from the condition of living in bodies and in time. But, importantly, vulnerability is also socially, politically, and economically created and differentially imposed. An acknowledgment of vulnerability, both shared and produced, can open a space of interconnection as well as a platform for responsiveness and resistance. Unlike trauma, vulnerability shapes an open-ended temporality—that of the threshold of an alternate, reimagined reality. In this vein, Ariella Azoulay has written about what she calls "potential history"—what might have been and thus what might yet be.[7] But to envision such different possibilities instead of a linear history would mean to envision different temporal trajectories and conflicting truths that would lead to alternate futures, and, counterintuitively perhaps, to alternate pasts as well.[8] Indeed, each past envisioned its own future in response to its own vulnerabilities, therefore vulnerable times can encompass many different historical moments and temporalities.[9] If we think of vulnerability as a radical openness toward surprising possibilities, then we might be able to engage it more creatively—as a space to work from as opposed to something only to be overcome.[10]

When the feminist legal scholar Martha Fineman and her colleagues adopted the notion of vulnerability for their initiative at Emory Law School, jettisoning the idea of "dependency" that Fineman had worked with previously, they wanted to counteract US liberal and neoliberal ideas of autonomy, self-reliance, and equality.[11] They aimed to create a space for a political discourse of interdependence and care in which active state intervention in human communities would not be seen as exceptional. The Emory group contests popular conceptions of vulnerability as a condition of weakness, victimhood, or stigma. Vulnerability, they claim, outlines our sometimes necessary reliance on social institutions that can enhance resilience and reduce susceptibility to injury. The recent workshop organized by Judith Butler and Zeynep Gambetti in Istanbul, on "rethinking vulnerability" from a transnational feminist perspective, built on Butler's work on precarity as well as her more recent writing on bodies on the street. Highlighting various socially imposed gendered vulnerabilities, the workshop aimed to mobilize these as resources for "developing new modes of collective agency . . . [and] alliance . . . characterized by interdependency and public action."[12]

Despite this promising recent feminist work with the idea of vulnerability and its potential use as a political platform of demand, however, the notion does have a complicated and also troubling history.[13] Vulnerability is widely used in the language of security and defense, and it has served as an alibi for arms buildup and violent conflict throughout the Cold War, the War on Terror, and various disputes around the globe. Talk of vulnerability to attack, terrorism, atomic threat, natural disaster, and crime is rampant and contributes to a crisis mentality that can always be invoked for political purposes, as we can see every time we step into an airport and dutifully take off our shoes, every time we discuss gun legislation in the United States or "security" walls on contested borders. An aspiration to invulnerability can elicit a defensiveness that shuts down debate and silences dissent—and we see this acutely in our contemporary moment.

These discourses of defense and denial are gendered and culturally marked. In fact, it is particularly among feminists that their purchase is being contested: claiming a disproportionate vulnerability for women, or for any socially disadvantaged group, brings with it a plea for protection that potentially signals weakness and the perpetuation of disempowerment.[14] At the same time, the appeal to a shared vulnerability as a fundamental species condition carries its own risks of ignoring differences of power and privilege.

These drawbacks notwithstanding, vulnerability has emerged as a productive concept in a number of seemingly unrelated fields—in studies of environment, social ecology, and political economy, on the one hand, and in developmental psychology, on the other. Here vulnerability is opposed not to invulnerability but to resilience. Scholars in these fields study the ability of people (particularly children), environments, and systems to adapt to shock and change. While "vulnerability" is used to describe the predisposition of people or systems to injury, "resilience" (from the Latin *resilere*, "to recoil or leap back") is a form of suppleness and elasticity that enables adaptation and recovery from shocks, surprises, or even slowly evolving changes or negative factors. In martial arts, moreover, the acceptance of vulnerability is seen to provide a source of passive power, and vulnerability is now similarly used in studies of leadership and pop psych theories of relationship. The openness created by the admission of vulnerability, it is said, produces strength and fosters connection.

This synergy between social-political fields and ecological-biophysical sciences in thinking about vulnerability is promising, pop psych truisms notwithstanding. But what can the humanities, and particularly literature and the arts, offer this paradigm, and what conversations might emerge between these diverse and distinct fields?

We might begin by considering the forms of responsiveness and vulnerability fostered by aesthetic encounters. Aesthetic encounters, I would suggest, elicit a sense of vulnerability that can move us toward an ethics and a politics of open-endedness and mobility, attuning us to the needs of the present, to the potentialities for change, and to the future. In our acts of reading, looking, and listening we necessarily allow ourselves to be vulnerable as we practice openness, interconnection, and imagination, and as we acknowledge our own implication and complicity. Aesthetic works, moreover, whether visual, literary, acoustic, or performatic, can serve as theoretical objects enabling us to reflect on the vulnerabilities they elicit within us.[15]

In my own work I have tried to map out an aesthetics of the aftermath as an aesthetics of vulnerability, looking particularly at representations of the Holocaust in the work of second and subsequent generations, but of other pain-

4.2 Christian Boltanski, *Autel Lycée Chases (Altar of the Chases High School)*, 1988. Black-and-white photographs, lamps, and tin boxes, 68×55 in. COURTESY OF THE ARTIST AND MARIAN GOODMAN. GALLERY, PARIS / NEW YORK. © 2014 ARTISTS RIGHTS SOCIETY (ARS), NEW YORK / ADAGP, PARIS.

ful histories as well.[16] The French artist Christian Boltanski, for example, has been instrumental in shaping such an aesthetic, one that, in his terms, is not "about" the Holocaust, but "after." His *Lessons of Darkness* installations are afterimages—blown-up faces cropped from school photos of Jewish schools in Vienna, Berlin, and Paris from the 1930s, mounted on boxes, with wires and lights that echo surveillance and torture.[17] Powerful works such as Boltanski's and their ghostly emanations incite us to ask how we might respond to the visceral knowledge of genocidal murder and mourning that these photographs carry forward from the past, and also to the complicity the artist signals with the technologies to which he is subjecting these children. How can we allow the knowledge of past atrocity to touch us without paralyzing us?

What aesthetic strategies might galvanize memory in the interest of activist engagement for justice and social change?

In developing the notion of postmemory to account for the aftermath of catastrophic histories, I have thought precisely about the ways in which we might make ourselves vulnerable to what Susan Sontag has called "the pain of others," whether our ancestors or more distant subjects, in the past or the present.[18] Postmemory describes the relationship that later generations or distant contemporary witnesses bear to the personal, collective, and cultural trauma of others—to experiences they "remember" or know only by means of stories, images, and behaviors. The contact with past or distant atrocities is thus mediated by imaginative investment, projection, and creation—by what Robert Jay Lifton has called "formulation."[19] Current pedagogies encourage students to respond to "the pain of others" through identification and empathy, but my work with postmemory has introduced a distancing awareness, emphasizing that although "it could have been me, it was, decidedly not me." I thus prefer to think in terms of a form of solidarity that is suspicious of an easy empathy, that shuttles instead between proximity and distance, affiliation and disaffiliation, complicity and accountability.

Postmemorial aesthetic strategies can offer ways in which we can practice vulnerability as a form of *attunement* and *responsibility*—responsibility not as *blameworthiness*, but in the sense that the legal scholar Martha Minow has so helpfully suggested, as the *ability to respond*:[20] a response working against an appropriative empathy, enabled by incongruities that leave space between past and present, self and other, open without blurring these boundaries and homogenizing suffering.[21]

The American artist Lorie Novak's 1987 composite projection *Past Lives* enables such an exercise in responsiveness. *Past Lives* superimposes two images: a picture of the children of Izieu, hidden Jewish children deported to Auschwitz by the Lyon Gestapo chief Klaus Barbie in 1943, and a well-known portrait of Ethel Rosenberg, executed as an atomic spy in the United States in 1953. Both are projected onto a picture of the artist as a child held by her mother in the early 1950s. When the artist who grew up in the shadow of traumatic histories that she did not herself experience literally grafts these onto her skin, is she identifying and empathizing with the victims?—is she appropriating their story? Or, rather, is she allowing herself to be marked by their stories, taking responsibility for their legacies and for her own implication, in the present in which Barbie was being brought to trial? In reframing archival images by making them more difficult to see, Novak's projections, like Boltan-

4.3 Albert Chong, *The Sisters*, 1993. Photograph with inscribed copper mat.
COURTESY OF THE ARTIST.

4.4 Lorie Novak, *Past Lives (for the Children of Izieu)*, 1987.
COURTESY OF THE ARTIST.

4.5 Marcelo Brodsky, *The Class Photo*, 1967, 1996, from *The Classmates / Buena memoria*. Hahnemuhle photo rag print, 49.25×72.75 in. COURTESY OF THE ARTIST.

ski's, paradoxically render visible what Roland Barthes has called the *champ aveugle*, or the "blind field" that exceeds the frame, and thus also aspects of the past that the images themselves render invisible.[22] Reframing, as well as holding and touch, projection and superimposition—these are some of the aesthetic strategies I find helpful in thinking through vulnerability and its complex temporality. But what do these entangled responses *do* in the present, what do they demand of their viewers?

Discussing these same strategies in different historical and political contexts certainly reveals the divergent vulnerabilities created by different forms of state violence and different possibilities of intervening in a present that is both retrospective and anticipatory. Take the aftermath project *Buena memoria*, by the Argentinian photographer and human rights activist Marcelo Brodsky.[23] His original image was also a school picture, Brodsky's own class photo from the Colegio Nacional de Buenos Aires, taken in 1967, several years before some of these children would be "disappeared" and murdered by the Argentine dictatorship. Each of the children's bodies in the image is inscribed with a brief text that brings their stories into the present. Some faces are circled, and others—the faces of the disappeared—are circled and crossed out. In *Buena memoria* the violent mark of erasure on the skinlike surface of

4.6 Marcelo Brodsky, *Memory Bridge 05*, 1996, from *Memory Bridge / Buena memoria*. Lambda color print, 19.75 × 27.5 in. COURTESY OF THE ARTIST.

the photographic print recalls the violence of selecting individuals out of the social body with the intention of annihilating them and their memory. The cross-outs transmit that violence, puncturing us as viewers.

But in this broadly exhibited installation, shown also in the very school building itself for current students to see, these lines of erasure transmit something else as well. Brodsky reunites members of the class, and he photographs them as they hold their class photo, literally holding their living and disappeared schoolmates' memory in their arms and close to their body, touching the photo and permitting it to touch them. Their touch touches us and moves us from personal grief and mourning to anger, defiance, and intervention. *Buena memoria* performs the determination to make visible and palpable the murder of classmates whose presence it asserts and whose memory it recalls. In a society suffering from what Diana Taylor has so aptly called "percepticide"—the self-blinding of a population living under terror—this aesthetic work provokes a politics of visibility and accountability, to be sure, but also a multisensory practice of affective engagement.[24]

Looking at images of people, and knowing, as in these images and installations, that some of them were violently kept from living the future they were anticipating when they stood in front of the camera, confronts us with the

4.7 Susan Meiselas, *Youths Practice Throwing Bombs in the Forest Surrounding Monimbó, Nicaragua*, 1978. COURTESY OF SUSAN MEISELAS, MAGNUM PHOTOS.

poignant irony inherent in still photography. Roland Barthes has termed this the "lacerating" *punctum* of time: the juxtaposition of divergent temporalities that confront what will be with what has been.[25] This juxtaposition is precisely what I have been calling vulnerable times. The photograph, Barthes writes, "tells me death in the future," but artists like Christian Boltanski, Marcelo Brodsky, Albert Chong, and Lorie Novak reframe the archival images so as to grant them multiple afterlives in which they continue to develop, making past injustices and atrocities newly visible so as to act in future presents. Still photography becomes a durational process, a relationship evolving over time.

To end this story I turn briefly to an aftermath project by the artist Susan Meiselas, whose images engage precisely in such forms of relation and collaboration. Meiselas's images of war and conflict in Nicaragua, El Salvador, Chile, and Kurdistan instantly became iconic, but her practice is not aimed at a single moment of witness and exposure, however intimate and concerned. Her durational work of return has provoked forms of responsiveness and political intervention directed to a future that looks back not just to extreme acts of destruction and violence, but also to fragile moments of hope.

Meiselas first went to Nicaragua as an American photojournalist during the popular Sandinista insurrection against the repressive Somoza regime in 1978. Her images recorded much more than a violent struggle, however. "In Nicaragua I experienced an extraordinary optimism," Meiselas writes, "a moment in which a whole society was mobilized, uniting together as they overthrew a dictatorship. The images I made came to stand for that optimism. If I've returned to Nicaragua so often, it has been to see what has remained of that hope among present generations, born after the revolution."[26] Iconic images are static. Even if they are recontextualized in myriad news outlets, they nevertheless continue to point back indexically and to be used to reinterpret the moment they were shot, a moment of political witness recorded by the camera.

Hence Meiselas returned to Nicaragua for the twenty-fifth anniversary of the overthrow of Somoza with a project called *Reframing History*. From among the images she took in 1978/79, she brought nineteen mural-sized photographs back with her and installed them at the very sites in which they had been taken. These public installations acted as provocations, prompting a set of conversations that reflected on the past and its legacies—both its atrocities and its promises of a more equitable life, largely suppressed and now forgotten. As images of violence and of resistance, brought back to their original sites, they acted as very different revenants than the faces of children discussed earlier. "The photographs were alive again," Meiselas writes.[27] In the twelve-minute film *Reframing History* and the longer documentary *Pictures of a Revolution*, still photographs are animated. We see these mobile memorials go up and engage in the present street scenes, we listen to the discussions, we watch people pass without looking.[28] Superimposing a moment of hope on a present of disappointment, these memorial images manage briefly to reaffirm that hope and to interrupt a trajectory of resignation and forgetting. But bringing memory back to a site means also to confront missed encounters, lack of recognition, oblivion, and loss. It is to try to live with the jarring physical beauty of a landscape that wants to but cannot forget a half-eaten corpse of a quarter century ago.

4.8 Susan Meiselas, *Residential Neighborhood, Matagalpa, Nicaragua*, 1978.
COURTESY OF SUSAN MEISELAS, MAGNUM PHOTOS.

4.9 Susan Meiselas, *Matagalpa, Nicaragua, July 2004 (Residential Neighborhood, 1978)*, from *Reframing History*. COURTESY OF SUSAN MEISELAS, MAGNUM PHOTOS.

4.10 Susan Meiselas, *Managua, Nicaragua, July 2004 ("Cuesto del Plomo," Hillside outside Managua, a Well Known Site of Many Assassinations Carried Out by the National Guard. People Searched Here Daily for Missing Persons, June 1978)*, from *Reframing History.* COURTESY OF SUSAN MEISELAS, MAGNUM PHOTOS.

If Meiselas is inviting us to return with her to a moment of hope, she certainly undercuts any possible nostalgia with a scene such as this. What are we to do with this disturbing incongruity between horror and beauty? How can we respond? Counterintuitively, the Polish poet Adam Zagajewski surveys a similarly disturbing scene and writes a remarkable poem, in the second person, asking us to "try to praise the mutilated world."[29] This poem has a particular reception history—it was widely disseminated in the aftermath of the 9/11 attacks on the World Trade Center—but Zagajewski wrote it in response to a trip he took with his father through Ukrainian villages in Poland, whose inhabitants were forced out during the population transfers following the Second World War.

Here also, in the call to memory and an intimate past, there is a nostalgic backward glance, but I think that this strange and haunting praise poem, like Meiselas's installations, is doing something else, something I hope we can use as we move forward from our own difficult present—something to do with trying to praise.

> Try to praise the mutilated world.
> Remember June's long days,
> and wild strawberries, drops of wine, the dew.
> The nettles that methodically overgrow
> the abandoned homesteads of exiles.
> You must praise the mutilated world.
> You watched the stylish yachts and ships;
> one of them had a long trip ahead of it,
> while salty oblivion awaited others.
> You've seen the refugees heading nowhere,
> you've heard the executioners sing joyfully.
> You should praise the mutilated world.
> Remember the moments when we were together
> in a white room and the curtain fluttered.
> Return in thought to the concert where music flared.
> You gathered acorns in the park in autumn
> and leaves eddied over the earth's scars.
> Praise the mutilated world
> and the gray feather a thrush lost,
> and the gentle light that strays and vanishes
> and returns.

What does it mean to praise the mutilated world? Perhaps to praise is to be responsive to and responsible for its contradictions, without trying to resolve them. Perhaps it is to embrace the potentialities of a vulnerability that is also resilient, "the gentle light that strays and vanishes and returns." Meiselas's and Zagajewski's aesthetic of vulnerability confronts us with the fragile beauty of hope and resistance, despite multiple and repeated assaults.

The encounter with these images and words enjoins us to hear the devastating stories they tell and the inspiring moments they come back to reclaim. This invitation, to praise, is an invitation to do what we have learned and what we teach, and what sustains us as scholars, teachers, and human beings—to read, to look, and to listen openly and vulnerably. And in thus inviting us to consider what might have been, these works also propel us to imagine and to fight for what might yet be.

4.11 Susan Meiselas, *Masaya, Nicaragua, July 2004 (Returning Home, September 1978)*, from *Reframing History*. COURTESY OF SUSAN MEISELAS, MAGNUM PHOTOS

Notes

This article is a revised version of my Presidential Address at the 2014 Modern Language Association Convention in Chicago: "Connective Histories in Vulnerable Times," 330–348. On this topic, see also the published version of the 2014 MLA Presidential Forum "Vulnerable Times," *Profession* (2013), http://profession.commons.mla.org/, with illuminating papers by Ariella Azoulay, Judith Butler, David Eng, Rob Nixon, and Diana Taylor.

1 See Asper, Kempin, and Münchmeyer-Schöneberg, *Wiedersehen mit Nesthäkchen*.
2 On the vanished German Jewish culture of Czernowitz, see Hirsch and Spitzer, *Ghosts of Home*. See especially chaps. 4 and 10 for the vicissitudes of the German language that continued to be spoken there after Czernowitz was annexed by Romania in 1918 and renamed Cernăuți.
3 See especially Caruth, *Trauma* and *Unclaimed Experience*, as well as Felman and Laub, *Testimony*.
4 See especially Laura S. Brown, "Not Outside the Range: One Feminist Perspective on Psychic Trauma," in Caruth, *Trauma*; Craps, *Postcolonial Witnessing*; Fassin and Rechtman, *The Empire of Trauma*; Rothberg, *Multidirectional Memory*; and Nixon, *Slow Violence and the Environmentalism of the Poor*. See also Suleiman, "Susan Suleiman Responds to Judith Herman."

5 For a discussion titled "Trauma, Memory and Vulnerability" between Susan Rubin Suleiman, Andreas Huyssen, Michael Rothberg, Maria José Contreras, and Anaya Khabir, see the 2014 MLA Presidential Forum papers collected in *Profession* (2013), http://profession.commons.mla.org/.

6 Hoffmann, *Time*, 45, 6.

7 Azoulay, *Civil Imagination* and "Potential History."

8 See Hirsch and Spitzer, "Vulnerable Lives," 51–67.

9 On such alternate conceptions of temporality, see, e.g., Walter Benjamin's writings about "incomplete history" and messianic time, "Theses on the Philosophy of History"; Agamben, *Potentialities*; Koselleck, *Futures Past*; and Wenzel, *Bulletproof.*

10 Susan Suleiman defines the contemporary in this sense of an open-ended future in *Risking Who One Is.*

11 Martha Albertson Fineman, *Vulnerability and the Human Condition*, February 14, 2014, http://web.gs.emory.edu/vulnerability/index.html.

12 Butler, *Precarious Life* and "Bodily Vulnerability, Coalitions and Street Politics"; Butler and Zeynep Gambetti, Workshop titled "Rethinking Vulnerability: Feminism and Social Change," Istanbul, September 16–19, 2013, http://socialdifference.columbia.edu/projects/rethinking-vulnerability-feminism-social-change.

13 See the important caveats raised by Ziarek: "Feminist Reflections on Vulnerability"; and Martha Albertson Fineman, Colin Dayan, Ilaria Vanni, and Ewa Ziarek, with moderator Elizabeth Castelli, "Theorizing Vulnerability Studies," panel at a conference titled "Vulnerability: The Human and the Humanities," Barnard College, March 3, 2012, http://www.youtube.com/watch?v=4NkT0QgJOpM.

14 See Butler, "Bodily Vulnerability, Coalitions and Street Politics."

15 The theoretical object, Hubert Damisch writes, "obliges you to do theory but also furnishes you with the means of doing it" (cited in Bal, *Of What One Cannot Speak,* 7).

16 This work has been part of a set of rich interdisciplinary conversations and collaborations with scholars, artists, and practitioners interested in memory studies across numerous histories and sites. For an account of my long-term engagement in this field, see Hirsch, introduction to *The Generation of Postmemory.*

17 Gumpert, *Christian Boltanski.*

18 Sontag, *Regarding the Pain of Others.*

19 Lifton, *Death in Life.*

20 Minow, "Surviving Victim Talk," 1442–1445, and *Between Vengeance and Forgiveness,* 118–147.

21 See Azoulay, introduction to *The Civil Contract of Photography*, for an argument in favor of a "civil" rather than an empathic spectatorial gaze elicited by photography.

22 Barthes, *Camera Lucida,* 57.

23 Brodsky, *Buena memoria / Good Memory.*

24 Taylor, *Disappearing Acts*, chap. 5.

25 Barthes, *Camera Lucida,* 96.

26 Meiselas, "Return to Nicaragua," 166. See also Meiselas, *Nicaragua*, and *In History*.

27 Meiselas, "Return to Nicaragua," 170.

28 Susan Meiselas and Alfred Guzzetti, dirs., *Reframing History* (*Susan Meiselas Photographer*, 2008), www.susanmeiselas.com; Alfred Guzzetti, Susan Meiselas, and Richard Rogers, dirs., *Pictures from a Revolution* (*Docurama*, 1991). See also Diana Taylor's discussion of *Reframing History* in "Past Performing Future: Susan Meiselas's *Reframing History*," in Meiselas, *In History*, 232–236.

29 Zagajewski, "Try to Praise the Mutilated World," in *Without End*.

....

CHAPTER 5

Barricades

Resources and Residues of Resistance

BAŞAK ERTÜR

We fight on the bridge cast between vulnerable being and its ricochet to the sources
of formal power.

—RENÉ CHAR, *Leaves of Hypnos*

The material recurrence of the barricade throughout the past several centuries and across the globe is complemented by its symbolic and figurative
force in vocabularies of resistance, where it has come to signify insurgency,
self-sacrifice, heroism, martyrdom, and a politics of antagonism. The more
recent return of barricades, from the Arab Spring to the European Indignados and various Occupy movements, allows us to appreciate anew the
spirit of the barricades in more varied terms attuned to the combination of
vulnerability and resourcefulness that has vividly marked these uprisings.
Taking my cues from the emergence of barricades and a number of other
dynamics during Istanbul's June 2013 Gezi uprising, I attempt in this essay to
explore the role of vulnerability in resistance in terms of its materializations
and afterlives. As a contribution to this volume's concern with vocabularies of resistance that do not deny vulnerability as a resource, I draw on the
language of monumentalization and countermonumentalization as a loose
analytical framework that brings spatial practice, representational strategy,
vulnerability, and its memory into conversation. As artifacts that embody a
good measure of anti-instrumentality and untimeliness, in addition to what
we may call an *ecstasis* of collective embodied action, barricades, I propose,
can be regarded as countermonuments of resistance. If I collapse metaphor
and matter, anecdote and evidence, in the course of this essay, I do so not out
of a commitment to analytical fallacies, but in an attempt to grasp something

about the relationship between vulnerability and resistance that often proves intransmissible.

The Gezi Barricades

Much has been written about the myriad issues and events that culminated in what has come to be known as the Gezi resistance, an uprising that began in Istanbul and spread rapidly across Turkey.[1] The immediate occasion was demolition works at Gezi Park in a blatant breach of planning permissions. The resistance began on May 27, 2013, with a few dozen people keeping watch over the park, and within five days it had snowballed into tens of thousands gathering together to defy the brutal force and tear gas that the police dispensed liberally so as to secure the unlawful demolition by cordoning off the park, refusing assembly there and in the abutting Taksim Square. Eventually, on the afternoon of June 1, when people forced the police to withdraw (predominantly through nonviolent means), Gezi Park, Taksim Square, and a large surrounding area became a state-free zone for ten days (figure 5.1).[2] This zone was demarcated by dozens of barricades of various sizes and styles. On Gümüşsuyu, the main artery that climbs up to Taksim Square from the Beşiktaş Stadium, there were close to fifteen successive barricades built with pavement stones, scaffolding materials, and corrugated metal sheets from nearby construction sites (figure 5.2). Surrounding the other sides of Taksim Square, in the streets and boulevards of Tarlabaşı, Talimhane, and Harbiye, the barricades featured reappropriated crowd-control fences with their *Polis* signs graffitied over to read *Halk* (the people), as well as materials from the major renovation works at Taksim Square, such as enormous cement pipes and iron rods (figure 5.3). The wide junction near Taşkışla, a historic building of Istanbul Technical University situated amid a cluster of five-star hotels, was blockaded with several burnt-out public buses parked sideways (figure 5.4). No matter how wide or narrow, every street in the area that would eventually lead to Taksim Square was striped with barricades.

The barricades were made collectively and spontaneously, as if one always built barricades with strangers on the streets, as if building barricades was just what one did. This knowing-just-what-to-do around barricades, even without any prior experience, is something of a mystery. In his study of European "barricade events" from the sixteenth century until the end of the nineteenth, historian Mark Traugott homes in on this enigma of a knowledge "that has been sustained, transmitted, and applied without the benefit of formal organization or institutional hierarchy."[3] He suggests that the "uncanny convergence in the

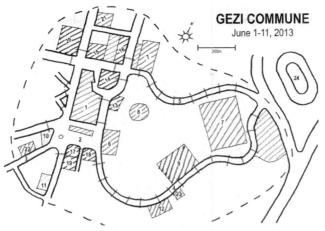

GEZI COMMUNE
June 1-11, 2013

1	Gezi Park	9	Military Hospital	17	Taksim Hill Hotel
2	Taksim Square	10	Taksim Mosque	18	Marmara Hotel
3	Istiklal Street	11	Trinity Church	19	Ottoman Palace Hotel
4	Barricade Road (S)	12	German Embassy	20	Armenian Hospital
5	Barricade Road (N)	13	Gezi Hotel	21	Indian Embassy
6	Atatürk Cultural Centre	14	Intercontinental Hotel	22	French Embassy
7	Technical University	15	Divan Hotel	23	Macedonian Embassy
8	Atatürk Library	16	Hyatt Hotel	24	Besiktas Stadium

5.1 Gezi Commune Map by Oscar ten Houten. Used under Creative Commons license: BY-NC-SA and modified slightly.

5.2 Photo by Başak Ertür: The view of the seventh barricade from the sixth. Gümüşsuyu, June 10, 2013.

5.3 Photo by Başak Ertür: Reappropriating the debris of the construction boom. Talimhane, June 10, 2013.

5.4 Photo by Başak Ertür: Barricade buses with resistance graffiti: "Does this bus pass by democracy?" Taşkışla, June 10, 2013.

behavior of individuals thrown together by their common desire to protest," and the expression of this convergence in barricades throughout the past centuries, may serve as a key to "the logic that inheres in even the most unstructured and chaotic instances of civic rebellion."[4] Barricades, then, embody the ways in which something of a structure emerges when bodies that are moved by or are beside themselves with indignation, desire, grief, or desperation act in concert. *Gezi Tune*, a short film released online one week after the encampment in the park was evicted, captures something of that strange coupling of spontaneity and structure, fever and sobriety involved in the collective labor of building barricades. Shots of pavement stones being lifted and passed from hand to hand in a long human chain are intercut with another chain transferring basic necessities and yet another moving together in a dance—resistance is depicted as a buzz of activity that creates its own measure and music as it unfolds.[5]

People who kept guard at the barricades day in and day out were mainly youth in their teens or early twenties, some of them members of radical Left factions, but most of them not.[6] This was an odd amalgam of the dispossessed from the surrounding neighborhoods and middle and upper class but otherwise disenfranchised kids—predominantly male, but there were also young women present in this tough-guy space. There were worries about undercover police activity at the barricades, as people reported plainclothes police infiltrating these spaces to provoke conflict with the uniformed police on the other side of the barricades, leading to arrests. The inevitable permeability of these structures was experienced in a different way at the park: for the first several nights after the police retreated, the park was still enshrouded in tear gas wafting up from the barricades where seemingly avoidable clashes continued to take place. Yet the barricades provided their regulars a point of participation in the resistance, a space of articulation at the threshold of the polity-in-making of the occupied zone. Compared to the life in the park, this was a somewhat marginal incorporation, but one that was given priority: those at the barricades were the first to receive their share of the daily medical provisions, food, clothing, and equipment that were donated to the occupation and redistributed from the self-organized central coordination at the park.

As the fighting subsided and their utility became less immediate, the barricades began to come alive in different ways. It appeared that they were in constant flux—undone, remade, fortified, beautified, and renamed so as to commemorate losses new and old. One morning, the occupation awoke to the smiling bricks of one barricade (figure 5.7). And then the bricks of another barricade had been neatly ordered into six perfect 1.5-by-1.5-by-1.5-meter cube

5.5 Photo by Yücel Kurşun.

5.6 Photo by Cevahir Buğu.

5.7 Smiling barricade, June 6, 2013.

structures. One barricade repurposed the frame of an appropriated billboard as a pedestrian gate "of freedom"; another ironically sported the "Opening Soon!" banner from a nearby shopping mall construction; another was played by drummers for an impromptu concert.[7] The inside of one of the blockading buses was painted all in pink, as if a public vessel for a collective psychedelic trip; another was painted sky blue. The barricades seemed to live and breathe as they pointed to an endless possibility of doing and undoing.[8] They testified to a magnificent and spontaneously self-organized collective labor, yet in addition to being permeable, it was obvious that they ultimately wouldn't stand a chance against the armory of the state. In that sense, they were both transient and inextinguishable. They embodied something of the vulnerability with and despite which the actual bodies in resistance stood against police violence.

Monumental Space and Strategy

It may be significant that the key sites of the majority of the recent uprisings were those that we may identify along with Henri Lefebvre as monumental spaces.[9] Lefebvre suggests that the didactic function of monumentality, the clear intelligibility of its simple message, masks "the will to power and the arbitrariness of power beneath signs and surfaces which claim to express collective will and collective thought."[10] This masking, however, is never total—"monumental 'durability' is unable to achieve a complete illusion."[11] So monumental spaces attract protest and oppositional political claims not only because they provide the most symbolically charged sites for the contestation of arbitrary enclosures of the political, but also because that's where the cracks are most easily revealed. Indeed, much like Cairo's Tahrir, Madrid's Puerta del Sol, Athens's Syntagma, and Kiev's Maidan, Istanbul's Taksim Square is the "emblematic site in urban public consciousness for the enactment, production, and regeneration of the political" in Turkey.[12] With Ankara designated as the capital of the new Republic in the early twentieth century, Sultanahmet, Istanbul's previous political center by virtue of its proximity to the palace, became obsolete. Taksim was reinvented as the monumental space of the Republic in Istanbul, the square where official ceremonies and election rallies were held. The symbolic weight of this space is propped up by a number of monumental structures, most importantly the Republic Monument, built in the late 1920s. Located just off the center of the square, this is the first figurative monument in Turkey to depict Mustafa Kemal Atatürk's founding of the Republic.[13] Another key monumental structure in the square is the landmark Atatürk Cultural Center (AKM), whose architectural style embodies the top-down modernization project of Turkish republicanism. Gezi Park itself shares this monumental aesthetics—it is elevated above street level, with stairs leading up to the park from all four sides and most majestically from Taksim Square, as if the park sits on a pedestal.

Over the past several years, it has become apparent that Tayyip Erdoğan's Justice and Development Party (AKP), in power since 2002, has its own monumental vision for Taksim Square. For example, the AKM building has been a major source of controversy since 2005, when plans to destroy and rebuild it were first aired. There has been a characteristic lack of transparency around the fate of the building, but government spokespersons have variously said that it will be replaced with a business conference center, a modernized cultural center, and, finally, as announced by Erdoğan during the Gezi uprising and much ridiculed since, a giant baroque-style opera house. Closed to public use since 2008 under the pretext of renovation in the aftermath of the controversy, the building, as revealed during the Gezi occupation, had been completely gutted and left to decay. Now plans are under way to build a mosque in Taksim, presumably partially to offset the powerful presence, just off the square, of Hagia Triada, one of the largest Greek Orthodox churches in Istanbul (one cannot help but see parallels with the building of the Sultanahmet mosque to overshadow the Hagia Sophia at the height of the Ottoman Empire). It has been reported that Erdoğan himself has been overseeing the revisions of the architectural design of the planned mosque, and his level of involvement and investment in this project is not entirely surprising given that during his time in office as the mayor of Istanbul in the mid-1990s, he was a key actor in the failed campaign to build a monumental mosque in Taksim.[14] Most tellingly, the Gezi protests themselves were instigated precisely by the current neoliberal government's monumental desire for Taksim, as the illegal destruction of the park was meant to make space for a shopping mall whose façade would be a replica of the eighteenth-century Ottoman barracks once located there.[15]

As with the fate of most monumental spaces, Taksim Square has been host-ing protests and mobilizations since the 1950s,[16] and the political claims that have found expression there over the past few decades have been quite diverse. But Turkey's Left has its own history with the square, a key moment which was May 1, 1977, when half a million workers and revolutionaries marched there. Paramilitary snipers, whose identity remains unknown, opened fire on the masses from nearby buildings; thirty-four people were killed and hundreds injured in the ensuing mayhem. The event serves as one of the milestones in the brutal repression and eventual crushing of the Left in Turkey. The period between the 1971 and 1980 coups d'état was one during which the Turkish state honed its expertise in developing calculated methods for unleashing incal-culable suffering. While most on the Left experienced this expertise in the unspeakable privacy of torture rooms, events like the Bloody May Day in Taksim publicly displayed the kind of violence that the state was capable of planning and executing. Since 1977, May Day rallies have not been officially allowed in Taksim Square, leading to annual unofficial marches countered by police brutality, except from 2010 until 2012. During those three years there was a temporary lull in the traditional May Day clashes: rallies were permitted in the square, and hundreds of thousands came to celebrate labor and commemorate the losses of 1977. Since 2013, however, the old state tra-dition has returned with a vengeance, as the measures taken by police to obstruct assembly in Taksim amounted to de facto exercise of martial law powers.

Notably, in the recent history of Left mobilization in and around the square, something akin to a fantasy of "taking back Taksim" is discernible as a driving force. This operates as if the square had once properly belonged to the people. But it is that very *as if* that testifies to the entanglement of monumental spaces with political imaginaries that yields particular forms of spatial practices. In Lefebvre's account, monumentality is a texture: it operates as a web of meaning, and monuments merely "constitute the strong points, nexuses or anchors of such webs."[17] Following Lefebvre, Rita Sakr suggests "looking beyond the site of the monument to the different acts of monumentalization and counter-monumentalization that occur phenomenologically and discursively across a range of macro- and microhistories,"[18] that is, to performances and practices that constitute and disrupt textures of monumentality. In this account, space is produced performatively. So when the imagined possibilities and spatial dynamics of protest are simply limited to "reclaiming the national, local or communal space and its symbolic attributes,"[19] the claim remains indexed to the monumental injunctions of a prefabricated space.

Although largely characterized by different dynamics, the Gezi occupation itself was not entirely spared from such monumentalizing longings. These were noticeable in various spatial practices in the occupied zone, as well as in articulations during Taksim Solidarity meetings.[20] The meetings were open to all, though they were mostly attended by representatives of the organized Left. Other politically identifiable constituents of the Gezi resistance, such as feminists, participants of the LGBT Bloc,[21] and representatives of Müştereklerimiz,[22] would also attend, but it is fair to say that the representative capacity of the meetings were off-balance: while the organized Left were in fact a minority in the occupied zone,[23] their representatives made up approximately half of the attendees at the Taksim Solidarity meetings. Significantly, from the beginning of the occupation onward, all Taksim Solidarity meetings were held outside Gezi Park, in the offices of a trade union in nearby Beyoğlu district. Among the other groups and unaligned individuals active in the occupied zone with various self-assigned tasks, there was a sense that the umbrella meetings were either too disconnected with the dynamics in Gezi, or simply too deadly dull to sit through.

Indeed, at these meetings during the first few days of the occupation, certain relatively urgent questions concerning infrastructural mobilization, such as coordination and physical security in the occupied zone (the latter was particularly vital as the space was partially a construction site), kept being bogged down in extended debates on the symbolic value of this or that practical move. Pragmatic proposals for supporting life at the occupation were repeatedly sidelined by concerns about the show of presence in Taksim Square, "taken," the rhetoric went, after decades of revolutionary struggle for the sake of which many lives had been lost. Such debates paralyzed the meetings for the first three

5.8 Monumental misinterpellation: "Did somebody say baroque opera?," Istanbul Pride Parade in Taksim, June 30, 2013.

days with regard to coordination efforts. Meanwhile, the occupation in the park set up infirmaries, distribution points for provisions, and a kitchen in entirely self-organized efforts loosely coordinated by groups such as the LGBT Bloc and Müştereklerimiz. The irony of the situation became particularly pronounced when at a Taksim Solidarity meeting on day 3, one man took the floor to proudly announce his party's first major expenditure for the sake of the occupation: they had ordered thousands of flags to be produced for distribution in Taksim Square, carrying not the logo of their party, but the image of Deniz Gezmiş, as a figure who, they had reasoned, all occupiers could share as an icon. But a sense of the tragic articulates itself to this irony of infrastructural ineptitude when we consider that for at least two generations on the Left, the 1972 execution by hanging of the revolutionary student leader Deniz Gezmiş along with two of his comrades is an event that has served as a similar

5.9 Photo by Başak Ertür: Atatürk Cultural Center on June 10, 2013.

point of cathexis as that of the Bloody May Day of 1977, publicly crystallizing an otherwise all too intimate knowledge of state violence. It appeared during the Gezi resistance that instead of providing a source of attunement to present vulnerabilities and the need to tend to them, the memory of past violence had benumbed its bearers into monumentalizing consolation.

On the other hand, the notion of countermonumentalization goes some way toward capturing the dynamics that characterized the Gezi resistance and its political aesthetics. This is not limited to what people did with the monuments themselves, though admittedly there was something of a paradigm shift in witnessing AKM and the Republic Monument being covered with banners and flags of various radical factions (figure 5.9); seeing people walking on the rooftop of AKM; walking past people sitting, lying, or pitching tents on the landscaping around the monument (previously so unimaginable as ground to tread on that it hadn't even required the usual warning signs for people to keep off); gathering around bonfires in the square; watching flags featuring the portrait of the imprisoned Kurdish leader Abdullah Öcalan wave freely there; and witnessing what came to be known as the "eternal *halay*," the literally ceaseless circle-dance of Kurds gathered around the tent of their party, the Barış ve Demokrasi Partisi/Peace and Democratic Party (BDP), in one corner where Gezi Park meets the square (the dance continued whether it was the height of midday heat or 5 AM). Lefebvre suggests that the usual spatial opposition between inside and outside is insufficient "when it comes to defining monumental space"; instead, "such a space is determined by what may take place there, and consequently by what may not take place there (prescribed/proscribed, scene/obscene)."[24] This begins to explain something of the paradigm-shifting effect of the material practices that transgressed the monumental injunctions of Taksim Square.

But these spatial practices were combined with other political dynamics, a countermonumentalization that we may identify with Meltem Ahıska as "inhabit[ing] and politically subvert[ing] the gaps and excesses within the assumed totality of the nation."[25] Many accounts not only of Gezi but many of the myriad uprisings of the past several years touch on this: the state-free zone became a site for a politics of contact between identities, groups, and organizations that previously would not and could not exist side by side. Explosive humor was another quality of the Gezi resistance that is often emphasized in accounts, similarly decisive in this dynamic of countermonumentalization— it took hold of the social media, covered the walls of the city, subverted the words of traditional leftist chants, seeped into the choreographies of spontaneous collective performance pieces, and was mixed into the bricolages of the barricades. Humor has its own peculiar way of disarming, and laughter, we found out, can go some way toward shattering the brittle categorizations that regulate the body politic. Those days in June allowed a glimpse of the political landscape that could emerge through a rearticulation of constituent power in its diversity, the unraveling of rooted prejudices and worn-out enmities, and the emergence of new subjectivities as visible and viable beyond the petrified subjects of the official nation-state ideology. This process might well be described as the countermonumentalization of political imaginaries.

Countermonumentalization: A Bricolage

In a 1992 essay, James E. Young contemplated the countermonument in light of the work of a number of artists exploring the possibilities for critical memorialization practices in Germany in the aftermath of the Holocaust. The challenge that these artists attempted to address was the incommensurability between the politics of the traditional genre of public monuments and the need to memorialize the nation's own victims, since conventionally monuments commemorate the victories, heroes, and martyrs of the nation itself.[26]

In traditional monuments of martyrdom, past vulnerability is anonymized and appropriated, reconfigured into a narrative of selfless sacrifice for the glory of the nation. In monuments of victory, past vulnerability is often erased altogether along with the erasure of the victims of the depicted triumph. The artists of the countermonument movement sought to produce public memorial artifacts that would neither erase nor appropriate the memory of violence in an anesthetizing closure that shores up the current order. Their works were instead meant to stimulate in their audience a responsiveness and liveliness to the very continuities of the conditions of political violence and vulnerability in the present.

As indicated, the notions of monumentalization and countermonumentalization lend themselves as nodes of a conceptual framework for addressing political dynamics beyond a strictly literal interpretation of these terms as simply indexed to the erection of monuments and similar spatial practices.[27] Ahıska describes countermonumentalization as "the visualization of a certain *aesthesis*" through oppositional social practices and movements. Here *aesthesis* refers to "the heterogeneous experiences of sensuous perception embedded in the fabric of life," which are otherwise repressed by the political aesthetics of monumental transmission.[28] Thus we can think of countermonumentalization as an undoing of the anaesthetizing stasis of monumentalization, a reclamation and reconfiguration of the ecstatic. This is intimately connected to the question of vulnerability, if we understand vulnerability, following Judith Butler,[29] as an ontological condition that marks the ecstatic dimensions of our being, the various ways we are always already outside ourselves. In Butler's account, vulnerability defines our inalienable unboundedness, our fundamental dependence on others and on infrastructures, the ways in which we are given over to pleasure and pain, to abandonment and sustenance, as well as to various affective states beyond our control. If, in addition to certain spatial practices, monumentalization names a framing of the body politic in ways that foreclose certain affective responses while marshaling others, countermonumentalization can be figured as resisting and subverting such foreclosures and imperatives. In this sense, countermonumentalization operates as a reclamation of vulnerability, a form of reattunement to vulnerability.

The conceptual framework of monumentalization/countermonumentalization further assists in attending to the aesthetic and political operations that forge the relation between the constitution of the body politic and political violence. This potential has been taken up by a number of legal scholars who have turned to the language of monumentalism and countermonumentalism to explore the affinities between memorial practices and constitution making,[30] to trace museological practices that approximate the truth of constituent power,[31] and to call for a countermonumental constitutionalism.[32] It is perhaps not entirely coincidental that this vein of work mostly pertains to South Africa, where constitutionalism has urgently and unavoidably been tied to the politics of memory or, more specifically, to a range of official efforts undertaken to address past political violence in ways that reconcile the victims to the present order and thereby bolster the conditions of cohabitation. Notably, critical legal works that draw on this vocabulary to inquire into the dynamics of constitutionalism tend to figure countermonumentalism as a form of fidelity to the liveliness, diversity, and ambivalences of constituent power, whereas monumentalism is used to capture the ossifications of constituted power: elective framing of constituent dynamics, exclusionary closures, and the redistribution of legitimate violence.

The jurisprudential significance of representational strategies also finds a relatively simple articulation in the "antimonuments" of the Mexican Canadian artist Rafael Lozano-Hemmer. His works use light, shadows, programming technology, and sometimes sound as medium, and urban public squares and buildings as sites. They crucially depend on the active participation of members of the public, to the extent that without their engagement the work cannot come to *be*—a quality that destabilizes the distinction between maker and audience. The antimonuments are designed to allow discreet individual participation while facilitating the emergence of collective patterns of self-organization among strangers who happen to be engaging with the work. As prototypes meant to capture and reflect structures emerging from collective action, these works can be understood on one level as inquiring into the dynamics and potentials of constituent power. Indeed, Lozano-Hemmer explains that he is working toward a "relational architecture" as an alternative to "the fetish of the representation of power,"[33] which we may in turn read as a figuration of the forcible frames and monumentalizing aesthetics of constituted power. Admittedly, Lozano-Hemmer's works bracket out vulnerability or, more specifically, the questions of violence and necessity that inevitably accompany constitutional processes, the former as threat and/or means, the latter as the necessity to provide basic infrastructure for the sustenance of lives. Then again, this bracketing brings to the fore another aspect pertaining to the ecstatic, namely, the ludic element of collective action and collective self-organization, something we rarely contemplate in attending to the serious business of the political.

Encountered in various guises in art history, memory studies, literary criticism, legal scholarship, and other fields, the concept of countermonumentalization may be productive for contemplating the historical possibilities for resistance today, as it gathers together a key set of issues including memory, violence, vulnerability, collective embodied/material/spatial practices, representational strategy, and the polity to come. The convergence of these questions is relevant in the immediate aftermath (if not midst) of a global wave of uprisings that no Left analysis foresaw and many Left analyses are quick to dismiss, either through hasty diagnoses or frustrated prescriptions. The weight of Left history sits heavily as monumentalized Left failure,[34] as so many elaborate analyses of the overwhelming entrenchment of the forces to be resisted, and as intimate knowledge of our vulnerability before the legal, hyperlegal,[35] and extralegal instruments of *raison d'état*. Then again, the barricades return.

So I return to the barricades in the remainder of this essay, as a way to probe into the lives and afterlives of vulnerability in resistance. As a long-standing "repertoire of collective action," barricades serve both as a materialization of and metaphor for resistance. They are temporary embodiments of collective agency that combine spontaneity and structure, and yet in doing so they resist a logic of "utility versus futility": they shield but only provisionally; they fail but only to return again. Young's description of the countermonument powerfully resonates with the significance of the barricade as an artifact of resistance in public space: "Its aim is not to console but to provoke; not to remain fixed but to change; not to be everlasting but to disappear; not to be ignored by passersby but to demand interaction; not to remain pristine but to invite its own violation and desecration."[36] Indeed, as edifices that defy monumental premises of representation, closure, fixity, stasis, continuity, durability, pristineness, as well as the traditional hierarchies between maker, object, and audience, barricades present themselves as countermonuments, embodying something of the ecstasis of resistance. Further, the associations of memory-work that the term "countermonument" evokes are not entirely lost on the barricade, as the phenomenon raises its own problems and paradoxes for memory, in its awkward combination of historical consciousness with untimely spatial strategy.

The Memory of Barricades

The tension between monumentalization and barricades was something that Walter Benjamin attended to in the Arcades Project. In Convolute E, titled "Haussmannization, Barricade Fighting," he gathers passages on the transformation of Paris in the mid-nineteenth century under Baron Haussmann, as well as a range of materials on barricades such as a passage from Friedrich Engels's notes on the barricade as strategy, several citations concerning the different materials used for building barricades, and descriptions of barricades from 1830, 1848, and 1871. The convolute betrays Benjamin's fascination with the numbers and ubiquity of barricades in nineteenth-century Paris, and the use of overturned omnibuses in barricade building. His juxtaposition of Haussmannization and the barricades is far from arbitrary: Haussmann's regeneration of Paris was an undertaking of "strategic embellishment" meant to destroy the architectural infrastructure that rendered barricade fighting effective. As Benjamin writes in the exposé of 1935, "The true goal of Haussmann's projects was to secure the city against civil war. He wanted to make the erection of barricades in Paris impossible for all time."[37] Benjamin also highlights the monumentalizing ambitions of this transformation: "The institutions of the bourgeoisie's worldly and spiritual dominance were to find their apotheosis within the framework of the boulevards. Before their completion, boulevards were draped across with canvas and unveiled like monuments."[38] In the revised exposé of 1939, he appends to this passage the following succinct critique of monumentalization: "With the Haussmannization of Paris, the phantasmagoria was rendered in stone."[39] The defiant return of the barricades during the Paris Commune, despite the new unaccommodating cityscape, seems to signify for Benjamin a triumph over monumentalized phantasmagoria: "The barricade is resurrected during the Commune, it is stronger and better secured than ever. It stretches across the great boulevards, often reaching a height of two stories, and shields the trenches behind it. Just as the *Communist Manifesto* ends the age of professional conspirators, so the Commune puts an end to the phantasmagoria holding sway over the early years of the proletariat."[40]

An aspect of the tension between barricades and monumentalization that does not find its way into the Arcades Project is the attempted erasure of the Commune's memory through the monumental architecture of Sacré-Coeur.[41] But there is another, perhaps more significant one: the monumental defensive structures that were built over several weeks by the Commune's Commission of Barricades, under the direction of shoemaker Napoléon Gaillard (the "stronger and better secured" barricades that Benjamin seemed to celebrate), actually performed disastrously in combat. Barricade historian Mark Traugott explains, for example, that the largest of these edifices, built on the corner of Rue de Rivoli and Rue Saint-Florentin, fell quickly when the Versailles army attacked, because it was easily outflanked and captured from behind. "By contrast, many of the spontaneous barricades set up on the spot by unorganized insurgent forces put up a fanatical resistance and long held out against overwhelming odds."[42] Eric Hazan notes a similar dynamic concerning the barricades of June 1848.[43] Indeed, we find that the military leader of the Commune, Gustave-Paul Cluseret, put his finger on the matter in his memoirs written in the Commune's aftermath. Here he insists on the necessity for the barricades precisely to *not* be like monuments: "The building of barricades was, first of all, to be carried out as quickly as possible; in contrast to the unique, well-situated, and centralized civic monument, whose aura derives from its isolation and stability, barricades were not designed around the notion of a unique 'proper place.' "[44]

While barricade histories teach us that the monumentalization of barricades hastens their fall, triumph at the barricades is in any case fleeting and rare. Most of the time, their best effect is to prove costly for and delay the machinery of state violence. Traugott notes that although barricades featured prominently in the 1848 revolutions and later insurgencies, their practical utility had already diminished by 1848 from a strictly military perspective. This is also the crux of Engels's notes on barricade fighting in his introduction to Marx's *Class Struggles in France*, though he dates the shift to after 1848. He states that all military, technological, and urban developments since then had made the conditions far more favorable for the arm of the state and far less so for barricade fighting. Reporting on the brief Hamburg uprising of 1923, Larissa Reissner chimes in to this chronology and laments the "old romantic barricade" of 1848: "As a fortified wall between revolutionary rifles and government cannon the barricade long ago became a specter. It no longer serves as a protection to anyone but solely as an impediment."[45] Then again, like a specter, the barricade keeps returning even if "its military effectiveness has fallen asymptotically over time to nearly zero."[46] Historian Dennis Bos notes a further irony: the barricade became internationally ubiquitous precisely at the same time as it became militarily futile.[47] So why is it that this specter keeps returning and roaming the world?

Notably, for both Bos and Traugott, the return of the barricade despite its tried and tested vulnerability can be explained by a kind of transmission that we may identify as a form of monumentalization. According to Bos, the recurrence of barricades across borders in the nineteenth and early twentieth centuries is an effect of the mythology of the Paris Commune in the international socialist labor movement. He lightly traces the disseminations of accounts, reporting, images, speeches, poetry, plays, songs, and other literature on the Commune across Europe to demonstrate how the barricade "transformed from matter into myth" along with the romanticization of the Commune in chivalrous and suicidal imagery: "Addressing socialists on a personal and emotional level, the barricade referred to an imaginary world of socialist chivalry. In many accounts the symbolic barricade functioned as a stage for acts of bravery or as the background for scenes of proletarian martyrdom."[48] In Bos's account, the enormous losses of the Paris Commune, the massacre of twenty thousand Communards within a week by the Versailles army, were mythologized into legends of virile heroism and self-sacrifice. He further suggests that later barricades could not shake off the key themes of this legend, neither in how they were inhabited nor in how they were represented: "There is no escape from the weight of an established tradition . . . Both in literature and in actual conduct there seems no choice but to conform to the stereotypes set by history and mythological representations."[49] We may read what Bos describes as a process of the monumentalization of resistance in socialist imaginary and memory: the ossification of unmourned loss in tales of self-sacrifice, the erasure of vulnerability in chivalry.

Traugott has a similar explanation for the spectral return: he suggests that we can explain the "miraculous" nondisappearance of barricades only by looking beyond the purely pragmatic considerations, thinking not only in terms of their material efficacy but also the more abstract functions they perform.[50] For this, he first turns to Eric Hobsbawm's explanation in the introduction to *The Invention of Tradition* of how the practical utility of an object or practice has to wane for it to be appropriated for symbolic or ritual purposes. Then he draws on Pierre Nora's concept of *lieux de mémoire* to suggest that "buildings, monuments, and battlefields are classic examples of the type of locations that help perpetuate a sense of connection to pivotal historical events. Barricades, which possess properties in common with all three, likewise exerted a powerful influence over the popular imagination."[51] In this account, the barricade keeps returning due to its "iconic status" as a symbol of the "revolutionary tradition."

It seems to me, however, that both of Traugott's references are ill suited to explaining the recurrence of barricades. Hobsbawm's idea of the invention of a tradition is largely a top-down affair: he writes of "imposing repetition," "formalization and ritualization," by either single initiators (i.e., Robert Baden-Powell and the Boy Scouts), official institutions such as armies and courts of law, and at the very least by private groups such as the Parliament or the legal profession.[52] This is very much at a remove from the spontaneous uptake of the barricade as a structure by insurgents across cultures and from a diversity of backgrounds who do not even necessarily identify with a particular ideological tradition. The concept of lieux de mémoire may be similarly counterproductive here: the comparison of barricades to buildings, monuments, and battlefields is flawed, as the latter are site-specific and relatively permanent. But even if we were to go with Nora's less spatially anchored examples of archives, festivals, anniversaries, treaties, depositions, and fraternal orders,[53] the concept still does not quite yield itself to the phenomenon of barricades. For Nora, lieux de mémoire "originate with the sense that there is no spontaneous memory";[54] what goes by the name of memory in modernity "is in fact the gigantic and breathtaking storehouse of a material stock of what it would be impossible for us to remember, an unlimited repertoire of what might need to be recalled."[55] Nora opposes this to what he provisionally terms "true memory, which has taken refuge in gestures and habits, in skills passed down by unspoken traditions, in the body's inherent self-knowledge, in unstudied reflexes and ingrained memories."[56] As idealized as it is (and perhaps Nora himself would not accept this nostalgic formulation's application to a phenomenon as untethered as the one under consideration), this formulation of "true memory" seems to capture more about barricades than his lieux de mémoire concept does.

The figure of the barricade has served as an emblem of and metaphor for resistance, and there are indeed entrenched political, rhetorical, and aesthetic traditions established around it. However, an account of monumentalized transmission based on the allure of mythology and iconicity misses all that is precisely countermonumental about barricades: their refusal to accommodate phantasmagoria, their resistance to monumentalization, their embodiment of an ecstasis of resistance. A more accurate account would be of countermonumentalizing transmission, one that would mark the role of vulnerability in resistance rather than disavowing it through mythologies of virility, fantasies of impermeability, iconographies of heroes/martyrs, or consolations of monumentalized failure. Hannah Arendt offers a clue here, borrowing a formulation from *Leaves of Hypnos*, the journal of prose poetry that René Char kept while fighting in the French Resistance: "Our inheritance was left to us by no testament." Arendt begins *Between Past and Future* and ends *On Revolution* with Char's fragment. An inheritance has been left, but without any prior testament. Something has been passed on, but it has been foreseen by no tradition.

In both texts, Arendt supplies her reading of this fragment with a number of other expressions that she gleans from Char, most importantly this: "If I survive, I know that I shall have to break with the aroma of these essential years, silently reject (not repress) my treasure."[57] Departing from Char's passages, Arendt playfully proposes that the history of revolutions "could be told in parable form as the tale of an age-old treasure which, under the most varied circumstances, appears abruptly, unexpectedly, and disappears again, under different mysterious conditions, as though it were a fata morgana."[58] Char's text does not readily reveal what this treasure may be, but Arendt is characteristically confident in her interpretation: the treasure is what was once known as "public happiness" or "public freedom." She explains that during the Resistance, Char and his generation of writers were forced into a political existence they had not planned or foreseen. Because they were moved to take it upon themselves to resist tyranny, they began to act in a public sphere of their own making. Arendt proposes that eighteenth-century political thought identified precisely this, the active participation in the making of the public realm, in terms of "public happiness" (in America) and "public freedom" (in France)—something she discusses in more detail in the earlier chapters of *On Revolution*. She expresses her preference for the American formulation: if they knew to call it "happiness," it is because they knew it through experience rather than merely in theory.[59]

Mark the gesture toward the ecstatic here, both as a resource and as the experience of resistance. In fact, Arendt often mentions in passing "the great ecstasy" of collective action.[60] In one place she formulates this ecstasy in terms of "the exhilarating awareness of the human capacity of beginning, the high spirits which have always attended the birth of something new on earth," as something those engaged in building a polity are bound to experience.[61] Something akin to what she is describing traverses the testimonials from the current wave of uprisings, where narratives of overwhelming emotion are common. For example, Yasmine el Rashidi writes of witnessing a "reservoir of emotions that I never thought I would ever bear witness to" in a number of encounters on Tahrir Square, including one with a man with missing teeth who sat on a sidewalk and wrote page after page of slogans, poems, and essays: "He had been in that same spot for two weeks and said he would stay until the day he died. 'I carry the emotion of a nation, not only my own.' "[62] In two beautifully written diatribes against the attempts by "experts of expertise" to render the Gezi uprising "knowable, calculable, measurable," Hazal Halavut writes of "the beautiful knowledge" of resistance as one gained through emotion.[63] Slavoj Žižek is not impressed: "The mass movements that we have seen most recently, whether in Tahrir Square or Athens, look to me like a pathetic ecstasy. What is important for me is the following day, the morning after. These events make me feel as one does when one awakes with a headache after a night of drunkenness."[64] But the trouble with this easy dismissal is that it fails to register the thought-defying diversity and extent of infrastructural mobilization that actually has emerged in the midst of the ecstatic in these uprisings. It is also shortsighted even if formulated as a mastery of foresight— why be *moved* to collective action if the morning after is to banish the ecstatic through such hasty claims to sobriety?

What moves us to collective action, even when it is most unexpected, is the felt necessity to reclaim anew a world that fails to contain the ecstatic dimensions of our being, a world that abandons us to our private political irrelevance, if not destitution. So in the spirit of Arendt's untimely "treasure," I would propose that barricades return not because but more likely despite entrenched traditions; not because we need heroes or martyrs, myths or monuments, but precisely to release the aesthesis foreclosed by such ossifications. Resistance, then, may be understood as a reclamation of vulnerability, even when it appears as its very defiance through heroic acts by ordinary people who put themselves on the line. In other words, we resist not just despite vulnerability, but perhaps because of it and for its sake.

Notes

I wish to express my gratitude to the editors and contributors of this volume for their careful engagement with earlier drafts of this essay, to Meltem Ahıska for the initial and continuing inspiration, to Stewart Motha and Alisa Lebow for providing thoughtful commentary, and to Hannah Franzki for luring me back into the *Arcades Project*.

1 A number of insightful collections include the pamphlet from San Francisco Bay Area Independent Media Center, "This Is Only the Beginning: On the Gezi Park Resistance of June 2013," October 2013, https://www.indybay.org/uploads/2014/03 /03/this_is_only_the_beginning.pdf; Yıldırım and Navaro-Yashin, "An Impromptu Uprising"; and Alessandrini, Üstündağ, and Yildiz, "'Resistance Everywhere.'"

2 The police lifted most of the barricades and repossessed Taksim Square on June 11, then evicted the camp at Gezi Park on June 15.

3   Traugott, *The Insurgent Barricade*, xi.

4   Traugott, *The Insurgent Barricade*, 11.

5   "Gezi Havası," *Vimeo*, June 22, 2013, 4:21, http://vimeo.com/68917094.

6   This is captured in a number of interviews at the barricades published in the Gezi special issue of the Turkish-language journal *Express*, no. 136 (June–July 2013): 52–55.

7   Hakan Vreskala and Taksim Gezi Direnişçileri, "Dağılın Lan," June 8, 2013, 2:56, http://www.youtube.com/watch?v=cjfoXoz69sw.

8   This sense of the barricade as a living being is found in Larissa Reissner's account of the 1923 Hamburg Rising: it "sprout(s) from the ground multiplying at an incredible rate" and then "courageously catches with its breast all the blind frenzied fire that troops rain down on their unseen enemy." Reissner, "Hamburg at the Barricades," 66–67.

9   Lefebvre, *The Production of Space*.

10 Lefebvre, *The Production of Space*, 143.

11 Lefebvre, *The Production of Space*, 221.

12 Navaro-Yashin, *Faces of the State*, 1.

13 Alkan, "Taksim'in Siyasî Tarihine Mukaddime," 150.

14 See Çınar, *Modernity, Islam, and Secularism in Turkey*, 114–118.

15 At first glance this seems like a generic choice for a symbolic return to the glorious days of the imperial past. However, it has been suggested the choice may have more to do with the government's own heritage of political Islam. Alkan, "Taksim'in Siyasî Tarihine Mukaddime," 148–149. The Taksim barracks were one of the key sites of the April 1909 counterrevolutionary uprising, which "spoke in the language of religion" against the constitutional coup of 1908, the latter being an important precursor to the secular republicanism of modern Turkey. See extended discussion by Sohrabi, *Revolution and Constitutionalism in the Ottoman Empire and Iran*, 224–283.

16 Alkan, "Taksim'in Siyasî Tarihine Mukaddime," 150.

17 Lefebvre, *The Production of Space*, 222.

18 Sakr, *Monumental Space in the Post-Imperial Novel*, 3.

19 Baykan and Hatuka, "Politics and Culture in the Making of Public Space," 55.

20 Taksim Solidarity is an umbrella formation of more than one hundred organizations, including numerous political parties on the Left, labor unions, chambers, and NGOs. Taksim Solidarity was established in March 2012, in opposition to the government's regeneration project for Taksim Square and environs. A full list of constituents can be found at Taksim Dayanışması, http://taksimdayanisma .org/, accessed on June 10, 2016.

21 LGBT Bloc did not exist as an entity prior to the Gezi uprising; rather, it named those that gathered around the rainbow flag at the resistance.

22 "Our Commons" is a relatively new formation of various activist groups, including local groups from neighborhoods threatened with eviction, ecologists, feminists, LGBTs, anticapitalists, and migrants, which started in Gezi Park

from the first day onwards, before the matter exploded into a popular uprising. See, Müşterekler, http://mustereklerimiz.org/our-commons-who-why/, accessed June 9, 2016.

23 In KONDA Research and Consultancy's survey of 4411 people over June 6–7 in Gezi Park, 6.4 percent identified themselves as "representatives of a group or formation" while the rest identified as "ordinary citizens." Further, 21 percent identified as "a member of a political party or a nongovernmental organization such as an association, foundation, or platform," while 79 percent had no such membership. KONDA, "Gezi Parkı Araştırması: Kimler, neden oradalar ve ne istiyorlar?," http://www.youtube.com/watch?v=5zP6TnfALQU.

24 Lefebvre, *The Production of Space*, 224.

25 Ahıska, "The Imperial Complex," unpublished paper, 2013.

26 Young, "The Counter-Monument," 270–271.

27 Ahıska, "The Imperial Complex."

28 Ahıska, "The Imperial Complex."

29 See, for example, Butler, *Undoing Gender,* 17–39; *Precarious Life,* 19–49; and *Frames of War,* 33–62.

30 Synman, "Interpretation and the Politics of Memory."

31 Douglas, "Between Constitutional Mo(nu)ments."

32 Spaulding, "Constitution as Countermonument"; Le Roux, "War Memorials, the Architecture of the Constitutional Court Building and Counter-Monumental Constitutionalism." For a similar spirit of inquiry that opposes memorialization to monumentalization see van Marle, "The Spectacle of Post-Apartheid Constitutionalism."

33 Lozano-Hemmer, "Alien Relationships from Public Space."

34 Brown, Hemmer, "Alien Relationship."

35 Hussain, "Hyperlegality."

36 Young, "The Counter-Monument," 277.

37 Benjamin, *The Arcades Project,* 12.

38 Benjamin, *The Arcades Project,* 11.

39 Benjamin, *The Arcades Project,* 24.

40 Benjamin, *The Arcades Project,* 12.

41 Harvey, "Monument and Myth."

42 Traugott, *The Insurgent Barricade,* 16.

43 Hazan, *The Invention of Paris,* 241.

44 Cited in Ross, *The Emergence of Social Space,* 36.

45 Reissner, "Hamburg at the Barricades," 67.

46 Hazan, *The Invention of Paris,* 241.

47 Bos, "Building Barricades."

48 Bos, "Building Barricades," 355.

49 Bos, "Building Barricades," 359.

50 Traugott, *The Insurgent Barricade,* 221.

51 Traugott, *The Insurgent Barricade,* 222–223.

52 Hobsbawm, *The Invention of Tradition*, 4–5.

53 Nora, "Between Memory and History," 12.

54 Nora, "Between Memory and History," 12.

55 Nora, "Between Memory and History," 13.

56 Nora, "Between Memory and History," 13.

57 Char, *Leaves of Hypnos*, 62. This edition reads, "Our heritage is not preceded by any testament." Arendt must have been quoting from the 1956 Routledge collection of Char's work, *Hypnos Waking: Poems and Prose*, which I have not been able to access. In this edition, the full fragment is: "If I escape, I know that I shall have to break with the aroma of these essential years, reject (not repress) silently utterly my treasure, reconduct myself to the very principle of the most indigent behavior as at the time when I sought myself without ever acceding to prowess, in a naked unsatisfaction, a hardly glimpsed knowledge and inquisitive humility."

58 Arendt, *Between Past and Future*, 5.

59 Arendt, *On Revolution*, 119.

60 For example, in *On Violence*, 49n17.

61 Arendt, *On Revolution*, 223.

62 El Rashidi, "Cairo, City in Waiting," 62.

63 Halavut, "Gezi ya da Uzanıp Kendi Yanaklarından Öpmenin İhtimali," http://www.5harfliler.com/gezi-ya-da-uzanip-kendi-yanaklarindan-opmenin-ihtimali/; "Gezi'nin Kalan'ı", http://www.amargidergi.com/yeni/?p=245.

64 Dutent, "Slavoj Žižek: The Eternal Marriage between Capitalism and Democracy Has Ended," http://www.humaniteinenglish.com/spip.php?article2332.

CHAPTER 6

Dreams and the Political Subject

ELENA LOIZIDOU

Compared with the reality which comes from being seen and heard, even the greatest forces of intimate life—the passions of the heart, the thoughts of the mind, the delights of the senses—lead an uncertain shadowy kind of existence unless and until they are transformed, deprivatized and deindividualized, as it were, into a shape to fit them for public appearance.

—HANNAH ARENDT, *The Human Condition*

All that we see or seem
Is but a dream within a dream.

—EDGAR ALLAN POE, "A Dream within a Dream"

A Start

I recall my late maternal grandmother, sitting in the back veranda of our house in Nicosia on a low stool, in a loose light black dress, and on various occasions saying: "I had a dream last night. I dreamt I was at the village, in Petra. I saw my home and the church and the river." My brother and I, in our teens then, were eager to find out more; we used to ask her: "How did it look? How did you get there?" She replied that the village looked "the same" and that she flew there.

My grandmother came from the small village of Petra, located in the valley of Soleas. The village was for a long time an intercommunal village, with Turkish Cypriots, Greek Cypriots, and Maronites living alongside each other. Petra (Πέτρα) means "rock." In 1958 the Turkish Cypriot community renamed the village Dereli, meaning "place with a stream," naming the village's second environmental element, the stream that carved through the rock. In 1975 the village was given the name Taşköy (village of rock) or Petre[1] by the Turkish

Cypriots, returning it to its first name. The first census—in 1831, when the island was under the Ottoman Empire's administration—records that there were 139 men in the village, of whom 53 where Turkish Cypriots and 86 Greek Cypriots. In 1960, the year of Cyprus's independence, the census shows that the total population was 1,034 inhabitants (men and women): 5 were Maronites, 63 Turkish Cypriots, and 966 Greek Cypriots. In 1973, again according to the census, the village was solely composed of 910 Greek Cypriots. Ever since that time, the census has shown no inhabitants. Soon after the Turkish invasion of 1974,[2] the village was flattened out, destroyed, and some parts of it are now used as a military base. The Turkish Cypriot population of the village had been displaced a decade earlier, between January and February 1964; they fled to the nearby Turkish villages of Lefka, Ellia, and Angolemi.[3]

My grandmother fled her village when the Turks invaded Cyprus of July 20, 1974. She returned though with a couple of her covillagers once, just after the invasion, to pick up stuff she valued: photographs and my parents' wedding wreath. At the time Petra or Taşköy was occupied by the Turkish army. While my grandmother managed to avoid being observed and returned to Evrihou, the village that was hosting her and not under occupation, the couple with whom they returned to Petra never came back and are still listed as missing. My maternal grandmother, Eleni Frangopoulou, died in 1985, a refugee, and without being able to return, except in those dreams that gave her a break from exile.

And a break from exile it was indeed. As she was telling us her flight dreams, her face used to lighten up. I could feel a sense of liberty embracing her: Eleni Frangopoulou was free again. She was at Petra, among familiar places and faces, away from everyday discussions about what came to be known as the "Cyprus problem." Since the Turkish invasion of Cyprus in 1974 there have been ongoing attempts by the Greek and Turkish communities respectively to find a peaceful solution and reunite the island. The bicommunal talks were constantly discussed and analyzed in the media, giving hope and then disappointment to all. The flight dream appeared to be her only gateway out of the trap of hope and disappointment; it gave her a sense of freedom that she otherwise did not have in her everyday waking life. In her dream the place where she grew up returned to give her access both to her past and to herself, to who she was, reconstituting a self that had been both disrupted and scattered as a result of the invasion and her refugee status. These flight dreams were dreams *of* freedom. Or, more precisely, they *were* freedom: the visual entry to a past, of a familiar self and environment, enlivened her, freed her from the present (a constant reminder of loss—land, familiar environment, independence, sociability), and enabled her to articulate her longing for a lost self.

The psychoanalyst Adam Phillips writes that "dreams are the way we talk about the unintelligibility of reality, and about the ways we acknowledge this. Desire, that is to say, makes sense only in dreams."[4] Dreams—not just through their symbolism, but also in the way we recollect them and recount them to others—give us the chance to recompose ourselves, even in the dream that is a nightmare. This very recomposition is an *act* of freedom.

This chapter, prompted by my late grandmother's flight dreams, explores the extent to which Hannah Arendt's political theory recognizes dreams (and not dreams as metaphors) as integral to political subjectivity. I argue that Arendt's formulation of politics—as a space "of self-making in which diverse individuals and groups interact to create themselves and to shape their common world"[5]—can't incorporate the dream into its definition, even though she explicitly talks about dreams in her book on Rahel Varnhagen, as in her essay "The Jew as Pariah: A Hidden Tradition."[6] In the chapter titled "Day and Night" from her book *Rahel Varnhagen: The Life of a Jewish Woman,* Arendt focuses on Varnhagen's dreams. As Elisabeth Young-Bruehl tells us, Arendt finds the reference to dreams useful, since they reveal that there can be an ambiguity in the struggle for identity;[7] nevertheless, she refrains from naming Varnhagen's dreams as part of the political sphere. As Young-Bruehl points out, Arendt found dreaming, poetry, and other sensory accounts introspective and thus felt they belonged to the private sphere, not the political.[8] We see this position replicated when Arendt engages with the role of poetry, literature, and dreams in her essay "The Jew as Pariah: A Hidden Tradition."[9] Here she explicitly refers to the world of sensation and literature as socially but not politically emancipatory.[10] Kathryn T. Gines, in *Hannah Arendt and the Negro Question*, also points out that Arendt refuses to acknowledge the sensual world as an integral part of politics.[11] In an otherwise congratulatory letter to James Baldwin for his publication of "Letter from a Region in my Mind," Gines points out, Arendt disagrees with his positioning love as a politically emancipatory concept:

> What frightened me in your essay was the gospel of love which you begin to preach at the end. In politics, love is a stranger, and when it intrudes upon it nothing is being achieved except hypocrisy. All the characteristics you stress in the Negro people: their beauty, their capacity for joy, their

warmth, and their humanity, are well-known characteristics of all op-pressed people. They grow out of suffering and they are the proudest pos-session of all pariahs. Unfortunately, they have never survived the hour of liberation by even five minutes. Hatred and love belong together, and they are both destructive; you can afford them only in the private and, as a people, only so long as you are not free.[12]

Arendt's position in this letter is that love and the entire sensual realm, including poetry and the arts, are like dreams: even if they animate the social and private realm, they have no place in politics and are not an integral part of political subjectivity.

This boundary may not always be sustained. Nevertheless, what persists in Arendt's writing is the stipulation that dreams and more generally the sensual realm can't be designated to the sphere of the political; at best they can re-veal a truth about politics. Recounting a dream, as my grandmother did, may bring about one's recomposition as a subject—it enabled her to raise herself up from the pains of being a refugee. This is the same recomposition of the body we observe in demonstrations, protests, and other political gatherings when standing up to the battering of the dominant orders or conditions of being. Here we can think of the dream (its experience and a recounting) as an extension of the overt political acts of demonstrations and protests, tracking the *flight* to freedom.

Dreaming and Subjectivity

The subject has been a long-standing problem of philosophy. Simon Critchley reminds us, "The subject is that which is thrown under as a prior support or more fundamental stratum upon which other qualities, such as predicates, accidents, and attributes may be based."[13] Moreover, the subject is the founda-tion by which "entities become intelligible."[14] More specifically, from Descartes onward, philosophy casts aside the belief that the world is made intelligible by something (i.e., God) that resides outside (wo)man. Instead, "the human subject—as self, ego, or conscious, thinking thing"[15]—becomes the protago-nist of the venture of trying to make sense of the world. The human subject thus becomes the "beginning point for an understanding of entities."[16] Since Descartes, disparate philosophical traditions have explained how the human subject is constituted. Here, as a way of expanding our understanding of who may count as a political subject, I critique Hannah Arendt's understandings of the subject. I have chosen Arendt rather than any other political theorists because of her rich engagement with the problematic of the political subject. More precisely, contra Arendt, I explain that dreaming is an essential element of our political subjectivity.

Arendt was not so much interested in identifying how the subject is constituted; rather, by taking on board constitutive elements of the subject (e.g., thinking, reflection, acting), she tells the story of how the subject moves into the world. Her writings offer us a biography of the movements of the human subject; most notably, in *The Human Condition* they are sketched as labor, work, and action.[17] In her other writings, we see the human subject described as moving in a variety of ways: thinking, acting, judging. In turn, each *movement* reveals to us a different *dimension* of the subject, moral, political, and aesthetic and simultaneously brings into view their corresponding modes of life (moral, political, and aesthetic); those modes of life both *relate to* and *articulate* those dimensions of the subject.

Arendt's way of marking the differences between these dimensions of the subject has become influential, and she has been able to point to (but not always able to sustain) the form and characteristics of these dimensions. Dreams appear in her political theory and work as part of the private and therefore apolitical realm, as I indicated earlier. Here I show how she maps these different dimensions of the subject and suggest that there is a need to consider the dreaming subject as integral to political subjectivity.

Arendt tells the story of the subject in a number of her writings, including *The Human Condition* and her essays "Civil Disobedience," "Some Questions on Moral Philosophy," and "Thinking and Moral Considerations."[18] The story of the subject is played out in her distinction between the effects of thinking and the effects of acting, or, to put it differently, through the ways that thinking and acting articulate the spheres of morality and politics:

> The main distinction, politically speaking, between Thought and Action lies in that I am only with my own self or the self of another while I am thinking, whereas I am in the company of the many the moment I start to act. Power for human beings who are not omnipotent can only reside in the many forms of human plurality, whereas every mode of human singularity is impotent by definition. It is true, however, that even in the singularity or duality of thinking processes, plurality is somehow germinally present insofar as I can think only by splitting up into two although I am one. But this two-in-one, looked upon from the standpoint of human plu-

rality, is like the last trace of company—even when being *one* by myself, I am or can become two—which becomes so very important because we discover plurality where we would least expect it. But insofar as being with others is concerned, it still must be regarded as a marginal phenomenon.[19]

Nevertheless, Arendt does not just differentiate the two spheres of life, the moral from the political, by attributing thinking to the ethical sphere and acting to the political. She also articulates a particular tendency in each of these spheres: the ethical sphere has an inclination toward thinking, the political toward acting. She does not claim that the political sphere is bereft of thinking, nor does she suggest that the moral sphere is empty of acting. Rather, she points out that their difference lies in their *form*. Thinking is an activity that takes place in isolation—yet when one is by oneself and thinks, reflects, and dialogues with oneself, it becomes apparent that this thinking singular self is also a split self. In her essay "Civil Disobedience,"[20] where she takes up the figure of the conscientious objector, Arendt unpacks further why such activity— objecting to unjust law, as Thoreau did, or refusing to defy punishment, as Socrates did—takes the form of politics. These may be morally accurate acts, but they cannot be properly political because they remain private acts.[21] By "private acts" she means that these are acts of singular selves, and as such they "cannot be generalized."[22] Further, it cannot be proved that every single person "possesses the innate faculty of telling right from wrong" or is interested in themselves in such a way that they want to hold themselves accountable for a failure of conscience.[23] Again, the central distinction between ethical and political acts is not so much the lack or presence of action per se, since objectors of conscience do *act*—Thoreau refused to pay his taxes in protest of the Mexican-American War and slavery. Rather, the actions in such cases do not appear to be congruent with the conscience of a plurality and cannot attest to the cognitive processes or interests of a plurality; in other words, they are *hidden* behind singular selves. Arendt consistently argues that the political subject is one that appears as a multiplicity in public to create in concert contestation and deliberation of a common world that would ensure a good life. While she has always been aware that the private is a constitutive feature of the political sphere,[24] Arendt maintained that only the uniqueness of each person, encapsulated by *speech* and *action* (what differentiates humans from animals), can make an appearance in public.[25] While every person is unique, this uniqueness can only distinguish itself in the context of plurality: uniqueness thus requires plurality to become visible at all. To put it otherwise, "who" we are can only be revealed when we are in a plurality and, more specifically, when we are acting in concert.

We may therefore conclude that for Arendt political subjectivity can be distinguished from moral by: (a) its form, plurality, (b) the activity of speech and action, (c) a spatial dimension that is public,[26] and (d) uniqueness of the self, which can be revealed through action and speech but not through thinking, for in thinking, as she points out, even if we have an "I" that is split into two (conversing with oneself, raising internal debates), this activity still remains singular and subjective. For Arendt the subject becomes political because of plural action. In the activity of thinking the element of a plural action is not present. For her it is primarily the plural action that registers the difference between moral and political subjectivity. The political subject is one that engages with other subjects and does so *intentionally* "to create themselves and to shape their common world."[27] It is the commitment to working out the shaping, even reshaping, of the world that belongs to a plurality of subjects that makes such actions political.

While it is true that Arendt's writing never managed to sustain the distinction between thinking and acting,[28] in some essays she seems to intimate that action can be bereft of thinking. And most importantly, she seems to claim that thinking and action *incline* toward a different formation of the subject—thinking inclines toward a singularity, action toward a plurality. We may view *Eichmann in Jerusalem* as critical of those who refuse the possibility that action can be devoid of Thinking.[29] Eichmann, as she argued, cannot be considered essentially evil, or monstrous;[30] rather, he should be considered a thoughtless individual, one who obeyed commands without reflecting on the justifiability of those commands or their effects. Perhaps it is because of her observations during the Eichmann trial that she returned to the relation between thinking and action in her essays "Some Questions of Moral Philosophy" and "Thinking and Moral Considerations." More precisely, in *Eichmann in Jerusalem,* Arendt witnesses Eichmann's failure to think of his responsibility toward the Jewish population executed and tortured in the concentration camps and concludes that Thinking (which generally belongs to the private sphere) and political Action (which belongs to the public sphere) need to go hand in hand. As I will explain below, in these essays she finds a way to connect thinking to action, singularity and subjectivism to plurality. Arendt follows Kant in allying thinking to action through the faculty of Judgment.

Again, Arendt's primal concern with thinking is not thinking per se but the subjective character of thinking, particularly with her claim that if thinking cannot be generalized, it cannot be plural. In "Thinking and Moral Considerations" she elucidates how thinking can be generalized, can become visible when linked with a plurality.[31] How then does she manage to show the generalizability of thinking? First, like Kant, she differentiates between the activity of thinking and knowledge. This differentiation is important because thinking is usually equated with knowledge, and because she wants to show how thinking is an activity that everybody engages with and is therefore generalizable, whereas knowledge is differentially distributed; not everybody has the same access to the accumulation of knowledge. Arendt then proceeds to show the *value* of thinking as an activity that has the tendency to undo fixed ideas and concepts all the time[32] without being visible to the senses.[33]

She undertakes to demonstrate this distinction by taking an ordinary man, Socrates, as an example. As it is known, Socrates refused to escape the sentence of punishment delivered against him by the judges (Athenian citizens) for allegedly corrupting the youth and practicing impiety. His refusal was based on a reflection and deliberation with himself through a form of philosophizing that enabled him to see that it was "better to be wronged than to do wrong" and that it would be preferable for a multitude of men to be in disagreement with him than for him to become someone who disagrees with himself.[34] The first reflection, as Arendt aptly writes, points out to us the subjective part of thinking—"I" prefer to be wronged than to do wrong.[35] And the second reflection brings to the surface the duality of a self.[36] How then does this dual self manifest itself, according to Arendt? If one does not want to be in disharmony with oneself, then there must be one self who tries to be in attunement with another self and which, by implication, is not the same self as the one that is trying become attuned: "The curious thing that I am needs no plurality in order to establish difference; it carries the difference within itself when it says: 'I am I.'"[37] For Arendt, these two Socratic reflections taken together reveal something even more fundamental: "For Socrates, this two-in-one meant simply that if you want to think you must see to it that the two who carry on the thinking dialogue must be in good shape, that the partners be friends. It is better for you to suffer than to do wrong because you can remain the friend of the sufferer."[38] In "Thinking and Moral Considerations," she reveals the plurality in thinking, a dimension not present in "Civil Disobedience." In "Some Questions of Moral Philosophy," she explains how thinking (which contains a split self) reveals itself in public, linked with action, the movement that distinctively defines politics.

In "Some Questions of Moral Philosophy" Arendt argues that thinking trespasses into the sphere of action through the faculty of judgment. To support this proposition she uses Kant's *Critique of Judgment*, or, more specifically, her critique of Kant's understanding of how judgment operates. For Kant, aesthetic judgment operates when we are faced with the particular: in such instances, "judging decides about the relation between a particular instance and the general, be the general a rule or a standard or an ideal or some other kind of measurement."[39] Arendt protests against this understanding of judgment, in which the particular is constantly subsumed to the universal.[40] To her mind, judgment, whether moral or aesthetic, is predicated on particular acts that become exemplary by not becoming subjugated to the general. Socrates's stance is to set himself up as an example of someone who will not do any wrong and would prefer instead to be wronged. By taking such a position, Socrates exemplifies moral decision making for others on the basis of a general maxim: "Some particular instance . . . becomes valid for other particular instances."[41] Aesthetic judgment (a form of thinking) in this respect becomes, or transgresses into, the realm of action or politics; in becoming exemplary, it escapes its subjective, private, and moral dimension. Its exemplarity also reveals to us the uniqueness of the "thinker" (who is always already more than one), but also the creative and reflective aspect of the process of judging itself.

As Judith Butler aptly explains in *Parting Ways*, Arendt's thinking/action distinction cannot always be sustained; the way Arendt accommodates thinking in the realm of action through the activity of judgment is one example.[42] Butler's observation offers an important intervention in the way we can read Arendt. Butler offers this opening:

Although it sometimes seems that she is separating two different modes of plurality, the one that is the self and one that is the self with others, she also lets us know that the distinction is not absolute. She has already told us that solitary thinking carries the trace of social company. But there is a stronger claim to be made here, one I wish she had made. Indeed, in my view without that animating trace of social company, there can be no self-reference, which means that sociality precedes and enables what is called thinking. One becomes capable of having a dialogue with oneself only on the condition that one has already been engaged in dialogue by others. Being addressed precedes and conditions the capacity for address.[43]

Butler releases Arendt's writing and thinking from a form that wants or needs action and thinking to be two completely separate activities, and ultimately she addresses Arendt's concern that thinking, because of the private character of its operation, may be apolitical. Butler does this not by collapsing thinking into action, but by drawing a configuration of the subject that is animated by other subjects. The subject is therefore constituted not just by itself or its own activities (thinking, action, judgment) but also from the outside, such that the boundary between outside and inside is much more permeable than the one offered by Arendt. In this instance Butler highlights this possibility by pointing to the sociality of thinking. Thinking, reflecting, judging—Socrates's "It is better to be wronged than to do wrong"—is already within plurality or a community. Socrates may be dialoguing with himself, but this dialogue stems from a legitimate communal question: How does one act if one's conscience is at odds with that of the community? Should one, like Eichmann, continue working toward the death of the Jewish population because some law commanded one to do so? Or should one act against the law and risk the consequences of harming oneself? The motif of the split subject also shows us that the split between inside/outside is not just always already in dialogue (because the boundary is permeable) but also constitutive of one's subjectivity: "Only as someone brought into language through others do I become someone who can respond to their call, and who can interiorize that dialogic encounter as part of my own thinking, at which point sociality becomes an animating trace in any and all thinking any one of us might do. Thus the dialogue that I am is not finally separable from the plurality that makes me possible."[44] If it is through language, or the fact that we are addressed by another in language, that we are constituted—if this is where thinking, dialogic with oneself (the split "internal" self), and acting take place—then the political-ethical dimension of subjectivity are inextricably linked. One can't split this nexus, nor can one really say when the one begins and the other ends. Butler makes visible in Arendt a different political subject than the one Arendt argues for, but one that nevertheless addresses her moral dictum that it is a necessity to act and live in accord with the fact that we share the earth with each other and that nobody can decide who or what population has more right to it than others.

Through Butler's rereading of Arendt's distinction between the thinking and acting subject or ethics and politics, we are able to see how the category of the moral subject (as Arendt calls it) may not be as private and apolitical as she considered it. We still of course do not get away from some of Arendt's other concerns, namely, that not everybody may respond to being addressed by another, or recognize how through language they are implicated in another's life, but that does not alter the fact of being addressed by a plurality. To put it bluntly, a response may not be guaranteed, but no one can avoid the fact that we do share language, we are addressed and respond to language, and it constitutes both our access to the world and a sign that we share the world.

Dream-Action

If we agree, then, that the political and moral might be linked in this way, where can we locate the dreaming subject (the one whose dream is a political landscape)? Is the dreaming subject part of this link? Can the dreaming subject, my grandmother in this case, be considered as an acting subject, a political subject? And if not, what may be at risk if we stop regarding dreaming subjects like my grandmother, who dreams of the dispossession of her land, as political subjects?

If we follow a strict interpretation of Arendt's views on these different dimensions of the subject, then dreaming subjects will not fall under the rubric of politics. The dreaming subject, whether it is my grandmother dreaming of flying over her occupied home, or whether it is the black colonized subject in Frantz Fanon's *Wretched of the Earth* dreaming of decolonization,[45] will not amount to a political subject. We can see why: dreaming appears to be a private, subjective activity that does not correspond to a plurality. Even if we follow Butler's rereading of Arendt, we may have some difficulties arguing that the dream is a response to an address coming from a sociality that may be formative of a political subjectivity, especially if we understand political subjectivity as subjectivity that is immersed in action in the form of plurality for making better a common world. If, as Phillips reminds us, the recounting of dreams is a way of making our reality more intelligible,[46] and if the subject is the way we make sense of the world, then we may say that Arendt's political subject is partial, based primarily on the conscious part of its subjectivity and not on the realm of the unconscious, where dreams live and enable us to make sense of an otherwise incomprehensible reality. In other words, the story Arendt tells of the political subject is only half a story. It does not take into account those processes such as dreaming that give us access to our desires, and so to the way our wishes inform our understanding of our realities. Dreams have always been very much a part of the political imagination; dreams of freedom and emancipation often appear in the literature of liberation and political struggle.[47] I am not of course suggesting that the dream as a metaphor or common motif in political uprisings is the same as other dreams one may have, but I am suggesting, along with Freud and Foucault,[48] that dreams are constitutive of the self and our wishes,[49] and to ignore or cast aside such an important part of self-formation in our understanding of politics, either because dreams are subjective or because they do not obviously connect to a plurality, limits our account of the political subject. At a more existential level, it may risk rendering invisible the dreamer's life and the way that dreamers account for themselves. Dreams may in fact be the *only* available way for some subjects to account for themselves. As I noted earlier, Arendt recognizes that the subjective element, *thinking*, is constitutive of *action*, but she nevertheless insists on the nexus "action-plurality"—in other words, that a political subject is one who appears in action-deliberating with others for the creation of a common world. I argue, instead, that no formation of plurality can be understood if we cut out the way singular selves are formed, and the account they give of themselves, which may include these "subjective" dream narrations. If we exclude dreams from our accounts of political subjectivity, we fail to account for the singularities of political subjects and not just the political potential residing in these singularities.

Demonstrating Dreams

I remembered my grandmother's dream only after I finished writing "Disobedience Subjectively Speaking,"[50] which offers a critique of Arendt's essay "Civil Disobedience" based on its repudiation of the idea that "subjective" disobedience[51] can be rightly categorized as politics.

In rethinking the concept and practice of disobedience and more generally politics, I found that one cannot really take the subject out of civil disobedience or reduce civil disobedience to a philosophy of the subject. In "Civil Disobedience" Arendt casts the acts of conscientious objectors as apolitical and subjective, but if subjective acts are subtracted from the category of civil disobedience, it is unclear how individuals become politicized. When people take to the streets, it cannot only be because they have calculated in a reasoned manner—what we may call deliberation—that there is no other way to make a political demand. And it cannot simply be the result of the faculty of judgment and the practice of judging that converts singular entities into political actors and thus to a plurality. I am of course not contesting the importance of action-plurality (or sociality, in Butler's language) and its direct relation to politics. But Arendt's account fails to articulate what moves one at a particular moment toward politics. Understanding what moves a singular subject toward politicization will enable us to see those subjects who reveal their politics (and political subjectivity) in various forms—dreams, poetry, art, and so on[52]—as well as in well-established and recognized forms (protest, dissent, deliberation).

....

It was Rosa Parks, the young black woman from Montgomery, Alabama, who on December 1, 1955, refused to give her seat in the black section of the bus to a white passenger (an act that rejuvenated the civil rights movement), who enabled me to understand and see the problem with Arendt's account of civil disobedience and, more generally, politics. More precisely, in reading an interview Parks gave in 1956 I became more aware of what I was already wary of in Arendt's account of civil disobedience and the restricted concept of politics that emerges from it.

In the interview Parks[53] gives an account of what happened on that day on the bus and distinguishes it from other occasions where habitually seats were given to white passengers on the demand or command of the driver or the white passenger. In the interview we hear Parks accounting for why on that day she was not obedient to such a command. She tells us first that she was pushed as far as she could be (indignation) and then that she was without fear and wanted to find out what rights she had as a human being. Rosa Parks's disobedient act, as we know, reinvigorated the civil rights movement. While Arendt asks us to consider disobedience outside subjective parameters, Parks brings us back to the subject, back to a particular prompt to action and the force and movement behind it. Parks cannot have been moved to action only because she was convinced (after deliberation with others) that segregation laws were unjust. She already knew that. Parks moved on that day because of indignation, fearlessness, and a curiosity to see how far the law could recognize her humanity. Parks refused to give up her seat; she ignored the authoritative voice of the bus driver, who was acting at that moment as an enforcer of the law. In staying put and being fearless (risking imprisonment and punishment), she put into action, or materialized, both her desire to have her humanity recognized (by law) and her indignation with the law.

Without the subject, without an understanding and sense of how the disobedient subject is formed, we are all the poorer. By subtracting the subject (ethics, imagination, sense) from politics—removing the *force* behind action, conscience (Socrates, Thoreau), indignation and fearlessness (Parks), dreams of a different world (Emma Goldman, Martin Luther King), anger and indignation and hope (Occupy in both the United States and the United Kingdom; Indignados in Spain, Greece, and Portugal; Gezi Park demonstrators in Turkey; "Spring Revolutions" in Egypt and Tunisia)—Arendt leaves us with a partial story.

Writing about the vulnerability of dreaming came directly out of my effort to give an account of the limits of Arendt's understanding of politics. Arendt pleaded for an understanding of civil disobedience bereft of the subject, while I was constantly encountering the subject on the road to political transformation, an embodied singular subject prompted to action not just because its voice could not be heard, not only because of injustice or legal and political roadblocks, but also as a result of dreaming, because of the imagination, because of indignation, because of anger. Like Rosa Parks, these subjects found themselves defying their fears and acting on their dreams to see their lives and polities morphing, proximating—sometimes temporarily, sometimes for a long period—(in)to a life other than the ones that were already given or, indeed, the ones they were commanded to live. Parks was commanded to leave her seat. Instead she stayed put, and through this inaction she mobilized her desire to have the law recognize her and other black Americans as human beings with equal legal standing. Occupy defied local laws that prohibited camping in Zuccotti Park. They temporarily set up a space where they both publicized the unequal distribution of wealth and attempted to live in a way that expressed the dream of a plurality: indeed, one of the publications that came out of Occupy is titled *Dreaming in Public: Building the Occupy Movement.*

All the invocations of the subjective experiences, like Parks's or individuals involved in Occupy, alerted me to the possibility that if we keep repeating certain well-used and frequently cited descriptions and accounts of phenomena (like Arendt's understanding of politics), we miss or may let go astray accounts that can't be consolidated within Arendt's understanding of politics—or, if they could be, they wouldn't reveal the difficulties and tensions that may vex such a category. By not taking into account the role of dreaming in the formation of the political subject and the role it can play in both sustaining and enlivening singularities and pluralities in/on their way toward building a world, we may be risking limiting our understanding of what politics is, who a political subject is. We may not notice that it is possible to build a fair and just polity that is not organized around written laws or on the model of a preexisting political system—indeed, what builds a polity may more closely approximate that which is revealed in a dream. Such wishful formulations may be distant from the neoliberal state we find ourselves in today.[54] So let me put this more directly: I want to see how we can avoid disavowing the subject, dismissing what the singular subject can tell us through a dream as without meaning for our understanding of the political subject.

Perhaps such worries may be unfounded. After all, even Descartes, in his First Meditation, allows dreaming to be an integral part of the subject. As he points out in this laborious meditation, dreams, despite their fictitious "character," still draw their images from reality and thus are grounded in reality. In her essay "How Can I Deny That These Hands and This Body Are Mine?" Butler reminds us that while Descartes in his First Meditation brackets out the body from, for example, the exercise of thinking/writing, as if the relation between writing and thinking happens automatically, without the pain of a headache, without a blockage—the body, nevertheless, makes an appearance in the invocation of the practice of writing in this very meditation.[55] Butler's critique of Descartes's meditation is even more poignant when we consider dreams that draw their images from what can be designated as nonreality.

Take, for example, the dream of flight, the dream whereby my grandmother saw herself flying over her village. As it is based on nonreality (so far we have not developed the ability to ascend to the sky without the aid of a mechanical device), we may for example render such a dreamer, my late grandmother, as a nonsubject (or more specifically as a nonpolitical subject), and by this I mean we may be removing their dream from the realm of intelligibility (political or otherwise) and may thus risk making them unintelligible and silencing them. The Greek word for dream, όνειρο, is composed of the words Όν (being/existence) and Είρω (to put together or narrate[56] the story of my being). If we follow the semantic links between "dream" and "story" that the Greek word όνειρο implies, we find that if we exclude dreaming from an account of a self, we risk excluding a very important way of accounting for one's political existence. Such an exclusion removes a fundamental aspect of one's political subjectivity—the part of the political that projects into one's imagining of what it means to be a subject and how one may live through one's political exile, dispossession, and vulnerability. An exclusion of dreams itself cuts out of the subject an account of one's existence. In one common type of dream, that of flight, what interests me most is not so much what the dream signifies but, rather, the movement of ascending that such a dream articulates and its relation to political subjectivities.

Troubling Dreams and Political Concealments

In her astute account and critique of neoliberalism and neoconservatism, Wendy Brown alerts us to the difficulties of grasping the present via the vehicle of the dream. At the start of her essay "American Nightmare: Neoliberalism, Neoconservatism and De-Democratization," Brown refers to a lecture that Stuart Hall gave in 2005, where he puts the "logic of dreamwork" at the heart of our understanding of the present and contrasts it with an account of the present marked by "a monological, internally consistent, temporally linear, and systematic frame."[57] At the same time, Brown worries not only that Hall's admirable aspiration would be difficult to put to work—dreams are polysemic and complex and reveal the contradictions within our political associations— but, moreover, that such method of analysis in our times may conceal for example the undemocratic aspirations of the Left and conjure the figure of the bad citizen on the Right, ignoring the ways in which neoliberalism may have affected the Left political subject as well as its politics. Brown worries that there is a possibility of leaving uninspected the tensions and problematic aspirations of the Left, which, as we know, is a political community to which she belongs (she makes sure in the essay to refer to the Left with the pronoun "we"). She also urges us to engage with the tensions that such dreamworking/writing may reveal:

> Hall's challenge to break with monological, totalizing, and linear accounts, then, is impeded not simply by intellectual hangover (from an episteme in which power was figured as unified, systematic, and purposeful) but also by difficulty in left desire. This is a difficulty we can redress only through willingness to reckon with the incoherent, multiply sourced, and unsystematic nature of political orders and rationalities on the one hand, and to avow identification and affinity with some of what we excoriate on the other. If, for example, many on the left share the rightist ambition to secure cultural and political hegemony and impose a moral order, such antidemocratic impulses bear careful scrutiny even, nay especially, as all sides adorn themselves in the robes of democracy.[58]

Brown raises important concerns about conflictual desires and aspirations in Left political movements. At an intellectual and scholarly level, a dream analysis of the present may run into turbulence, since we may find in dreams some problematic aspirations that the Left may be holding onto, even a set of questionable desires it seeks to put into action once it seizes power. Nevertheless, Brown's concerns may conflate political desires (the Left gaining power and doing away with democratic safeguards) and the dream per se.[59] Gaston Bachelard suggests that when, for example, somebody dreams of flying, it does not necessarily relate to a desire to ascend in society and may not be a metaphor for the achievement of some aspiration; rather, it is related to some movement in her instinctual world and her dynamic imagination.[60] In other words, Bachelard's theory of dreams diverts the interpretation from content or symbolic interpretation, that is, oriented toward a revelation of some deeper, unconscious meaning, or goal, something that Freud follows in *The Interpretation of Dreams.*[61] Instead Bachelard urges us to view dreams in general, and the dream of flight in particular, on their surface; to understand and follow the dynamic movement they produce in the soul, understand it as an internal movement that shakes the soul and deforms reality—the reality of our inability to fly. If we follow Bachelard's philosophy of dreams, and specifically his analysis of the flight dream, then we can also see Brown's concern: the possibility that dreamworking/writing may turn into a disaster of a dream (the Left taking power and undoing democratic safeguards). Such a consequence does not follow from the dynamic and psychical aspects of the dream, which as she correctly notes are characterized by nonlinearity, nonconsistency and nonsingular logic, but rather from the desire to *execute* the dream, realizing it in a particular way that subtracts from the amorphousness of the dream and its openness. As we know, executions are also bloody events.

Is there, though, a possible way out of this dilemma (rather than by simply restating it)? Can we dream singularly or even collectively without falling into the traps to which Brown alerts us? To investigate such a possibility let's turn first to some categorizations of dream. Foucault informs us that Artemidorous, in his pioneering work *Interpretation of Dreams* (Ονειροκριτικα), talks of two types of dreams. The first is *enypnia*, "dreams that express the present affects of the individual" and reflect back to the dreamer the reality of his life.[62] For example, a person suffering from indigestion may dream of vomiting. As Foucault points out, such dreams reflect the present state of affairs of the dreamer.[63] The second type, όνειρο (*oneiro*), draws on three etymologies; the first "'tells what is real'... what is already inscribed in time's unfolding and will come true as an event in the not-too-distant future"; the second refers to the deforming and reshaping of the soul, where "it leads it [the soul] into dispositions and induces movements in it corresponding to what is shown";[64] and the third refers to the name of a beggar from Ithaca.

Enypnia and όνειρο (oneiro) are diametrical opposites, with different loci of operations and effects:

> The first [enypnia] speaks of the individual, the second [όνειρο] of events in the world; one originates in the states of the body and the mind, the other anticipates the unwinding of the temporal chain; one manifests the action of the too-little and the too-much in the domain of appetite and aversions, the other alerts the soul and the same time shapes it. On the one hand, the dreams of desire tell the soul's reality in its present state. On the other hand, the dreams of being tell the future of the event in the order of the world.[65]

I would argue that my grandmother's dream, flying over her occupied village, falls within the category not of enypnia but of όνειρο. In the novel of Chariton of Aphrodisias, which Foucault offers as an example of an όνειρο,[66] Challirhoe "near the end of her trials" dreamed of returning to Syracuse to the temple of Aphrodite, signifying that she was protected by the Gods and she was to be rewarded with marrying Chaereas, an event that was to take place in real life (similar to my grandmother's return to her village by flying). There is a great deal in Artemidorous's dream analysis that may not at first glance directly correspond to my grandmother's flight dream. Such dreams, Foucault tells us, are *anticipations* of a future event. But we may say, for example, that the anticipation of a solution to the "Cyprus problem" was not something that was expected to happen soon. Nevertheless, at a second glance, everyday public discussions in the media made such nonexpectation a possibility. This very possibility wrapped itself in the form of a never-ending hope, making the distant reality of such an event into a hopeful possibility for the near future. There was always hope, of course, that God, the Christian God, would by a miracle facilitate the return of the refugees to their homes. Again, this drew on the tropes of miraculous interventions, which might never happen but also might happen at any time.

Artemidorous's account of όνειρο, a movement that reshapes the soul, is close to the etymology of the word όνειρο, narrating one's existence. I recall my grandmother sitting on the low stool at the back of our home in Nicosia telling us her dream, her feet well planted on the floor, her posture solid and serious. Her words were light, narrating the dream where she saw herself doing something that is impossible for any human being to do. Bachelard tells us that dreams of flying require us to look away from the *form* of the flight (e.g., flying with wings) and from the symbolization/signification of the content of the dream.[67] Instead we follow the movement that such dreams introduce in the dreamer; a "journey for its own sake, an 'imaginary journey' that is more real than any other since it involves the substance of our psyche."[68] And when we focus on what the flight dream *does*, we notice an ascending, a deformation of reality, exposing us to an imagination that is not bound to a form ("frees us from the tyranny of forms, and restores us to substances and to the life of our own element")[69] and to the desire of the soul to ascend, to unburden itself from the formal restrictions—or, as he puts it, the flight dream transforms the motion of the soul into the "whole soul in motion,"[70] to the joy that we gain from the fear of falling (indeed, according to Bachelard, the flight dream teaches us not to be afraid of falling).[71] It is only then, as he suggests, that we may be able to see what the flight dream is: "a future with a vector breaking into flight."[72]

If we follow Bachelard's analysis of the dream of flight, we may see in my grandmother's flying dream, her flight to her occupied village, *not* a desire to reterritorialize, not a land claim to take back what has been taken away from her (after all, she sees from above her village, she does not land on it, even while, by contrast, her dearest waking concern was whether she would be able to be buried in her village when she died), but, rather, a return to a lighter way of living—a familiar way of life where she could reenact her intimate life—to have an ocular access to a past that was not in her present. Or even, and this may be closer to Bachelard's analysis, her flight dream may show us a movement in her soul that put in motion her whole soul. If dream etymologically in Greek refers to the narration of one's being, then we may say that this flight dream enabled her to utter αρθρώνω in Greek, to rise through speech, to unburden herself from the legal category of the refugee,[73] which she often found heavy to bear (after 1974) in Cyprus; it was not uncommon for the refugees, before they were given accommodation in state building houses, to find themselves discriminated against by their fellow Greek Cypriots. The word "refugee" was often used derogatorily and instigated differential treatment: for example, property owners refused to rent to those who bore that status.

In *Giving an Account of Oneself* Butler alerts us to the fact that our survival may lie or reside in (as the title suggests) giving an account of oneself, of opening to the other and simultaneously registering not only our mutual dependence on each other but also our survival. Accounts of oneself can be delivered in various ways, including through dreaming.

Flight

Bachelard writes that the height of the soul that such a dream enables "is materially, dynamically and vitally moral."[74] We may want to question his invocation of the morality of heights/flights; we may also want to question its political efficacy and effects. Wendy Brown may have been thinking of this problematic in pointing to the erasure of tensions and ambiguities that could derive from the uncritical realization of the dream-work.

Then again, if we bracket the subjective element (and thus the singular in Arendt's words) from politics, we may actually fail to recognize the deeply differential politics of such a gesture: we may exclude precisely from politics a mode of speaking (dream speaking), of accounting for oneself that allows populations and individuals who have been beaten down to the ground by politics to start to ascend, to come into being. To express one's being through dreams (or art, or poetry, or feelings) allows one to raise/elevate one's body and voice above the chains of exclusion, formalization, discipline, and differential treatment. This may be the only way certain subjects can account for themselves: the disavowal of their dreams may mean the disavowal of their political subjectivity.

Indeed, in their documentary film *Women of Cyprus*, Katrivanou and Azzouz introduce us to Turkish Cypriot women and Greek Cypriot women's accounts of the "Cyprus problem." They all talk of their dream of return to their "homes" and offer us their own solutions to this problem: one suggests, for example, that the Cyprus problem could be solved if we focused attention on pain, for pain is what is shared by both ethnicities and communities.[75]

Similarly, Colin Dayan in *The Law Is a White Dog* tells us that the art created by the prisoners in US Supermax prisons is not allowed to be sent to their loved ones on the outside. According to one prison official she interviewed, such correspondence is believed to contain "coded information" that may threaten the prison's security: "They beg to send this art home to their families. Maybe they spent a month or two doing it. But we take it and hang it on this wall. Once they're in SMU, it's not their property. These guys are suspected gang members. There's gang symbolism in these pictures."[76] We can question the conclusion that the prison official comes to regarding prisoner art—we may regard the belief that they contain coded messages to their families as paranoid—but we can certainly agree that art, a subjective expression, contains an account of oneself, and is to this extent a political articulation of oneself. The suppression of the posting of such art to the outside world underscores even more that such articulations (paintings, dreams, etc.) are political.

Art, as Bachelard points out, allows ascension, the flight of the soul, and the expression of one's very being above the form—which here takes the form of political institutions, politics, and institutions of justice; it allows one to deform the formal story of the authorities. And deformation, like dissent, is deeply political. It raises the body. And the raising of the body is dangerous. The raising of the body deforms the official account of oneself—contests it and rewrites it. And this raising may be seen in dreaming, in poetry, and elsewhere as well. The "Standing Man" on Taksim Square may just be another embodiment of this flight, this ascent, "a future with a vector breaking into flight."[77]

Notes

1 PRIO Cyprus Centre, "Petra."

2 After Cyprus gained its independence from Britain on August 16, 1960, some Greek Cypriots believed that Cyprus should be united with Greece. They have formed a group called EOKA B. On July 15, 1974, EOKA B, along with the national guard, instigated a coup on the island directed by the Greek military dictatorship. The Cypriot president Archbishop Makarios III was removed. Makarios was committed to keeping the island and its different communities—Greek, Turkish, Armenian, and Maronite Cypriots—united. In response to the coup and as one of the guarantors of the Cypriot independence (the other two were Britain and Greece), on July 20, 1974, Turkey invaded Cyprus to protect the Turkish Cypriot community. For critical accounts of the events leading to the 1974 invasion of Cyprus by Turkey and the political negotiations since then, see Navaro-Yashin, *The Make-Believe Space*, and Constantinou and Papadakis, "The Cypriot State(s) In Situ."

3 As Constantinou and Papadakis, "The Cypriot State(s) In Situ," and Navaro-Yashin, *The Make-Believe Space*, inform us, this displacement took place after the flare-up of interethnic violence in December 1963. Cyprus was granted its constitution in 1960 after a national struggle waged against British colonialism. The constitution created two positions of authority: president (Greek Cypriot) and vice president (Turkish Cypriot) and a council of ministers, seven Greek Cypriot and three Turkish Cypriot, and a parliament that was to be constituted according to this ratio: 78 percent Greek Cypriots, 18 percent Turkish Cypriots, and the remaining 4 percent Cypriot Latins, Maronites, and Armenians. The president and vice president had a veto over all matters other than taxation in Parliament and the council of ministers. The Turkish Cypriot community was unhappy with aspects around taxation. The Republic's president tried to address

them by proposing thirteen amendments to the Constitution. This sparked in-terethnic violence. As a result Turkish Cypriots who lived in mixed villages left. See PRIO Cyprus Centre, "From Solea to Morphou," for an account of how these two communities interacted prior to the war. Constantinou and Papadakis suggest that the "Cyprus problem" stems from the failure of both Turkish and Greek Cypriot communities to stop looking at either Greece (Greek Cypriots) or Turkey (Turkish Cypriots) as their respective motherlands or a failure to decolonize.

4 Phillips, *Side Effects*, 128.

5 Kaplan, *Sexual Justice*, 151.

6 Arendt, *Rahel Varnhagen*; Arendt, *The Jewish Writings*, 275–297.

7 Young-Bruehl, *Hannah Arendt*, 89.

8 Young-Bruehl, *Hannah Arendt*, 87.

9 Arendt, *The Jewish Writings*, 275–297.

10 Arendt, *The Jewish Writings*, 276, 278–279.

11 Gines, *Hannah Arendt and the Negro Question*, 1–13.

12 Gines, *Hannah Arendt and the Negro Question*. HannahArendt.net, "The Meaning of Love in Politics: A Letter by Hannah Arendt to James Baldwin," September 2006, http://www.hannaharendt.net/index.php/han/article/view/95/156 (Hannah Arendt, November 21, 1962).

13 Critchley, *Ethics-Politics-Subjectivity*, 51.

14 Critchley, *Ethics-Politics-Subjectivity*, 53.

15 Critchley, *Ethics-Politics-Subjectivity*, 53.

16 Critchley, *Ethics-Politics-Subjectivity*, 53.

17 Arendt, *The Human Condition*.

18 Arendt, *The Human Condition*, "Civil Disobedience," "Some Questions on Moral Philosophy," and "Thinking and Moral Considerations."

19 Arendt, "Some Questions on Moral Philosophy," 106.

20 Arendt, *Crises of the Republic*, 50–102.

21 Arendt, *Crises of the Republic*, 64.

22 Arendt, *Crises of the Republic*, 64.

23 Arendt, *Crises of the Republic*, 64.

24 Honig, "Toward an Agonistic Feminism," 221; Isaac, *Arendt, Camus and Modern Rebellion*, 230; Kaplan, *Sexual Justice*, 151.

25 Arendt, *The Human Condition*, 176.

26 See, e.g., Brennan and Malpas, "The Space of Appearance and the Space of Truth."

27 Kaplan, *Sexual Justice*, 151.

28 Butler, *Parting Ways*, 172.

29 Arendt, *Eichmann in Jerusalem*.

30 Arendt, *Eichmann in Jerusalem*, 275–288.

31 It is uncertain why she does not consider the generalization of thinking made in "Thinking and Moral Considerations" in a subsequent essay, "Civil Disobedience."

32 Arendt, "Thinking and Moral Considerations," 173.

33 Arendt, "Thinking and Moral Considerations," 167.

34 Arendt, "Thinking and Moral Considerations," 181.

35 Arendt, "Thinking and Moral Considerations," 183.

36 Arendt, "Thinking and Moral Considerations," 184.

37 Arendt, "Thinking and Moral Considerations," 184.

38 Arendt, "Thinking and Moral Considerations," 185.

39 Arendt, "Some Questions on Moral Philosophy," 137.

40 Arendt, "Some Questions on Moral Philosophy," 143.

41 Arendt, "Some Questions on Moral Philosophy," 144.

42 Butler, *Parting Ways*, 172.

43 Butler, *Parting Ways*, 173.

44 Butler, *Parting Ways*, 173.

45 Fanon, *Wretched of the Earth*, 15.

46 Phillips, *Side Effects*, 128.

47 See, e.g., Fanon, *Wretched of the Earth*, 15; Lang and Lang/Levitsky, *Dreaming in Public* (2012); King, "I Have a Dream."

48 As Tyrus Miller writes, "For Michel Foucault . . . dreams [are] a dimension of human existence under the sway of destiny and fate." Miller, "From City-Dreams to the Dreaming Collective," 96.

49 Freud, in *The Interpretation of Dreams*, 404, talks about flying or floating dreams as fulfillments of specific wishes that the dreamer may have.

50 Loizidou, "Disobedience Subjectively Speaking."

51 Arendt, *Crises of the Republic*, 49–102.

52 Miller, "From City-Dreams to the Dreaming Collective," points to Walter Benjamin's exploration of the dream as a way of understanding political collectivities. Benjamin's writings in the *Arcades Project* draw on cultural artifacts, art, houses, streets, and the city more generally to unravel the memories and hopes of collectivities.

53 Parks, "Rosa Parks Interview."

54 Brown, "American Nightmare."

55 Butler, "How Can I Deny That These Hands and This Body Are Mine"; Loizidou, *Judith Butler*, 140–149.

56 *Oneiro* has its roots in the words *on* (being) and *eiro* (which could mean "drawing connections" or "narrating"). See Vlahou, "ονειρο . . . ον +ειρω', τα ονειρα."

57 Brown, "American Nightmare," 690.

58 Brown, "American Nightmare," 691.

59 It is important to note that Brown's concerns about the way in which dreams are or may be used by the political Left or Right are similar to Arendt's concerns about how to incorporate the subjective into her understanding of politics. As we can see, Brown is concerned about the impossibility of having a dream motif that is general (after all, there can be multiple interpretations). Arendt too was concerned that conscientious objectors' acts can't be generalized because they are acts of singular selves.

60 Bachelard, *Air and Dreams*, 57.

61 For the difference between Freud on Dream and Bachelard see Loizidou, "Dreams of Flying-Flying Bodies."

62 Foucault, *The Care of the Self, vol. 3*, 10.

63 Foucault, *The Care of the Self, vol. 3*, 10.

64 Foucault, *The Care of the Self, vol. 3*, 10.

65 Foucault, *The Care of the Self, vol. 3*, 10–11.

66 Foucault, *The Care of the Self, vol. 3*, 14.

67 Bachelard, *Air and Dreams*, 22.

68 Bachelard, *Air and Dreams*, 24.

69 Bachelard, *Air and Dreams*, 26.

70 Bachelard, *Air and Dreams*, 48.

71 Bachelard, *Air and Dreams*, 34.

72 Bachelard, *Air and Dreams*, 21.

73 The aspiration of legal recognition—an aspiration that we noted in Rosa Parks, for example—may not sustain one's elemental, as Bachelard would have put it, aspirations for their *being*. Emma Goldman in her essay "The Tragedy of the Political Exiles" points to the burdens, exclusions, and restrictions in mobility that the introduction of the passport, a legal document, has created. Similarly, the category of the refugee may be a desired legal category for those who have been displaced by occupation, war, or natural catastrophes, but with it comes the burden of the formality of law, which restricts to a great extent the way one can utter or account for one's being. Moreover, it can induce and promote prejudices within the wider society. See Arendt, *The Jewish Writings*.

74 Bachelard, *Air and Dreams*, 62.

75 See, e.g., Katravanou and Azzouz's documentary *Women of Cyprus*.

76 Dayan, *The Law Is a White Dog*, 93.

77 Bachelard, *Air and Dreams*, 21.

CHAPTER 7

Vulnerable Corporealities and Precarious Belongings in Mona Hatoum's Art

ELENA TZELEPIS

In this essay I look into Mona Hatoum's art of vulnerable corporealities in order to think about what kinds of bodies are formed and deformed in times of loss, displacement, and occupation. How do these bodies come to embody and witness what is lost? How do they relate to other bodies? How do they live on between past and present, as well as between life and death? I am interested in unraveling the ways that the precarious and dismembered belongings enacted in Hatoum's art trouble the fantasies of invulnerable sovereignty, including the sovereignty of fixed place. Hatoum's feminist aesthetics bring forth a bodily representation of vulnerability, alerting us to both the disembodiment induced by mass political violence and the embodied potential for resistance and self-determination.

Hatoum's art offers an account of corporeal subjectivity attuned to a living cartography of nomadic passages whereby nomadism denotes multilayered histories of displacement and vulnerable (un)belonging rather than free flow and open access. Her art-making evokes her exilic and diasporic biography and performs a critical engagement with the destructive violences of occupation and containment. She was born in exile in Beirut, Lebanon, in 1952, of Palestinian Christian parents who were forcibly dispossessed of their households and sources of livelihood in Haifa and displaced to Lebanon as a consequence of the Arab-Israeli War in 1948. Growing up in Beirut, she attended French school, so her childhood was immersed in the polyaccented Arabic lived language (in its Palestinian and Lebanese versions) and the French learned language. Her experience of place involved reference to another place and another language; her experience of language, to recall Jacques Derrida, was "nonlocatable."[1] She was cast as a pariah, the Palestinian Arab and stateless exile with neither Lebanese nor Palestinian citizenship documents, but, in her case, with a British passport acquired as a result of her father's long period of employment as a civil servant—director of customs—in Palestine under the British Mandate. For those from the ethnic community of Palestinians who had fled in Lebanon, their citizenship was withdrawn en masse, but they were not given an alternate form of documentation. Even though citizenship is not the only mode of belonging, especially as it does not refer to linguistic and sociocultural forms of relations, it is a forming experience, especially when it is *"precarious, recent, threatened,* and more artificial than ever."[2] In this light Jacques Derrida—a Franco-Maghrebian Sephardic Jew whose French citizenship was abruptly and violently taken from him by the French state's unilateral decision and who had to wait years before they granted it back to him—describes his multiple names/identities not as a richness, but as a "disorder of identity." Does this "disorder of identity," Derrida asks, "favor or inhibit anamnesia? Does it heighten the desire of memory, or does it drive the genealogical fantasy to despair? Does it suppress, repress, or liberate?"[3] And he suggests: "All of these at the same time, . . . the contradiction that set us in motion. And has us running to the point of losing our breath, or our minds."[4]

This "losing one's mind" is a feeble and nontotalizing knowledge extending to self-knowledge. It indicates a failure in comprehension, an uncertain thinking that errs. The uncanny duplicity that marks the etymology of "erring," both as a directionless wandering and as a cognitive failure, is suggestive in this respect. As a "wandering," it departs from the same and drifts toward "missing," a movement that does not lead to completion, totality, or accumulation. Erring as a failure in cognitive mastery is ultimately a failure to reproduce sameness, a failure to conform and complete. Both as a diversion and as a failure to conform, erring is open to otherness and difference. It evokes the aporia as a nonpassable border, one that bears the name of the other and denotes the unexpected and the subversive. It points to the forces that invert, pervert, and subvert the oppositional schemas of presence/absence, identity/difference, propriety/impropriety, interiority/exteriority. Such errant performativity emerges in effect from Hatoum's lived and artistic exiled cartographies. Hatoum was exiled for a second time when, as she was visiting London in her twenties, the Lebanese civil war erupted in 1975. Stranded in London, she would watch Lebanon being torn apart, with her family members living in homes very close to the Green Line and abruptly finding each other on opposite sides of the divide. Even though London was supposed to be a short visit for her, it eventually became a new place of residence; she studied and still lives and works there.

Hatoum's site-specific artwork, moving in between "East" and "West," traces pathways across different spaces, borderlands, and bodies as well as artistic genres and media. Her avant-garde installations, performances, videos, and sculptures are marked by a bodily and sensible unconventionality, as well as an unsettling political engagement with questions of borders and boundaries, exile and belonging, confinement and displacement. Working with bodily material and waste, barbed wire, sandbags, brass, soap, maps, furniture, kitchen utensils, calligraphy, Muslim prayer mats, embroidery, Arabic folk lanterns, and digitalized genres of contemporary media, to name only some of her prototype materials, she re-collects the political genealogies of the familiar and the estranged. Hatoum enacts belonging not as a static site of comfort and territorial being or being-together, but rather as a discomforting embodied performativity through which borders and bodies are constantly displaced, re-collected, and re-embodied.[5] For Hatoum, there is nothing direct and commonplace about belonging, which becomes, rather, a complicated process of reconfiguring place as commonplace. In her installations, even domestic space emerges as constitutively discomforting, and not only under circumstances of explicit dispossession and forced displacement. Used domestic objects become de-formed and even harmful in ways that contest their original functions and homely settings. The domestic environment is not stable and spatially fixed, but uncharted and continuously shifting territory.[6] As a nomadic artist as well as an artist of the nomadic, Hatoum activates her own passings and crossings, both forced and chosen ones, to translate between different cultural imaginaries and to disrupt the "commonplace" of displacement and confinement.

Drawing on the historical specificities that inform Hatoum's art, I would like to ask here: does exile work to disrupt the notion of topos/place, or does it inscribe the desire to produce another place? Is exile a perennial nonplace, an out-of-place, injurious and utopian at once, or does it seek a place and, in that sense, remain within the bounds of an ontology of place? How might exile unsettle the metaphysics of place and trouble the fantasies of an invulnerable sovereignty of place? And perhaps more significantly: to what extent is this kind of reflection affected by the ongoing struggles of those without a place of their own? Furthermore, how is the grammar of vulnerable belonging marked by the resistance of those stripped of the rights of freedom and belonging? What kinds of belonging and unbelonging, figured through tropes of gendered, sexualized, ethnicized, and racialized vulnerability, could allow us to think the resistant potential of ascribing to art the task of relating to loss, finitude, and vulnerability? Hatoum visited Palestine for the first time in 1996 during an artist residency in Anadiel Gallery, a deteriorating space previously used as a book-binding business and located in a working-class neighborhood in the northwestern old part of Jerusalem. It was in that multilayered space that she created the floor installation *Present Tense*, a grid composed of twenty-two hundred squared soap bars from the Palestinian Nablus factory, which, while it was still in operation during Hatoum's residence, was ultimately shut down by Israeli forces. Into the transient underlying structure of this local olive oil soap produced by traditional Palestinian methods, she outlined, by means of minute red glass beads, the borders of the disjointed and isolated zones carved out of historic Palestine and intended to be the future Palestinian state according to the 1993 Oslo accords. The Palestinian Occupied Territories hold an emblematic position in Achille Mbembe's conceptualization of "necropolitics," which accounts for zones of death where populations are subjected to conditions of life conferring upon them the status of living-dead.[7] In the "death-world" of the Palestinian occupation, the territorial fragmentation and the web of intricate internal borders and isolated cells render any movement impossible, while these disjointed zones are related to each other through surveillance.[8] As the historicity of the Palestinian dispossession is constantly being disavowed, Hatoum intervenes with a "homemade" map whose mnemonic scent evokes Palestine's affective history and culture. As spatialized relations of power are played out at the expense of Palestine's human geography, she seeks, as she characteristically noted in a conversation with a viewer during the exhibition at the gallery, to wash her hands of the matter with this soap. The title *Present Tense*, and the very materiality of the installation, address both the ambivalence of a state of tension and suspense and the urgency for action in the present time.

Living-Dead Bodies

Hatoum created her performance piece *The Negotiating Table* in 1983 (at the time of her residency at the Niagara Artists' Centre, at the Western Front in Vancouver) and presented it for the first time in the SAW Gallery in Ottawa in 1983, that is, during the ongoing Lebanese civil war and the year after Israel's invasion of Lebanon—a moment of brutal aggression against Palestinians in Lebanon. During the years of isolation and subjugation of Palestinians in Lebanon, a Palestinian national movement and a newly formed national (as opposed to merely colonial) history emerged to which Israeli invasion forces reacted by destroying Palestinian archives, private libraries, homes, and cultural artifacts, to ultimately instigate the massacre of Palestinian civilians in

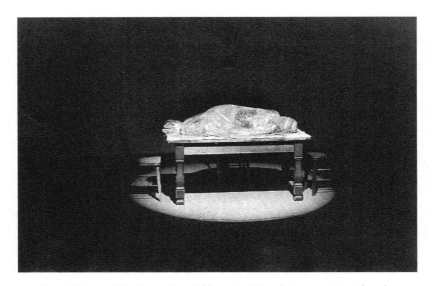

7.1 Mona Hatoum, *The Negotiating Table*, 1983. Video documentation of performance. Color video, sound, 20:33 minutes. PHOTO BY ERIC METCALFE. COURTESY MONA HATOUM AND WESTERN FRONT, VANCOUVER.

Sabra and Shatila in 1982.[9] In *The Negotiating Table*, the body of the artist herself, blindfolded, stained in blood, bound by ropes, and covered with surgical gauzes and animal entrails, is curled in a transparent plastic body bag thrown on the top of a table in a dimly illuminated room for three hours. The performing body is immovable, barely breathing, almost frozen between the violence of war and the diplomatic devices of negotiation and exoneration. This is a body made utterly susceptible to its consumption by the world's gazes of sedimented anesthesia. It is this spirit of banalized complacency that the hypnotizing sound of the performance evokes. Audio recordings of mainstream Western political news reports, politicians' speeches, and peace negotiations in the background indicate that the dispute resolutions take place over the confined, wounded, disposable, racialized female body. Denoting the dehumanized and destroyed dignity of the victim, the performer's naked body looks like a monstrous mass of an ambiguous but certainly brutalized materiality, residing in the liminal realms between life and death, public and intimate, as well as human and nonhuman. She cannot be identified as herself and can barely be recognized as human; at the same time, the amorphous and dismembered mass signals wounded human flesh—anonymous and unrecognizably disfigured—exposed to extreme violence. Her body is hardly recognized as female, yet it insinuates the forces of gendering and racialization that structure the damage inflicted on gendered, racialized bodies as inert and disposable bodily matter. As Luce Irigaray and Judith Butler have influentially shown, "matter" is deeply embedded in power genealogies of racism, gender, and sexuality. In this macabre portrait of a living corpse, Hatoum associates matter with the passivity and exclusion imposed by international agencies of "negotiation" and diplomatic machinery to secure or exonerate persisting injustices of political violence, occupation, and racism.

Injurability refers not merely to a generalized human condition of vulnerability, but to a political distribution and regulation of the terms of exposure, or thrownness, to injustice; and these terms are gendered, sexualized, ethnicized, and racialized. In this piece, the horror of the battlefield, which is enacted by the artist's violated body, and the complicit carnage of policy-making negotiations, which are performed in the uncanny background sound of propagandistic conversations about the war's "opportunities for creative diplomacy," are considered from the perspective of vulnerable and disposable civilian victims. The sensuality of suffering, simultaneously public and private, is addressed as the abjection of violated bodies and their reduction to formless waste, in all its connections with a gender and race politics of disposability. Inhabiting both humanity and animality, the artist's body becomes a site of categorical liminality. Through the becoming-carcass of the artist's body, political suffering comes to involve animality and human animality at once, thus interrogating the relation between them, and implying various questions: How do animals suffer, and how does their suffering bespeak the rawest forms of human precarity? And what does it mean politically to become a zoomorphic body suffering *like* an animal in between language and the impossibility of speech? The artist's body embodies "the aporia between . . . the human and the inhuman produced in the language of sovereignty."[10] At the same time, this utter political violation and dehumanizing dismemberment is ambivalently embodied as not only the death but also the resistant, albeit precarious, living-on of the female artist as witness. The bleeding and broken body, exposed in public to the gaze of others, becomes a site of resistance and an agent of protest against geopolitics of injustice and cultures of anesthesia. The broken and exposed body of the performance is not quite owned (only) by the performer; rather, the performance itself is utterly disposed of. In its crossing the bleeding borders of intimate and public, it implies vulnerability and resistance, abandonment and relatedness. This is an embodiment that manifests how "the place of the body, and the way in which it disposes us outside ourselves or sets us beside ourselves, opens up another kind of normative aspiration within the field of politics."[11]

Hatoum's ambivalently (sub)human remains thrown on the negotiating table signal the intertwinement of differential human vulnerability with the condition of "becoming pariah" that is operative within, despite, and against the cruelty of persisting legacies of colonial, racist, gender, and class domination. The feminist theorist Eleni Varikas uses the itinerant concept of pariah as an emblematic metaphor of alterity and exclusion: as a figure deprived of both the common human status and the status of individual singularity.[12] The status of pariah, Varikas reminds us, is always defined by the sovereign One, in accordance with normative criteria beyond which lies the disdained abnormal and the monstrous. The social and political exclusion of the pariahs is legalized through jurisprudence, but also through epistemic violence. And as their social and political exclusion is established, the suspicion for their humanness grows: this is about "the loneliness of the hybrid." Emotions of shame are inflicted on pariahs, Varikas reminds us, as they are considered threateningly vulnerable and unpredictably resilient. Yet pariahs do reverse normative violence and structures of domination, turning their exclusion into a positive mark of their reclaimed subjectivity. They come into being as subjects who revolt against the disavowal of their desires and demand their dignity. From the realm of being injured and marginalized, they performatively figure in the center by protesting against social injury and injustice. What can we learn about the universality of humanness and rights from a point of view marked by the outrage and the traumas of those expelled and exempted from this conceit of universality? Hatoum grapples with this question in light of historical exigencies, which enable and afflict, at once, the possibility of art. Her *Negotiating Table* embodies a creative contradiction between art's melancholia (signaled here by the artist's becoming-carcass) and revolutionary potential, especially its transformative capacity to endure, inscribe in, and actively mobilize collective struggles contesting domination, displacement, and occupation—in all their connections to the gendered division of labor. As Ewa Ziarek notes, in reflecting on Virginia Woolf's writing as a site of "feminist aesthetics of potentiality," we might find ourselves asking about the intimate relation between the agential potential of female artists to create artworks of freedom and "the collective task of women's struggle for freedom, which in turn assures the future possibility of female art."[13]

In attempting to tackle the question of violence from the perspective of those exposed to it, Adriana Cavarero coined the term "horrorism" and drew our attention to the violence that aims at deteriorating the uniqueness of the singular body.[14] The provocative neologism itself implies the lack of linguistic means through which contemporary violence, in all its diverse manifestations, might make sense, be conceived of, and be articulated. Cavarero is interested in violent acts that assault and injure at an ontological level—namely, the bodily irreducible singularity—and thus destroy the subject's dignity. She propounds "vulnerability" as our constitutive ontological condition of being reciprocally exposed to each other's power for care or harm. Horrorism, then, from her perspective, denotes the violation of dignity, the violation of bodily vulnerability in all its singularity. This singularity, however, is not just attached to, or individually owned by, a particular body; rather, it is shared with, and exposed to, "everybody" of human singularity: "On the scene of horror, the body placed in question is not just a singular body, as every body obviously is; above all, it is a body in which human singularity, concentrating itself at the most expressive point of its flesh, exposes itself intensely."[15] Hatoum's *Negotiating Table* is the mise-en-scène of horrorism par excellence. Horrorism, as Cavarero tells us, dismembers the victims at the level of their existence. Furthermore, it specifically expropriates the female body, morphing it into a site of death. It is through these horrorist enactments, however, that the injured body does not stay in its place, even though horrorism works to freeze it in place, and becomes an occasion for politicizing vulnerability and its pervasive genealogies.

In Hatoum's *Negotiating Table*, death is the ultimate form of domination, but it also becomes an occasion of resistance-generating power, or "necropower" in Mbembe's terms.[16] I saw Mona Hatoum's performance *Negotiating Table* in crisis-ridden Athens in the spring of 2012, when economic hardship, deprivation, and disparities were escalating amid harsh austerity measures with particularly adverse effects on equality and democracy. The performance was hosted and curated by a private institution of contemporary art, during a period when public space was abandoned by the state and dispossessed by corporate power. In recent years, Greece has become a contemporary biopolitical and necropolitical site of injured and broken bodies due to neoliberal aggression. "Crisis" involves a complex circuit of governmentality, of austerity, securitization, de-democraticization, and the erosion of welfare systems. The violent logic and logistics of crisis have brought to the fore the contingencies of everyday life, such as a growing sentiment and a raw reality of precariousness. It has also brought to the fore various enactments of resistant embodiment. Furthermore, it has instigated new articulations of questions about belonging, marginality, and the contested boundaries of Europe. Hatoum's performance in Athens, amid neoliberal and de-democraticizing conditions of impoverishment, homelessness, and a growing number of suicides related to the crisis but also emergent and persistent protest collectivities, worked to reposition and reframe a body performed through the other. *The Negotiating Table* uncannily echoed in an Athenian scene of a homeless person who was lying on the pavement, his body covered by the body of a stray dog. The two intertwined bodies formed an amorphous disposed mass of wounded materiality, residing in the interstices of life and death, public and intimate, as well as human and nonhuman. Outside of the sheltered institutional settings of the art market, in the context of neoliberal political horror, the exposure of bodily vulnerability to international machinery of debt "negotiation" is not limited to human embodiment.[17] Political suffering comes to involve animality and human animality at once, thus pointing to new enactments of precarity and unhomeliness but also cobelonging and companionship.

Troubling Invulnerable Resistance

In Hatoum's art, nomadic subjectivity signals not a flight from, but rather an engagement with, the political horrors of occupation and containment. If nomadic subjects challenge hegemonic subject formations from within, working to destabilize the dominant subject positions of the "center" as the emblematic site of all fantasies of origination, the question enabled by Hatoum's work concerns the embodied political performativity at work in the exigencies of nomadic subjectivity.[18] Judith Butler's theorization of performative and transformative agency enables us to capture the potentiality of such nomadic subjectivity for the purposes of interrupting the normative and exclusionary standards of belonging and opening up alternative possibilities for political and affective sensibility. According to this rendition of the politics of performativity, subjects are persistently and incalculably interpellated by the reiteration of sedimented norms whose materialization is socially compelled and yet always incomplete. As they reflexively appropriate these injurious terms and respond to their demanding call, subjects incorporate and bring into being the conditions that discursively form and enable them. Performativity, in this sense, involves an interminable interplay of vulnerability and potentiality, incorporation and resistance. If incorporation is to be understood as an incomplete and unattainable materialization of regulatory ideals, can we think of the body as the medium of the spectral finitude and futurity of the performative?

Hatoum's work could be taken to imply this question as she reactivates bodily performativity from the position of postcolonial horrorism, as it is interminably marked and fissured by a diverse array of cartographies of uprootedness, diasporic culture, gendered exile, and responsiveness.

Hatoum's work provides a suitable occasion for rethinking the disjunctive temporalities at the heart of performative agency as responsiveness to the persistent eventualities of racism and imperialism. As a figure of exile, whose topos of performative engagement is simultaneously within and against the power and knowledge apparatuses that produce colonial sovereignty, Hatoum has been moving across countries and languages, semiotic systems and cultural signs. She has lived, in Edward Said's words, a "nomadic, decentered, contrapuntal [life]; but no sooner does one get accustomed to it than its unsettling force erupts anew."[19] That she is extraterritorial, multilocal, and culturally heterogeneous also means that she has experienced the intrusion of violent colonial histories and politics into the intimate quarters of her life. These in-between, indeterminate, affective spaces of here and there, of past and present, as well as of unsettledness and reclamation, allow for modes of living across temporal and spatial distance and, at the same time, in close proximity with other sites of emplacement and displacement. It is in these interstices of vulnerability and resistance that nomadic subjectivities with transformative agency emerge, producing unexpected spaces of signifying, commemorating, and contesting. Hatoum's art provides an occasion for addressing and representing the aporias of emplacement and displacement in their shared but also conflictual processes of reimagining community based on the condition of vulnerability.

In her installation work titled *Keffieh* (1993–1999), made of cotton fabric and human hair, Hatoum (mis)appropriates the disembodied modernist grid of representation in order to create her own version of the keffieh, the scarf usually worn by men, which has become the symbol of the Palestinian struggle for freedom.[20] Suggestively, she started working on the piece the year that the Oslo accords were signed. More specifically, for the purposes of that work, she had the traditional fishnet pattern on the black-and-white cotton cloth of keffieh (*keffiyeh* or *kufiya*) embroidered with women's black hair, in a way that allows the hair to stick out from the border-frame of the keffieh. The black-and-white checkered keffieh, worn by Palestinian men of any rank, was Yasser Arafat's trademark headdress and has become a symbol of Palestinian struggle for self-determination. Although the keffieh is mainly a male symbol of Palestinian resistance and is associated with Arab masculinity, Leila Khaled, a female member of the armed wing of the Popular Front

7.2 Mona Hatoum, *Keffieh* (detail), 1993–1999. Human hair on cotton fabric, 120×120 cm. PHOTO FLORIAN KLEINEFENN. COURTESY MONA HATOUM AND CHANTAL CROUSEL, PARIS.

for the Liberation of Palestine, has been represented wearing the keffieh, this time in the mode of a Muslim woman's hijab, wrapped around the head and shoulders. Hatoum intervenes in these thick genealogies of embodied resistance and revamps the keffieh by weaving a tactile piece that is "an abject and precarious web of human tissue."[21] As weaving is typically considered a feminine practice in conventional systems of division of labor, weaving women's hair in a keffieh adds a dissonant voice, or an inappropriate/d corporeal sign of uncanniness, to the unifying discourse of the struggle of freedom and its implicit gendered strategies of representation and misrepresentation. The uncontrollable materiality of women's bodily fiber trespasses and disrupts the fixed architectonics of the male resistance symbol. In so doing, it interrogates the conventional presumptions that posit resistance as male. Thus, a sign of bodily vulnerability is reappropriated and deployed to trouble the heroic conceits often operative in iconographies and practices of resistance.

The women's bodily fiber that trespasses the checkered pattern of the keffieh and complicates the genealogy of the resistance symbol works as a gesture of resistance to male representations of resistance. I would like to suggest, however, that, in contaminating the maleness of the keffieh with fragmented and displaced traces of female hair, Hatoum does not merely create an opposition between sovereign patriarchy and subjugated womanhood. The victim's discourse that focuses on objectification reinscribes the sexual politics it seeks to undermine by establishing an illusory antithesis of desiring male subjectivity and desired (or, undesired) female objectivity. Subject and object are not to be theorized as antithetical structures, though, but as positions reciprocally immersed, determined by heteronomous power relations that include class, race, gender, and sexuality. The division between subject and object, which has crucial implications for capturing materialities that matter, provokes the question of the abject as the rejected remnant of materiality that calls into question the borders and limits demanded by the symbolic, and as that which establishes a threatening precariousness and ambiguity in the subject's constitution of self and identity. "We may call it a border; abjection is above all ambiguity," writes Julia Kristeva, drawing on anthropologist Mary Douglas's groundbreaking analysis of purity and defilement.[22] Neither subject nor object, neither inside nor outside the body, the abject is the terrifying and contaminating "matter out of place" that is jettisoned beyond the boundaries of the symbolic order; it is quintessentially rendered other and cannot be assimilated. It is extended past what is conventionally possible and thinkable. It is disavowed and expelled from social rationality, discharged as excrement, and declared to be a nonobject of desire. The abject "fascinates desire, which, nevertheless, does not let itself be seduced. Apprehensive, desire turns aside; sickened it rejects."[23] To put it differently, the boundary-constituting taboo that Kristeva calls abjection attests to the construction of the culturally intelligible speaking subject through expulsion and repulsion, or, to invoke Cavarero's language again, horrorism. To return to *Keffieh*, then: women are constitutively the ideological boundary of the national body politic. Their abjection is needed for the formation of the public political sphere of desiring and active male subjects. In representing the female body as abject, then, Hatoum calls for a relation to women and their struggles as that which remains other but also as that which is to come in ways unanticipated and inappropriable, including an unanticipated modality of anticolonial struggle for self-determination.

In a different but related vein, Hatoum's uncanny textility in *Keffieh* resonates with the cultural performance of Muslim women's veiling, a multilayered practice complexly associated with piety and social status. Hatoum accentuates sexual difference as particularized and localized, disrupting the stereotyped perception of "women" as a universal and homogeneous category of shared oppression. Importantly, *Keffieh*'s corporeality alludes to a difference or dissonance in culture and power, which introduces a caesura into the discursive space of belonging and its gendered modalities of authorization. *Keffieh* comments thus on the transformation of female veiling into a typical mode of Western orientalist fantasizing of the Middle East as seductive and dangerously mysterious, in its supposedly nonsecular and nonmodern essence. Further, it unsettles Western discourses of veiling that work to signify Muslim women as perennially victimized, helplessly vulnerable, and in need of compassion and salvage.

The Micropolitics of the Body (Not) at Home

What kinds of homely and unhomely corporealities are then brought forward in living enactments of displacement and containment? The body in Hatoum's work seems to have lost its homely modalities of embodiment, but as it seeks to reground itself in new diasporic intimacies, it opens up to the possibilities of mutual vulnerability and precariousness. Thus, belonging becomes a matter of intimate and precarious embodied relationality. In *Corps étranger* (1994), as the viewers enter a white cylindrical wooden shell, they direct their sight down to a circular video screen grafted on the floor. They find themselves watching an endoscopic medical camera persistently moving through intimate details of bodily interiors and orifices. Fragmented and scattered on the floor, this is in fact the artist's own body, in physical discomfort, susceptible and trespassed on the other as the foreign object of camera, the medical intervention, or the viewers' gazes. Distressingly enlarged are skin folds, mucous membranes, hair, teeth, and pupils. Sounds of breathing and heartbeats accompanying this video stress an audio-materiality of life. The body, represented as a place with visible, audible, and palpable qualities, lies in the interstices of intimate and foreigner.

7.3 Mona Hatoum, *Corps étranger*, 1994. Video installation with cylindrical wooden structure, video projector, video player, amplifier and four speakers, 350×300×300 cm. PHOTO PHILIPPE MIGEAT. COURTESY MONA HATOUM AND CENTRE POMPIDOU, PARIS.

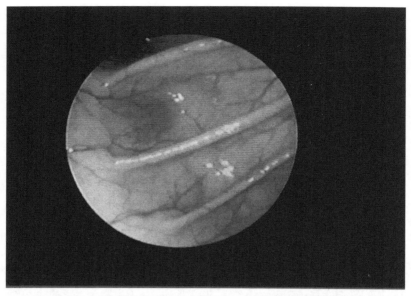

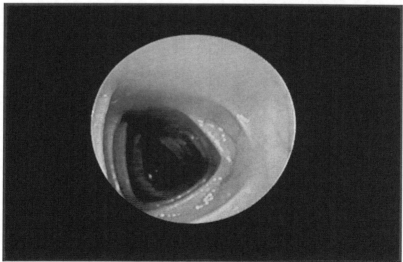

7.4–7.5 Mona Hatoum, *Corps étranger* (detail), 1994. Video installation with cylindrical wooden structure, video projector, video player, amplifier and four speakers, 350×300×300 cm. PHOTOS PHILIPPE MIGEAT. COURTESY MONA HATOUM AND CENTRE POMPIDOU, PARIS.

Hatoum's mise-en-scènes of corporeality, in all their vulnerability and horrorism, echo the work of Jean-Luc Nancy, for whom the body is an open space that is more spacious than spatial; it is a place, a place of existence.[24] As it is equated with the multiple eventualities of the skin, which is variously folded, refolded, unfolded, invaginated, exogastrulated, orificed, invaded, stretched, relaxed, excited, and distressed, the body makes room for existence.[25] Similarly, the skin becomes for Hatoum "the place for an event of existence."[26] It bespeaks the corporeal eventness of performativity—an awkward materiality that eludes any programmatic figuration or calculable materialization and opens up to a certain disposition of the self toward the other. The corporeal subject is enacted as fundamentally social in its sensual openness, vulnerability, and physical interrelation to the other. Incorporating the other, the subject opens up—and gives room—to the radical contingency of engagement where the other is not reduced to the proper logic of possession. On the contrary, the other seems to have a knowledge of her own and emerges in new, intimate, and unforeseeable ways. It is suggestive, in that respect, that the endoscopic camera and the medical gaze expose the artist's own body in its most intimate details. Again, as in *The Negotiating Table*, body becomes utterly disposed of itself: a *corps étranger*, or "foreign body."

The theme of bodily exposure and its ambiguous un-homeliness emerges also in Hatoum's fifteen-minute video work *Measures of Distance* (1988), where the artist shows slides of her mother taking a shower, as she simultaneously superimposes on them letters in handwritten calligraphic Arabic that were exchanged between Hartoum and her mother during the period of civil war in Lebanon, while the artist was exiled in London. The interplay of textuality and corporeality (and, in particular, the forces and the vulnerabilities of eventuality erupting from this interplay) compels a rethinking of the mutual dependence—albeit not mutual reduction—between language and the body. The writing, as it is inscribed on the mother's exposed body, acts as an ambiguous border of simultaneous intimacy and alienation between the two women. The (m)other's body is veiled and mystified, turned into a text of deferred and misfired communication. It emerges as a spatio-temporal threshold of partaking with and partitioning from. Hatoum claims an unending longing for another whose distance is measured by the incommensurable intricacies of bodily sensibility. Synchronically, in the ambient acoustic background of the video work, the artist is both conversing with her mother in Arabic and translating her mother's letters in English. In the midst of this polyphony, a nonsemantic and rather confusing sound landscape is produced,

7.6–7.7 Mona Hatoum, *Measures of Distance,* 1988. Color video, sound, 15:30 minutes. A Western Front Video Production, Vancouver. COURTESY MONA HATOUM.

implying an embodied politics of vocal relationality. The multilayered *phone* of the mother tongue embodies the "measures of distance." Adriana Cavarero has pointed to the multiple ways in which the Western metaphysics of "devocalizing" logos has erased the singular sounds of voices and embodied uniqueness.[27] To the traditional philosophical prioritization of semantics versus *phone* (voice), she responds with an alternative narrative that reverses this hierarchy and stresses the authenticity of the subject in her embodied voice. Cavarero's conceptualization of relational politics is premised on the reciprocal interdependence and exposure of singular persons.

Hatoum doubles the author when she reads her mother's letters, and we, the viewers, become its recipients too. Looking and hearing, as well as reading and writing, are replayed in this work as sites of identification and disavowal in colonial discourses. Placed in between the racializing forces of voyeurism and surveillance, a dialectics so crucial to the colonial cultural text, Hatoum's mother describes how her husband—the artist's father—was angered when he found out about her naked body being exposed for the purposes of the filming. In her own words, he felt that she had taken from him something that belonged exclusively to him. Engaging with the visual and auditory imaginaries of colonial power, Hatoum traces back her life in Lebanon to only reinvent its moral and sensible inscriptions. Above all, she captures and estranges the fictions of fantasy and desire, including the properness of oedipal family values and gender hierarchies, as they are translated into the conventional boundaries between private and public, and as they are encompassed in the question what can be exposed publicly and what is to remain hidden from sight in the gendered and sexualized anatomy of colonial discourse.

Epilogue

Hatoum claims a body in anticipation and beyond anticipation, an undetermined and exposed body, and, eventually, an unhomely body whose departures and distances are measured by the incommensurable intricacies of collective bodily vulnerabilities and resistances. It is this political performativity of the body that informs Hatoum's art, from *The Negotiating Table* featuring the indiscriminate, defenseless, and disfigured casualties of the Palestinian carnage, to the keffieh of the gendered complexities of the struggle for self-determination, the corps étranger, whereby the intimate details of bodily interiors are under biopolitical surveillance and control, and the measures of distance where the exposed body of the artist's mother materializes and defers, at the same time, the relationality of the mother tongue. Within the different moments of her work, what is at stake in Hatoum's work is not merely the individual body, but the poignant iconographies and actualities of plural corporealities that are at work in the horrorism of our contemporaneity. While *The Negotiating Table* performs the destruction of the human body's integrity, thus exposing the utter superfluity and disposability of the confined bodies of Palestine's occupation, in *Keffieh* the figural integrity of the symbol of Palestinian struggle is performatively undone and expropriated for purposes of expanding and complicating the political vocabulary of resistance by dismantling the stereotypical images of the helpless female body. Engaging either with unarmed instances of disposability or with resistant responses to it, what Hatoum's art brings to the scene is the singularity of vulnerable bodies as they are exposed to the other. This is, indeed, about the political circumstances and potentials of a common—albeit unevenly distributed—condition of vulnerability.[28]

Notes

This is an expansive and differently focused version of an essay that appeared in "Migration, Gender and Precarious Subjectivities in the Era of Crisis," ed. Athena Athanasiou and Giorgos Tsimouris, special issue, *Greek Review of Social Sciences* 140–141 (December 2013).

1 Derrida, *Monolingualism of the Other*, 29. An exile from the philosophy of logocentrism, as Richard Bernstein puts it (Bernstein, *The New Constellation*), Derrida, like Hatoum, inserts the nomadism, travels, and secrets of his autobiography in the corpus of his work. In *Monolingualism of the Other: or, The Prosthesis of Origin*, he grafts his renderings of cultural belongings, language, and desire on lost languages of origin while he reminisces on his childhood and adolescent years in French colonial Algeria before he sailed across on a boat for Europe and metropolitan Paris. He grew up monolingual, speaking only French, even though he would hear Arabic spoken in his surroundings: his "access to any non-French language of Algeria (literary or dialectical Arabic, Berber, etc.) was *interdicted*" (31). Arabic for Derrida is the elided language, the expelled speech of the other. And Algeria is his place of belonging and loss—his "nostalgeria," as he names it. For him "French was a language supposed to be maternal, but one whose source, norms, rules, and law were situated elsewhere" (41). So his access to French was "*also interdicted*, in a differently, apparently roundabout, and perverted manner" (31). The interdiction, Derrida suggests, is not negative and "does not incite simply to loss. Nor is the amnesia it organizes from the depths, in the nights of the abyss, incited to perdition. It ebbs and flows like a wave that sweeps everything along upon the shores that I know too well. It carries every-

thing, that sea, and on two sides; it swells, sweeps along, and enriches itself with everything, carries away, brings back, deports and becomes swollen again with what it has dragged away" (31).

2 Derrida, *Monolingualism of the Other*, 15.

3 Derrida, *Monolingualism of the Other*, 17–18.

4 Derrida, *Monolingualism of the Other*, 18.

5 For Ranjana Khanna, Hatoum's art is paradigmatic in that it treats (un)belonging moving away from modernist literary and artistic revered representations of exile and turning to the concept of asylum, a site of hospitality and potential hostility. Khanna, "Technologies of Belonging."

6 See Ahmed et al., *Uprootings/Regroundings*.

7 Mbembe, "Necropolitics."

8 Mbembe, "Necropolitics," 27–28.

9 Said, *The Politics of Dispossession*, 72.

10 Athanasiou, "Reflections on the Politics of Mourning," 51.

11 Butler, *Precarious Life*, 26.

12 Varikas, *Les rebuts du monde*.

13 Ziarek, *Feminist Aesthetics and the Politics of Modernism*, 88–89.

14 Cavarero, *Horrorism*.

15 Cavarero, *Horrorism*, 19.

16 Mbembe, "Necropolitics."

17 It would evolve a lengthier discussion regarding Mona Hatoum's art in relation to the market economy and capitalization of artwork. A significant contribution to this perspective has been made by Bojana Kunst's writings on how performance and contemporary live arts are in proximity with capitalism and yet resist the capitalist appropriation of art (Kunst, *Artist at Work*, 2015). In Kunst's analysis, performance art creates forms and representations of contemporary capitalist exploitation or articulates images that critique capitalist models of activity, productivity, surplus value, and doing more, as well as the successful and teleological completion of the goal. In *The Negotiating Table*," Mona Hatoum's inactive or passive performance—lying down on the table or sleeping—is ultimately an aberration between work and nonwork, between production and "doing less." She is unrecognizable, in between nonhumanness and humanity, slipping into the dystopic others of eventuality and temporality. Contrary to any programmatic logic and future-related goals, her performance is an occurrence of heterogeneity, impurity, contamination, and alterity invoking the malleable limits of humanity. Ultimately, Hatoum's vulnerable embodied practices of passivity and eventuality in *The Negotiating Table* point to what is to still come (hence its value cannot be accessed) rather than conceptualizing (and commodifying) the future. So it can be argued that Hatoum's work, in its plural materialities and materializations, enacts possibilities that do not work to reproduce, but instead occasionally resist, the capitalization of artwork.

18 Braidotti, *Nomadic Subjects*.

19 Said, *Reflections on Exile*, 149.
20 On Mona Hatoum's renderings of modernist tropes, see Mansoor, "A Spectral Universality."
21 Mansoor, "A Spectral Universality," 49.
22 Douglas, *Purity and Danger*; Kristeva, *Powers of Horror*, 9.
23 Kristeva, *Powers of Horror*, 1.
24 Nancy, *Corpus*.
25 Nancy, *Corpus*, 15.
26 Nancy, *Corpus*, 15.
27 Cavarero, *For More than One Voice*.
28 Butler, *Precarious Life*.

CHAPTER 8

Precarious Politics

The Activism of "Bodies That Count" (Aligning with Those That Don't) in Palestine's Colonial Frontier

REMA HAMMAMI

It was the day they were clearing the villagers of Mufaqara from their land. The soldiers were pushing and shoving people around, hauling off their belongings and dumping them. . . . The children screaming as their homes were being bulldozed, people trying to save a few of their belongings, people who barely had anything. That day I felt totally depressed. Defeated. You ask yourself, where is the world? Where is the press? There was no one there. No one saw what was happening to us. That was the moment I realized that we were totally alone.
—HISHAM, leader of the Popular Resistance Committee of Southern
Hebron Hills / Masafer Yatta

This essay focuses on a particular site of struggle and strategy of activism that involves the coming together of intelligible and unintelligible bodies in an attempt to resist the necropolitics of Israeli settler colonialism in the West Bank / Palestine. The strategy of building solidarities with "bodies that count" is analyzed in relation to the way Israeli sovereign power and imperial geopolitics operate to distribute precarity unevenly both across and within Palestinian space in the West Bank, relegating the Palestinian communities of Masafer Yatta to a zone of hyperprecarity and elimination. As such, in this zone, the struggle of the communities has become centered on the possibility of existence itself. The analysis here focuses on how the active solidarities of grievable bodies (those recognized by sovereign power as rights-bearing subjects, or indeed as fully human—here Israelis and Euro-Americans) entering this zone attempt to produce countervisibilities and connection in the face of the erasures and isolation deployed by Israeli colonial violence. In contrast to the wider literature on "protective accompaniment" that tends to foreground the voices and agency of white, western subjects in their narratives of these types of activisms, here I reverse the usual order and put Palestinians from the communities at the center.

Imperial Peace / Colonial Space

In 1999, at the height of the Oslo "peace process" between Israel and the PLO, the Israeli military (Israeli Defense Forces, or IDF) issued an evacuation order against the twelve Palestinian communities of Masafer Yatta in the occupied West Bank. The military had designated the land on which the communities existed in an arid and isolated part of the southern Hebron Hills an IDF training area, "Firing Zone 918," and the residents of the communities were charged with "illegally" residing there. Over the period of October/November 1999, the IDF systematically expelled more than seven hundred families from their lands, demolished their homes and cisterns, and poured cement down their wells.[1]

Over the course of the 1990s within the settler colonial cartography of the West Bank and the Imperial geopolitics of the Oslo "peace process,"[2] the villages of Masafer Yatta had become reterritorialized into a zone of hyperprecarity known in diplomatic language as "Area C." The 1994 Oslo Accords subdivided the once seamless territory of the occupied West Bank into three zones marked by varying degrees of Palestinian "autonomy" from Israeli control. Palestinian towns and cities (Area A) became zones of Palestinian Authority (PA) "full responsibility," and PA "security control" over the population within those areas was the signal mark of "autonomy." Palestinian villages within their municipal boundaries became categorized as "Area B," zones in which the PA had civilian responsibility over the population, while Israel continued to hold full rights of "security" control over them. The remaining 64 percent of the land, the lightly populated territory surrounding the 166 separate islands of Areas A and B, was deemed "Area C"—the area that crucially contains both the majority of Palestinian farm and pasturage lands, along with Israeli settlements and IDF military installations. To this day, Area C remains under direct Israeli civil and military control and is where the Israeli military is the literal sovereign. Through this violent process of reterritorialization, Palestinians in towns (now Area A) and villages (Area B) of the West Bank were brought under a form of imperial trusteeship under the tutelage of a global assemblage of peace and state-building actors and institutions that mediated the direct necropolitics of Israeli sovereign rule, while those inhabiting Area C found themselves plunged into a zone of abandonment on what was now Israel's settler colonial frontier. One Area C resident described it this way:

> Look around you, under that tent is the house we built—two small rooms with no doors or windows, of course without a permit, that's why we covered it in a tent—to hide it. They came last week and said there is a demolition order on it. . . . And [laughs] this tent we're sitting in—there's a demolition order on it too. What's there to destroy? Some iron poles and a tarp! They've even made our access to the breeze illegal—they don't want us to get any air! (Um Bahjat, al Mufaqara)

In Area C approximately two hundred thousand Palestinians live in 230 scattered communities, side by side with three hundred thousand Israeli settlers in 135 settlements and another 100 "settlement outposts."[3] The majority are small herding and farming communities and Bedouins who often do not have the basics of modern infrastructure (water, electricity, accessible roads) and also lack the most basic social services (schools and health clinics). Housing is often "temporary" and includes caves, shacks, and tents. This dearth of modernity is due not to "underdevelopment" but to active "de-development" by the Israeli authorities, who prevent even the most basic forms of permanent construction and thwart all attempts at creating the infrastructure for "livable life."[4] Along with the constant surveillance/destruction of the communities' attempts at making an infrastructure of existence by the Israeli military, there is the constant threat of and actual "frontier violence" undertaken by settlers against them. Humanitarian and human rights reports regularly describe a range of Israeli mechanisms that lead to what they call the population's "vulnerability to displacement," including restrictive planning and zoning; house demolitions and mass eviction; the creation of military firing zones and closed military areas; access restrictions to land, water, and pasturage; and the near constancy of settler violence.[5]

Necropolitics, Settler Colonialism, Erasure

The ramified system in place in South Hebron, like everywhere else in the Occupied Territories, exists for one and only one purpose—to steal land and to make the owners of this land disappear. Everything, and everybody, on the Israeli side is fully mortgaged to this single aim.

—DAVID SHULMAN, Israeli Ta'ayush activist

In his seminal article "Necropolitics," Achille Mbembe extends and transforms Giorgio Agamben's theorization of the state of exception from the camp to the colony: "The colony is the location par excellence where the controls and guarantees of the judicial order can be suspended—the zone where the violence of the state of exception is deemed to operate in the service of 'civilization.'"[6] By focusing on the colony as a formative site of the state of exception, Mbembe brings racism and its translation into different economies of violence over bodies and territory into the genealogy of contemporary forms of governmentality and the biopolitical. In this reading, the colony and sovereign power are coconstitutive: in the colony a permanent state of emergency reigns where law is displaced by arbitrary and discretionary rule and where in the management of native populations modern biopolitics is superseded by its constituent logic of necropolitics. Or, as Hunaida Ghanim puts it in relation to the native, "From the moment that power is directed to destroying, eliminating, and dismantling their group, the decision about their life becomes a decision about their death."[7]

In understanding the specific form that colonial necropolitics takes in the context of Masafer Yatta, it is useful to read Mbembe in conjunction with Patrick Wolfe's more historicized account of settler colonialisms. Wolfe has noted that the deep logic of settler colonialism is the elimination of the indigenous population in order to settle their land, a process that has adaptively involved different technologies of violence across different colonial formations and historical periods (such as assimilation or mass displacement—and not solely genocide).[8] As a structure that unfolds through time (and space), elimination is also shaped by the balance of power between indigenous populations and the colonizing power.[9]

In Israel's case, the technologies of "elimination" through mass expulsion and ethnic cleansing that marked its founding in 1948 gave way to the modalities of military occupation after the 1967 capture of the West Bank and Gaza. As Richard Falk noted, Palestinians "find themselves being colonized by an alien power against their will and under the pretext of 'belligerent occupation.'"[10] In the contemporary West Bank, these logics are now refracted through the differential "protection" offered by the presence of what constitutes an imperial trusteeship over the Palestinian Bantustans of Areas A and B, operating within the wider logics of Israeli settler colonial necropolitics—producing what Mbembe describes as "late colonial occupation": "a concatenation of multiple powers: disciplinary, biopolitical and necropolitical."[11] Thus, in Area C, where the Israeli military is the literal sovereign, the logics of elimination are free to unfold relatively unimpeded; there modern biopoliti-cal techniques (urban planning, land use, residency procedures) in the service of necropolitics, bound by military "law," operate in tandem with the frontier violence of the colony's shock troops: its settlers. And as Wolfe notes, there "the murderous activities of the frontier rabble constitute the colonial state's principle means of expansion."[12]

Hyperprecarity / Nongrievable Life

That precariousness is an ontological condition common to all life is the start-ing point for Judith Butler's arguments for situating contemporary ethical politics around a recognition of mutual vulnerability and interdependence. Precariousness refers to and follows from our social existence as bodily be-ings, always dependent on others for the needs of our survival. Precarity refers to the political conditions that follow when these needs of survival are not addressed: it "designates that politically induced condition in which certain populations suffer from failing social and economic networks of support and become differentially exposed to injury, violence, and death."[13] For Butler, pre-carity also refers to the situation of populations forcibly exposed to forms of state-sanctioned military violence whose condition is exacerbated by the fact that their only option is to seek protection from the very state that targets them with violence.[14] To highlight this twofold condition of precarity, the spe-cific political condition induced by Israeli necropolitics in Masafer Yatta (and for Palestinians in Area C generally), I refer to its situation as hyperprecarity.[15]

The differential distribution of precarity across populations relies power-fully on representational regimes that delimit whose lives are worthy of suste-nance and protection and whose lives are perceived as disposable or not even human. The distinction between lives that are recognizable, as constituting the human "us" in dominant Western (and colonial) norms, Butler (building from her social ontology of precariousness) refers to as "grievable," in contrast to those "ungrievable" others who are made unintelligible by the racist opera-tions of these same norms. The loss of a Palestinian life is grieved by those intimately close and often by those farther away. But a Palestinian life, though grievable within its own community, becomes ungrievable across ontologi-cal divides that foreclose it from being recognized as human—a process that is innately political. To grieve someone thus moves from being a personal experience of loss to becoming the basis for sustained political acts of rec-ognition and mutual interdependence. As will become clear in what follows, these ethics are centrally embodied in the forms of resistance politics at work in Masafer Yatta.

To Exist Is to Resist

To get in the way of settler colonization, all the native has to do is stay at home.
—DEBORAH BIRD ROSE IN WOLFE, "Settler Colonialism"

The people here are doing their own story—they are really saving themselves. We are a part of this story, but really it's the people, the communities themselves.
—ANNA, Italian activist, Operation Dove

The subhead above, "To Exist Is to Resist," is the slogan of the Popular Resistance Committee in Masafer Yatta, in the South Hebron Hills. Given the settler colonial logics of elimination, as the slogan points out, simply continuing to exist as bodies and communities in Masafer Yatta is itself a resistant act. But maintaining existence is not simply about staying put—to do so in such circumstances results in the ongoing erosion of the infrastructure necessary for "livable life." As such, over three decades the constant and persistent efforts of the villagers themselves to create this infrastructure has been the core of resistance. The everyday and constant work of just "being" is made up of the multitude of acts of making life possible in and through the everyday. The persistent acts that make home and livelihoods, of going out to plant and harvest wheat, of herding sheep in the hills, collecting water in cisterns, planting trees and harvesting olives, of children walking miles to the closest schools, of men and women continuing to marry, of women to give birth and raise children—when targeted with elimination become simultaneously the underlying logic of resistance to it. One might call this a politics of subaltern persistence.

As Butler has noted, an awareness of one's own precarity leads to an acknowledgment of one's dependence on others: "Precariousness implies living socially, that is, the fact that one's life is always in some sense in the hands of the other. It implies exposure both to those we know and to those we do not know; a dependency on people we know, or barely know, or know not at all."[16] For situated communities of hyperprecarity, this awareness that one's survival depends on so many others is an everyday doxa, and in Masafer Yatta it probably has deep historical roots in surviving in and through the harsh environment. Even before the occupation and the settlements came, this was always a vulnerable project that could not be accomplished without mutual dependence and an ethic of mutual care with both neighbors and strangers. It is this mutuality that has created the identity of "community" and actually instantiates it in the absence of the usual mechanisms of state municipal designation or public buildings. When this long-standing doxa of interdependence becomes faced with the logics and mechanisms of settler colonial elimination, it becomes politicized. In Masafer Yatta one constantly hears a statement to the effect of "My struggle is not just mine"—that is, I am not struggling to save only my home; I am struggling for my community's existence, because without it my home means nothing.

But this politics of subaltern persistence was ultimately no match against the fully unbridled logics of elimination that became so brutally clear in the events of 1999. In Hisham's description of those events in the opening quote of this essay, he points to two crucial absences he identified in that moment that had enabled the villagers' everyday struggles of creating livability to be so easily defeated: visibility ("no one saw what was happening to us") and connection ("There was no one there"). The logics of elimination both rely on and produce differential visibilities through which the colony can be instantiated and normalized and the native's presence can be erased.[17] Settlements are actively visibilized in space in terms of both location (on hills) and architecture (red roofs).[18] They are marked on regular road maps and planners' charts and are signposted on the roads and highways.[19] By contrast, the Palestinian communities of Masafer Yatta are actively invisibilized—they do not exist on maps and plans, nor are they marked by road signs. To locate them one has to look for the markers of the neighboring Israeli settlement. Their residents are forced to build "invisible" homes—to live in the caves of their grandfathers or, if above ground, to keep buildings low and squat or hidden under tarps.

The violence involved in this process is differentially visibilized as well: that inflicted on the native in the process of rendering the "empty landscape" for colonization remains unseen, while the violence incurred by soldiers and settlers is made (spectacularly) visible and deployed in a politics of mourning that further fuels the logics of elimination.[20] As Hisham puts it, "Look, we all know how the occupation works. They want to evict us and at the same time they use violence to try and make us react violently. If we're violent, it's easy for them—they can just get rid of us."

But more fundamentally, this regime of visibility rests on the same grounds as the colony: the ontologies and their attendant epistemologies that mark off Palestinians as racialized noncitizen subjects/others from the rights-bearing

Israeli citizen subjects who are their colonizers. Captured within these imperial/colonial frames of being and representation, Palestinian personhood is unintelligible, Palestinian suffering is invisible, and regular demands for rights and recognition are already foreclosed.[21] Regular modes of political resistance also become absorbed into and occluded by these operations of power, reducing them to forms of self-defeat.[22]

As such, the isolation that Hisham speaks of was not simply a practical political state, but a more profoundly ontological one. Thus, finding a politics of the possible meant finding ways to emerge into the intelligible by creating forms of countervisibility and connection that could open up a geopolitical space in which the struggle might break into realms of recognition/recognizability.[23]

Enabling Existence: Alter-Geopolitics and the Practice of Possible Resistance

Before they came, our struggle was just going round and round in circles.
—HISHAM

The communities' strategies to create countervisibility have centered on actively seeking and making linkages with intelligible bodies—with those who are recognized by sovereign power as grievable,[24] or with what Jennifer Hyndman has called "bodies that count."[25] Struggles that foreground connections between grievable and ungrievable bodies are what Sara Koopman has called alter-geopolitics.[26] She locates this in the tradition of insights from feminist geopolitics that emphasize bodily practices and the making of everyday securities in the face of militarized violence. For her, "groups doing alter-geopolitics are making connections, often across distance and difference, which focus on the safety of bodies (often by moving bodies) and ground geopolitics in everyday life."[27]

Koopman writes about alter-geopolitical struggle within the framework of "protective accompaniment," a growing form of global human rights–based political practice that brings First World bodies into sites of armed violence to both monitor human rights violations and "protect" human rights workers. "Protective accompaniment" originated in the Indian nonviolent struggles for independence and the American civil rights movement, continued during the Latin American "Dirty Wars" starting in the 1980s, and has persisted into the present, and it also encompasses other contemporary locations of violent conflict, such as Sri Lanka.[28] Though the best-established global groups are often animated by religious or secular ethics of nonviolence, all frame their work within a discourse of human rights. Theorizing the politics of protective accompaniment is still in its nascence. But at the center of debates that have emerged among activists themselves is the obvious problematic of whether deploying racial privilege and hierarchies of corporeal value against sovereign violence simply reproduces the same racial and corporeal distinctions that the sovereign violence rests on.[29]

The practice of "alter-geopolitics" in Masafer Yatta involves some of the tactics (and dilemmas) of protective accompaniment but ultimately encompasses a wider array of practices (and bodies) in confrontation with the nature of Israeli sovereign power operating there. Taken together, these practices have attempted to create forms of connection and countervisibilities in an attempt to "internationalize" the space of Masafer Yatta in ways that can open a space in which the ongoing struggle for existence can become a struggle for recognition.

Grievable Bodies, Visibilities, Cameras

Rather than detail the history of how "bodies that count" came into the space of Masafer Yatta joining the communities' struggle, I want to concentrate on how the presence of these grievable bodies works in this particular space. What types of visibility and connection does their presence produce? Does activism based on placing grievable bodies next to ungrievable ones simply reproduce the same hierarchies of corporeal value that it depends on? Or does it and can it work to break them down?

There has been more than a decade of actions, links, and everyday practices of alter-geopolitical activism in Masafer Yatta. A rich and diverse network of activists and solidarity workers from an array of backgrounds have linked themselves with the struggle for existence by the communities. The vast majority have actually spent time in the communities, some staying as part of ongoing projects of accompaniment, others routinely coming to participate in a variety of ongoing actions. People from the villages have an extensive vocabulary of acronyms for the range of groups that have spent time there (ISM, Ta'ayush, CPT, etc.) as well as human rights and other organizations (B'tselem, ACRI, COMET, etc.) that have become part of the dense network of actions and relationships. A wide array of reports, blogs, and videos produced by this range of actors documenting events and actions taken in the communities have been produced and circulated through the Internet. Some communities (al Mufaqara and Susiya) now have their own dedicated websites. In practical terms, both activists and the community distinguish between the everyday bodily work of accompanying shepherds to their fields, or children to the school, versus the role bodies play in moments of mass action. Israeli and international activists are involved in both types of accompaniment. Although Israeli activists were the first to come to the villages, it is international activists who form a permanent presence of living in the communities.[30]

The main aim of everyday accompaniment is to enable shepherds and farmers to access lands that settlers through the use of violence have tried to deny them entry to and that the military enforces. By denying the communities access, settlers advance their own goals in two ways. First, the already meager economy of the villagers becomes unsustainable, leading them to abandon their communities in search of a living elsewhere. And, second, if settlers can keep them from accessing grazing and other lands under the law of the colonial sovereign for over a period of ten years, these lands will revert to the state—and therefore the colony:

> The conflict is over the land; the shepherd's lands and the farming land— the settler wants them both. So it's up to us to make sure that the shepherd is on his land and the farmers are on their land every day. The conflict is every day. Everyone is involved. If I go on my own [to the land], I'm weak but if I go with others then we can work on the land and stop the settler from taking it. (Hisham)

> I suppose you could say I work appointments and emergencies [laughs]. So the shepherds they call me, we are on twenty-four-hour call, and say, "I am going with my sheep to this valley tomorrow." Almost all of the sites, settlers try and stop them or the military does. So that's an appointment—we go with the shepherd to that valley, create a presence and monitor. Then there are the emergencies, I get a call that a shepherd is somewhere and settlers are coming—so we try and get there as quickly as possible. (Anna, Italian accompanier, Operation Dove)

The act of going to the land in defiance of settler threats and the military has become the logic of a persistent everyday activism that through constant repetitive performance attempts to keep remaking and securing livable space for the community, and prevents its reterritorialization as a settlement. But to move one step beyond this—to create "the new" (or, more often, re-create it)—takes forms of "mass action." Only through a mass of bodies in action together can the physical infrastructure that marks existence and collectivity be (re-)created. Here, the Palestine Solidarity Project reports one such action:

> On Saturday, May 26th, 2012, locals together with more than thirty-five Palestinian, Israeli and international activists built a third single story prefabricated building in the village of Um Faqara [al Mufaqara], South Hebron Hills. . . . The construction of the three new structures was organized by the Popular Committee and activists with the aim of peacefully resisting the Israeli occupation by affirming the right to live of the community of al Mufaqara.[31]

In both situations there are multiple ways that visibility is both used and created by "bodies that count" that also operate across different scalar levels. First is the way they work "on the ground" in the day-to-day intimate and always potentially explosive encounters when Palestinians are confronted by soldiers and settlers. In these encounters, the presence of the Israeli or international activist bodies (as people from the community and the activists describe it) serves not to protect Palestinian bodies, but to deflate the always potential violence of the military (and to a lesser extent that of the settlers) that would be exerted on Palestinians if they were "alone." Activists are intelligible to soldiers: they share the same ontological ground and therefore have shared normative scripts. Activists invoke this shared ground in their interactions with soldiers who are then forced to affirm those norms—a process of reminding and recognizing that is impossible for Palestinians to invoke:

> The [foreign] girls is [sic] better with the soldiers, I try and talk to them about the occupation but with the girls they say, you know, like where do you come from? What do you do? [laughs] and the girls can use that. (Sandro, Italian activist, Operation Dove)

> It's good, it allows us to try another way, the soldiers try to make it personal but we can use this to try and take it in another direction—we can then talk to them about the occupation. (Luisa, Italian activist, Operation Dove)

> Having heroically driven the flock down toward the wadi, the soldiers and policemen pick their way over the rocks toward us.
> "You are now in a Closed Military Zone. You have fifteen minutes to get out of here."
> "And just where are we supposed to go?"
> "Down into the wadi, past that curve in the hills."

"And why are you doing this?"

"I work for the brigade commander. Ask him."

"I'll be glad to ask him, but he doesn't want to talk to me."

"You now have fourteen minutes."

"You know what you are doing is illegal," we say. "The Supreme Court ruled in 2004 that the army cannot declare a Closed Military Zone arbitrarily, and it is expressly forbidden to do so if this means denying Palestinian shepherds and farmers access to their lands." (David Shulman, Israeli Ta'ayush activist)

But perhaps the more important way that foreign bodies work to "bring down the violence" of the military and settlers is through countersurveillance and the production of countervisibilities. Through their presence, and increasingly through the use of cameras, they attempt to make the violence entailed in erasure visible. One activist explains it this way:

> When there's an action against, for instance, demolishing a home, everyone is there (activists, the community, soldiers), and the soldiers can get violent. So we do nonphysical interposition to try and keep down the violence of the situation, try and lower the tension. If you use a camera, the soldier is less likely to be violent because he knows it is all on camera. Having a camera, staying close to the Palestinians to make them feel safer, and try and talk to the soldier. (Anna, Operation Dove)

Hisham and the international activists use the human rights language of "documentation" when talking about these countersurveillance measures. And indeed, the texts and videos produced are posted on websites and blogs, written up as reports sent to human rights organizations and other official and nonofficial addresses, and constantly circulate far beyond the spatial confines of Masafer Yatta. Soldiers and settlers fear that reports and images of their violence may become visible to specific circuits where they may actually face consequences for it.[32] This fear then becomes used as a tactic by activists and the communities on the ground, who constantly use cameras in daily accompaniment as well as in mass actions. Here are two descriptions of the operations:

> If I go on my own, it's different how the soldiers act—he'll be in your face, and if you answer him he'll start pushing you around, beating you, but when there's a foreigner filming, his behavior changes completely. He starts behaving better. (Maher, schoolboy shepherd, Atwaneh village)

You know, the video camera, it depends on the situation. If you point the camera in the face of soldiers or settler, they can become more violent, but if you use it further away, it can bring down the level of violence or tension. . . . But also we use it in legal work. We can take evidence, and then their lawyer can't say "No, you are a liar." You can't do nonviolent action without it. (Sandro, Italian activist, Operation Dove)

"Waaargh!!!" the older settler roars and charges us with a rock in his palm. I am afraid, finding myself behind the camera at a settler attack once again. . . . "Stop them!" I shout to the soldiers in the jeep down in the wadi. The settler runs past us to throw the stones at the shepherds. . . . "I will butcher you!" he screams at GH and throws a big rock towards him. GH dodges the rock, thank goodness. I get it all on tape. (Amitai Ben Ami, Israeli Ta'ayush activist)

The soldiers' and settlers' fear that their violence will be caught on tape and potentially made visible becomes a possibility that both activists and the community employ in everyday resistance. Attempting to visibilize the violence of Israel's occupation to especially Israeli but also international publics through popular media has increasingly become a programmatic strategy of activists as well as human rights organizations across the occupied West Bank and Gaza. The Israeli human rights organization B'tselem has since 2007 run a video activism project—giving hundreds of cameras to communities at risk, like those of Masafer Yatta across the West Bank. But catching settler and soldier violence on camera and getting the evidence onto Internet sites is no guarantee that their violence will actually become visible. Kuntsman and Stein have shown how such activist media in the Israeli context enters into a dense field framed by what they call "digital suspicion," a long-standing interpretive practice deployed to undermine Palestinian claims.[33] In the current context these older discourses now couple with the technological realities of digital media and produce competing forms of knowledge and conflictual interpretive communities that open varying political possibilities for both state institutions and activists.[34]

As Stein notes, most of the activist videos from the field are not even posted online.[35] Those that are often remain un-noted save by the communities of activists themselves. And the few who do break through the dense layers of Israeli apathy/suspicion about the occupation's evils and become viral (and therefore visible to Israeli publics) do so because they transgress the dominant frame—and show violence being enacted against the legible or grievable bodies of international and Israeli activists.

The other circumstance in which settler or military violence breaks into visibility within Israeli publics is when the nature of the violence performed by Jewish Israeli bodies transgresses racial and gendered norms of Jewish/Israeli identity. In these cases the identities of the victim remain irrelevant. Thus, one of the few activist videos taken in Masafer Yatta that became viral in Israel was a clip of four settler youth carrying clubs, descending a hill, and coming toward a shepherd and his wife, who they then mercilessly beat. The video created a huge debate in Israel, not because of the beating of the shepherd and his wife, but because of what the settlers were wearing: head coverings that mimicked the iconic and feared image of Palestinian militants.[36] In both of these cases, the violence visited on Palestinians can momentarily appear, but only as the background or shadow of the main subject of the violence—either to grievable bodies or to norms of Jewish/Israeli identity. Outside of these conditions, only in extraordinary instances have Palestinian victims of Israeli violence been able to appear as human to Israeli publics. In the limited cases where they have, it is because they appear as something other than Palestinian (either as an *extremely young* individual child or as an extremely vulnerable individual woman).[37] In both instances, their humanity is individual, exceptional, and singular. An activist named Hisham describes the difference as follows:

> When the settlers tried through violence to stop the kids from reaching the school, we went to Hebron and asked for some of the international solidarity workers there [to come]—they were Americans. . . . The next day the settlers attacked them—the kids and the solidarity workers. People went to hospital—so what happened?—there was media pressure, you know. Americans were attacked and ended up in hospital in south Hebron. . . . Palestinian kid gets attacked, given that he's Palestinian its normal, no one's interested. But because he's an American it's a different situation. (Hisham)

Palestinians from the communities are aware of the way the politics of visibility continues to operate unequally across race and to a lesser extent across gender within activist media practice. Hisham and others prefer to focus on more immediate and critical priorities and achievements: that cameras at the direct level of activism in the field (where they are most successful) can temper and deflect violence and be used to provide counterevidence to the always trumped-up charges used by the police and military when detaining young men from the communities. But a politics of hope also animates the use of cameras and the potential impact of their more mediated effects: the hope that the films produced help rally support and solidarity for their struggle across diverse activist networks and communities and one day may become part of wider projects of making evidentiary claims against the military and settlers.

Gendered Bodies

The differential order of corporeal value at work in Masafer Yatta uses both racial and gender logics. Masculinist norms associating female bodies with vulnerability are clearly operative across the varying bodily encounters and their particular configurations of race, violence, and power—but are constantly opened up to new possibilities and reinscriptions in daily life. The following quotations offer a sense of this process:

> The women and the girls are strong, praise be to God, very strong. When they [soldiers] take a boy we [women] go after them and don't let go until we've taken him back. Even if they use violence we stay with them. Have another biscuit, come on, I'll be upset if you don't. (Um Bahjat, al Mufaqara)

> The first time it was 2002, I remember, the men had gone down to a valley . . . to plow the land, and then the settlers came from the caves and started attacking them with stones. There were lots of people injured— nine people ended up in hospital. When the soldiers came, instead of stopping it they let the attack continue and then started arresting people. From that day women started facing the soldiers and the police, intervening, and trying to stop the men from being arrested. There'd be fewer men taken. It started automatically, and then after that we began to organize it. (Sumaya, head of the women's committee, Atwaneh)

> The Palestinian women defy the military and sit down in front of them, quickly starting a small fire and beginning to make tea. The soldiers push and kick and force them up. For a short eternity they kept on driving the group arbitrarily up the hill past the closed zone. (Amitai Ben Ammi)

Women from the communities are often described as being the front line of collective actions. In demonstrations they are always in the lead, or when someone (usually male) is arrested by the military, it is women who engage physically with the captors in order to "steal back" the captured body. The possibility of using female bodies in this way is based on exploiting the normative order, according to which the female body is invested with a sexed and gendered vulnerability; at the same time, the act works to subvert these norms. Soldiers, Palestinians, and Israeli and international activists all share to varying degrees these heteronormative scripts. Women's bodies, especially orientalized ones, pose a challenge to the masculinist/militarist norms of the soldiers that are framed by masculine defense of the vulnerable/feminized home front. In this equation, women regardless of race become civilianized—and if they are "passive, oppressed Muslim women" this actually works to enable their inclusion into the category of civilian.[38] Thus when these "civilian" female bodies come into confrontation with male military bodies, the sex/gender/racial order that defines "defensive" versus "offensive" bodies becomes completely confounded and threatened. In this encounter, soldiers are left unable to lay claim to their normative truths of masculinist protection of the vulnerable feminine—instead, the whole logic of a settler colonial military might be laid bare for what it is. "And it's like, when we defend and intervene, we women just feel great," Amal of Atwaneh explains. "We can do something—and we've done something."

In the interactions within the community of solidarity (among solidarity activists and men and women from the communities), norms about "local custom" and the importance of respecting their sex/gender boundaries are often invoked. Women from the communities themselves regularly invoke and reproduce these local norms in relation to "outsiders." But when they relate the instances when they have broken them by using them against the soldiers, it is with a jubilance that often accompanies acts of feminine subversion:

> The settlers don't differentiate, they don't care, they'll attack a girl, a woman, but the soldiers have this thing, they freak out if there are foreigners filming there and a settler is attacking a woman or girl. Soldiers will attack or arrest guys, but not women, or only rarely. They're scared of the reaction in the media. But in Mufaqara, when the girls were defending the mosque from being destroyed they arrested them—OK, I mean at the end they don't really differentiate either. (Amal, Atwaneh)

While the military is loath to transgress any female body—including the visible bodies of international and Israeli female activists—the settlers operate according to a different set of norms. All bodies not operating according to the logics of elimination are threats to the collective body of the colony, regardless of sex/gender or race. Anna's comment speaks to this point:

> Now we [international accompaniers] are five women and one boy [sic]. It's the same in other fields—though sometimes it's more equal women and men. . . . The (Palestinian) men here have had to work on themselves. It's not easy to be able to trust twenty-year-old Italian women to accompany them. They are all very respectful—they trust us and we work to deserve their trust. (Anna)

Nonviolent resistance undertaken against settler colonial violence as well as the strategies of protective accompaniment linking ungrievable to grievable bodies all speak to a resistant politics congruent with the feminist geopolitical ethics identified by Koopman.[39] Simultaneously, the work of female bodies protecting male ones in the face of militarist violence suggests how gender norms are transgressed both in the dynamics of everyday resistances to elimination and also in the production of resistant masculine subjectivities—particularly Palestinian ones. Palestinian male bodies are the most directly targeted by and thus most vulnerable to Israeli colonial violence. In addressing the politically subjugated Palestinian masculine body, Julie Peteet has argued that masculine subjectivity reframed humiliation and beatings as rites of passage to manhood in the first Palestinian intifada—a move that reinstated subjugated male bodies as sites of resistant virility.[40] In the orientalizing discourse of aid agencies, Palestinian men, powerless and humiliated by the occupation, reclaim their masculinity by engaging in domestic violence (a claim agencies continue to produce despite all evidence to the contrary).[41]

> All my respect to them [women and girls], it's something to be really proud of. Guys are always the most targeted with imprisonment. . . . When the girls and women come and they sneak in from here and from here and take you back [while being hauled off by soldiers], well, that's a victory for us. Instead of [ending up] being imprisoned and fines and all of that. (Maher, schoolboy shepherd, Atwaneh)

Both of these claims view Palestinian masculine subjectivity as unitary and limited rather than as polyvalent, and open to multiple interpretations and subject positions. In the context of Masafer Yatta, colonial violence enacted against Palestinian male bodies is the norm, and is part of the everyday of being male in this environment. As such, attempting to elude violence while continuing to push back against the politics of elimination becomes prioritized as the more successful act of resistance. One body saved from a beating or a capture while it is involved in retaking stolen land or rebuilding a demolished home becomes in itself a victory when resistant bodies (especially Palestinian male ones) are targeted by sovereign violence. In this understanding, the male body no longer belongs to a separate domain of the masculine; rather, it becomes a site invested with the entire political ethic of the community in resistance, opening up the possibility of reordering norms of masculine/feminine and vulnerability/protection.

As the quotation above by the young Italian female accompanier (Anna) suggests, however, the deordering of normative masculine and feminine subjectivities in the process of struggle (which is necessary for it to succeed) is something that activists and the community are both readily aware of and attend to carefully. And it is particularly in these instances of handing one's body over to another, especially when it is a male body to a female one, that vulnerability opens itself into trust.

Conclusion: Crossing Boundaries / Remaking Spatial and Political Imaginaries

The types of visibilities produced through the activism of using "bodies that count" seems to rely on rather than challenge the racial hierarchies that frame and actively produce Masafer Yatta as a space of hyperprecarity. One might argue that the slippages that occur, those brutal self-images that are usually cast off as "an aberration," might through their constant repetition begin to break open a space in which Palestinians begin to appear as legible, as mournable, as having equal worth to an Israeli or Euro-American "us." But it is actually in the everyday coming together of grievable and ungrievable bodies in the space of Masafer Yatta that we can see how the constant defiance of hierarchies of corporeal value begins to break them down:

> What I mean is, the settlers, when they see the Israeli activist, it brings out more violence in them. The settler, he sees a Palestinian and an Israeli together, and he leaves the Palestinian and goes after the Israeli. (Hisham)

> After a while one of the soldiers begins to scream curses, sharp and thin in the desert air. "You ruiners of Israel, *ochrai yisrael*, you are aiding the enemies of the Jews, degenerates"—he is waving his gun, threatening us [the Israeli activists], fingering the clip. (David Shulman)

"Are you an Arab?" one of the settlers approached Muhammad. "Get out of here!" And then to me: "Are you my brother, or his brother?" (Neve Gordon, Israeli Ta'ayush activist)

Israeli activists pose a profound political challenge to the military and settlers and their racial/spatial imaginary of Masafer Yatta as containing the "us" of (Jewish) Israelis versus the "them" of Palestinians. Not only are they bodies "out of place" (as Israeli/Jewish bodies who are not soldiers or settlers); they are also "our" bodies that have unraveled from "us" and woven themselves into "them," the enemies we aim to eliminate. The rage of soldiers and settlers toward Israeli activists is not simply about their being on the wrong side, but of quite literally embodying an existential threat to the Zionist nationalist imaginary of an ethnically bounded Jewish Israeli nation. Instead, Israeli activists are a constant reminder (or, in the eyes of settlers and soldiers, a nagging insistence) of a possible national future that is not based on ethnic privilege and exceptionalism. Hisham asks, "Before they [Israeli activists] came, what Israelis did we know? Settlers, soldiers, they were the Israelis for us."

Israeli bodies that link themselves to Palestinian ones also subvert the binary ethno-religious logic, increasingly suffusing Palestinian nationalism. On the one hand, there are the effects of Israel's spatial policy of ethnic separation, making the physical interaction between Israeli Jews and West Bank and Gazan Palestinians virtually impossible. In tandem with this, there has been a rise of Islamist rhetorics about the conflict with Israel being "civilizational" in nature. Both have led to a Palestinian nationalist imaginary that increasingly mirrors the ethnic exclusivism of Zionism.

But beyond these more obviously political effects, there are the ways the activists and communities themselves still bounded by these hierarchies and binaries increasingly begin to elude them in relation to each other. And this process opens a space in which transformative relationalities begin to emerge:

We both know that us and the Palestinians—for the world our lives are not worth the same. But the fact that I live in this house, and I sleep and eat like you and run when you call me, and we eat the same food and listen when you want to tell me something—this really tells us both that I do not believe your and my life are not worth the same. Maybe this isn't clear at first—but happens over time. . . . This way of being in a conflict is a way that you become part of it and that really changes those dynamics. We share everything, we share daily life—OK, we share stories about problems with settlers and soldiers, but we also talk about problems of kids and of boyfriends and love problems, or problems of the sheep's milk. . . . And that changes everything. . . . That sharing of daily life inside the conflict—that changes everything. (Anna)

A passport is a good tool with soldiers and police, but what makes your action work here is your total commitment—if you're not committed you are no use here. So what works here is not our passport but our commitment. (Pippo)

Do they offer protection? No, the Israelis and internationals can't protect us. But what they do, let me find the right words . . . They make our existence possible. (Hisham)

"So, who would you say are better here [at struggle]? The [Palestinian] men or women?" Reply: "They're the same." (My joking question and the response of a young man from al Mufaqara)

Week after week, on Saturday morning, we follow him to the fields. Today, like every week, there are women and children—the wonderful, impish children . . . marching with him. We head over the hill and down into the wadi and straight into the fields, which the thieves have plowed. . . . The soldiers are ready. They come at us, they bark, threaten, order us to stop . . . but Sa'id keeps walking until he has crossed the wadi and moved halfway up the next hill. . . . All I can say is that I'll follow Sa'id wherever and whenever he wants me. (David Shulman)

The foreigners here have really helped. They got our story out to the world. When they first came it was strange for people. People were suspicious: Who are they? What do they want? . . . A year passed and then people understood. Now they're like one of the families in the community: there's a wedding and they should come; someone's cooked something special, they send a dish over to them. They've become part of us. (Sumaya, head of the women's committee, Atwaneh)

What I've learned from the people here is how to trust. To trust strangers. To trust in the future. To expect the worst but do the best. (Pippo)

I've learned a lot from Palestinians; maybe the most important is being able to see the future as a huge possibility. Being able to wake up every day and forgive the past and the present and to see a big future ahead. (Anna)

Notes

The narratives used throughout the text are differentially ascribed. The Palestinian and international accompaniers I have given pseudonyms to protect their anonymity; the former for obvious reasons, the latter because their identification could result in summary deportation by Israel. The Israeli activist narratives I have taken from various blogs and activist sites where the authors have felt free to use their full names.

1 See the Israeli human rights organization B'tselem's webpage on "Firing Zone 918" at http://www.btselem.org/publications/fulltext/918, accessed May 3, 2016; also see UN OCHA, "Life in a 'Firing Zone.'"

2 As will be evidenced by the discussion below on the unfolding of the Oslo Accords, I put "peace process" in quotes to demarcate that in the case of Palestine (as in many other cases), peace was simply a different modality for perpetuating violence and dispossession.

3 See various reports on Area C by the United Nations Office of the Coordinator for Humanitarian Affairs, Occupied Palestinian Territories (UN OCHA), including "Displacement and Insecurity in Area C of the West Bank"; "Area C Humanitarian Response Fact Sheet"; and "Restricting Space."

4 This fact is captured well by Peter Lagerquist, whose aim, however, is to show how Israeli human rights lawyers instrumentalized the "false primitivism" of the communities, on behalf of their legal defense. See Lagerquist, "In the Labyrinth of Solitude."

5 See UN OCHA, "Area C Humanitarian Response Fact Sheet"; "Displacement and Insecurity in Area C of the West Bank"; "Life in a 'Firing Zone'"; and "Restricting Space."

6 Mbembe, "Necropolitics," 26; see also his *On the Postcolony*; Agamben, *State of Exception*.

7 Ghanim, "Bio-power and Thanato-politics."

8 Wolfe, "Settler Colonialism," 387–409.

9 Wolfe, "Settler Colonialism," 387–409.

10 Falk, *Unlocking the Middle East*, 114.

11 Mbembe, "Necropolitics," 29. However, what Mbembe's account misses in terms of Palestine is how the constituents of this concatenation are unevenly distributed across different spatial zones of the imperial protectorate's presence and nonpresence in the West Bank and Gaza.

12 Wolfe, "Settler Colonialism," 392.

13 Butler, *Frames of War*, 25.

14 Butler, *Frames of War*, 25–26.

15 In the context of Palestine, Gaza is another zone of hyperprecarity, but one where Israel uses different modalities of violence for its production.

16 Butler, *Frames of War*, 14.

17 For a feminist reading of this process in the context of Palestine see Shalhoub-Kevorkian, "Palestinian Women and the Politics of Invisibility."

18 Weizman, *Hollow Land*.

19 At the same time, plans and money and the whole military/political-economic machinery that builds settlements are kept, if not invisible, opaque. A number of Knesset inquiries have sought to uncover the hidden and complex webs of money, plans, and permissions that connect governmental and extragovernmental organizations and route money from supranational Zionist organizations and philanthropists to the settlement project. All of the settlements have been built through this bureaucratic opaque-ness—a sleight of hand through which the Israeli state's colonial designs that breach international law can be undertaken without directly embarrassing their imperial allies.

20 For an example of how the settler politics of mourning operates see Feige, "Jewish Settlement of Hebron," 323.

21 Butler, *Frames of War*.

22 It seems almost banal to state that any form of Palestinian armed resistance is immediately transposed into the frame of "terrorism" and Israel's "right to defend itself." "Terrorism" becomes a master signifier that occludes and absorbs not only acts of Palestinian armed resistance but a host of other Palestinian nonviolent resistant acts and speech. Attempts to gain membership to the United Nations, and BDS—the movement for boycott, divestment, and sanctions—have all been declared forms of terrorism by various Israeli politicians and their supporters.

23 Butler, *Precarious Life*; Butler, *Frames of War*.

24 Butler, *Precarious Life*; Butler, *Frames of War*.

25 See Hyndman, "Feminist Geopolitics Revisited." The communities of Masafer Yatta are not the first or only West Bank and Gaza communities that have mapped themselves into these new forms of embodied global solidarity politics. The best-known solidarity actions are the weekly actions in the village of Bil'in and other communities attempting to resist land and livelihood dispossession by Israel's "Separation Wall." The global symbol of these on the ground solidarities in Palestine is the American activist Rachel Corrie, who was killed by an Israeli military bulldozer in March 2013 while she and other international activists were trying to prevent the Israeli military's ongoing devastation of Palestinians' homes in Rafah, Gaza. On these activisms in Bil'in see Jawad, "Staging Resistance in Bil'in," 128–142; Roei, "Molding Resistance." For critical self-reflections by Euro-American accompaniers on the politics of bodies that count in Palestine see Stamatopoulou-Robbins, "The Joys and Dangers of Solidarity in Palestine."

26 See Koopman, "Alter-geopolitics."

27 Koopman, "Alter-geopolitics," 202

28 For an overview of the ethics and history of the protective accompaniment movement see Mahoney and Eguren, *Unarmed Bodyguards*.

29 Along with discussion of these problematics in Koopman's "alter-geopolitics" see

also her "Cutting through Topologies," 825–847, as well as " 'Mona, Mona, Mona!' " See also Henderson, "Citizenship in the Line of Fire"; Coy, "The Privilege Problematic in International Nonviolent Accompaniment's Early Decades" and " 'We Use It but We Try Not to Abuse It.' " See also Hyndman, "Feminist Geopolitics Revisited."

30 Since 2004 the communities have had a constant presence of young Italians sponsored by a Catholic-linked organization, Operation Dove, which also has accompaniers working in Albania and Colombia. Israeli activists with jobs and lives just over the Green Line come regularly on Fridays or Saturdays.

31 See "PSP Activists Join Building Project in Um Faqara," *Palestine Solidarity Project*, http://palestinesolidarityproject.org/2012/05/27/psp-activists-join-building -project-again-in-um-fagara/, accessed May 4, 2016.

32 This fear by (most) soldiers and (many) settlers rests on a number of grounds. Most fundamental is the Zionist imaginary of belonging to the liberal West and the desire to protect this in its own self-representation as well as in projections of it globally. The huge and ongoing investments by the Israeli state in its global image maintenance attests to this. The Israeli military has a double investment in the protection of its liberal humanist image given that in a number of countries (the United Kingdom, Spain) there are standing indictments against specific Israeli generals for war crimes. Fear of indictments for war crimes among the senior military has not only led to the creation of a huge legal apparatus within the Israeli military to inform what actions might be indictable internationally; it has also led them to create strong internal military sanctions against foot soldiers whose acts are caught by visual media or posted on social media. For such cases see "Israeli Soldiers are Fighting for their Right to Point Guns at Young Palestinians," *Vice News Online*, https://news.vice.com/article/israeli-soldiers-are-fighting -for-their-right-to-point-guns-at-young-palestinians, accessed May 4, 2016; "Fleeing Soldiers Claim Officers were Afraid of Media Photos," *Israel National News Online*, http://www.israelnationalnews.com/News/News.aspx/163017# .VOcvy8bLBpl, accessed May 4, 2016; "Anger Over Ex-Israeli Soldier's Facebook Photos of Palestinian Prisoners," *The Guardian Online*, http://www.theguardian .com/world/2010/aug/16/israeli-soldier-photos-palestinian-prisoners, accessed May 4, 2016.

33 Kuntsman and Stein, "Digital Suspicion, Politics and the Middle East."

34 Kuntsman and Stein, "Digital Suspicion, Politics and the Middle East."

35 See Stein, "Viral Occupation Cameras and Networked Human Rights in the West Bank."

36 Another infamous example is the video of a settler woman chanting "Inti sharmuta" ("You are a whore") through a mesh screen at the Palestinian woman living next door to the settlement in Hebron. See " 'Sharmuta Video'—Settler Harassment of Palestinians in Hebron," *Youtube*, https://www.youtube.com/watch?v =KUXSFsJVo84, accessed May 4, 2016.

37 In terms of violence against Palestinian children, the July 2013 arrest of a five-year-old boy in Hebron (captured on camera by B'tselem) was the first time since the

killing of Muhammad al Durra in 2001 that the Israeli military's violence toward children broke into visibility. "Settlers Attack Palestinian Woman in Hebron," a video from 2011, most likely broke through the frame because the settlers in question were themselves children, including girls.

38 In Israeli discourse, the tenacity of the sexual/orientalist trope of the Palestinian woman as passive, vulnerable, and victim of Islamic patriarchy is so powerful as to reinscribe the female suicide bomber as such a vulnerable victim. See Hasso, "Discursive and Political Deployments by/of the 2002 Palestinian Women Suicide Bombers/Martyrs," 535–566. And in both Israeli wars on Gaza, the IDF's body count of Palestinian civilian deaths was composed solely of women and children. Palestinian men were by definition "armed combatants."

39 Koopman, "Alter-geopolitics."

40 Peteet, "Male Gender and Rituals of Resistance in the Palestinian Intifada."

41 For the most insightful and sustained critiques of this donor "common sense" on Palestinian domestic violence see Johnson, "'Violence All around Us'" and "Violence, Gender-Based Violence and Protection."

CHAPTER 9

When Antigone Is a Man

Feminist "Trouble" in the Late Colony

NÜKHET SIRMAN

In this essay I attempt to think through feminist theory and activism in Turkey in light of the challenge posed to it by an armed political movement that is in the process of writing and practicing its own feminism. It is about a man on hunger strike who accepts his role as an "Antigone," and it is about a politics of transgression and vulnerability. It looks into the questions raised by such acts of transgression and vulnerability, and how these subvert accepted theories of gender, the subject, and the subject of rights. It describes a set of events, acts, and discourses that require a complex analysis of a gendered political practice that has been developed by the Kurdish movement, especially by women. It tries to trace the intricate flux and reflux from vulnerability to transgression, back to vulnerability and then to resistance. The aim is to think vulnerability in tandem with transgression rather than strength or impermeability. The essay argues that every transgression is a willingness to open up to a vulnerability that is also a claim to another way of establishing relations with the world. It is a form of transgression that places the subject outside the terms of accepted politics, whether feminist, leftist, or nationalistic. The subject thus becomes vulnerable to blows from all sides, including the academy. It is a vulnerability that the subject embraces willingly, ready for the destruction as well as the creation that it will bring. Hence it is difficult to write about as an academic, in an academic publication, aimed at an academic audience.

This is a difficult piece to write because of trouble regarding the subject of transgression, or its being posited as an ontological fact, especially in conditions of the late colony, where one is compelled to transgress. The question that the notion of vulnerability raises is a question about the subject: who or what is vulnerable, or is vulnerability always an issue of the subject? In their discussion on dispossession, Athena Athanasiou and Judith Butler debate whether dispossession is an ontological state or whether it is more appropriate to talk about a *becoming dispossessed*.[1] Similarly, I would like to be able to talk about the becoming vulnerable not of a subject, but of a position, a relation to power, that brings with it unintelligibility and thereby vulnerability. This position of vulnerability follows from the act of transgression, an act that is not necessarily taken up as a form of performative politics, but as an act that one is compelled to perform because of the place one occupies in the existing scheme of power and intelligibility. The question then becomes: what or who is compelled to perform/act in a particular way? Thus, what follows will be about subjects compelled to act in particular ways. These actions will count as a political performance only after a history of struggle, transgression, and vulnerability has marked them as subjects capable of political performance. Otherwise, they *are* not. It is thus that I talk about subjects whose transgression makes them vulnerable.

I will first single out the different modes through which transgressions are effected: I first look at the case of a man who demands that the state return the remains of his dead guerrilla brother, and then goes on a hunger strike when his request remains unheeded, at which point a woman journalist links his act to Antigone and finally the man ends up by accepting the Antigone name. I then look at the agonistic relation between feminists from the Kurdish movement and feminism as practiced by feminists in Istanbul within and outside the academy who adopt a largely European second-wave approach to women's issues. By looking at the reactions of Istanbul feminists—who, although by no means homogeneous, have by and large constructed the hegemonic feminist discourse and practice in Turkey to date[2]—to the texts published by Kurdish feminists, I show that mainstream feminism is unable to address the problems posed by the kind of vulnerability assumed by Kurdish feminists. This, I hope, enables me to ask questions about the possibility of a politics of justice and equality based on acts and discourses that transgress the limits of intelligibility, plausibility, and feasibility established by the sovereign. In other words, the issue at stake is whether or not there are limits to a politics of vulnerability, whether or not such a politics becomes an obstacle to being recognized by other forms of politics carried out in the name of justice and equality.

Acts of Transgression

On May 16, 2011, more than three hundred members of the Peace and Democracy Party (BDP)[3] crossed the border with Iraq to retrieve the bodies of twelve Kurdish Workers Party (PKK)[4] guerrillas killed by the Turkish armed forces. The military had declared that they would not bring the bodies back for burial and would shoot anybody attempting to do so. On September 4, 2013, the Nusaybin BDP mayor Ayşe Gökkan declared to the daily *Radikal* that on Sunday, September 1, the remains of a guerrilla who had just been buried in a newly established guerrilla cemetery in Urfa's Suruç province had been taken by the military forces and forty-three tombs belonging to PKK guerrillas had been desacralized. She was then reported as saying, "That body belongs to all Kurds, not just to the family, and the people will not be silent in the face of such treatment of remains that they feel belong to them. An apology has to come forth."

These are just two examples of the struggle that has been going on in Turkey in the context of the multifaceted war/fight/struggle between the Turkish state and the PKK. They show the extent to which this struggle is about which lives are deemed to be sacred—in other words, human and therefore grievable. The slashes in the previous sentence can be repeated with every word and phrase used when talking about this struggle, and to a large extent, this essay is concerned with these different ways of naming—with the power to name and assign intelligibility to different bodies and actors. Another slash can be introduced regarding the parties of the struggle. According to the Turkish establishment, the army is fighting with terrorists, while according to the PKK, the Kurdish people are fighting the Turkish state. This struggle is now almost thirty years old and has been punctuated by many cease-fires; the last started sometime in January 2013.

The struggle led to almost 50,000 dead (mostly Kurds—civilians as well as guerrillas); 1.2 million people underwent forced migration: approximately 4,000 villages were emptied of their inhabitants by the armed forces; between 1990 and 2001, 5,000 civilians died violent deaths (including death in custody, disappearances, summary executions, murders by "unknown perpetrators") according to official figures; and between 1997 and 2012, 363 women, 264 of them Kurdish, reported rape and sexual harassment in custody.

As usual, though, these figures do not mean much. They are the sort of commodity states usually transact in. More descriptive is the struggle over dead bodies described above, a struggle which indicates that, as with Creon's denial of a burial to Polynices, the sacredness accorded to the human is denied by state security forces to Kurdish insurrectionists. Overall, the words quoted by Achille Mbembe to describe what he calls the late colony are a much more accurate description of what happened especially from the 1990s onward:

> To live under late modern occupation is to experience a permanent condition of "being in pain": fortified structures, military posts, and roadblocks everywhere; buildings that bring back painful memories of humiliation, interrogations, and beatings; curfews that imprison hundreds of thousands in their cramped homes every night from dusk to daybreak; soldiers patrolling the unlit streets, frightened by their own shadows; children blinded by rubber bullets; parents shamed and beaten in front of their families; soldiers urinating on fences, shooting at the rooftop water tanks just for fun, chanting loud offensive slogans, pounding on fragile tin doors to frighten the children, confiscating papers, or dumping garbage in the middle of a residential neighborhood; border guards kicking over a vegetable stand or closing borders at whim; bones broken; shootings and fatalities—a certain kind of madness.[5]

Indeed, according to sociologist İsmail Beşikçi, Kurdistan is what he calls an "international colony," as it was divided into four pieces after the First World War.[6] Ever since the establishment of the Turkish Republic in 1923, Kurdish rights have been a vexed issue, often erupting in uprisings and massacres.[7] Kurds had been organized in tribes forming the buffer zone between the Ottoman and Safavid Empires, and with the establishment of the Turkish Republic they not only lost the relative autonomy they enjoyed locally, but also were put under more and more pressure by the centralized government to accept the political and cultural system of modern Turkey.[8] The official nationalist discourse in Turkey denies difference to Kurds, claiming that they are not really a separate ethnic or political entity and that it is impossible to talk about colonization of territories that have been under Turkish rule since the eleventh century. These claims and counterclaims turn the very assertion of the status of colony into a transgressive act.

The Kurdish movement also maintained until 1999 that Kurdistan had been a colony since the days of the Ottoman Empire. Since his capture in 1999, Abdullah Öcalan, the imprisoned leader and major theoretician of the PKK, has stopped using the colonialism argument, concentrating instead on what he calls a "democratic" instead of a "nationalist" nation and locating its main demands within a framework of human rights rather than independence. On its part, the Turkish security forces have inflicted all of the acts described by Mbembe on the Kurdish population, acts which in their totality amount to what the Kurds call "the nineties." Indeed, in return for claiming a separate Kurdistan, the Kurdish population as a whole has been living in a necro-politics, or a life subjected to the power of death only possible in conditions of the late colony.[9] The Kurdish movement[10] has responded to this form of subjugation in various ways, including military operations of a guerrilla variety, forms of civil disobedience of the sort depicted above (the crossing of the border), academic and political journals that popularize the various theories of resistance produced by Abdullah Öcalan, various newspapers and news agencies that offer a genuine alternative to the press in Turkey, and a series of legal political parties that have maneuvered within the terms of the rather stringent antiterrorist laws of Turkey yet still have been declared unlawful by the Turkish courts.[11] The armed wing of the movement began to attack the Turkish armed forces in August 1984, and this inaugurated a protracted war that has lasted more than thirty years. Many young people from villages in the Kurdish regions have taken up arms against what they saw as the oppression of the state.[12] The result was what the armed forces have called a low-intensity war in the rural areas with no prospect of reaching a definitive end.[13] Since its switch in perspective from national independence to a democratic nation, the movement has articulated demands within the field of political and cultural rights and has diverted more and more of its attention to creating bottom-up forms of politics at the level of the village and the neighborhood, such as new forms of municipal government and new forms of academies within which every minute aspect of everyday life is scrutinized and divested of what have been called forms of capitalist modernity.[14]

The acts of transgression that I describe above have been accompanied by a powerful discourse of liberation and ethnic rights. "That body belongs to all Kurds," the statement by Gökkan, is an example of the kind of transgressive discourse I want to talk about. This is a discourse that effects a double motion: on the one hand it claims those traditional forms of organizing the passage of the person between life and death, yet by claiming possession of the body in the name of an ethnic group, it transgresses those very forms that assign the body to the genealogical family. This act of transgression makes sense in the context where the Turkish security forces have often not allowed families to bury their dead, thus marking the bodies as terrorist and ungrievable.[15] This essay will deal with one form of the gendered political practice that this resistance has produced.

Antigone Is a Man

Hüsnü Yıldız started a hunger strike in the province of Tunceli in the northeast of Turkey on June 10, 2011, in order to obtain the remains of his brother, Ali Yıldız, a guerrilla who had been killed in 1997 during a confrontation with the Turkish armed forces. Hüsnü Yıldız had learned that his brother had been buried in a mass grave on military soil, and had tried in vain to retrieve the remains through the courts. He then wrote a letter addressed to intellectuals, writers, and journalists. Yıldız, in this letter, describes his efforts to retrieve his brother's remains and says, "My family does not possess tanks and cannon. We do not have the power to enact laws nor make [public] decisions. We have our bodies. So it is that I have turned my body into a weapon of struggle and started a hunger strike. Because I do not possess any other weapon." The letter, by juxtaposing the dead guerrilla who struggled with his weapons and Yıldız, himself, as his brother, having no weapon other than his body, already poses a challenge to the discourse of the state, which treats dead guerrillas simply as terrorists trying to destroy the unity of the nation. He states that, as an elder brother, he wants to have the remains of his brother returned to him, and he claims that everyone has a right to have a proper tomb. Yet he also demands that the state opens all mass graves, and thus, like Gökkan, speaks in the name of all dead guerrillas and does not limit his act to a kinship obligation. Moreover, Hüsnü Yıldız is not the only person who had to struggle to obtain or bury the remains of Kurdish fighters.[16]

On August 1, fifty days into Hüsnü Yıldız's hunger strike, Sennur Sezer, a feminist leftist poet and activist, wrote a column in the newspaper *Evrensel* titled "An Antigone in Dersim"[17] in which she summarizes the plot of the play and quotes Yıldız's letter at length. She describes Antigone as a heroine who knew that all deaths require a burial and asserts that Antigone is killed for fighting for this right. She concludes by saying, "The only thing I can add to this [Yıldız's letter] is that after 2500 years Antigone still lives and still struggles for the right to a tomb."[18] For Sezer, the gender of Antigone does not seem to matter even though she defines herself as a feminist. That is not the case for other feminists who took up the case and who saw in Antigone the power of women to resist the sovereign, but even these feminists continued to hail Yıldız as an Antigone.[19] Finally Yıldız himself also declared that Sezer was correct in saying that Antigone lived on this soil and that all he wanted was the remains of his brother.

When Antigone is a man, it raises the question of what transgressions have been effected by this gender switch. This transgression operates through a reformulation, a reiteration, a fixation that expands the debates surrounding the figure of Antigone. That Antigone represents transgression is a point that has been underscored by numerous readings. For Lacan and Irigaray, Antigone signifies the bloodshed or "the zone from which the unspeakable truth about the criminal nature of the law might be spoken."[20] For Butler, Antigone stands for a crisis of representation of the classical structural accounts of familial arrangements, thereby transgressing the norms of kinship.[21]

What does the figure of the male Antigone transgress, displace, and deform? Is Hüsnü Yıldız, the man seeking his brother's remains, involved in an impersonation of Antigone, a gender reversal meant to highlight the vulnerability of the self? The action that Hüsnü Yıldız is an agent of is the hunger strike. He has put his body in peril in order to expose the immorality of the actions of state security forces. This is an act that places the actor in a position of vulnerability and is in line with other such acts deliberately committed by the Kurdish movement, such as hunger strikes, refusals to give evidence in courts in Turkish, addressing public audiences in Kurdish, refusing to describe the PKK as a terrorist organization, refusing the legitimacy of state justice by solving disputes and petty crimes within party structures, and sitting in Galatasaray Square in Istanbul to demand the punishment of state security forces responsible for the disappearance of their kin. What these actions undertake in response to necropolitics is to remove the repressive policies from the domain of the political and place them within the domain of the moral. This amounts to an attempt to delegitimize the state itself, as it is presently constituted. The immorality of denying a proper burial becomes equivalent to letting a man die a little every single day in full view of the public. This act, of which Hüsnü Yıldız is the subject, is a repetition of similar hunger strikes undertaken by numerous other Kurdish actors, including members of Parliament, political prisoners, and even a mayor. In each case, the protest is saying: I/we are human. And with each repetition, the hunger strike ceases to be the action of one subject and becomes instead the action of a whole population. The "I" slides easily into a "we" who is/are also saying "you leave me/us with no other option but to put my/our bodies in peril." In other words, these subjects become subjects by subjecting their own bodies to the same kind of treatment they face in their everyday lives. The policies pursued by the state, including forced evictions from villages, crop burning, destroying winter supplies, and closing off pasturelands to grazing, all amount to destroying the means of livelihood of the rural Kurdish population and hence are a way of starving them.[22] Refusing to treat patients if they cannot speak Turkish, refusing to rent houses to forced migrants, and not employing Kurds for menial jobs are urban ways of not letting Kurds live, and these amount to a more indirect consequence of state-backed militarist discourse against the Kurds. It is in this sense that Kurds are compelled to act in the way they do; they are, in other words, compelled to transgress. In the process, they become collective subjects rather than individual self-present actors in possession of their bodies.[23]

When Sennur Sezer labels Hüsnü Yıldız as Antigone, another move is effected. On the one hand, Hüsnü Yıldız's act is individualized and then placed within the framework of a rights discourse. He becomes a man seeking the right of a dead brother to a proper burial. But at the same time, a confusion of genders is created that allows a reading based on transgression.[24] If Antigone occupied the place of the man in deciding to bury her brother, Hüsnü Yıldız seems to occupy the place of the woman in claiming the right to bury his brother's remains. In other words, the disruption caused to gender identity transgresses both gender and kinship norms,[25] and, I would argue, also raises questions about who the subject of rights might be. Judging by Mayor Gökkan's words, it is not only the immediate family that has the right to see the dead properly buried, but a larger collectivity defined by its acts of resistance. This is not simply an ethnic group or a political party, but all those who have been united by common suffering at the hands of the same immoral power. Thus, the right is no longer possessed by an individual, as in Sezer's version; rather, it raises the whole question of who the proper bearer of rights might be.

Finally, apart from confusing the subject, the apparent gender reversal also raises questions about the ontology of gender itself. The political practice of the Kurdish movement indicates the direction such a questioning must take. When PKK guerrillas were killed over the border, the first to go to retrieve the bodies were in fact women, accompanied by members of the BDP, thus putting into effect once again a becoming-Antigone, though it does not get named as such. Women have been sitting every Saturday in Galatasaray Square in Istanbul for five hundred weeks or more to demand that the state release information about their disappeared relatives. Women have also stood for peace, by throwing on the ground between fighting parties their white head scarves, the traditional way women were to stop fighting.[26] An organization called Mothers of Peace was established during the 1990s, when murders and disappearances were daily events in the Kurdish regions and in Istanbul.[27] This turning of Kurdish women into icons of resistance was accompanied by the large number of young women recruited to the fighting units of the PKK and to the legal and semilegal parties, journals, and associations working in Turkey. Finally, as described by Handan Çağlayan, the party placed women at the center of its ideological practice, first as goddesses representing the identity of the Kurdish nation, and then as true comrades-in-arms, so that now women stand for the true revolutionary figure of the Kurdish movement, a force that could transform the whole society, if its power was understood.[28]

Next I turn to this discourse of feminization to address other sorts of transgressions and vulnerabilities that the Kurdish political movement undertakes.

Outside the Canon: The Culture of Rape and *Jineoloji*

Naming Hüsnü Yıldız as Antigone has to be placed within the context of the gendered politics of the Kurdish movement.[29] A man seeking the proper burial of his brother's remains is feminized in the sense that he becomes as vulnerable as a woman. Becoming vulnerable, in the political practice of the Kurdish movement, is nothing but the enactment, or perhaps performance, of a vulnerability to which one has already been subjected.[30] Being vulnerable and becoming vulnerable are merged in a political practice that places the troubling term "woman" at the center of its discourse and practice. According to Handan Çağlayan, the Kurdish movement sees woman as "the slave of slaves," and to eliminate slavery from the society as a whole, he urges women to renounce all the kinship ties that pin them down, bringing down the whole society and men with them. In this sense, the liberation of women is also the liberation of Kurdistan.[31] These ideas are articulated in texts that circulate widely within the Kurdish women's movement and are related to two concepts that have been put forward by Abdullah Öcalan and that end up by placing Kurdish feminists outside the feminist canon articulated by Istanbul feminists, whose discursive and political practice can be depicted as the hegemonic feminism of Turkey. Locating themselves in this outside, Kurdish feminists once again raise the issue of vulnerability as a becoming that is willingly embraced.

One of these concepts is summarized by the term "culture of rape" and has been used to designate the morality with which the Turkish state waged war against the Kurdish movement. Established, as it is, on the basis of patriarchal ideology, this morality is characterized by force, appropriation, usurpation, seizure by violence, dispossession, and militarism. "Institutionalized sovereignty" is the way a woman from the movement describes the concept:

Our guide Apo [Abdullah Öcalan] has depicted the ideological infrastructure of the culture of rape when he said that: "gender ideology has, since its inception, denoted sovereign ideology. It is closely related to the formation of class and of sovereignty." Sexism and its ideology is the counter-revolution of the natural community and its woman-led free culture. It is a counter-revolution effected on the person of the woman and it is a counter-revolution carried out against the woman, and with her, against society. This counter-revolution has changed the course of history.[32]

These propositions are based on a grand narrative of history that claims that the culture of rape has been around for five thousand years and that capitalist modernity is its latest version. It is a mode of violent appropriation of nature, of the people and their labor, and of women. It is a practice, a mode of sovereignty, and an ideology that only begins with the rape of women; in reality, the whole society becomes the subject of rape, and in societies where a politics of countering this culture is not put into action, society undergoes this sort of rape on an everyday basis. The culture of rape signals the breaking of a people's will. Kurdish women are called to struggle against this culture of rape, and this will mean struggling for the freedom of both their gender and their national identity. Thus, in this formulation, women are asked to fight for their genders as well as their nation, the subordination of which takes place through identical means. In this view, what is called institutionalized masculinity is a form of colonialism that targets women as well as other assets of the natural community, and women are called upon to rebel against this masculinity, which manifests itself through child brides, the exchange of sisters, honor killings, and all kinds of violence against women, including domestic violence and forced prostitution.

The notion of the culture of rape makes sense only within the larger framework of a new revolutionary science within whose terms the Kurdish movement sees itself as acting. *Jineoloji*, the second term introduced by Öcalan, is the science of woman, and it is supposed to refer not just to women but to all areas of life, including politics and morality. Emine Ayna, previously BDP MP for Diyarbakır, introduces the concept in a newspaper interview in the following way:

Struggling in the domain of politics is not sufficient if we want to struggle against the system to solve the problem. This patriarchal system organizes itself in all domains of life, ranging from science, religion, politics, to philosophy, art, and aesthetics. The only way to struggle against all of these is to revise history from its beginnings. We need to revise all areas of science, the social sciences, the natural sciences, the medical sciences, to overhaul its literature, write a completely new literature. *Jineoloji* is what will realize this project.[33]

This attempt to rethink the very terms of the academy, including all social sciences, borrows largely from Öcalan's reading of Murray Bookchin, an ex-Marxist who had put forward a theory for an ecological, democratic society which he called "communalism."[34] This society, renamed "democratic confederalism" by Öcalan, could be brought about only through a thorough debunking of the "analytic, objective, experimental, cold-blooded and rationalist science."[35] This thinking led, according to the editor of a special issue on *jineoloji* of the journal *Demokratik Modernite*, to a dichotomous form of thinking based on the subject/object distinction, which, in turn, made it possible to produce male sovereignty and the exploitation of women by men, of slaves by the master, and of society by the state. This amounted to a man's science, to which the Kurdish movement had to respond by positing a woman's science.[36] But, rather than an already established science, jineoloji is proposed as an open-ended call to all women's organizations to develop together the terms of this new science that will have to be, above all, moral.

On the basis of this call, members of the Democratic Free Women's Movement (DFWM), organized as it is as an autonomous entity within the Kurdish movement, have, by calling meetings and circulating texts that explained the concept, sought to engage the feminists of Istanbul to respond.[37] However, feminists and feminist academics unequivocally rejected this call, baffled by a terminology that was totally foreign to them.[38] They were angered by what they felt was an attempt to encompass all feminisms and thereby assert a kind of domination over groups and initiatives that prided themselves on being autonomous from any other political project.[39] The majority of feminists writing in the journals that influenced feminist thought described themselves as antimilitarists and were already quite critical of the use of violence by the Kurdish movement. They felt that the term "science of woman" fixed and essentialized the category "woman," and that as such it was a form of violence and would buttress another form of power.[40] Having come from leftist organizations of the 1970s, many influential feminists had long claimed that the only way to struggle for women was to stop thinking in terms of major revolution and to concentrate on the everyday. After all, the personal was political! The Kurdish women, by contrast, seemed to argue that feminism was to be the true revolution, that it provided the tools that would act as the spring-board from which all areas of life could be reorganized.[41] Taking the term "science of women" to mean "science *about* women" rather than "science *by* women"—that is, by those who have been subordinated by science—feminists were confused about a move that both criticized science and at the same time claimed it. Feminists in Istanbul were also disappointed with the kind of criticism Kurdish feminists brought to bear on feminism. They argued that feminism already encompassed many of the issues raised by the concept and that the critique of feminism it developed was a result of an ignorance of feminist theory, which they saw as a critique of the male-centered knowledge/science institutionalized in the academy. Ultimately, they felt, this was another move revealing the nationalism inherent in the Kurdish movement.

The concept of the culture of rape fared no better. Some, such as anthropologist Sibel Özbudun, maintain that the phrase makes an erroneous use of the term "culture" both politically and academically, since cultures are psychosocial deposits that change very slowly and that calling rape a "culture" means accepting that it would be very difficult to eradicate.[42] Other feminists have claimed that the Kurdish movement has misunderstood not only what culture is, but also what gender is all about. They argue that the formulation repeated the male view that equates women with the soil, with nature and with the home, trapping women within a specified location in society.[43] Most of these critiques stem from the political practice of the feminists in Istanbul that traces its intellectual antecedents to the second-wave feminism of Europe and have largely not made postcolonial forms of feminist struggle part of their political practice despite their acquaintance with it.[44] Furthermore, many feminists were quite unhappy with the fact that it is a man, the leader of the Kurdish movement, who articulated what was claimed to be feminist theory. Finally, feminists felt that new concepts such as jineoloji and "culture of rape" served to draw the attention of the rank and file away from "real" feminism, which would necessarily entail confrontations between men and women within the Kurdish movement.

Women belonging to the DFWM countered these criticisms by repeatedly asserting that only with the science of jineoloji can they feel they are the subject of political discourse. In their view, feminist discourse, centering as it does on domestic violence, cannot address the violence that women suffer under conditions of necropolitics, but the notion of the "culture of violence" does. Explaining within a single theoretical framework the atrocious conditions women have lived under, both now and in the traditional kinship order, imparts a sense of satisfaction and agency to Kurdish feminists.[45] Thus, to the despair of Turkish feminists who seek strategic alliances with them, they are deeply grateful to their leader. But whatever they are, the women of the Kurdish political movement are not just vulnerable—they do not only resist. They are in the process of imagining and materially instituting another kind of society, while at the same time daring the Turkish authorities by placing themselves in situations of vulnerability.[46]

These comments bring us back to issues of transgression and vulnerability. I take the women from the DFWM as calling on other women to recognize that their transgression is a product of their vulnerability and that a feminism that does not address this condition can be of no help to them. Nazan Üstündağ, a sociologist, in an article in the Kurdish daily, *Özgür Gündem*, claims that through the term *jineoloji*, the DFWM is engaging in a postcolonial discourse and practice.[47] If, as Stuart Hall has argued, the colonial is both an ontology and an epistemology, then the postcolonial means making terms such as "culture," "science," and "woman" "operat[e] under erasure"—that is, "subject[ing them] to a deep and thorough-going critique, exposing their assumptions as a set of foundational effects."[48] It means going on using these terms but only in their deconstructed form, knowing that they are terms through which colonialism has maintained its domination, and therefore using them against or alongside their subjugating content. Thus, rather than fixing the term of "woman" in the "science of woman," women in the DFWM search for "different ways of staging the encounter between colonizing societies and their others" and attempt to "go beyond" the terms set by colonial forms of science and knowledge.[49] For the DFWM, "woman" is not simply the object of their new proposed science but is both its object and its subject; in other words, they imagine a form of knowledge where the dichotomy between subject and object will no longer hold. "Under erasure," "woman" is, to use the terms proposed a long time ago by Teresa de Lauretis, both the "Woman" of representation and the "woman" of the real that is unrepresentable.[50] Like the subject of feminism as described by de Lauretis, the women of the DFWM move in and out of gender as ideological representation, this time exposing not only the terms of the "sex-gender system," but also what de Lauretis calls the "space-off"—the space not represented yet implied (unseen), of the (white?) feminist discourse articulated by Istanbul feminists.[51] But since the party no longer describes the situation of Kurdistan as a colony, Kurdish feminists, like their Turkish counterparts, do not work with concepts from postcolonial feminist theory. Their Marxism and their universalism preclude them from seeing themselves marked by any form of indigenousness or blackness (as in the case of black feminism).

To live under "late modern occupation,"[52] then, is to be compelled to fall outside the feminist canon, to risk being unintelligible and therefore to transgress the limits of feminist discourse. It is to say that Antigone is a man and that a science of woman should be possible. It is to claim that Kurdish women are not like the earth or the hearth, that is, vessels who will faithfully develop the seed, while also affirming that, indeed, that is what they are in representation. It is saying that women are at the same time both the Kurdish woman depicted as the victim in representation who has been raped, tortured, and displaced and the smiling fighter defending Kobanê, the small Kurdish town on the Turco-Syrian border under attack by the Islamic State. It is to become because one is, and to be, because one has become. It is to live with these contradictions, which are both the causes and the effects of their vulnerability as colonized subjects. It is to introduce trouble in feminist discourse and make it productive.

Conclusion

When Antigone is a man and the leader of a guerrilla force is a feminist who talks about the culture of rape and proposes a science of women as a way of revolutionizing society, the effect is one of transgression. What is transgressed at the immediate level are the gender norms of the nation, and of kinship. But there is also a transgression of the language of science, which is written in the excessive mode, with none of the caution and the caveats of the language of the academy. It is a language that poses as science and thereby exposes all science as saying more than it claims to have said. Finally, the language of feminism is transgressed in the name of feminism. But, as I have also claimed, each of these moves, every one of these transgressions, leaves the subject of this language in an even more vulnerable position.

Charting the trajectory taken by three feminine figures in representation, I have demonstrated that these figures cannot enjoy unchallenged presence, since they have to be treated as operating "under erasure." The figure of a male Antigone raises the question of whether Antigone is necessarily a woman and a self-present subject. The notion of the culture of rape puts into question the figure of the Kurdish woman as victim in colonial representation. Finally, the category of "woman" itself is rendered unstable through the proposition of a science of woman. All of these terms—"culture," "science," and "woman"—as well as notions of the subject, terms central to the tenets of science and of feminism, are deployed so as to reveal the space-off from which they have been articulated with certainty. As the position of power that science and feminism occupy are exposed, the insistence that the chains of signification they set into motion are not closed off signals an invitation to think through these chains together and offers the possibility that the dialogue about representation and the everyday may be conducted differently.

One final question remains. When Antigone is a man and the phrase "culture of rape" is meant to describe both the depletion of the environment by the state and the violation of women under custody, and "jineoloji" denotes the science of women, which is meant to go beyond feminism, will the Kurdish political movement be aligned with justice and equality? In this essay I have argued that, under conditions of the late colony, vulnerability and transgression may very well operate in an endless chain of claustrophobic causation. This almost inevitable concatenation, I would suggest, is what we call resistance. This form of resistance does not produce subjects of resistance, or objects of knowledge, but places these positions in constant ambiguity, creating both unintelligibility and unease in the canon. The unease is about a becoming. Feminist fears that the becoming-woman of a man and the becoming-sovereign of the Kurdish political movement may lead to more concentration of power in the hands of Kurdish nationalism cannot be totally ignored. Becoming, after all, is a movement that can be understood not as a movement in only one direction, but as a series of movements that are reversible and that have been reversible, dependent, as they are, on whatever else happens in their vicinity. This "whatever else" includes alliances with feminists as well as other developments in the Middle East, such as the opportunities and the problems presented by the Syrian conflict. In other words, Antigone as a man signals a state of vulnerability that keeps open both the possibility that masculinity, science, and culture will be questioned and the possibility that they will be reasserted. Vulnerability as a state of instability will always keep questions open, make decisions reversible, and allow the formation of new configurations of power and resistance.

Notes

1 Butler and Athanasiou, *Dispossession*, 5.
2 Istanbul has, since the 1980s, been the center from which feminist theory and practice have been produced in Turkey. Journals such as *feminist, Kaktüs* in the

1980s, *Pazartesi* in the 1990s, and *Amargi* and *Feminist Politika* in the 2000s have set women's unpaid labor and domestic violence as the main issues that feminism would be dealing with. The subordination of women within the gendered role of wife and mother has been the main concern of this feminism, which takes the state as the main actor that perpetrates this subordination.

3 In Turkish the Peace and Democracy Party is the Barış ve Demokrasi Partisi.

4 The Partiya Karkerên Kurdistan, or Kurdish Workers' Party, is a guerrilla force that has been involved in armed insurrection in Turkey since the early 1980s. See Güneş, *The Kurdish National Movement in Turkey*, for a recent account.

5 Hass, *Drinking the Sea at Gaza*, quoted in Mbembe, "Necropolitics," 38–39.

6 Beşikçi, *Devletlerarası Sömürge Kürdistan*. Beşikçi has been jailed for seventeen years for maintaining that Kurdistan exists. He argues that Kurdistan is not even a colony, since its identity and language have been denied by the Turkish state and by international actors.

7 The first uprising took place in 1925 and was led by a cleric, Şeyh Sait, who demanded the restoration of religious law. He was hanged in Diyarbakır's main square. The next took place in the border with Iran in 1930 and led to the massacre of fifteen thousand people, it is claimed, in a valley named Zîlan. Sometimes the massacres did not follow an uprising, as was the case in the Dersim provinces in 1937–1938. The number of villagers murdered ranged from nine to twelve thousand; numerous girls were taken away and given to officers as home workers in what amounts to another "lost generation." The Kurdish political movement claims to have started in 1984 the twenty-ninth Kurdish uprising against colonization and exploitation.

8 The Turkish nationalist discourse claims that Kurds are in a dire state of barbarism, which they will transcend with the help of Turkish modernity, thus articulating a discourse much familiar to colonizers. A good example involves honor killings attributed to Kurds. See Sirman, "Kinship, Politics and Love: Honour in Post-Colonial Contexts."

9 Mbembe, "Necropolitics," 39. For that reason this text retains the concept of the late colony.

10 This term is used by the Kurdish extraparliamentary opposition—politically active Kurds as well as those close to the PKK—to denote all sections of a complex political, military, and administrative organization with varying ties to a central steering committee located in the Qandil mountains in northern Iraq.

11 In Turkey, whether pro- or antigovernment, the established press, news agencies, and TV channels are all pro-state. The Kurdish movement produces its own newspaper, journals, and other publications, which generally are not read by the public at large. These publications have suffered various offensives by the state security forces, especially during the 1990s. See Bayram, "Another Story of the Daily Circulation of *Özgür Gündem*," for a study of the daily *Özgür Gündem*.

12 This oppression included unannounced house-to-house searches, destruction of winter food supplies, summary arrests, and bastinadoes, as well as the interdic-

tion of the Kurdish language in any form in public spaces. Many people remember listening in secret to cassette recordings of performers who sang resistance songs and laments for the massacres.

13 The rural population suffered terribly during the 1990s but has, by and large, continued to support the guerrilla movement. When in 2013, the PKK and the government agreed to a cease-fire whose terms meant the withdrawal of guerrilla forces from the rural areas, the population, rural and urban, was very sorry to see them go as, for them, the presence of the guerrillas seemed a protection against the small everyday abuses of the Turkish armed forces. See Women for Peace Initiative, *Report on the Process of Resolution.*

14 For a study of how municipal politics have been reconfigured, see Gambetti, "The Conflictual (Trans)Formation of the Public Sphere in Urban Space." On the basis of the writings of the movement's imprisoned leader, Abdullah Öcalan, the academies of the movement have produced guidelines to create what they call "the democratic nation" and its new forms of politics, culture, and ethics. Some of the cultural and especially linguistic rights demanded by the movement have been granted by the government during Turkey's process of accessing to the EU.

15 See Özsoy, "Between Gift and Taboo." Özsoy argues that the dead are an affective force for the Kurdish movement that symbolize Kurdish identity "as a sacred communion between the living and the dead" (Özsoy, "Between Gift and Taboo," viii).

16 In his PhD dissertation, Özsoy recounts the law suits and the verbal abuse suffered by the mayor of Diyarbakır in 2005 when he sent ambulances belonging to the municipality to retrieve the bodies of thirteen deceased guerrillas. Özsoy, "Between Gift and Taboo." The Saturday mothers of Galatasaray Square in Istanbul are others who have been demanding the remains of their kin since 1995. See Ahıska, this volume.

17 The erstwhile province of Dersim had a population of largely Kurdish Alevis that was brutally "pacified" in 1937–1938. After this massacre, the name of the province was changed by the authorities from Dersim to Tunceli. Today calling the province Dersim counts as an act of transgression.

18 Sezer, "Antigone Bu Topraklarda Yaşıyor." Translations from the original Turkish are all mine unless otherwise indicated.

19 One such piece, titled "Neredesin Antigone?" ("Where Are You, Antigone?"), written by Ayşe Kilimci, claimed Antigone understood that a tomb was the womb of the earth and could not be denied to people. A woman whose son had "disappeared" in police custody and who sat with the mothers of the disappeared every Saturday to demand the remains of their loved ones, replied to Kilimci's query: I am here and have been here since August 2004 (the date her son disappeared). See "Sahi, NEREDESİN ANTİGONE?," *Kadinmedya Online,* http://www.kadinmedya.com/kose-yazilari/sahi-neredesin-antigone.php, accessed May 4, 2016.

20 See Das, *Life and Words,* 61.

21 Butler, *Antigone's Claim*, 23.

22 Refusing to treat patients if they cannot speak Turkish, refusing to rent houses to forced migrants, not employing Kurds for menial jobs are urban ways of not letting Kurds live that are a more indirect consequence of state-backed discourse.

23 Butler and Athanasiou, *Dispossession*, 7–9.

24 In her comments on this essay at the CGC Istanbul workshop, Athena Athanasiou wondered whether such a gender switch may be seen as a form of catachresis rather than a kind of transgression and then suggested that Antigone is not necessarily a woman, since, according to Butler, her act prompts others to regard her as manly. Whatever reading we prefer, Antigone remains a figure that puts some established order into crisis. I would like to thank Athanasiou for her comments, which have helped me rethink the question of Antigone's gender.

25 Butler, *Antigone's Claim*, 6.

26 Because this act amounts to baring the head in a society where married women need to cover their hair in the name of decency, it becomes an act that signals distress and indicates that the normal order of society is under threat.

27 See Aslan, "Politics of Motherhood and the Experience of the Mothers of Peace in Turkey."

28 See Çağlayan, "From Kawa the Blacksmith to Ishtar the Goddess."

29 Sezer, the first to use the name Antigone in this way, is not part of the Kurdish movement directly, but is part of women's feminist organizations who have close links with the Kurdish women's movement. Many in the Kurdish movement itself subsequently adopted the notion as a way of talking about the right to a grave.

30 Athanasiou and Butler distinguish between becoming dispossessed by the action of others and becoming dispossessed by the actions of the self. Butler and Athanasiou, *Dispossession*, 4. "Vulnerability" and "dispossession" as discussed by Athanasiou and Butler are terms that are akin to one another, and elaborating their difference requires more work than is possible here.

31 Çağlayan, "From Kawa the Blacksmith to Ishtar the Goddess," 9–10.

32 Aryen, "Kurumlaşmış Egemenlik" ("Institutionalized Sovereignty"). The term "natural community," in Öcalan's writings, refers to the primitive communism of Marxist thinking, in which a matriarchal society was supposed to exist.

33 *Diha* news agency, June 10, 2013. Women in the Kurdish movement have readily adopted the term *jineoloji*, especially as the word *jin* means "woman" in Kurdish.

34 Biehl, "Bookchin, Öcalan and the Dialectics of Democracy."

35 Editör, "Hakikatin Arayışında Jineoloji," 4–5.

36 Editör, "Hakikatin Arayışında Jineoloji," 5.

37 The DFWM has, as of January 2015, transformed itself into the Free Women's Congress (Kongreya Jinên Azad). It is at the moment producing a journal called *Jineoloji* and has invited feminists from within Turkey and outside to take a place on the journal's advisory board.

38 "Woman is not just the other half of society. Woman is also the basic force providing meaning to society and to social[ized?] nature. The real force that imparts meaning and value to social life is woman's nature which makes up the reality of material and spiritual culture by having been imbricated from woman's material and spiritual life." These statements, which open the Kurdish women's movement statement on *jineology*, are examples of texts which are pretty unintelligible to the feminists. No author, "Jineoloji Kadın Bilimi," http://m.friendfeed-media.com/822f0720d12225c69d6b2db47f7b68d169b0b3a2, accessed September 13, 2013.

39 Bayraktar and Özdemir, *Feminizm Tartışmaları*, 49–82. Having been present at the discussions recorded in this volume, I was also convinced at the time that this was a discourse of power.

40 In an interview published in *Yeni Özgür Politika* on March 13, 2014, feminist Ayşe Düzkan implied that inventing a new term for feminism is one way Kurdish women articulate their national identity.

41 See Tekeli, "Women in the Changing Political Associations of the 1980s."

42 Sibel Özbudun, " 'Tecavüz Kültürü' mü?," *Kadın Hareketi*, http://www.kadinhareketi.org/content/view/744/1/, accessed May 4, 2016.

43 Writers such as Audra Simpson and Andrea Smith have constructed similar links between the rape of the land and the rape of Native American women. See Simpson, *Mohawk Interruptus*, and Smith, *Conquest*. However, it has to be underlined that the Kurdish movement, for its part, does not accept the term "indigenousness" to describe its position with the Turkish polity, maintaining that this term has no universal relevance and harks back to primordial loyalties.

44 In effect, this kind of "white" feminism has to date been seriously challenged only by Kurdish feminists. Very recently, some women identifying themselves as Muslims have also begun to articulate a different kind of feminism in internet blogs such as *Reçel (Jam)*, composed of women who claim they cannot make jam. These women have also been active during the Gezi protests. See Gambetti, this volume. Whether this is the beginning of what Morris calls, "alternative histories that might [be] written—not as the disclosures of a final truth, but as the assemblages of utterances and interpretations that might have emerged from a different location," is yet to be seen. Morris, "Introduction," 3.

45 The reference here is to what the DFWM, following Öcalan, refers to as the conditions of near slavery under feudalism. This refers to notions of patriarchal domination in tribal organizations. That this is a rather extreme depiction is attested to by anthropologists who have studied tribal organization. See Yalçın-Heckman, "Kurdish Tribal Organisation and Local Political Processes."

46 These acts include such innocent things as going on marches with Öcalan's poster in hand, repeating slogans banned by the security forces, wearing the red, green, and yellow colors of the Kurdish flag on every part of their clothing, and the like.

47 Nazan Üstündağ, Jineoloji Konferansı, *Özgür Gündem*, March 7, 2014.

48 Hall, "When Was 'the Post-Colonial'?," 255.

49 Hall, "When Was 'the Post-Colonial'?," 247.

50 De Lauretis, *Technologies of Gender*, 20.

51 De Lauretis, *Technologies of Gender*, 26. As Letitia Sabsay pointed out in her review of this essay, it is ironic to turn to a canonic feminist's writings to make my point when there have been many ways of speaking about the location from which women can speak (or can speak but not be heard). Women have, like the Kurdish women, been left out of both the national imaginary and its feminist critique, as Spivak argued in her 1988 essay which has been seen "as an episteme-changing text, a landmark in the necessary displacement of second-wave feminism." Morris, "Introduction," 11. I have turned to de Lauretis's depiction not just because of Kurdish feminists' universalism, but because it specifically addresses not the production of feminist subjects through ideology, but, through the notion of space, the way feminist locations are produced and then hidden from view. According to Morris, "The subaltern (as woman) describes a relation between subject and object status" of aporia that includes all women living under conditions of imperialism and globalization; for this reason, I think that de Lauretis's words can very well be read as the unheard language of the subaltern. Morris, "Introduction," 13.

52 Mbembe, "Necropolitics," 39.

....

CHAPTER 10

Violence against Women in Turkey:
Vulnerability, Sexuality, and Eros

MELTEM AHISKA

Dünya yerinden oynar kadınlar özgür olsa!
[The world would move out of
its joints if women were free!]
—Current feminist slogan in Turkey

While I was writing and rewriting parts of this chapter, new cases of violence against women and also new measures suggested against such violence continued to busy publics in Turkey. Among the interventions creating controversies and confusions was the petition of a male lawyer to the Turkish Parliament in February 2015 suggesting that a monthly allowance be paid to single men to enable them to "satisfy their sexual needs," as a remedy for the problem of increasing violence against women.[1] The lawyer thinks it is unsatisfied sexual needs that cause men to be violent against women; interestingly, his argument hints that male desire can be murderous. On the other hand, a group of women's organizations made a public declaration around the same time to protest their exclusion from meetings with the parliamentary commission formed by the government that "interrogates the reasons of violence against women in order to take precautions against it."[2] The exclusion of the knowledge and experience of women's organizations who have been fighting, some of them for more than thirty years now, against violence committed by men is notable in its own right. Sexuality, violence, and politics are intricately and dangerously linked. In this chapter, I approach the problem of violence against women in Turkey by problematizing this connection between sexuality, violence, and politics from an angle that remains invisible, if not imperceptible:

What does violence against women, and the dominant forms of representing it, tell us about women as desiring subjects?

Violence against women, including various forms of denigration, battering, harassment, rape, and killing carried out by men, has become quite visible in Turkey. Different feminist groups joining in platforms such as Kadın Cinayetlerini Durduracağız Platformu (We Shall Stop the Women's Killings Platform) or Kadın Cinayetlerine İsyandayız Platformu (We are Revolting against Women's Killings Platform) continue to protest violence against women, particularly women's killings by men. They stage big public demonstrations that feature slogans like "The love of men kills three women each day!" But feminist groups are not the sole actors giving visibility to the problem. Several campaigns organized by the government, municipalities, and various nongovernmental organizations, by leading newspapers and television channels, and the support given by celebrities contribute to addressing violence against women as a grave and urgent question. I will discuss some of these campaigns later in the chapter. The way feminist discourses have been appropriated and transformed by different actors, including the state, already points to a problematic terrain.[3] At the same time, the connections between violence against women and other economic, social, and political facts, such as forms of state violence and the gendered division of labor, are severed, leading to a certain decontextualization of the problem. The huge inequalities between women and men in the existing regime of power are not generally addressed. On the contrary, the idea of gender equality is dismissed by fetishizing the sexual difference of women.[4] The question I want to focus on here, however, is not the highly complex historical, social, and political context of violence against women in Turkey. Instead, I would like to address a particular problem: Why does violence against women continue with no impediment despite the seemingly high awareness, and why is it almost normalized in society?

Each day we wake up to a new tragic incident of a woman being killed or beaten by her husband or kin, or a woman raped most often by a man she knows. The statistics on violence against women—especially the killings of women, albeit problematic in their own right—show an exponential rise, implying that something akin to a massacre or, in other words, a *femicide* is going on.[5] The recent legal reforms and the new shelter initiatives by the government are far from solving the problem. The vulnerability of women has not necessarily been lessened; instead, paradoxically, it seems to grow.

I would like to raise a series of questions to explore the seeming "mystery" of this paradox. The first question concerns the connections between visibility and violence. What schemes of intelligibility are evoked in the public representations of women's "victimhood"? Here Judith Butler's discussion about representation and vulnerability is of key importance. Butler argues that there are "two distinct forms of normative power: one operates through producing a symbolic identification of the face with the inhuman, foreclosing our apprehension of the human in the scene; the other works through radical effacement, so that there never was a human, there never was a life, and no murder has, therefore, even taken place."[6] Yet the dominant representations of women's killings in Turkey fit into neither form. The faces of women are neither rendered as "inhuman" enemies nor completely effaced; in fact, they are highly mediatized in sentimental ways.

Women are represented in legal, political, and media discourses—including some feminist versions—as victims that should be recognized and protected by society, yet one needs to attend to the very form of representation of violence in this context in order to understand how women's vulnerability is reproduced and fixed. The representations that evoke the victimhood of women cancel the multiple temporalities of vulnerability—that is, how women as subjects have differently lived, desired, and struggled through the experience of violence. When no desire for living, and living differently, is allowed for women in these representations, victimhood is petrified and fixed in time, and hence normalized. As a consequence, mourning for the loss of women's lives is hindered. In these representations it is as if women contain two selves that are played against each other: one is the sublimated figure of *the woman*, and the other is the vulnerability that is "naturally" associated with sexual difference, with being a woman. If the first equation poses the woman as the ideal *object* of love in the family—that is, as the mother (both to her children and to her husband) who has no sexuality other than the duty of reproduction—the latter evokes women as *abject*, as thoroughly and infinitely sexualized beings whose uncontrolled desire is threatening and dangerous. The status of subject is granted to women through this bipolar coding.

My second question derives from this bipolarity and leads to another tension—that between *individuality* and *anonymity* in legal, political, and media representations of violence against women. For example, women seem to be individual subjects with rights before law, while at the same time they are subjected to the social and sexual arrangements regarding "woman" as a category in the society through judicial and/or extrajudicial practices. Similarly, media representations of violence against women evoke individuality in the visual display of victimhood yet reproduce women as an anonymous category in their appeals to stop violence. I contend that the *perverted* relationship between individualization and anonymity is sustained not only by erasing the desire of women but also marking it as a site of danger.

Then how can we connect the representations of violence against women to the barring of female desire foreclosed by the idealized images of womanhood and normative family? This of course raises the huge and ambiguous question "What is female desire?" I find Herbert Marcuse's distinction between *sexuality* and *Eros*[7] particularly useful for discussing desire from a broader perspective, due to its transformative capacity. For Marcuse, Eros cannot be reduced to the sexual act; rather, it is desire for life in all its dimensions, extending to knowledge, beauty, creative work, and politics. I contend that Marcuse's conceptual intervention provides a significant vantage point for critically rethinking the connections between vulnerability and sexual difference established within the compartmentalized and highly regulated discourses of sexuality. Finally, I will suggest some preliminary ideas toward thinking new forms of engaging with women's experiences and memories of vulnerability. Before I address these challenging questions, let me give a general background regarding the discursive constructions of violence against women in the last decades in Turkey.

Discursive Constructions of Violence against Women

There are practical and theoretical difficulties with regard to doing feminist politics targeting the question of violence against women. First, although violence against women is a widespread phenomenon around the world, it takes different forms in different cultural contexts. In other words, it has its localized and culturalized forms and terms of existence, legitimization, and problematization. Therefore, it has been a matter of debate among feminists whether a *specific culture* or a *general form of patriarchy* is responsible for it.[8] Second, it is not only feminists (and there are different kinds of feminisms, of course) who are talking about violence against women, but also a range of other actors, including state institutions, academics, and experts—both men and women. A proliferation of representations and discourses surround the phenomenon, the articulation of which is not independent of power positions. What constitutes a genuine feminist perspective has thus been an issue of contention. Third, women's own accounts of violence are mostly unrepresentable in the hegemonic publics due to their liminality;[9] these stories reveal a complex web of emotions—not only of bewilderment but also of ambiguity due to women's own conflicting loyalties and divided identities. A broader question concerning *what it means to be a woman,* and a huge practical as well as theoretical complexity, appear in these accounts.[10] Yet despite the complexities, the individual accounts and memories of women regarding vulnerability and violence are mostly generalized by the leading representations, and women are shown as *victims* of violence needing help, which in turn legitimizes certain actors with a certain authority to describe, analyze, and solve the problem to *help* these women. The "woman problem" that has been on the agenda of the Turkish state and society since the 1920s[11] re-presents itself in this case as a problem of women.

Yet the increasing visibility of violence against women in Turkey is not easy to contextualize. It may well be argued that violence against women has always existed in Turkish society, albeit behind closed doors, within the realm of the private. Feminists' organized struggles, especially against domestic violence, from the 1980s onward have contributed to its *visibility* as a social problem, and that is why it surfaces in various governmental discourses, in media and academia today. It is also possible to argue that violence against women has actually *increased* due to several social and political factors in the society.[12] However, what seems more important for the scope of this chapter is to understand the discursive constructions of violence against women—that is, its conditions and modes of visibility.

Yeşim Arat and Ayşe Gül Altınay note in the comprehensive nationwide survey they conducted in 2007 on domestic violence in Turkey that "since the early 1990s there have been significant changes in the ways in which domestic violence has been addressed in the public arena. Whereas 20 years ago, being opposed to domestic violence would have been considered a strictly radical feminist stance to take, today such violence is commonly condemned and those who practice it are punished by law."[13] Presenting a progressive history, the authors point to significant changes, ranging from legal reforms to preventive measures and policy making, that have aided to raise a general awareness in the society. They wholeheartedly acknowledge the role of the women's movement in this progress but also emphasize the importance of the cooperation of the women's organizations with the state.[14] They are optimistic that "deterrent sentences against violent offenders will prove that the state in no way approves of such violence."[15] However, they are also skeptical, stating that it is imperative that the reforms, such as the new Penal Code, "which was drafted with significant contributions on the part of the women's movement in Turkey, be strictly enforced, *so that progress can be achieved in actuality and not just on paper.*"[16]

Indeed, beginning in the early 2000s both women's organizations and the state started to employ funds, particularly European Union funds,[17] to conduct research on issues related to the discrimination and violence against women in order to develop *projects* for countering it.[18] In the 2000s municipalities around Turkey opened shelters for women.[19] Following the official circular of the government on the question in 2006, and declaring the prevention of violence against women as a state policy, there have been several joint ventures of state institutions with media and different NGOs for designing campaigns using television, film, newspapers, and billboards in order to create a general awareness in the public, and a variety of educative activities targeting women as well as men, including policemen and soldiers.[20] However, as Arat and Altınay note, much remains to be done to put what has so far been on paper into practice.[21] It seems that the history of progress is interrupted by "something" unknown that produces a gap between what is achieved in "actuality" and what remains "on paper."

Legal Reforms: The Complicity of "Tradition" and "Modernity"

Most of the above-mentioned attempts and projects are represented within a particular framework, namely that of *modern development* and *democratization*, if not directly initiated by it. Turkey's EU candidacy engendered the imperative for structural reforms in the 2000s. Under the European imperative to improve the democracy in Turkey, violence against women has been marked as a fundamental social *problem*, and the incoming EU funds were used mainly by various NGOs in collaboration with the government and the media for targeting the problem and expanding its visibility all around Turkey. I would say that the perspective of democratization geared to and framed within the negotiations with the EU has instrumentalized this issue, among others, to a great extent causing a huge abyss, a dangerous one indeed, between what is said and what is actually done.[22]

Looking at the impact of some reforms in the field of law might give us a better sense of the "failures in practice" despite the changes "on paper." The influence of the EU can also be traced in the field of law, along with various women's groups' determined struggle and agency that should be acknowledged in the consequent reforms in the law.[23] In the 2000s, both the Turkish Civil Code and the Penal Code were altered, eliminating some articles that justified men's naturalized dominance over women in the family and dated back to the foundation of the Turkish Republic.[24] One of the most prominent changes is in the former article 462 of the Turkish Penal Code, which deemed the situation as *undue provocation* if the perpetrator (say a husband) had discovered or was convinced that one of his first-degree relatives (say, his wife) was involved in an illicit relationship. "If the person then committed murder, the punishment could be reduced by one-eighth. This article was used often in combination with other articles, such as Article 51, which offers a second legal argument for leniency. The latter holds that if a suspect has committed murder because of 'uncontrollable grief' or as a result of provocation, the sentence could be reduced by two-thirds. The effect of the two articles together resulted in substantially reduced sentences."[25] Furthermore, the emphasis on "family honor" in these codes resulted in the interpretation of violence against women with regard to "moral and familial order" rather than addressing women as individuals.[26] Series of legal reforms starting from 2004 eliminated most of these dubious articles. The most important change was that women now would be treated as *individuals*, and the crimes against them would be defined not within the *familial order* but in terms of crimes against personal rights and liberties.

More recently, in 2014, Turkey signed the Istanbul Convention, which addresses violence against women by laying out highly important and comprehensive measures, including prevention, protection, prosecution, substantive law, and monitoring.[27] However, both the ongoing practices of law and the apparent *reluctance* of the authorities (if they are not openly siding with the perpetrators) to implement the new legal and policy changes surely cast doubt on the potential effectiveness of the convention. Cemre Baytok gives a vivid account of several court cases in the last few years (in which feminists intervened as third parties) where the male perpetrators tried for violence against women, including killing, were favored and enjoyed acquittal or reduced sentences justified by various moral judgments on women.[28] Showing that the former clause of "provocation" still provides a substantial argument that works against women, Baytok argues that killings of women are systematic and cannot be reduced to individual and deviant acts, demonstrating the failure of "rights talk." She also reinforces the feminist assessment that women killings are political and that law has a crucial role in sustaining the system.[29]

It is noteworthy that the Ministry of Women and Family was restructured in 2011 and was renamed the Ministry of Family and Social Policy. Similarly, the new law enacted in 2012 is titled "The Protection of Family and the Prevention of Violence against Women." A contrast then, reappears between the new focus on individuality on the one hand, and the persistent emphasis on familial order on the other. In many court cases "moral and familial values," albeit revoked, are being reactivated through the *commonsensical* judgments of legal professionals. Dicle Koğacıoğlu, who has studied the social reception and interpretation of law in Turkey, thereby interconnecting legal texts and practice, illustrates this through an interview with a judge who notes: "No, we do not judge a woman's honor here. Who are we to do that, after all? It is something personal. *But, of course*, when you are entrusting a minor to a woman, you want to make sure she has certain characteristics. For instance, it wouldn't be appropriate to hand her the child if she sleeps around all the time. She has to behave in socially accepted ways, in line with what is *customarily* considered to be a good mother. Honor, *after all*, is a very important virtue. We cannot expect women to be without it."[30]

So customarily, in the judge's terms, a woman's conduct needs to be in harmony with the socially accepted norms. If not, she can be denied her rights, and she can be easily and "justifiably" turned into an object of violence. I would like to draw attention to the phrases used in the judge's account above, such as "but of course" and "after all." These phrases indicate how the recently emerged discourse of individual rights for women refers to its *supplement*— the social and political realm within which laws are enacted, interpreted, and applied.[31]

The law's elusiveness concerning the protection of women as "individuals" is discussed by Veena Das in a highly illuminating way. Das argues that "the judicial discourse splits into the poles of grammar and semanticity. The legislative level is the level of grammar without content, while the adjudicatory processes relate to the level of judicial verification through which content is given to the judicial grammar."[32] In this double process social reality is mediated through the judicial discourse. Das contends that, particularly in cases of rape, the law is concerned less with protecting women's bodily integrity and more with regulating sexuality along the rules of social alliance. Similarly, Dicle Koğacıoğlu points to the complicity between "modern" institutions and so-called culture and tradition in the case of what are named as "honor crimes"[33] in Turkey. According to Koğacıoğlu, the "tradition effect" produced by civilizational discourses obscures the role of "modern" institutions, including the law, in mediating and perpetuating violence against women. Hence the gap that seems difficult to address, the gap between what is legally and officially articulated and what is actually done, is a relation of complicity between the grammar and the semantics of law, in Das's words. This gap cannot be analyzed within the existing frameworks, within the antinomies of modernization and tradition. On the contrary, the very antinomy makes a loop between terms and their meanings in judicial practice, creating a mystery that clouds the dynamics of gender and power relations, which in Koğacıoğlu's words has to be "identified and *de-mystified*."[34]

I contend that the *anonymity* of individuals—especially of women, in the grammar of law, which occludes the gendered "place" of individuals within the system of alliance—is significant for creating the mystery that the legal reforms do not lead to substantial changes. Despite the "modern" emphasis on individual rights, the judicial discourse constructs anonymous subjects—who have hypothetical abstract rights, which have been always already substantialized, circumscribed, and differentiated by social and political presumptions. The anonymity of women in judicial discourse also entails the objectification of their bodies and the abjection of their desire. Das makes a significant point about the anonymity of women with regard to their sexuality and their "positioning . . . *in relation to men* as either available for sex or protected within a system of alliance" that she identifies in court cases about rape.[35] Through this positioning, "the courts construct male desire in a manner that leads to either the naturalization of rape as legally consensual, or to its criminalization as a challenge to patriarchal alliance systems."[36] Thus, "women are not seen as desiring subjects in the rape law."[37] Furthermore, "women who show 'illicit' desire become consensual objects of male desire even against their will."[38]

Although heterosexual marriage in this context appears to be an important protective factor, we should add that the distinction between acceptable and illicit female desire is highly contingent and slippery, as can be seen in women killings within marriage and family in Turkey, usually claimed to be "provoked" by unacceptable signs of female desire, such as women wearing tight trousers, carrying love poems in their bags, going out without permission, wanting a divorce to start a new life, and so on.[39] Even mere laughing can be a symptom of threatening female desire, as scandalously declared by the former vice prime minister Bülent Arınç: "Women should be honorable. They should not laugh out loud in public!"[40]

When the female desire is prohibited, it follows that the male desire is not desire for a particular woman, as Das would argue. *It is for a generalized, standardized female body.*[41] This is, for example, what makes the collective violence against women possible and permissible in wars.[42] The female desire is recognized and defined as a *threat* in the act of violence, and as *provocation* during the processes of the judicial assessment of violence. Women are thoroughly sexualized, and their embodied sexual difference is ultimately threatening and deserving of violence unless it is totally contained and regulated within the established regime of gender and sexuality. Thus, individualization in the dominant legal and political discourses constructs and delineates sexual difference in a normative way based on the existing "social alliance." Since norms are categories protected from the challenge of the diversity of life, consequentially the woman is posited as a uniform anonymous object. Yet the discursive boundaries of the woman as an object are difficult to maintain. As Judith Butler argues, "Norms cannot be embodied without an action of a specific kind, and they cannot continue to enforce themselves without a continual action."[43] The continual action of the norms in this case is to reenact the constant "provocation" and "threat" that comes from living women's desire. Women are subjectivized in this way with reference to their "essential" exposure to potential violation. They are defined as vulnerable.

Heterosexual marriage and privileged class positions may occlude the vulnerability of women to a certain extent by creating "special women" who are treated as token women-individuals. However, these positions are also extremely fragile in the face of male violence, for example when upper-class professional women become "victims" of violence, their "individual career" immediately collapses, leaving behind a helpless and wounded body surrounded by "scandalous" personal stories. The same perversion regarding the individualization of women can be observed in the media representations of violence that are explored in the next section. Here we see how the violence, especially violence that results in death, *individualizes* women in the public. In other words, it is noteworthy that women are turned into individuals when they are murdered, having been contained under an anonymous category while alive. The anonymous and the individual are finally and "safely" reconciled in a woman's death, since the dead body seems to be free of the threats of living desire.

Representation, Visibility, and Violence against Women

The specific cases of murders of women are visualized so as to constitute a lesson and warning to others—the general category of women. It is no coincidence, then, that although the visibility of women's living bodies is highly monitored in the society, the existing campaigns to stop the violence against women in Turkey mostly show the pictures of women's mutilated dead bodies, turning their stories of death into "emblematic cases."[44] Through this tidal dynamic of individuality and anonymity, of life and death, *vulnerability* appears as the ultimate truth about women; it almost becomes the general defining character of being a woman; it proves women's individual existence as vulnerable subjects, evoking the necessity of the discourses about womanhood associated with normative motherhood and family. Thus, it is also no coincidence that the Turkish government, while seemingly being alert to the issue of violence against women, has constantly declared the importance of family and motherhood.[45]

Asa Elden and Berna Ekal raise important questions about the current visibility of violence against women in Turkey by reporting the results of the conference they organized on male violence, visibility, and media.[46] They state: "Among the main actors of the discussions about male violence today, there are not only those who struggle for women's rights, but also the state and the media. Then isn't it timely that we start thinking about the character and results of this visibility?"[47] Indeed, recent examples of visibility in the awareness campaigns organized by governmental agencies call for further thinking.

On March 8, 2013, the Beyoğlu Municipality organized an open-air exhibition on Istiklal Street, Istanbul, commercially and politically one of the most central and visible public places in Turkey—a place for tourist and shopping activities as well as demonstrations, further marked with the Gezi protests a few months later.[48] In that exhibition for the Women's Day, the contours of the bodies of the murdered women were drawn on the ground with their names, ages, and the "reasons" for their murder scripted beside them. The women were depicted as prototypical victims of murder using the standardized visual idiom of the police, while being individualized at the same time with their names, ages, and the brief histories that brought them to a "tragic" death. Another municipality-sponsored exhibition at Galatasaray Square on Istiklal Street showed newspapers' gruesome pictures of women's killings under the general title "There Is No Excuse for Violence." There were many other similar visual representations of women's killings around the country, especially for International Women's Day, that either cited the names of victims or exhibited newspaper clips or portrait paintings to create awareness about violence against women. In all of these, very different from the active gatherings of women in the feminist demonstrations,[49] violence against women appeared as an abstract social problem, fixed in time, with no "before" or "after." But more importantly, the particular images and names of dead women provided evidence that women are killed, paradoxically implying, in my view, that they can be killed, that they are *vulnerable*. These representations, because of their very modality, created an alarm not to activate women against violence but to threaten them with violence.

The most popular performance in 2013 in that respect has been a project sponsored by the Ministry of Family and Social Policy, comprising eight women celebrities posing as eight murdered women selected among the numerous cases for the purpose, with the title *Eight Women Eight Lives*. With the help of heavy makeup the celebrities attempted to act out the expressions of these women at the moment of their death. The photographs of these portrayals, which were taken by a well-known photographer and were no different from scenes in a horror movie,[50] were publicized in various media, highlighting the emphatic connection of these celebrities with the murdered women. The celebrities were shown saying, "It could have been me!" Interestingly, the campaign was later popularized in the media, and that sentence was transformed into "It could have been you!" In the public spots on TV, the images were animated and accompanied by the slogan "Awake before death arrives!" I find the particular mode of visualization in this project very telling.

How to interpret the schemes of intelligibility in these images? By portraying the tragic deaths of particular women, these images at first seem to invite the audience to recognize and mourn the wasted lives of the murdered women. But apart from evoking the individual cases, the whole project aims to promote a general awareness concerning the killing of women. As I have argued before, it both individualizes and totalizes women as a sexualized category. The crude formalism involved in the project (eight women, eight lives, March 8), together with the specific mode of realization, are significant for discussing what is at stake in this very form of representation. The photographs aiming to portray the faces of particular women are realized through the role-playing of celebrities. Looking at these transformed faces, you first recognize the celebrity, then realize that she is acting out a murdered woman. The temporal gap, as it were, in the reception of these images creates a distance from the representation, enhanced with the aesthetic abstraction that the crude formalism provides. You have to negotiate between the past and the present, between the significations of the murdered woman and the living celebrity, in order to perceive the message. But what could the message be, especially when anchored with the phrase "It could be me!" or later popularized as "It could be you!"? These images only address women, absenting the men as actual and potential perpetrators. Yet the men are invisibly there not only as perpetrators but also as sovereign norm setters.

These images are highly disturbing, yet they do not create "dissonance."[51] In other words, they do not break the framework of familial gaze within which violence is located; instead they contribute to its survival. By showing the extreme cases of disorder leading to women's abjection, they create an urgent need to bring back and consolidate the order for which women should be responsible. The public spots call on women to awaken before dying, but this rather vague and abstract slogan combined with the other elements in the representation implies that women must "behave" or else it could be them! Through the exaggerated images of abnormal death, these representations of violence impose the normativity that reigns in the society. In that way, the images attempt to reestablish the "familial gaze" by highlighting the excessive vulnerability of women.[52] The personification does not necessarily mean humanization, as Butler argues.[53] Similar to what happens in the judicial discourse, women appear in these modes of personification not as human beings with a capacity of life, but merely as "consensual objects of (murderous) male desire," vulnerable by definition.

In the dominant representations of violence against women, we see that murdered women have double selves, which becomes more apparent in the "Eight Women Eight Lives" project. The individuality therefore is twofold. The idea of the "normal" and surviving woman, for example the image of the celebrity as a woman, is compounded with the abject figure that signifies general sexual difference and vulnerability. The signification produces a "myth," in Roland Barthes's terms,[54] which does not hide something but only distorts it. It removes history from the sign by way of naturalization. In other words, the lives of murdered women are stolen or "derealized" in the image while it also makes the meaning that sustains the myth of "normal" family. But at the same time, the forms of female desire that breed life are once more murdered and justified by the frozen images of death. Here survival is a key theme. The survivor women have to position and reposition themselves against the threat of violence, which means they have to submit to the regime of gender within which female desire is equated with dangerous sexuality, and hence violently regulated to the point of death.

The representations of male violence against women are not of course limited to the governmental agencies. Feminists and women's organizations also attempt to find the most effective ways of representing violence against women, particularly killings of women, to create a sense of urgency in the society. Yet there is a tendency in these too to prioritize the death of women over the affirmation of female desire. The project "Anıt-Sayaç"[55] (the Monument-Meter) is significant in that respect. The project is a website produced in 2008 that aims to be a "digital monument" dedicated to the women killed by men. The data collected through news media regarding killings of women are updated each day in the form of a meter that counts the number of dead women. The names of the women appear as lists in different colors for different years, and when you click on the specific names you get basic information regarding the given reasons of killing, who killed her, and in what way. The newspaper clip about the murder, usually with a horrifying image, also appears on the screen. The introduction to the project states that this meter shows the continuity of violence against women, and as the meter ticks our hope is lessened. No doubt the intention to create a sense of emergency and awareness, and with some creativity, is there; yet I would like to argue that this feminist project is not altogether different from the governmental ones, which objectify women as a general and vulnerable category by way of canceling their desire for life. How these women wished to live, what kind of pleasures they sought in their lives, not only becomes impermissible but also unthinkable. Once again, the figure of death allies with the dominant time-consciousness in society, imposing resignation and submissiveness before what seems to be the inevitable end: the continuity of violence. The possibility of the equality of women and men, in all their differences, is dismissed from imagination. Thus, the monumentalized claim to remembrance produces its opposite: forgetfulness. The survivor women are invited to forget that the heteronormative family structure that requires women to be obedient to men, and mostly to the men they "love," is what feeds violence: "To forget is also to forgive what should not be forgiven if justice and freedom are to prevail. . . . The wounds that heal in time are also the wounds that contain the poison."[56] The poison lingers in the memories of survivor women, tragically contributing to an atmosphere of cynicism in society that, despite all its visibility, confirms violence against women, confirms that it is fate and not one that deserves mourning.[57]

Thinking about Eros and Alternative Ways of Engaging with Women's Vulnerability

Most feminists declare that male violence is systematic, structural, and springs from the reigning patriarchy. But diagnosing and naming the structure is never enough. How does the structure sustain and reproduce itself? For example, how is it possible that the widely practiced violence against women continues despite its visibility, and its visible persistence does not create a shock of awareness of, say, a "massacre" in Turkey? As Wendy Brown proposes, women do not constitute a category like "race" that is regulated through a discourse of tolerance, which of course bears in itself the potential of violence against the differentiated group. Instead, Brown argues that women are incorporated into modern society by being subjected to an essential divide, primarily between their public and private modes of being. The subordinating difference of women is secured by a heterosexual social and familial order, "thus, woman's difference—as body, as maternity, as sexuality, as subject and sign of the household—remains outside the language and purview of equality, thereby leaving open the possibility of naturalization and subordination. Female difference, within a presumed heterosexual sexual order, is incorporable by men to the extent that it is cast as a difference of inherent subjection."[58] The vulnerability of sexual difference is not externalized but embodied internally within the very "normal" order of things, such as love and family. However, it is important to note that women have aspired and still aspire for equality just because of the elusiveness and fragility of this discursive boundary, as demonstrated in different feminist struggles throughout modern history. The gender mystery finds one of its first expressions in the words of Mary Astell in the beginning of the eighteenth century: "If all men are born free, how is it that all women are born slaves?"[59] and continues to resound till this day.

I suggest rethinking the paradox of visibility and violence against women that I have attempted to delineate above, in relation to the *infinity* of female desire that cannot be perfectly captured and submitted to a "natural" subordination. I cannot possibly review and discuss the wide and controversial literature concerning female desire and sexuality in this chapter. Instead, I would like to focus on a conceptual distinction—between *sexuality* and *Eros*—which I find significant and worthwhile for critically discussing female desire, violence against women, and alternative forms of engaging with women's vulnerability.

Foucault's genealogical analysis succinctly shows how the modern discourse of sexuality constructs its subjects and objects within a web of historical power relations, although he does not exclusively attend to how sexuality is primarily gendered.[60] We also know that Foucault's work has inspired and continues to inspire critical research and politics, which question the hegemonic modalities of sexuality, queer studies being one of the most significant today. Yet from another perspective, despite the critical emphasis on the discursive construction of sexuality, our cultures seem to be obsessed with "sexuality" and "sexual liberties." Herbert Marcuse, before Foucault, drew attention to the provoked "release of sexuality," along with "the increasing sexualisation of a commercially driven culture,"[61] as a repressive reversal of sublimation. Finn Bowring argues that this is a less discussed aspect of Marcuse's work, since he is known for his critique of Freud's theory of sublimation, in which Marcuse associated sublimation with repression. However, Marcuse's theoretical arguments advance a radically different position than merely celebrating sexual liberation as desublimation. Bowring states that Marcuse insisted on "distinguishing the socially organized release of suppressed sexuality from the free self-sublimation of libido. The latter presupposes fundamental social change; the former merely assimilates sexual relations to the existing social relations: 'sexual liberty is harmonized with profitable conformity.' "[62]

In that respect Marcuse makes an important distinction between *sexuality* and *Eros*. In the repressive order of our societies, says Marcuse, sexuality is "confined to leisure time and directed to the preparation and execution of genital intercourse,"[63] paradoxically producing the desexualization of the body. In this particular organization of libidinal energy, a "surplus-repression" arises necessitated by the "performance principle," which "de-sexualizes the body in order to make the organism into a subject-object of socially useful performances."[64] The nongratifying oppressive work relations and the disembodied tyrannical reason that dictates the performance principle in capitalist society constrain and channel libidinal energies. *Sexuality*, then, is a limited realm reduced to the pleasure derived from the marked genital organs of the body, functioning within the existing and fixed inequalities and hierarchies, rather than evoking a pleasurable relation and activity between people. *Eros*, on the other hand, concerns a whole way of life in relation to others, thus expanding the field of pleasure. Marcuse argues that the conceptual transformation of sexuality to Eros "involves not simply a release but a *transformation* of the libido: from sexuality constrained under genital supremacy to eroticization of the entire personality. It is a spread rather than an explosion of libido—a spread over private and societal relations which bridges the gap maintained between them by a repressive reality principle. This transformation of the libido would be the result of a societal transformation that released the free play of individual needs and faculties,"[65] thus defining a new reality as well as a new reality principle for the nonrepressive sublimation of life instincts. Eros, in Marcuse's understanding, could go beyond the corporeal love of one and extend to the field of knowledge, beauty, creative work, and politics, thus undermining the established binaries of mind/body, private/public, and work/pleasure. What he calls the self-sublimation of sexuality into Eros is a "nonrepressive sublimation" through which "the body in its entirety would become an object of cathexis, a thing to be enjoyed—an instrument of pleasure. This change in the value and scope of libidinal relations would lead to a disintegration of the institutions in which the private interpersonal relations have been organized, particularly the monogamic and patriarchal family."[66]

Marcuse does not particularly dwell on how women can aspire to *Eros* in the present patriarchal societies. Yet if we reflect on the ambiguous question of female desire with the specifications of the conceptual transformation of sexuality to Eros that Marcuse thought-provokingly discusses, we can step beyond the gendered power trap of the discourse of sexuality in order to raise new questions. Female desire is hegemonically translated to the dominant male codes of sexuality very much structured by the patriarchal and capitalist society. As I discussed above, women already represent sexuality—their bodies are thoroughly sexualized and subjected to the sexual difference—and the general standardized sexual difference makes women vulnerable both in private and public realms. The threat of vulnerability associated with sexual difference is pivotal for the continual normative action that stresses "provocation" in order to contain women's sexuality under a "useful" purpose, that of heterosexual marriage and reproduction. However, there is never a perfect containment; the proliferating images of murdered women continue to haunt society in a way that provokes further violence. Butler's words in another context may be relevant here too: "Violence renews itself in the face of the apparent inexhaustibility of its object. The derealization of the 'other' means that it is neither alive nor dead, but interminably spectral."[67] I would argue that what is spectral in this context is not the woman per se, but the interminable yet unrecognized *female desire*.

I agree with Rosi Braidotti that "desire is what is at stake in the feminist politics of pursuing alternative definitions of female subjectivity."[68] But what is female desire? It is interesting that the recent research of sexologists on female sexuality and desire come up with perplexing results. It seems that researchers cannot agree on the object of female desire; it is highly ambiguous.[69] In Braidotti's understanding, the notion of female desire is not a prescriptive one and does not entail a specific content; instead, she focuses on "women's desire to become, not a specific model for their becoming." In line with this proposition to rethink female desire as an open-ended becoming, I suggest that perhaps it is time for us to leave aside the question about the *object* of female desire, which echoes Freud's question "What does a woman want?," and embrace the ambiguity. The inexhaustible and infinite female desire that "provokes" male violence is not solely about sexuality in its instrumentalized and reduced meanings. The threatening female desire that provokes male violence concerns *Eros*—the libido that extends to beauty, knowledge, creative work, and politics, as well as corporeal bodies. One of the feminist demonstrations as part of the Gezi resistance in 2013 provides a perfect example for this. Against the government's preaching "At least three children," the protesting women wore banners that read, "At least three songs," "At least three books," "At least three lovers," and so on, affirming that female desire cannot be bound within the dominant idioms of sexuality.

In another vein, Ferhan Özenen, a Turkish psychoanalyst, makes this inspiring comment in a conference paper on the obscure object of desire that particularly focuses on *Orlando*: "Despite Woolf's conscious obscuring of sexes, it seems striking to me that Orlando rediscovers and finishes the long awaited oak tree poem as a woman. For Orlando poetry is '*a voice answering a voice . . .*' That might also be an answer to the question of what women want. . . . As Jessica Benjamin (1988) says, '*a woman wants to want, to have a sense of agency and desire: she wants sexual subjectivity.*' "[70] A woman *wants to want*, and this is exactly what is denied to her through violence, and what haunts us in the representations of violence against women.

The dominant representations of violence against women do not communicate what the murdered women have aspired to and dreamed of in their lives. Even in the "Eight Women Eight Lives" project, despite the emphasis on "lives," the addressed women do not confront the lives of murdered women, only their appalling death. We cannot mourn the murdered women because we cannot grasp the singularity and complexity of their desire. We cannot really sense what is lost for them, and what we have lost by their death. We are *desensitized* and *petrified* by the monumentalized horror. Instead of "submitting to a transformation" that is a vital aspect of mourning according to Judith Butler,[71] we are cautioned to surrender to our selves as "vulnerable women." We become the survivors, avoiding the vital question *what does it mean to survive?*[72]

So a series of very important questions remain: What is the way for feminists to engage with the vulnerability of women in alternative ways? For example, how do we assert and reassert possible forms of female desire as Eros in order to struggle against the "naturalized" subjection of women without reproducing the status of victimhood? How do we address the multiple temporalities of vulnerability, and thus construct a political memory of women—as vulnerable subjects—in order to fight against the forced amnesia? How do we collectivize and locate this memory in feminist theory and politics? I have no concrete answers to these questions; they are to be found within the struggles of women, if they are not already there in fragments. I contend that memory plays an important role in imagining and assuming a new politics that foregrounds Eros. Lynne Huffer, who discusses the eros of ethics with reference to Foucault's *ars erotica*, suggests that listening to the voices of alterity that continue to haunt us is crucial for the self-transformation of the subject of ethics and politics, and for practicing the new arts of living. But she reminds us that "the erotic practices of new arts of living will not be found in any specific discursive form" or "in a conception of present that papers over the otherness of history."[73]

Remembering leads to the awakening of the senses. The acknowledgment of women's vulnerability can invite a different kind of memory, not one monumentalized as fate but one that continues to pulse in the moments of our individual and collective struggles for life. We can then embrace the vulnerable memories that affirm the desire for another kind of life liberated from false antinomies such as help and victimhood, law and society, reason and body, vulnerability and violence, and so on. Memories have a political power not because they provide established alternative narratives to counter the existing histories, but because they can evoke instances of life in the past that may bring back the shadowed dreams and expectations. The coming back of the past dreams and expectations may be disturbing because of the violence involved in the betrayal or barring of desire. Nevertheless, this could also enhance the political potentials for transforming women's life and subjectivity in the present. Feminists must have a "libidinal investment," a phrase Dori Laub uses for hearing the testimonies of survivors of trauma, to devise political ways of holding the memories of libidinal quests, of both the murdered and the survivor women, which may include the feminists themselves. As Laub puts it, "There is so much destruction recounted, so much death, so much loss, so much hopelessness, that there has to be an abundance of holding and of emotional investment in the encounter, to keep alive the witnessing narration."[74]

Notes

I would like to thank the editors of this volume, and all the participants in the "Feminism and Vulnerability" workshop in Istanbul in 2013, for the most nourishing and illuminating discussion and comments. I also thank Banu Karaca,

Gülnur Savran, and Cemre Baytok for reading the draft, and making very important suggestions. I hope I do some justice to their valuable feedback.

1 Çolak, "Bekar Erkeğe Cinsel İhtiyaç Ödeneği Verilsin."
2 "Kadına Yönelik Şiddet Kadın Örgütlerinin Bilgi ve Deneyimi Yok Sayılarak Sonlandırılamaz!" ("Violence against Women Cannot Be Stopped by Excluding the Knowledge and Experience of Women Organizations!"), press release, *Sivil Toplum Geliştirme Merkezi*, February 16, 2015.
3 The most striking example for this comes from the government national action plan for 2012–2015: "The domestic violence against women came to the fore in the 1980s in Turkey. From the 1980's onwards, various campaigns, street actions, demonstrations led by the women's movement have provided the significant steps for making domestic violence visible. In our day, work around violence against women has become a field that is under the responsibility of the state that solicits the support and cooperation of all parties." *Kadına Yönelik Şiddetle Mücadele Ulusal Eylem Planı 2012–2015*, 13. Feminist politics is absorbed here without accounting for the antifeminist discourses propagated by the same government.
4 In his public speech in the First International Women and Justice Summit organized by KADEM in Istanbul on November 24, 2014, President Recep Tayyip Erdoğan declared that women and men cannot be equal due to their natural differences, adding that feminists do not understand what it means to be a mother. The speech attracted a big reaction from feminist women's groups. "Erdoğan: Kadın-Erkek Eşitliği Fıtrata Ters," *BBC Türkçe*, November 24, 2014.
5 The statistics regarding women's killings exist in a scattered way in different sources: the Ministry of Justice officially reported that between 2002 and 2009 the number of killings of women increased by 1,400 percent. While the number of women killed was sixty-six in 2002, the number increased to 953 in the first seven months of 2009. "Kadın Cinayetleri 14 Kat Arttı," *Bianet*, September 15, 2011.

Kadın Cinayetlerini Durduracağız Platformu, in their international petition for stopping the women killings in Turkey, declares that a total of 4,000 women have been killed since 2005 ("'Kadınlar yaşansın diye' kısa sürede 25 bin imza" ["25 thousand signatures collected in a short time for 'letting women live'"], http://kadincinayetlerinidurduracagiz.net/haber/919/kadinlar-yasasin-diye-kisa -surede-25-bin-imza, accessed October 12, 2014). The same platform states more recently that in 2014 a total of 294 women were killed by men ("Kadın cinayeti gerçekleri" ["Facts of women killings"], http://kadincinayetlerinidurduracagiz .net/veriler/1878/2014-yili-kadin-cinayeti-gercekleri, accessed February 18, 2015).

Yet we must note that there is no systematic keeping of the statistics regarding the violence against women. Many feminist scholars who work on the subject point to the absence of statistics and research. For example, in "The Tradition Effect" Dicle Koğacıoğlu argues that the absence of reliable data makes the topic vulnerable to speculation. Similarly, Yeşim Arat and Ayşe Gül Altınay emphasize that there is limited data regarding women's subjection to violence over the years;

for a long time existing research consisted only of "small-scale studies of particular organizations, localities, or regions, or studies conducted by women's organizations themselves" (*Violence against Women in Turkey*), 1. In another vein, sociologist Emrah Göker contrasts the increasing visibility of women killings in mainstream media with the failure of state institutions to file and report the detailed trends of violence against women, which he deems important for developing effective policies. According to Göker there are temporal gaps, and the statistics provided by the state institutions are unreliable. He also directs attention to another very important problem in the reporting of women killings: the existing official statistics only concern "domestic" violence; they exclude the murders of unmarried women and trans women. Göker, "Kadın Cinayetleri ve 'Veriye Dayalı' Siyaset."

6 Butler, *Precarious Life*, 147.

7 Marcuse, *Eros and Civilization*.

8 Chandra Talpade Mohanty's intervention has been very significant in problematizing both the "cultural" and "universalist" approaches of Western feminist scholarship to women's issues, including violence against women. According to Mohanty, these approaches produce a "third world difference" that "Western feminisms appropriate to 'colonize' the fundamental complexities and conflicts that characterize the lives of women of different classes, religions, cultures, races and castes" in non-Western contexts. Mohanty, "Under Western Eyes," 19.

9 I use the term "liminality" here in order to point to the in-betweenness of the authorial voice in these narratives: in between the reaffirmation of the construct of womanhood as a woman who has survived male violence, and the emerging instability of being a woman due to the cracks and wounds opened up by the experiences of violence.

10 Powerful examples of such accounts can be found in the book produced by the feminist foundation and women's shelter Mor Çatı (Purple Roof), *Şiddete Karşı Anlatılar*.

11 For an illuminating discussion of the "woman question" in Turkey in the first years of the Turkish Republic see Libal, "Staging Turkish Women's Emancipation."

12 See Ahıska, "Kadına Yönelik Şiddet'le Uğraşmak, Kadınlık Hallerine Nasıl Bir Ayna Tutuyor?" for a debate on this question among the consultants of Mor Çatı that entails two different arguments. Each argumentation has a valid basis: as we know from cases in other countries, it is difficult for women to reveal their experiences of male violence in public, and the feminist struggles can have a big impact in breaking the silence. At the same time, the new forms of state violence, militarization, and poverty in the age of neoliberal governmentality surely aggravate violence against women, not only in the domestic setting but also in other contexts, such as sexual violence under custody or sexual violence as a means of warfare.

13 Arat and Altınay, *Violence against Women in Turkey*, 35.

14 They write: "Indeed, women, who during the 1980s organized in protest actions *against* the state, have in more recent times begun to seek dialogue and

cooperation *with* the state. Women's organizations have had a significant impact in achieving many of the steps which have been taken in the struggle against violence, from the drafting and passage of Law No. 4320 to the revisions of the Civil Code and the Penal Code. Passage of the new Penal Code has been a major step towards ensuring that domestic violence is no longer viewed as an acceptable, 'ordinary' phenomenon but rather as a 'crime.'" Arat and Altınay, *Violence against Women in Turkey*, 69.

15 Arat and Altınay, *Violence against Women in Turkey*, 69.

16 Arat and Altınay, *Violence against Women in Turkey*, 69, emphasis added.

17 Starting in the mid-2000s, around 135 projects for supporting women's employment in Turkey were funded through what the EU calls preaccession assistance, amounting to a budget of approximately 24.5 billion euros. From 2008 onward, approximately 3 billion euros were distributed to around twenty NGOs in Turkey for projects with the aim of providing support to women exposed to male violence. Göker, "Kadınlara Yönelik Şiddetin Azal(tıl)(a)mayışı."

18 Some feminists, such as the Socialist Feminist Collective, have criticized this as "projectism." Hacıvelioğlu, "Kadın Kurtuluş Hareketini Sınırlayan Bir Dinamik."

19 See Diner and Toktaş, "Women's Shelters in Turkey," for a recent study on women's shelters in Turkey.

20 Some international actors in joint venture with Turkish NGOs had already started other campaigns during this period. For example, Amnesty International, as part of its global campaign "Stop Violence against Women" in 2004, not only produced a detailed report on the current situation regarding violence against women in Turkey, but also designed a petition to be signed by Turkish citizens and directed to the prime minister. This petition demanded that more shelters should be opened; help lines for enabling women to report crimes should be established; a public awareness should be created through a wide-reaching media; and legal institutions, legal professionals, police, and gendarmerie should be subject to a mandatory education for protecting women against violence, and those who have failed to carry out their duties in this respect should be penalized. Amnesty International, Turkey, Uluslararası Af Örgütü, "Kadına Yönelik Şiddete Son İmza Kampanyası" ["Petition for stopping violence against women"], http://www.amnesty.org/en/library/asset/EUR44/013/2004/en/1a0d2faf-d5ed-11dd-bb24-1fb85fe8fa05/eur440132004en.html, accessed October 25, 2014.

21 Arat and Altınay, *Violence against Women in Turkey*, 4.

22 I have discussed a similar instrumentalization of Turkey's so-called democratic reforms, in 2002, related to the aim of joining the EU. See Ahıska, "Occidentalism."

23 Baytok, "Political Vigilance in Court Rooms."

24 For example, an article of the Civil Code of 1926 read that "the head of the family is the husband, the husband represents the family, and the wife's residence should be the husband's." The article was changed in 2002, since it contradicted the UN's CEDAW treaty (the Convention on the Elimination of All Forms of Discrimination against Women), which Turkey had already signed in 1985, to intro-

duce equality among spouses. The CEDAW treaty specified that both spouses were now responsible for material sustenance and decision making in the family. It is worth noticing that the treaty was signed in 1985, but the code was only changed in 2002, when the effort to join the EU was at its peak.

25 Koğacıoğlu, "The Tradition Effect," 123.

26 For example, "if the members of the 'dishonored' family abandon an illegitimate child, the punishment was reduced to somewhere between one-sixth and one-third of the regular punishment for child abandonment." Koğacıoğlu, "The Tradition Effect," 123. Another example: in cases where a woman is raped, if the person convicted of rape marries the victim, his punishment will be postponed and canceled after five years of "successful" marriage, so that moral and familial order is restored. http://www.dezavantaj.org/index.php/haklarimiz/73-kadin-haklari-/1296-tuerk-ceza-kanunu-kadnlara-neler-getiriyor-, accessed October 25, 2014. One can see that in this case the women are doubly victimized, first raped and then forced to marry the rapist. It is as if "successful marriage" has been regarded as an ultimate containment and punishment both for women and men!

27 See "WAVE's Press Release Regarding the Istanbul Convention," *Mor Cati*, https://www.morcati.org.tr/en/home/268-wave-s-press-release-regarding-the-istanbul-convention, accessed October 22, 2014.

28 Baytok, "Political Vigilance in Court Rooms."

29 Baytok, "Political Vigilance in Court Rooms."

30 Koğacıoğlu, "The Tradition Effect," 124, emphasis added.

31 Nükhet Sirman similarly poses a challenge to the current interpretations based on the notion of individual human rights, arguing that honor and the family set the frame for all social, cultural, and political relations at the level of the everyday in Turkey. Sirman, "Kinship, Politics, and Love."

32 Das, "Sexual Violence, Discursive Formations, and the State," 396.

33 Koğacıoğlu, in "The Tradition Effect," has raised an important argument that the so-called honor crimes were associated with traditionalism along the modern/traditional binary, which was projected onto the eastern parts of Turkey, namely the Kurds. Following a line of critique in this vein, the majority of feminists in Turkey now avoid using the phrase "honor crimes," and instead employ the term "women killings."

34 Koğacıoğlu, "The Tradition Effect," 141, emphasis added.

35 Das, "Sexual Violence, Discursive Formations, and the State," 416.

36 Das, "Sexual Violence, Discursive Formations, and the State," 416.

37 Das, "Sexual Violence, Discursive Formations, and the State," 419.

38 Das, "Sexual Violence, Discursive Formations, and the State," 419.

39 O. Meriç Eyüpoğlu, as a practicing feminist lawyer, cites these as some examples presented as evidence of "provocation" for killing women in different court cases in Turkey. Eyüpoğlu, "Şiddet Değil Erkek Şiddeti."

40 "Bülent Arınç: 'Kadın herkesin içinde kahkaha atmayacak,'" *CNNTürk*, July 28, 2014.

41 Das, "Sexual Violence, Discursive Formations, and the State," 420.

42 Das, "Sexual Violence, Discursive Formations, and the State," 420.

43 Reddy, "Troubling Genders, Subverting Identities," 117.

44 Elden and Ekal, "'Amblem Vakalar' ve Erkek Şiddetinin Görünürlüğü," *Bianet*, July 26, 2013.

45 Recep Tayyip Erdoğan, Turkey's former prime minister and now its president, has been the main spokesperson for disseminating the moral values of family and is notorious for his harsh speeches against abortion and his belief that women should produce at least three children.

46 Swedish Research Institute in Istanbul, "Amblem Vakalar' ve Erkek Şiddetinin Görünürlüğü" [Emblem cases' and the visibility of male violence"] February 15, 2013, http://www.bianet.org/biamag/kadin/145142-amblem-vakalar-ve -erkek-siddetinin-gorunurlugu, accessed October 29, 2014.

47 Elden and Ekal, "'Amblem Vakalar' ve Erkek Şiddetinin Görünürlüğü."

48 The resistance started during May–June 2013 in Istanbul, at Gezi Park near Taksim, with a group of people protesting against the cutting of trees and the illegal confiscation of a public park, at the heart of Istanbul, and against resurrecting an Ottoman military barracks in this place to function as a hotel and a shopping mall. The protestors occupied Gezi Park and Taksim Square, and soon the movement spread to other parts of Turkey, with differing political agendas. The protestors were attacked with brutal police violence, causing severe injuries and deaths.

49 Particularly on the International Women's Day, March 8, or on the International Day for the Elimination of Violence against Women, November 25, feminists raise demands for the equality of women, point to men as perpetrators of violence and the state as the protector of men's violence, protest ideologies and practices that hold women's bodies captive, and cry for the liberation of women in solidarity.

50 See "8 kadin 8 hayat" [8 Women 8 Lives], *En Son Haber*, http://www.ensonhaber .com/galeri/8-hayat-projesinden-carpici-fotoflar/4, accessed October 29, 2014.

51 Felman and Laub, *Testimony*.

52 Marianne Hirsch argues that "the dominant ideology of the family, in whatever shapes it takes within a specific social context, superposes itself as an overlay over our more located, mutual, and vulnerable individual looks, looks which always exist in relation to this "familial gaze" (*Family Frames*, 11). The frame of the familial gaze produces: "individualization, naturalization, decontextualization, differentiation within identification, and the universalization of one hegemonic familial organization" (Hirsch, *Family Frames*, 54).

53 Butler, *Precarious Life*.

54 Barthes, *Mythologies*.

55 See the online monument counter that commemorates women who have been killed by domestic violence. "Monument Counter," *Anit Sayac*, http://www .anitsayac.com, accessed October 27, 2014.

56 Marcuse, *Eros and Civilization*, 212.
57 One eerie example for such cynicism comes from a recent television show in September 2014. A man who had married five times and killed two of his wives participated in a television show starring Seda Sayan, a TV celebrity known to make television programs related to "women's issues." Sayan had invited this person to the program on Show TV knowing that he had been kicked off of another show, *Marriage Show*, on Flash TV because he was seeking a new wife after already killing the two. Sayan's comments—such as "Have you ever seen such a good-humored murderer?"—led to loud reactions from different segments of the society, including the feminists of course. Nevertheless, this episode points to the fact that killings of women can be and often are lightheartedly underrated. "İki Eşini Öldüren Adam Seda Sayan'a Konuk Oldu," *Milliyet*, September 3, 2014.
58 Brown, *Regulating Aversion*, 72.
59 Cited in Hilda L. Smith " 'Cry Up Liberty,' " 204.
60 Foucault, *The History of Sexuality, Vol. 1*.
61 Bowring, "Repressive Desublimation and Consumer Culture," 16.
62 Bowring, "Repressive Desublimation and Consumer Culture," 16.
63 Marcuse, *Eros and Civilization*, 182.
64 Marcuse, *Eros and Civilization*, 182.
65 Marcuse, *Eros and Civilization*, 184.
66 Marcuse, *Eros and Civilization*, 182.
67 Butler, *Precarious Life*, 33–34.
68 Braidotti, "Embodiment, Sexual Difference, and the Nomadic Subject," 6.
69 For an amusing review of such research see Bergner, "What Do Women Want?"
70 Özenen, "That Obscure Object of Desire."
71 Butler, *Precarious Life*.
72 Cathy Caruth relates this question to a death drive in psychoanalytic terms, which implies that the formation of history in this case bears the endless repetition of previous violence. Caruth, *Unclaimed Experience*, 63.
73 Huffer, "Foucault's Ethical Ars Erotica," 141.
74 Cited in Hirsch, *Family Frames*, 34.

CHAPTER 11

Bare Subjectivity

Faces, Veils, and Masks in the Contemporary
Allegories of Western Citizenship

ELSA DORLIN

From the History of the Face
to the Historicity of Bareness

In 1994 Jean-Jacques Courtine and Claudine Haroche published a book that has since become a classic: *Histoire du visage: Exprimer et taire ses émotions XVIe début XIXe siècle* (History of the face: Expressing and repressing emotions, XVI–XIXth C). At the crossroads of several fields (philosophy, history, linguistics), this work has shown how the face has come to take on a complex, scrutinized, and disciplined meaning of personality at the turn of the seventeenth century. While the face is understood in a semantic relationship to the interior, it takes part in the very production of this interiority—an invisible relief of the self—and has become consubstantial with the very definition of the modern individual and with what characterizes its relationship to the world, as well as the distinction between public and private, intimate and political, personal and communal. Therefore, during the seventeenth century the face became the "corporal translation" of the individual in the sense that the face is how the individual is known, how its soul and its innermost self can take shape and be known but can also be confused. The face has thus become the "unveiled" side of the self, the side that is supposed to master social interaction. Hence, civility (which includes not only the rules of etiquette but also the very act of *making society*) could be defined as this art of the shown and the hidden, the visible and the invisible, the explicit and the implicit, which is primarily social play. This play is circumscribed in specific space-times, granting the self moments when it can "let go" and keep its face out of sight.

In line with the work of Michel Foucault, Philippe Artières, and Alain Corbin, but also the sociologists Norbert Elias,[1] Max Weber, Erving Goffman, and Richard Sennett, Courtine and Haroche set out a history of physiognomy, decorum, and politeness, or classical philosophical anthropology and the history of emotions that is nothing less than a history of the birth of subjectivity. Yet in 2011, in an academic French context where visual studies are not often represented, in an article titled "The Forbidden Invisibility" Claudine Haroche proposed a new extension to the 1994 book and opened her remarks with a statement that radically changed the conclusions. In the contemporary period, according to her, one sees a spread of a *"command to be continuously visible"* for individuals who tend to eliminate the false bottom of subjectivity: interiority. Under the influence of the development of information and communication technology, the individual is constantly subjected to an order of being transparent, constantly compelled to obscenity, ordering them to unveil their intimacy to the point that it runs out (and has no place or time to be replenished).[2] From this perspective, it becomes entirely impossible to "save face," making it totally unbearable to live in the social space.[3] New biotechnologies of identification, profiling, traceability, social networking, and so on are interpellations to unveil.[4] From this statement, Claudine Haroche goes on to say that what could describe the very functioning of a certain type of contemporary power is that the "repeated exhibition of self" prohibits invisibility, while the latter appears to be the very workings of social exclusion. "The command to be socially and mentally visible which is contextualized by the development of societies of control [is] concomitant of the extension of massifying social invisibility as well as of an empowerment of mechanisms."[5] Following Paul Virilio's remarks here, Haroche thus defines the postmodern condition as one of *overvisibility*, which participates in the commodification of the individual and announces the very depletion of subjectivity as we know it.[6] Unquestionably, *Histoire du visage* and the research that this book inaugurated constitute the starting point of this essay on the dialectic of the visible and the invisible as a complex apparatus of power that reveals bodies and exposes them: the "bare face" becomes the ambiguous target *and* effect of governmentality.

To introduce my main hypotheses, I must first conceptualize nudity or bareness in a specific contemporary context—especially when the dialectic between "see," "be seen," and "be unseen" has defined social recognition and social life or *livable life*. To this end, I begin with a text from Giorgio Agamben.[7] My first hypothesis concerns a critical history of civility: I go back to the French "veil wars" (especially the "burqa affair" of 2009), which have opposed at least two conceptions of the secular Republic for the last twenty years. This hypothesis is formulated through the definition of a "hegemonic subject," which I conceptualize as an "immodest citizen" in relation to an epistemological analysis of the face.

Second, I examine why it could be relevant to link the question of immodesty to the question of violence and social justice, and how some faces *mis à nues* or "made bare" become socially vulnerable. Here it is important to highlight the coexistence of several regimes of violence, existence, and visibility in the public democratic sphere.

Third, we look at how media, comics, and video games constitute the privileged material for what we could understand as a contemporary allegorization of the self as well as the continuous production of the frontier between citizens and others. In this "Wonder Woman hypothesis," I underline the historicity of this dialectic between the visible and the invisible and the representations of justice and truth in order to foster an understanding, for instance, of how an allegorical representation of justice depicted with highly visible facial characteristics and yet also blind or veiled has coexisted with equally consensual but more prosaic references, staging an entire myriad of law-upholders and heroes who are masked or veiled, but also gifted with supersight.

In light of these elements, how are civil rights redefined, particularly with regard to contemporary Western European laws that have prohibited concealing the face in the public space, but also to the mediatic construction of minorities as veiled or masked and thus as conspiring persons that the state must unveil or unmask? How do the multiple representations relating to the concealment of the face in Western popular culture and the different counter-conducts (*contre conduites*) that have fallen under the term civil disobedience these last years (e.g., Anonymous) allow us to trace the contours of an immediate history of new modalities of *subjectivation*? I illustrate this last point through several references chosen from the *cultural history of injustice* and the study of two popular representations of vigilantes (the polysemous character of Wonder Woman and a feminist video game called *Hey Baby!*).

Bare Face: Elements for a Historical Ontology of the Contemporary Self

Persona originally meant "mask." During antiquity, in Rome, individuals had no social existence apart from belonging to a lineage, which was represented by a prominent forefather's wax mask that each family of note kept in the atrium of its home. From this etymology, it is important to keep in mind that the social individual is communally represented as an actor that assumes a role and is separate from the moral person. "As for the slave, just as he had no ancestors, no mask, no name, he could no more hold 'personhood' or a legal standing (*servus non habet personam*). The struggle for recognition is thus each time a struggle for the mask, but this mask coincides with the 'personality' that society recognizes for each individual (or 'character' that it makes of him with his more or less reluctant complicity)."[8] Thus, to take measure of the revolution that would be identification techniques, legislation on recidivism (particularly in France and England), and photography, we must distinguish between *the recognition of the person* and *the identity of the individual*. It is only from the latter that the political history of the face could "begin."[9] In fact, since the late nineteenth century, the face is the flesh of individuals' identity. To narrate the history of the face is to launch an ontology of individual identity, and a historical ontology of sorts, which is based on the assumption that by becoming the target of individual identification techniques, the face was produced as the seat of individuality, the subject, and the ostensible materiality of the self. The development and dissemination of modern identification techniques developed by Alphonse Bertillon's judicial anthropometry were thus the birth of the face—photographed and archived. And yet criminals were the first to inherit an identity and a face (and not "just" that),[10] while the rest were still social individuals interacting in the policed frame of civility, which implies a discipline of body and a control of emotions and a game of mutual recognition, rules of decorum, a code of honor and offenses, and so on. However, this conception of public life, where morality renders laws useless, would eventually lead to the spread of the biometric control of individuals:[11] citizenship defined as "an identity without personhood."[12] Recognition has replaced the control that produced civility, in which individuals are kept in the illusion that they could from then on "assume all the masks, all the second and third possible lives. . . . Added to this is the sharp and almost contemptuous pleasure of being recognized by a machine without the burden of affective implications, which are inseparable from recognition by another human being. The more the citizen of the metropolis has lost intimacy with others, the more he has become unable to look his fellows in the eyes; the more virtual intimacy that he has had with this system, which has learnt to deeply scrutinize his retina, is consolatory."[13] Agamben concludes that we must seek this face beyond the mask as "biometric faces *that we still fail to see*."[14] This is a quite enigmatic conclusion. Which of our faces are still unable to be seen? Which of our faces are seen, are visible, and *matter*?

The Niqab and the Dialectic of the Visible
and Invisible: A New Regime of Civility

On June 22, 2009, the president of the French Republic declared in front of the members of Parliament: "The burka will no longer be welcome on French soil." When the so-called burka was targeted, a more salient set of issues emerged that had not appeared during the previous cases of what could be called the "veil wars" in France (1958, 1989, 1994, 2004):[15] that of frightening dissimulation. Described by a politician as "itinerant ghosts," those women who covered all or part of their face had become, in the space of several months, hideous figures or counterexamples of the new standard of social existence based on the generalized skin-baring among individuals. As such, laws against wearing the veil could be carried over to other measures, such as the "anti-face-mask" decree adopted in June 2009, which prohibited demonstrators from hiding their faces in public; or even the vague attempts to ban cross-dressing (in Belgium, for instance). On April 11, 2011, the proposed law banning the concealment of the face in public became definitive in France: it required any person covering her or his face to pay a fine of 150 euros. Alongside Belgium, France has thus become one of the first countries to adopt such legislation implicitly targeting the wearing of the full-face veil and so on, and Italy, the Netherlands, Spain, and Canada followed suit.

On a more complex level, a double standard is being used by the French authorities and proponents of the ban on the niqab in French public spaces. Indeed, there are two overlapping discourses that echo each other and finally merge into a single discursive device. The first discourse relates to the "disturbing concealment"—the impossibility of identifying women who wear the full-face veil.[16] In this context, it is a matter of guaranteeing the nudity of the face, which we might qualify as the seat of the biometric contemporary "personality," the target and product of surveillance technologies, with the help of a new offense—the offense of concealment. Here we are referred to the wider debate on individual freedom and societies of control (see infra). However, a second, slightly different discourse operates in parallel and complements the first. It consists of the claim that the Muslim veil and the full-face veil in particular constitute not a security or policing problem, but a civic, philosophical, and political problem that turns an individual religious practice into a challenge to secularism and the political pact at the foundation of Western democracies.[17] Those who defend the law banning the niqab from this standpoint are referring to a tradition they consider typically "Western" and specific to Renaissance humanism: that of civility. Thus, women who conceal their faces in public are considered to be a threat to the democratic order because they are making themselves unrecognizable to the political community with which they are supposed to have entered (or must enter) into contract. The veil would thus eliminate the very possibility of a social pact, made obsolete by the nonreciprocity that concealing the face entails.[18] Yet it is precisely this nonreciprocity between *seeing* and *being seen* that appears to contradict a supposedly universal ideal of civility that has come back into style.[19] From this point of view, we need to pay special attention to the highly controversial concept of "modesty" that today is the subject of a strong ideological debate and reveals a postcolonial double standard of sexual morality.[20] It generates bodies that can legitimately appear in the democratic public space, or describes the normative framework inside which some bodies are regarded as civilized, as citizens who have "nothing to hide" and are worthy of being defended and protected.

Faces That Matter

Yet what appears to be the single most original aspect of this question is not so much the question of civic reciprocity as that of contemporary representation of the political community, the social pact, and citizenship. The French controversy surrounding the veil perfectly reveals how the contemporaneous conceptualizations of the social pact and civic duty borrow their narrative style and symbolization from the direction of sight as an apparatus of power (which includes several well-known and frequently studied technologies of surveillance) as a moral and social economy of vulnerability. Until very recently, the dominant Western representation of the political community, conveyed by its founding political philosophy and theory, has been precisely based on the idea of blindness: the political pact is made between persons considered as such through the suspension of any regard that scrutinizes the affiliations and differences embodied by each individual. In the same way, the French Republic of freedom, equality, and fraternity was originally articulated in a speech about blindness—see articles 1 and 2 of the French Constitution (and hence the refusal to politically recognize borders, religions, races, hierarchies, and identities), which would precisely allow a political vision of community harmony and social justice, as well as a transcendent vision in relation to the "affiliations" of individuals. And this discourse accompanies an entire metaphorical history of the Republic, which, because it is blind to

11.1 "The Republic lives / sees itself with an unmasked face": Official public campaign posted since April 2011 in front of all French institutions–schools, social service offices, embassies, and so on. This campaign is a concrete application of the law of October 11, 2010, prohibiting dissimulated faces in the public sphere, adopted under Nicolas Sarkozy's presidency (2007–2012).

differences, acquires this political oversight capable of perceiving the public good. To a certain extent, women wearing the niqab come across as a truly monstrous figure insofar as they systematically invert this classic and mythological representation of the French Republic. I therefore conclude that the "burka affair" was the opportunity to re-create, to actualize, a myth, precisely as it is described by Roland Barthes.[21] In a depoliticizing process, it is a matter of opposing a semiology of blindness (but increasing the number of biometric technologies of control and surveillance) against a phantasmagoria of veiling as democratic conspiracy.[22] And indeed, in each public French institution we can see a poster with an almost topless Marianne and the slogan "The Republic lives / sees itself with an unmasked face."

Finally, by continuously showing images of women wearing the niqab in France, one is also building a monstrous representation of the minority fighting for (non)recognition: here, basically no recognition is being demanded in terms of visibility. The niqab even institutes a form of invisibility—a highly visible and accentuated invisibility. As Axel Honneth points out, this is just the opposite of the sentence in the prologue of *Invisible Man* (1952) by Ralph Ellison ("I am an invisible man").[23] For Honneth, Ellison describes an experience that demonstrates the dual regime of invisibility and nonrecognition. It seems unlikely that the niqab would be included in this "phenomenology of invisibility," which Honneth attempts to theorize, due to its divergence from Ellison's narrator's experience: he is invisible because people refuse to see him and their gaze pierces him, goes right through him. The experience of women wearing the niqab comes across as completely different: they are invisible because they cannot be observed; it is impossible to pierce or gaze through these "social specters." From this reflection on the controversy surrounding the veil as well as the paradigmatic example of the full veil, I broaden my study by taking interest in "the faces that matter" in the public space and visual culture.[24] What may help to shed light on this approach is the idea of a recognition policy through a system of visibility (being visible) and civility (see and be seen) discriminating citizens and spectra (social spectra). There are faces that we look at and others that are not even worth a glance (that of a homeless person sitting on the sidewalk, the beggar in the subway, the cashier, etc.), looks that we cross and do not "touch." These visible but powerless faces (sensorily powerless and socially nonsensical) that address others but that these others ignore thus remain invisible. Yet it is precisely by becoming invisible that they can to a certain extent resist against this social contempt. Therefore veils—like other practices aiming to make the face invisible—are forms of resistance/response against social nonexistence that, in their practice of unrivaled anonymization, come to address their claims and requirement for social justice.

The Immodest Citizen: or, Civil Existences and Other Appearances

It could be useful at this point to evoke the political history of incarnations and conceptualizations of civic existence (what it means to be a citizen), or even civic appearances (how it is possible to appear in public space?), not only through the systems of representations and allegories—for example, those found in the French public space through architecture—but also through a discussion of works on political theory understanding minorities as ghost categories, regarding their unrecognized existences as spectral existences.[25] In other words, we must question not so much who is visible and who is not, but the normative framework and scheme of intelligibility that makes individuals visible as citizens. To do this, I propose a working hypothesis with an episte-mological dimension.

Beginning with this observation, still to be refined, I would like to explore this other regime of civil and civic existence that I identify as unrivaled. My hypothesis takes inspiration from Donna Haraway's *Modest Witness.*[26] I pro-pose to make a connection between the "modest witness," as that figure is de-fined by Donna Haraway, and what I would like to hereafter define as the "im-modest citizen." The founding stage of the relation between the subject and object of knowledge specific to modern science generates a regime of truth. It is the regard of the subject of knowledge (self-constituted as a modest wit-ness), which, in the scientific process, becomes the condition that makes the production of the scientific fact possible. *The man of science*—as a disembod-ied figure, whose body is made invisible—is the only one who can modestly disappear in order to testify with authority about "what is." However, women remain mere spectators with no authority (they can look, but cannot testify—incidentally, their right to bear witness in civil suits was acquired only recently). The body is constantly creating a barrier, screening the truth. Women also become archetypal objects of knowledge: deemed immodest by their bodies' exposure and permanent availability, which they are incapable of "neutraliz-ing," they are objectified.[27] In parallel, this overexposure of women's bodies on the modern scientific scene goes along with a reclusion into the private space and therefore an exclusion from public life. In other words, the virile modesty of men of science, their invisibility, and their transparency goes side by side with a visibility—an omnipresence as a social individual. In the public arena, gender relations reverse the regime of the visible and the invisible. We thus observe a double standard for modesty, which works as an operator of power (the power to tell the truth and the power of domination) and defines immod-esty as a specific quality of civility—of community harmony. The immodesty of men, and their omnipresence and omnipotence in the public sphere, causes women's cloistered bodies to pass for obscene (in the sense that something that should remain hidden is being displayed). What strikes me as important is that the theater of science and the social theater are not two separate stages, but two illustrations of the same narrative of modernity. These two illustra-tions are embodied in the same allegorical representation, which, from the mid-nineteenth century, has associated bourgeois virility with female obscen-ity (breaking from the androgynous and eroticized ideal of the revolutionary citizen) and which progressively uses obscene female nudity to signify virile civic immodesty. Finally, we are faced with a problematic definition: to have citizenship or be a citizen is to be self-visible, and as a result, being a citizen means not having to demand to be seen, to be recognized, and to exist publicly.[28] And, in this context, it is necessary to discuss obscene minorities and invisible minorities if we want to accurately capture the mechanics of power. It is in this context that women wearing the niqab enter the stage, thereby changing the scenery and the text: they embody a dual foil, a counteremblem to the Republic. On the one hand, due to a paroxysmal modesty, a uniquely feminine modesty, it is their very invisibility that becomes highly visible; we are witnessing a kind of parody of the separation of the public and the private, and of gender boundaries. In the same way that the face of the white, bourgeois, immodest, male, and highly visible citizen in the public republican arena is veiled by female allegorical representations, here the veiled body is overexposed and becomes the focal point of attention, an overexposed target. On the other hand, fully veiled women are a negative allegory of this "French Republic," where citizen immodesty is also another representation of the citizenship compared to universalism; for instance, where citizen representation was well known as a form without content. The French "veil wars" appear as a symptom: the niqab seems to be a kind of perverse prism that reverses the voyeuristic relationship. Here the object being scrutinized is indeed the immodest face of the citizen, taken without its dual allegory, which acts as a screen (see the "sexy" body of the Republic in 1968, when Brigitte Bardot was chosen as model to be "Marianne," the classical symbol of the French Republic), an immodest entire body whose gender, color, class, and sexuality become obscene in turn: a visible body, observed and controlled, that no longer has a grasp on its own mode of appearance.

Democratic Obscenity: The Right to See and the Privilege to Disappear

This monstrous inversion of the republican allegory between visibility and invisibility of the face and between modesty and immodesty of the "national body" between citizen and spectral existence is the narrative thread of a certain definition of contemporary citizenship.[29] In this representation, though, it would be too simplistic to conclude that there is a tacit social contract—constitutive of citizenship—preceded by a precontract: a "global" command to do a striptease of self. Especially in the context of the *Charlie Hebdo* tragedy (on January 7, 2015, two men killed eleven journalists at the French satiric weekly newspaper *Charlie Hebdo* offices in Paris): at the beginning of 2015, day after day, we saw the faces of the authors of the attacks as our TV screen was used as a magnifying glass revealing the pretended blunt truth of them.[30] These men became "monstrous" because they appeared constantly, close to the spectator. There are of course various basic visual scenes where faces appear that contribute to producing *and* alienating who is seen and who is seeing (the "face-free" body, the blurred face, the black blindfold indistinctly used for children, witness, dead persons, anonymous, mole, etc.). A few weeks after the Paris attack, during Dominique Strauss-Kahn's French trial on charges of abetting prostitution, a double regime of visibility took place: a judicial one that is supposed to protect the identity of accused and witness (and only newspaper cartoonists can offer an obsolete, *désuete*, figuration of the identity), and a mass mediatic one. In this last visual regime, Strauss-Kahn's face progressively disappeared from the screen and finally became an evanescent silhouette—and again "respectable"—when he was finally acquitted and got into a car with tinted glass.[31]

Indeed, in contemporary media representations, the concealed, veiled, or masked face holds a complex meaning that marks the practices considered deviant or criminal but also refers to an entire popular imagination that stages the struggle against injustice. Thus, the vigilante or masked avenger figure should be defined as a contemporary political myth. From this point of view, there are two types of corpus we can build from. The first includes works conducted on the right of self-defense, justice, and taking the law into one's own hands, and on vigilantism.[32] The second consists of works conducted on Western popular culture, especially North American, in a globalized world context: those on children's literature and comics—Justice League of America, Marvel comics, film, video games, and so on—and on studies of the story of heroism from a gender and broader intersectional perspective.[33]

Whether or not they have superpowers, the masked vigilantes or avenging superheroes always possess an extrasensory view that allows them to capture the very essence of justice because it occupies the place of the observer, not blind but *located*. The benefits of a reflection like the one outlined here may find the theory of justice and cultural studies of interest, but also standpoint theory insofar as the critical study of superheroes and their standpoint allows for reworking the question of supervising power relations from the margins: it can indeed be done, and the double life—practices of anonymity, alias, and so forth—makes it possible.[34] Finally, this cultural history of superheroism and extrapower can be used as heuristic material in constructing a political history of the senses or *ordinary agency*.

From Blind Justice to Heroic Supersight:
The Wonder Woman Hypothesis

The figure of the masked vigilante is an illuminating case study. The style of modern representations of democratic justice is centered on vision as the political sense allowing for impartial judgment. We know to what extent blind justice is variously invested in the ancient and modern tradition. Contemporary political philosophy has significantly reworked this tradition and the visual metaphor of judgment as a neutral and disinterested judgment. Proposing the "veil of ignorance" device, Rawls allows individuals to choose fair principles of justice: the masked eyes symbolize the act of adopting apparently good principles, or at least the best possible for me and thus also for others.[35] In Rawls's scheme, even I do not know the social status and material conditions of existence that will be mine in a society that requires me to identify the principles that are the best *for all*. Criticisms of this model have been particularly rich and teeming (especially those from canonical feminists).[36] Our aim would be to limit ourselves to the overthrow of this model: under what conditions is the superhero another metaphor of justice? The superhero is the opposite of the blind (the figure of the ignorant observer, above all not knowing his future place in society).

Defining blindness as a principled position of justice allows for determining a position from which one judges in soul and conscience the principles on which a democratic society can be built. By contrast, the masked hero occurs once society is essentially founded and after the principles of justice have been adopted. It is clearly a "restorative" figure of injustice (because of bias in the principles of justice, their disclosures, etc.). In this context, vigilantism's or superheroes' "restorative" justice is represented not in the guise of a blind (or blindfolded) figure but as a *masked* one: vigilantes or superheroes are neither seen nor recognized (their face is unrecognizable either because of the mask they wear or because of their transformation into a superhero); moreover, it grants them "superpower" vision. This "superpower" vision implies that they perform justice in situ and are able to understand it just not because they are neutral, but because they are involved in social relations and live and observe them from within (in the case of Zorro, Superman, Batman, Spiderman, etc.).

In the procession of popular representations of masked heroes there are few female characters. Basically, the authentic popular figure of the female avenger in the contemporary Atlantic era and the first female superhero is Wonder Woman. Yet Wonder Woman is one of the very few superheroes who is not masked. Wonder Woman was created in December 1941 by William Moulton Marston (his work appears in issue 8 of *All Star Comics* under the pseudonym Charles Moulton, then in issue 1 of *Sensation Comics* in January 1942) based on two observations: (1) there was no leading female character in DC Comics, and (2) no "girl wants to become a girl" because the characteristics of femininity were disparaged and devalued in society, incarnating the very essence of vulnerability. He then made a sort of Amazonian Princess Diana with magical powers that were not her own. It is her bracelets that protect her from bullets and above all her unbreakable, expandable "magic lasso" (forged from Aphrodite's belt and bequeathed to her mother, who in turn gives it to her) that makes those around her tell the truth and takes away any will to resist. Moreover, Wonder Woman sees love as the most powerful force ("submission through love") and clearly wants to rehabilitate the evildoers she faces. From this belief emerged Transformation Island—near Paradise Island (home to the Amazons)—where she subjects the malicious to a "rehabilitation program."

The Wonder Woman character has been much commented upon in feminist theory and gender studies circles: she is the symbol of a kind of mainstream contemporary "feminist" mythology, but the saga for which she plays the heroine is simultaneously a reflection of gender power relations (for example, in the 1940s she was relegated to secretary of the League of Justice; in 1972 Samuel R. Delany was commissioned to write the scenario for six of the series' issues, but only #202 and #203 would be made due to a debate with feminist activist and essayist Gloria Steinem) and the most misogynist fantasies.[37] While these discussions speak to my broader intention, my specific purpose in this essay lies elsewhere. Actually, the creator of Wonder Woman is also the inventor of one of the best-known judicial technologies of the twentieth century: the lie detector. A doctor of psychology, in 1928 William Moulton Marston penned *Emotions of Normal People*, a kind of postmodern physiognomy. In this same period, he worked on the connection between blood pressure and emotions, and created the first machine recording the changes in blood pressure as they occur. By creating just a few years later the figure of Wonder Woman, an unmasked avenger, Moulton Marston shows a representation of justice through a figure of *transparency*: Wonder Woman is a perfect woman in that she has no psychological complexity or density. The normalized—stereotypical—femininity embodied by Wonder Woman helps here to better show the order to which all of society and not only women, is subject: to tell, to confess the truth.[38]

Wonder Woman simultaneously describes a norm of subjectivation and a mechanism of subjection (*assujettissement*). She is the savior, the mediator, *and* the survivor.[39] She seeks the truth; she tells the truth; she is innocent and does justice; she wants goodness and thinks love. Wonder Woman is an old-fashioned monstrous figure of truth. She could also be understood as the heroine and herald of a disciplinary society that is prone to exposing ourselves and the forming of our life ideals and ethics. Wonder Woman is both the spooky representation of a subjectivity to come (and even already there), a totally unmasked and emptied and flat subjectivity: an ideal, idealized, and formatted profile. As a technology of control (she detects lies), Wonder Woman is like the face of all disciplinary devices that produce truth of and about ourselves. She is a continuous confession machine, but here the confession generates no more interiority, no intimacy to target: because everything is shown and told, there is just a *bare subjectivity*. [40]

Impure Justice, Tragic Resistance:
First-Person-Shooter Heterotopia

Popular fiction and culture are emerging as a framework within which contemporary social movements maintain a *citational* rapport. A paradigmatic example could be the Anonymous movement: this coalition is a privileged entry point for reflecting on the question of contemporary forms of resistance.[41] In 2006, by taking the *unidentified* (not identifiable) identity of anonymous Internet profiles without portrait photos, activists with masked faces turned anonymity into a real *counterconduct*. Anonymous call for anarchism and ecology through a culture of piracy and hacktivism; they are not a defined group, but a collective with shifting and temporary boundaries. Invisibility (unseen, unspeakable) has (re)become a strategy of political subjectivation. They particularly go after countries that have draconian Internet policies and that censor the Internet or sites hostile to movements like Occupy Wall Street (during one of the rallies, one activist's sign read: "The corrupt fear us. The honest support us. The heroic join us"), or WikiLeaks. But they are also and more directly a fantastical representation of revenge in intimate relation with the fictional world of the comic *V for Vendetta* (by Alan Moore and David Lloyd and inspired by the story of Guy Fawkes, the main instigator of the Gunpowder Plot in 1605 to restore a Catholic monarchy in England). The Anonymous practice a policy of revenge that is precisely to *unmask* the dominant and their interests (e.g., nations), to make the details of historically anonymous groups or activists public (the Anonymous recently gave out the contact information for the office and members of the Ku Klux Klan), or even perpetrators and their crimes: for instance, the Anonymous posted on Facebook the name and contact details of those alleged to have caused the death of Amanda Todd, a sixteen-year-old girl who committed suicide on October 10, 2012, after posting a video on YouTube describing the sexual harassment and blackmail she had suffered for years. In the case of Amanda Todd, part of the extreme brutality of sexual harassment consists in the maximal exposure of her own lynching, as she said in her tragic confession video testament, where she chose to show not her face but several sheets of paper with sentences she wrote.[42] Amanda Todd tried to protect herself, but even after her death and because of the data memorized by the Internet and social networks, her suicide is repeated and infinitely duplicated.

I conclude with a final *heterotopia* of an invisible and avenger self. On her way to work on a winter morning in 2008, someone called out "Hot Ching Chong!" to Suyin Looui. Shocked, she decided to create the video game *Hey Baby!*, in which women are the heroes. Entering the game, you find yourself in the streets of such cities as New York or Montreal, armed with a gun. You are accosted by men, most of them young: "Hey baby, nice legs! . . . Do you have time? . . . Wow, you're so beautiful . . . I like your bounce, baby . . . I could blow your back out . . ." Here you have a choice: you either answer "Thanks" and continue on your way (the harasser appears to leave you alone, but will meet you again a few seconds later) or draw your firearm and shoot until the harasser is dead. The man lies in a puddle of blood and will quickly be replaced by a tomb inscribed with whatever last words he addressed to you. There are no prizes (there is an infinite number of harassers) other than the chance to walk freely in the streets.

Joining several other contemporary visual projects,[43] the game *"Hey Baby!"* represents women's avenger fantasy: going out on the street carrying a weapon. From this perspective, *"Hey Baby!"* runs counter to the imaginary conveyed by the vast majority of portrayals of violence against women, which tend to comprehend women, and to a certain extent rightly so, as "obscene" defenseless victims of sexism.[44] The ambiguity of the sadistic satisfaction in playing *"Hey Baby!"* brings us face to face with a lack of culturally explicit representations of scenarios in which women assume positions of agency when facing harassment. Through an FPS apparatus, *"Hey Baby!"* produces another narrative of vulnerable subjects[45]—when the few games featuring female characters are in the third person, where it is difficult to identify with a character with exceptional, and especially aesthetic, qualities (the best example being the *Lara Croft* series). However, as an FPS game, *"Hey Baby!"* adopts the characteristic point of view of "war" video games, in which the player sees the action through the eyes of a virtual protagonist.[46] Most FPS games recruit "gamers" into an ultraviolent militarist and capitalist imaginary, blurring the boundaries between imperial techno-science and science fiction. This imaginary is also highly gendered and racialized, as shown both by the target audience for this type of mass culture product and by the norms of gender, sexuality, color, and race that it helps to produce and reify. Indeed, while the enemies have a concrete identity (often the living dead, Nazis, aliens, communists, Mafiosi, or even Islamic terrorists), the main character is a universal contentless Subject that we could define here as an invisible omnipotence (especially because in this game you can't be injured and you can't die; moreover, in all video games, you always can restart the game). By applying this FPS mechanism to *"Hey Baby!,"* Suyin Looui allows *us* to play a feminist urban guerrilla in the first person, but she constructs a heterotopia where we fight back violence in a virtual solipsism.[47] She invents a space-time in which we can derive pleasure from fighting violence with violence, whatever our identities, physical and psychological capacities, or capital, skills, and social resources.

What are the limits of this heterotopic experience of our agency? First, if *"Hey Baby!"* creates a true living experimentation of our agency, it breaks precisely with what is alluring about FPS games insofar as it quickly becomes boring to so easily massacre ordinary sexists (and the endless game is incredibly boring). This repetitive feature of the game thus shows the repetitive dimension of sexist violence as well as the futility of the excessive response: how useful is an Uzi if the harassers never stop coming? Then, the sexist *interpellation* of the harassers turns a woman into a(n) (armed) *Subject*: a pure, indefinite subject who is perfectly transparent, who does exactly what She feels, thinks, wants, and imagines.[48] There is no inhibition, no dilemma, no moral awareness anymore and this *subjective gap* partly illustrates a relevant critique of the patriarchal permissive violence in the public sphere. But the Feminist First-Person Shooter of the *"Hey Baby!"* game also resembles a contemporary Wonder Woman: a monstrous figure of truth, an allegory of justice. Indeed, the fact that the game's heroine is armed to take the law into her own hands constitutes precisely a second limit of this feminist experimentation. In this game, the weapon is what restores bodily and sexual integrity (paradoxically, the weapon restores the right to be invisible in public space), but it is what I always see *as mine, as myself,* too. In the game, we find ourselves touring the world through the viewfinder of a firearm, as if our only *devenir sujet* was to be an Uzi. The pure Subject is embodied in the gun sights. Here the weapon is not a way to protect myself or my body; the weapon acts as a substitute for the security state (or the law that fails to "protect" me as the game encourages us to believe in a juridical-political mythology), but in fact no one is protected now because nobody is standing behind the sight, peering in;[49] we are the sight itself.

Notes

1. "The basic pattern of the image of the self, and of man in general, thus continues to be based, even in the most advanced types of . . . individualization that have emerged so far, on the idea of an 'inside' which is separated from the world 'outside' as if by an invisible wall." Elias, *Society of Individuals*, 125.
2. Haroche, "The Forbidden Invisibility," 77; McLuhan, *The Gutenberg Galaxy*.
3. Goffman, *Interaction Ritual*, 14.
4. Mattelart and Vitalis, *Le Profilage des populations*.
5. Haroche, "The Forbidden Invisibility," 79. See also Arendt, *The Origins of Totalitarianism*; Anders, *Nous Fils d'Eichmann*; Deleuze, *Pourparlers*.
6. Virilio, *L'accident original*.
7. Agamben, *Nudités*. Due to space restrictions, I am unable to include here a commentary on Giorgio Agamben and Judith Butler's discussion of "bare life" and sovereignty. See Agamben, *Homo Sacer*; and four works by Butler: *Parting Ways*, *Psychic Life of Power*, *Precarious Life*, and *Undoing Gender*.
8. Agamben, *Nudités*, 82.
9. The classical, medieval, and early modern history of the face will be of course deeply relevant to the modern history of the face. See Ariès and Duby, *Histoire de la vie privée en 5 volumes*.
10. Agamben touches quickly on a point: at the same time Francis Galton set out an alternative method to Bertillon's *spoken portrait* with digital fingerprints that might be imposed in England, he was stating that the process was perfectly suited to the indigenous of the colonies, whose faces merge and look alike.
11. Torpey, *The Invention of the Passport*.
12. Agamben, *Nudités*, 91.
13. Agamben, *Nudités*, 92.
14. Agamben, *Nudités*, 94.
15. Fanon, *The Wretched of the Earth*; Nordman, *Le Voile islamique en question*; Chouder et al., *Les Filles Voilées Parlent* [Veiled girls speak]; Tévanian, *Le Voile médiatique* [The media veil]; Dorlin, *Sexe, Race, Classe* [Gender, race, class]; Scott, *The Politics of the Veil*; and Bouyahia et Sanna, *La Polysémie du voile*.
16. Dorlin, *Sexe, Race, Classe*.
17. Fraser, "Rethinking the Public Sphere"; Scott, *The Politics of the Veil*.

18 It was the position of a meditatic French essayist Elisabeth Badinter (see Dorlin, *Sexe, Race, Classe*, note 16).

19 The same research question could be developed on imperial war or the phenomenon of drones (see Chamayou, *Théorie du drone* [Drone theory]).

20 See Mohanty, "Under Western Eyes"; Mahmood, *The Politics of Piety*.

21 Barthes, *Mythologies*.

22 Brown, *Edgework*.

23 Axel Honneth ("Recognition: Invisibility") cites this sentence ("I am an invisible man") from the prologue of *Invisible Man* (1952) by Ralph Ellison.

24 "Faces that matter" paraphrases Butler, *Bodies That Matter*. See also Sontag, *On Photography* and *Regarding the Pain of Others*; Butler, *Precarious Life* and "Bodies in Alliance"; and Butler and Athanasiou, *Dispossession*.

25 Butler, *Gender Trouble*.

26 Haraway, *Modest Witness*.

27 Linda Williams, *Hard Core*; Schiebinger, *The Mind Has No Sex?*

28 Honneth, "Recognition: Invisibility"; Ellison, *Invisible Man*; Le Blanc, *L'Invisibilité sociale*.

29 Salmon, *Storytelling*.

30 Sontag, *On Photography*.

31 Only a topless FEMEN activist came to disturb this scene of moral and national rehabilitation of Dominique Strauss-Kahn (DSK). In fact, rather than disturbing the scene the presence of the FEMEN group has contributed to this mediatic ceremony of rehabilitation. The FEMEN collective was created in Ukraine in 2008, and in 2012 its two main founders moved to France, where they continued their highly mediatized actions following the notoriety awarded to them during the DSK affair. FEMEN have contributed to defining the DSK affair as an exceptional case of sexism, as a residual phenomenon of sexual violence in Western societies. Using the political and cultural burden of gender and racial nudity of the body as a classical activist tool, FEMEN seek through mediatic impact to criticize the French government and overcome its lack of commitment to protect or means of protecting women against ordinary violence, supposedly perpetuated mainly by Muslim men. According to FEMEN leaders, topless direct action should be performed by activists handpicked for their *beauty* (that is, a racist and capitalist definition of aesthetic criteria and hegemonic norms). From this perspective, I regard FEMEN and their imperialist Marianne embodiment rhetoric as a feminist imperial vigilantism.

32 Klockars, "The Dirty Harry Problem"; Culberson, *Vigilantism*; Abrahams, *Vigilant Citizens*.

33 Heer and Worcester, *Comics Studies Reader*.

34 Harding, *Standpoint Theory Reader*.

35 Rawls, *A Theory of Justice*.

36 See Okin, *Justice, Gender and the Family*; Tronto, *Moral Boundaries*.

37 Steinem, *Wonder Woman*; Robins, *The Great Women Superheroes*; Lepore, *The Secret History of Wonder Woman*.

38 See Alcoff and Gray, "Survivor Discourse."

39 Alcoff and Gray, "Survivor Discourse." From a Foucaldian perspective, Linda Alcoff and Laura Gray offer a genealogy of the mechanism that builds the survivor discourse as a confession. They further analyze how, for example, victims of childhood sexual abuse are encouraged by and through a media staging to detail their abuses and their traumatic consequences socially and psychologically. Three characters come into play: the mediator (a "dispassionate" confessor, p. 280), the perpetrator, and the survivor. All three enact a dichotomy between experiences, judgments, emotions, and reasoning that leads to empowering the mediator (the one who listens to and/or watches the victim confess) with an expertise that is nothing less than a power to validate or invalidate what the victim says. The goal is to figure out whether the victim is lying or making up stories, and as a result the mediator has a power of veridiction. While the survivor is forced to confess within and by a controlled universe of discourse, the perpetrator of violence appears only in a discourse that protects him in a way that clears him and his actions, all the more since the survivors will only be heard if they stay within the boundaries of an autobiographical causality where the traumatic event (here sexual violence) sheds light on their own intimacy and turns the aggressor into an "accidental cause" of a hyperbolic interiority.

40 Foucault, *Discipline and Punish*; Butler, *Gender Trouble*.

41 See Coleman, "Hacker Politics and Publics"; Ruiz, *Articulating Dissent in the Public Sphere*.

42 See @AnonymousPress (http://twitter.com/anonymouspress), October 15, 2012.

43 We can also refer to another initiative, Hollaback New York, an LGBTQ community now found in most American and European cities that offers to photograph or film harassers and post the pictures on their blog (http://hollabacknyc .blogspot.com/), which also offers a wealth of practical and theoretical information against heterosexism. We can also refer to Sofie Peeters's documentary *Femme de la rue*, about sexual harassment in Brussels (August 2012, https://www .youtube.com/watch?v=iLOi1W9X6z4) or Shoshana Roberts's documentary *10 Hours of Walking in NYC as a Woman* (October 2014, https://www.youtube .com/watch?v=b1XGPvbWnoA). In Egypt, see the HarassMap collective (http:// harassmap.org/en/) and the short video *Creepers on an Egyptian Bridge*, a documentary by Tinne Van Loon and Colette Ghunim (September 2014). In January 2015 an online video ad by Everlast (a company that sells boxing and martial arts gear) showed men catcalling their own mothers in Lima (Peru).

44 In France, a number of the public campaigns against domestic violence or violence against women shown on television channels and the Internet or posted in public transport stations have used three main motifs: first, by picturing battered women in tears with prostrate and bruised faces, one motif plays on a demonstration of the aggressor's power and on one's sense of empathy and morality ("Do unto others as you would have them do unto you"). Yet inversely it removes

all agency from the victim, who becomes mute, degraded, and annihilated but whose eyes often invoke the viewer/abuser's pity.

45 This is also true for the Hollaback collective: they show the perpetrators from the victims' standpoint, not the victims themselves.

46 See Jessy Ohl and Aaron Duncan, "Taking Aim at Sexual Harassment."

47 Merleau-Ponty, *Le visible et l'invisible*.

48 Althusser, "Ideology and Ideological State Apparatuses."

49 To be clear, nobody ever *was* behind the sight.

....

CHAPTER 12

Nonsovereign Agonism
(or, Beyond Affirmation versus Vulnerability)

ATHENA ATHANASIOU

"The atmosphere was suffocating. Everyone was living normally, however, as though nothing had happened. A lot of people were rejoiced at the things done in their name. And we were exhausted, unwashed, sleepless, overworked, and, above all, deeply sad that we were unable to do anything to change the situation. We felt outraged. Jeered. Put aside." While pronouncing these last words, Saša took in her hands her personal archive—a collection of notes, photographs, fliers, and drawings. She pulled out a black-and-white photograph to show me. "Notice how wretched and angry we look," she said. The picture was riveting, indeed. It portrayed a small women-only public vigil against the siege of Sarajevo: a few black-dressed women, standing in the central square of Belgrade, looking rather isolated yet wholly engrossed in the exigencies of the situation, and holding a sign: "Not in our name." In my friend's words, "I don't know what had happened that time, but it was just three of us at the square. Because of the intense cold? Because of the war? In any case, only the three of us appeared. You cannot imagine the atmosphere and the reactions. Three women standing at the center of the city, protesting against the war. Passersby were cursing us, spitting on us. But I was so devastated that I did not care. It was like a breeze that was saving my life, again and again, every Wednesday."

In a conversation with me, my friend Saša Kovačević offered a dissonant account of the collective state of "normality" despite and against which she and her comrades took to the streets, arousing anger in their nationalist opponents. Since October 1991, when the Women in Black weekly actions started in Republic Square of Belgrade, the element of stasis as standing still and in dissent emerged as a crucial aspect of these activists' repositioning of their political bodies at the center of the city. Every Wednesday at half past three in the afternoon, the silence of the standing women was accentuated by their slogans, either written on banners or drawn on the pavement in the bustling square: "Women, traitors of war, protest for peace," "We are disloyal," and "We mourn all victims." Standing in the street to protest the militarized ethno-nationalism of one's own country was a risky business at those times of national fervor promoted by the ruling elite. In the context of the wars in former Yugoslavia and their aftermath, these activists have been bringing intolerable memories into public view. They have been doing so by mobilizing a sign of improper mourning, one which embodies their own and others' ambivalent and precarious belonging vis-à-vis the demarcation lines of the polis.

The principal theoretical question of this text is about agonistic mourning as performed despite and against the biopolitics of warfare and its accompanying interpellating lines of militarist and heteronormative national sovereignty. I would like to ask: How might we understand the politics of contested grievability as a means to refigure political subjectivity beyond sovereign accounts of agency and beyond the biopolitical distinction between natality and mortality? In what follows, I take up Women in Black feminist and antimilitarist action of dissent in post-Yugoslavia, in order to reflect on the relation between feminist political subjectivity and what we might call (perhaps with a little trepidation) "vulnerability." In exploring these political subjects' enactments of unthinkable mourning for the dead of the "other side," my interest lies in taking a closer look at vulnerability as aporia: what does this concept render admissible and what does it render inadmissible regarding feminist political subjectivity? As I unravel in this essay, vulnerability, and, more specifically, vulnerability to (the potential for) loss, implicates a work of mourning. Mourning, in its crucial reliance on the question of "what the other we have lost has been to us,"[1] furnishes a sense of common, and yet decidedly uncommon, vulnerability. It affirms and at once displaces the ethics and politics of shared "finitude"; I put the word in quotation marks simply to signal that "there is no finitude in or of itself."[2] The infinite fusion of divisibility and sharedness is the mark of finitude. As Jean-Luc Nancy has shown, finitude is not about an absolute limit.[3] Rather, it is about both the impossibility of being one with oneself and the radical corporeal precariousness of being as being-with, in terms of mortality.[4] Vulnerability, theorized alongside the im/possible work of mourning, performs a sense of politics and political subjectivity whereby "being-with escapes completion and always evades occupying the passage."[5]

I argue that the claim of Women in Black (hereinafter WiB) is an interminably aporetic call for another politics of vulnerability: different from, and critical of, both nationalist and liberal schemes of the ordinary binary autonomy-vulnerability, but also activity-passivity. I try to show that these activists define a mode of political subjectivity whereby a politics of vulnerability is enacted in terms of nonsovereign critical agency (akin to what Hannah Arendt called the "nonsovereign" character of human action). As I deploy it here, the problematic of vulnerability signals a challenge to the conceits of the autonomous and constituting subject. I am not interested in the condition of vulnerable affectability as such, then, but in how this perspective of finitude in reference to infinite exposure and responsiveness to the other (rather than in reference to natality versus mortality, as it is typically understood and I will develop later) incites us to think and work with/in body politics.

What does it mean to work politically through finitude as openness to the other and what kind of body politics would such work entail? WiB activists use the sign of mourning to publicly acknowledge the disposable victims of the "other side," those declared as "enemy," and to counter the biopolitical economy of enmity and disposability, with all its racial, ethnic, and gender inflections. In occupying the position of the internal enemy, which has been conferred upon them as a status of abjection, they depart from where they (un)belong in order to relate and respond to those estranged as external enemies. It is through this performative self-estrangement that they become the phantom residues of those who have gone out of presence in the polis. And this is how an agonistic configuration of the body politic is made possible.

Undoing Grief as Language-in-the-Feminine

WiB emerged in Jerusalem in January 1988, one month after the beginning of the first intifada, when a small group of Israeli Jewish women on the Left, actively supported by Palestinian women and men, started marching into the West Bank to protest against the occupation. They also initially organized vigils in Jerusalem. Dressed in black, they would stand every Friday, usually for an hour in the afternoon, at some prominent place in the city. The hallmark of those gatherings would be wearing placards with the phrase "End the occupation," accompanied by a raised black hand. Gradually, the movement spread from Israel/Palestine to become a worldwide feminist movement opposing militarism, racism, social and economic injustice, "humanitarian wars," and the "war on terror."[6] Since its inception, WiB has become an international movement of women who hold vigils, usually at rush hour in central squares, at busy intersections, or in front of major buildings and monuments, to protest against ethno-nationalist violence, militarism, imperialist power, capitalist injustices, racism, sexism, and homophobia.

In this vein, Žene u Crnom protiv Rata (Women in Black against War) emerged in 1991 in Belgrade, as part of the resistance movement against the regime of Slobodan Milošević. Their politics, openly feminist and firmly antinationalist within a wider landscape of an anti-Milošević coalition which was not univocally antinationalist (nor always feminist), was signposted by two suggestive mottos: "Not in our name" [*Ne u naše ime*] and "We will not be seduced by our own [people, nation] [*Ne dajmo se prevariti od svojih*]." The WiB network became known mainly through its weekly vigils in the center of Belgrade, where these political subjects mourn in protest, for others and with others. The sexually and nationally marked idiom of mourning, predicated upon the relegation of the female to the maternal as a means for honoring the nation's reproductive aims, is catachrestically appropriated by them: mourning is enacted beyond and against the proper meanings and "common places" of home and homeland. Instead of remaining attached to a discursive genealogy of "care for others" as a socially ordained virtue historically associated with the privatized, liberal morality of middle-class white femininity, the signifier "woman" is performatively queered as a catachrestic referent for subjectivities abjected from the discursive order of intimate belonging.

A propos of her work on Antigone's claim, Judith Butler has tackled the problematic of mourning as a layered figure of political catachresis critically engaging with the hierarchies of grievability.[7] The mourning of WiB, which might be termed "mourning" only by virtue of a political catachresis, has deauthorizing effects in the national and gendered matrix of grief. I would contend that catachresis in this context implies both incompleteness and impropriety; it is understood as an act of dismantling the apparatus of loyalty related to the politics of grievability and the discursive normativity that makes women-as-mothers stand for the idealized suffering of the nation. At the same time as they repeat and differ, these political subjects break through conventional allegiances of gender, sexuality, and nation. Their mourning is disloyal, not at home with itself. Disloyalty is construed, in this context, both as performative interruption of established chains of reiteration and as noncompliance to the ordinances of gendered and sexualized national intimacy.

Becoming an Enemy: Memory as Unbelonging

Mourning is typically prescribed to remain within the bounds of home as a "female duty" following the norms of blood relations, or to enter the public realm as an expression of honor for the nation's dead heroes in accordance with the codes of martial masculinity. What has mourning been doing, however, out at the Republic Square of Belgrade since the early 1990s and how has it been mobilizing the question of who gets to inhabit public space? How is the political memory of the "others" of the national ideal witnessed in this neuralgic public space of the Serbian (once Yugoslav) capital? How do assembled female bodies come to enact such an impropriety? What limits do they mark and at what price?

WiB activists enact the eccentricity of mourning, its exteriority to itself. Through the performative introduction of this impropriety into the square, the epitome of the open and the outside, they enlarge the sign of mourning to encompass the contingency of its subversive reappropriations. The historical center of Belgrade, the Republic Square [Trg Republike], has been the emblematic site for WiB street actions. The square has also been the central rallying point for different kinds of political gatherings—from the prodemocracy and antiwar demonstrations in the 1990s to protests organized by supporters of Milošević when the former Yugoslav president was extradited to The Hague on June 28, 2001. A few days after the Milošević extradition, several LGBTQ groups attempted to hold the first gay pride march at the square, but the event was violently attacked by a huge crowd of opponents.

WiB congregational actions take place at the Republic Square in suggestive juxtaposition to the sublime Prince Michael memorial [Knez Mihailo], which occupies an inaugural place in Serbia's national master narrative. Dedicated to exalting the birth of the Serbian nation, and at the same time to marking the designated space and time of national commemoration, the vertical monument depicts the national hero on horseback and with his hand allegedly pointing to Constantinople, indicating to the Ottomans the direction to leave the city, in a defiant gesture echoing the liberatory national ideology of the nineteenth century.[8] In this embattled arena, where the monumental architecture seems to immortalize the constitutive role of self-aggrandizing masculinity in the production of national remembering, the action of the black-dressed women temporarily interrupts the stream of pedestrian crossings. The activists' performativity of unbelonging in the 1990s often ignited enraged attacks and injurious speech by extreme right-wing militarist groups.

In putting their bodies on the line, the protesters have been becoming strangers and castaways, according to their attackers, who shouted "whores," "lesbians," "Yugoslavs," and "You are the shame of Serbia!" against them in the summer of 2004, when WiB held the performance *Maps of Forbidden Remembrance* to mark the ninth anniversary of massive ethnic cleansing of Bosnian Muslim civilians in Srebrenica. Time and again, they become strangers, as they take up the site of abjection and change its terms.

As these activists embody the figure of enemy in light of stratified vulnerability to loss, their mourning is depleted of its historically authorized foreclosures and is deployed against the nationalist and heteronormative conventions that pose vulnerability as a synecdoche for proper femininity. This suggests not only resistance through vulnerability, as a means of mobilizing solidarity against the normalization of violence, but also resistance to the normalizing violences that sustain the connections of vulnerability to gendered, nationalized, and racialized subjection. "I do not belong to anything and anyone, only to WiB," an activist told me once. My interlocutors, WiB activists, posited disloyalty both in terms of ethno-national lines and critical political subjectivity: "We, the traitors, don't do what we are prescribed to do: either lamenting at the tombs or being nurses." Their stories, as they narrated them to me, were stories of precarious belonging and performative foreignness. Their poetics of bodies emerging out of place and affirming relationality with others situated out of place raises the specter of contestation in the polis.

Spectral Spaces of Countermemory

Saša and her comrades not only expose their bodies to the polis's space of intelligible appearance. They also expose this space as layered through their embodied engagement with the spectrality of appearing and disappearing, assembling and dissembling. In appearing out of place, their memory for those who cannot appear is not enacted as recovery but rather as *trace*: that is, as the mark of loss and testimony, which always affects the survivor—the one who becomes homeless in the world after the other's death. The polis, writes Hannah Arendt, establishes a space where "organized remembrance" may take place.[9] And yet, what about displaced and disavowed memories that haunt the ways in which the polis comes to organize its remembrance? How does the political action of reclaiming a public space for remembering others—and otherwise—work to spectrally traverse and transfigure the polis and its inscribed order of memorability?

The work of haunting the polis's "organized remembrance" raises anew the problem of *emerging* in the polis, in all its gestural, affective, and socio-symbolic layers. The polis, for Arendt, is enacted as a relational "space of appearance": one which, as Judith Butler has significantly emphasized, happens performatively "only 'between' bodies."[10] In other words, it is the contingent actuality of the assembled bodies that brings the polis into being. Although the spatial component is crucial to the coexistence that brings the polis into being, the polis is not to be reduced to the physical space of appearances: it can be always and continually recreated anew through the actuality of people gathering "no matter where they happen to be."[11] In this sense, the polis is a *"potential* space of appearance":[12] "Wherever people gather together, it is potentially there, but only potentially, not necessarily and not forever."[13] In other words, the polis is an indeterminate and continually re-created potentiality arising from plural bodies getting together. And yet, if the polis requires people being in some sense and in particular ways present in a public space, I suggest that we further complicate the conditions of "being there" and "belonging together" through the emergent potentialities of (dis)appearing and (dis)assembling.

"Appearing," from the perspective of the political subjects with whom I worked, refers to the agonistic eventness of reclaiming a public space for remembering others and otherwise in the face—and in the aftermath—of militaristic state violence and war. It indicates lingering in spaces rendered uninhabitable. This reclaiming of public space involves bodies appearing out of place and yet reappearing and being exposed in political space, bodies meant to be eclipsed, bodies whose presence appears not to be present, disconcerted bodies, and, to be sure, bodies on the line: in other words, bodies to which "appearance" is never simply available and sharedness is always at stake. So, the register of the emergent that is played out here is indelibly marked by spectral iterations within the affective space of the polis. The political subjects of this study opt out of certain schemes of appearance as a way to contest the conditions of emergence that turn public space into a fixed and immutable landscape of memorability. By transmitting differently positioned memory claims, they reclaim a public space for making themselves and others vulnerable to memories out of place, and, ultimately, to the emergence of the other in the polis's "organised remembrance." In so enacting public space, they become subject to violence, arrest, alienation, or, especially in post-Yugoslav times, state paternalism; their resistance affirms and reanimates a shared sense of fragility, but also affection and camaraderie, in risky and courageous ways that resist injurious modes of gendered, sexualized, nationalized, and racialized appropriation of vulnerability.

In reading Arendt's conception of the polis, Butler has importantly asked: "On this account of the body in political space, how do we make sense of those who can never be part of that concerted action, who remain outside the plurality that acts? How do we describe their action and their status as beings disaggregated from the plural; what political language do we have in reserve for describing that exclusion?"[14] I would like to attend to this question of how we reckon politically with the enforced effacements that render political space a space for appearing and visible bodies, which is, for me, also a question of how to politically reckon with vulnerability and finitude but also with visibility tropes—such as those ascribed to sex and race—and their relevance to power and control. And so I ask what kind of polis would emerge from performing the spectral potentiality of displaced and disconcerted memory: an occurrence of memory that, contrary to appearances, incalculably complicates—albeit not incapacitates—the way in which people "come together"? Countermemory, in this context, becomes a performative force that registers that not everyone can emerge into the space of emergence, but also that not all "appear"—in the sense of being seen and becoming worthy of attention—according to the dominant frames of visibility, recognizability, and representability. Accordingly, not all appearing and assembling subjects act in concert with one another, nor do they share the same political positionalities and pursuits, nor are they propelled by homogeneous propensities and desires to set something in motion. The "space of appearance" is divided and apportioned:[15] that is, an agonal space implying the horrors of subjection and yet not devoid of agonistic action;[16] a space emerging both as a power effect and as a possibility for critical agency. Being-with-others-in-the-world does not indicate, I would like to suggest, an ontological category— that is, the human capacity of natality and plurality, in Arendt's parlance—but rather situated, contingent, and unevenly allocated conditions of possibility for performing common action in uncommon ways. This modality of political performativity insinuates possible and multiple ways in which appearing as reinhabiting the uninhabitable unfolds itself in unpredictable contingencies of political subjectivity.

On March 8, 2012, the year of the twentieth anniversary of ŽuC, a street demonstration stopped at 49 Jovanova Street, and a commemorative plaque was placed at the house where Ksenija Atanasijević lived from 1940 to 1981. The plaque described Atanasijević as a "philosopher, feminist, pacifist and antifascist." Instead of the solemn formality of commemorative public rituals that are habitually linked with national identity and are embodied in the monumentalist manifestations of historic sites and public sculpture, this was an event marked by the agonistic spirit of a political protest. This gesture was part of a struggle to install a different, hitherto unclaimed, memory at the center of the city's public topography: a struggle that involves public performances of embodied countermemory, such as vigils at the central square of the city, a demand to change militaristic place names in Serbia, actions of commemoration at the points where atrocities were committed in the name of the nation, and actions of commemoration-as-recuperation, like the one dedicated to Atanasijević (1894–1981), a major philosopher and feminist thinker, member of the Women's Movement Alliance and editor of the first feminist journal in the country, who in 1924 became the first female university professor to be appointed to the Arts Faculty of the Department of Philosophy at the University of Belgrade. Through these dissenting acts of performing irreconcilable memories in the city, in ways that reconfigure the gendered and ethnicized apparatus of belonging, WiB activists seek to trouble the sedimented intimacies of the nationalist archive.

A few months later, on June 27, 2012, after subsequent attempts to organize pride marches had failed due to either official banning or violent attacks by antigay protesters, Gay Pride finally took place and activists of WiB, Belgrade Pride, and Queeria Center held banners at the Republic Square: "I have the right to love," "My parents kicked me out of the house," "I was beaten up at this square." One of the banners was dedicated to LGBTQ people who were expelled from the public space—those who had to leave the country and those who had committed suicide because of homophobic and transphobic violence and repression: "I am no longer here." That uncanny reminder of disappearance registered the sociality of those uncounted who were expelled from one's uninhabitable world, gave up their place, or were banished from the polis. My respondents' ephemeral appearances in public evoke what it takes to make *these* present absences count.

Such instances of countermemory evoked the spectral presence of minor events and bodies that seemingly had not left any impressions on the normalized and normalizing site of archived history and, nevertheless, returned to trouble the ordered regularity of this history. I would like to make clear, however, that spectrality, as I use it here, does not denote by any means a status of being unreal/unrealized or being outside the political realm itself.[17] Rather, it seeks to signal an emerging and enduring state of appearance within, despite, and against existing political arrangements that make certain appearances of bodies in political space impossible or invisible. Specters, as we know, recur to haunt the *interior* of edifices, ontologically upsetting their terms of possession and making them susceptible to other inhabitations.

For our discussion of *this* configuration of mourning, we might think what politics is involved in the forces of spectrality. WiB memory-work constitutes an act of responsiveness to the other bodies of the archived memory, those with no place in the logics of national trauma. As they emerge to haunt collectively the national mnemonic and monumental space, these political subjects enact the performativity of becoming-ghostly: that is, the performativity of becoming responsive to the eventness of (nonpresent, nonrepresentable) others, in their plural singularity. Contrary to considerations of the event in terms of an unprecedented, apocalyptic appearance, we are thus impelled to reckon eventness through the figure of performative repetition as manifested precisely in the unauthorized appearance. Through this perspective, the polis becomes more than one and other to one: "plus d' un," to evoke Derrida's formulation.[18] It is, in other words, multiple and nonidentical to itself. It relies on the agonism that establishes ongoing and always contingent spaces of appearance beyond the epistemological premises of "appearance"—that is, visibility, transparency—that have been abundantly used to reify political subjectivity. As we try to make sense of the bodies that assemble in public space and are interpellated to fulfill the conditions of possibility for their appearance through norms of gender, sexuality, nationality, raciality, ablebodiedness, and ownership, we might find ourselves shifting from an analytics of *spaces of appearance* to one of *spacing appearance*.[19] In Butler's words, "the collective actions collect the space itself, gather the pavement, and animate and organize the architecture."[20] Indeed, collective action *animates* the space it yields. These acts of collecting and re-collecting space are inextricably bound up with the gestural dimension of taking space, also conceived as taking position. In this perspective, I propose a theoretical framework for understanding agonism beyond the biopolitical logic underlying the reductive dichotomy between "natalism" and "mortalism."

Agonism beyond Natalism versus Mortalism

In seeking an alternative to treatments of Antigone as figuring a "politics of lamentation," which might easily slide into a "lamentation of politics," Bonnie Honig has argued that Antigone's dirge and eventual death are political acts pointing "in the direction of an agonistic, not a mortalist, humanism."[21] Seeking to challenge the assumptions of mortalist humanism, which signals, in her perspective, a position premised upon an underlying commonality of finitude and liability to suffering, Honig turns to Hannah Arendt in order to propose that focusing on natality—the principle of Arendtian action—"may generate new commonalities while orienting humanism differently than mortality does."[22] I would like to ask, however: Is our analytics of agonistic politics doomed to reinscribing and perpetuating the humanist binaries between natalism and mortalism as well as agonism and vulnerability? Why would one need to move away *from* mortality *to* natality in order to argue for agonism or engage with agonistic politics? And why would one seek to analytically remove agony or agonal action from the register of agonistic engagement? I suggest that it is important to address, again and again, how politically consequential it might be to invoke the trope of natality—in all its religious and reproductive undertones that bespeak an *arché*—in order to make sense of the political praxis of "bringing something into being," as though it is purely inaugural and free of determination. Furthermore, by evoking natality as a theme that underpins the notion of human action, we remain by and large within the bounds of biopolitical and maternal logics, which has scripted motherhood as an absolute universal, a synecdoche of newness, and a paradigmatic signpost of self-negating relationality. But also, more broadly, the political consequence of turning either mortalism or natalism into essential traits of "human nature" is that humanness would thereby be universalized and depoliticized, thus working to legitimize and enhance the ruling assumptions of liberal humanism.

In a different vein, I insist on interpreting vulnerability and finitude here as thoroughly political and politically contingent themes, indeed as highly contested and differential occasions of intense politicization, rather than as humanist touchstones. I am interested in a performative agonistic poetics that is not devoid of the multiple potentialities of agony, and points toward a contextually situated—at once limited and incalculable—capacity and desire to engage and intervene in this world, and cuts across the binary between affirmative militancy and regressive grief; a binary often conventionally inscribed in terms of political, proactive natalism versus reactive, depoliticizing mortalism.[23] Once one subscribes to the terms of mortalism versus natalism, it is hard to avoid reductive conceptions of mortalism as powerlessness and natalism as pure inventiveness. Drawing on my fieldwork material, my suggestion is that once we challenge such configurations, we might be able to begin to make sense of the incalculably complicated and politically enabling ways in which these activists stage mourning as a site of agonistic resignification, however suffused with friction, in order to interrogate the hierarchies, injustices, and foreclosures upon which the authorized—gendered, racial, economic— frames of vulnerability and grievability are sustained.

Sovereignty, Finitude, Nonsovereign Agency

How might working on the register of uneven loss and mourning attend to the experience of becoming a political subject engaged in pursuits of critical agency? How might we think sovereignty and finitude together in articulating the possibilities for political subjectivity? It is in considering such overarching questions that I ponder, propelled and compelled by my ethnographic material, what it means to per/form a mode of nonsovereign political subjectivity in opposition and resistance to the logics of abjection, racism, and militarism. However, let me make clear from the start that the notion of nonsovereign subjectivity I seek to elaborate here, while clearly involving the modalities of mutual susceptibility and vulnerability, does not refer to a subjectivity identifying with, or reduced to, suffering and destitution. Nor should it be equated to self-negation, although it decisively relies on relationality and it questions the liberal devices of individual selfhood. Although my point is indeed to remain critical of self-sufficient unity, indivisible oneness, and absolute self-authorization, qualities in which the "ontotheology of sovereignty"[24] is anchored, I certainly do not mean to do away with all sovereignty *tout court*, especially insofar as it is tied to collective claims and courageous struggles of self-determination (no matter how problematic this notion might be in certain contexts). The perspective I am offering here might enjoin us to reinscribe self-determination as determination by and with the other, as an interminable and indeterminate finding of oneself with/in the other. So my point is to ask how we might think of sovereignty differently; namely, alongside the intricacies of finitude. The notion of finitude enables us to do so, and, as I argue here, in ways that open (rather than close) the space of the political. That said, the performative point of my critique is to call for a concept of political subjectivity and the political in general, which would require a troubled notion of top-down sovereignty, or, put differently, which may generate trouble in sovereignty.

This trouble in sovereignty—as a central category of modern political thought—has been efficiently occasioned by various strands of critical theory. Arendt, for one, has evoked a nonsovereign classical form of politics as well as nonsovereign quality of freedom. Sovereignty, conceived as a politically pernicious force of "self-sufficiency and mastership"[25] that is contradictory to plurality, undercuts a public-political realm and functions through mechanisms of exclusion and containment.[26] Derrida shares with Arendt the attempt to get away from a thinking that reduces the political to the assumptions and principles of sovereignty. If Arendt turns toward classical, presovereign forms of politics to evoke a nonsovereignty that would designate a plurality acting in concert, Derrida inquires into the political future of democracy as always deferred and yet present as an iterative and disruptive potential in the here and now.[27] In examining the history of the concept of sovereignty in its inseparable but contradictory relation to democracy, he delineates it as a form of power which is situated above the law and decides on what is proper to the human. In this context, "nonsovereignty" defines the impossible—albeit transformative—possibility for democracy without sovereignty, or *démocratie à-venir* ("democracy to come").[28] However, in registering a restless ambivalence vis-à-vis sovereignty, which is consonant with Arendt's own ambivalent attitude, he has significantly argued that: "In a certain sense, there is no contrary of sovereignty, even if there are things other than sovereignty. Even in politics (and the question remains of knowing if the concept of sovereignty is political through and through) the choice is not between sovereignty and nonsovereignty, but among several forms of partings, partitions, divisions, conditions that come along to breach a sovereignty that is always supposed to be indivisible and unconditional."[29]

Either as indivisible self-mastery of the subject or as an autarchic modality of power, sovereignty makes difference and sharing impossible. In her reading of Arendt and Derrida's accounts of political authority and resistibility, Honig has put it aptly: "Like her [Arendt], he [Derrida] refuses to allow the law of laws to be put, unproblematically, *above* man, but he recognizes, more deeply than does Arendt, that the law will always resist his resistance. His unwillingness to passively accept that is a commitment to politicization, resistibility, and intervention."[30] In this vein, what I am looking for is not a metaphysics of the outside and the beyond, which would be exemplified in an idea of pure nonsovereignty, either presovereign or postsovereign. Rather, what motivates me is a demand not to succumb to the logic of sovereignty as the only possible form of, and normal basis for, (the subject of) politics. Thus, I seek to account for the possibility of nonsovereign political agency: a notion of agency that is not bound to an antecedent sovereign self, not attributable to the individual's internal possession, and not reducible to intentional self-expression, will, and (conventional understandings of) autonomy. Instead, it remains immanent to power, socially involved, formed, and compromised; at once potent and vulnerable; a sovereignty without sovereignty.

What new imaginaries of the political would be prompted by this plurality of nonsovereign dispositions, then? Through the space opened by the WiB political subjectivity, I am led to rethink subjectivity outside the "sovereign" hold of sovereignty; beyond fantasies of mastery, and yet not as privation of the possibility of agency. I argue that WiB political subjectivity, as a spectral plurality of nonsovereign dispositions, decenters both defining orders of sovereignty: the one of unilateral and militarized national sovereignty and the one of subjectivity based on the model of self-grounding, phallogocentric, occasionally violent but distinctly inviolate, sovereignty.

Between Stasis and Ek-stasis

The WiB modes of nonsovereign agency in the wake of sovereign violence in former Yugoslavia implicate the contentious embodied intimacy of standing-in-public [*stajanje*] and enacting stasis as inhabiting the polis through discord. At the same time, they involve the potential to stand critically beside the normative matrices of "standing" as a presupposition of self-sovereign subjectivity. In other words, for WiB, *stajanje* entails standing in place but also standing beside oneself vis-à-vis the nationalist banality that led to militarist violence in what has become the former Yugoslavia. Hence, by positioning their bodies at the center of the city in solidarity with those turned into enemies by dominant ordinances of appearing, these political subjects actualize the multilayered modalities of stasis as a means of embodying their own and others' dissident belonging.

Stasis, usually denoting disanimation and disaffection, here signals animating the specters of unqualifiable losses—losses of bodies, communities, and possibilities—that haunt, and agitate, the common intelligibility of memorable life. It is about a mode of protest that compels a response and creates affective spaces for responsiveness and dissent—or, responsiveness *as* dissent. Therefore, *stajanje*, as stasis and standing, emerges as a precarious but defining moment of suspension that yields a new actuality of embodied loss and remembrance: one that derails, if only partially and temporarily, the normative presuppositions of what and who can "appear" in public in times of war exigencies and postwar normalization.

In standing at and across the border, in its multiple tropes of external and internal frontiers, enclaves, refugee camps, routes of mass expulsion, and states of siege, these political subjects embody the polis in ways that echo what Nicole Loraux has described as "the divided city." Division, which constitutes the founding moment of the city and the constitutive condition of the political, pertains to the always imminent, even if officially disavowed, possibility of internal division, or stasis. Internally divided, the city is constituted on the basis of that which it disavows. As marked subjects of gender, women, Loraux argues, performatively embody the awareness of this internal stasis—as division and revolt.[31]

The subjects I worked with in the course of my research actively engage with a labor of standing up as revolting and as enduring; above all, as repartitioning and reconfiguring the political realm of appearance. Slavica Stojanovic recalled her experience of standing at the square as an experience of responding to the enforced erasure from the polis's space of appearance: "I remember the feeling of such isolation, like we didn't exist, we were completely ignored. People passed, passed, and passed by. That was an awful feeling of not-existing, of being just erased." And she referred to violence as a mode of erasure from the polis's matrix of empathy: "Attacks happened later. At the beginning, people's reaction was apathy. They could not understand what we were doing there, in silence and dressed in black. Nobody would see us. Maybe they looked at us but they did not see us. It was all about erasure and denial." Erasure from the polis's available space of appearance is the price for stasis. At the same time, however, this erasure works as a performative occasion for another collective belonging, however precarious this might be, which speaks back to conventional discourses of both precariousness and collective belonging.

Slavica's narrative pointed not only to the traumas but also to the *ek-static* potential of standing against the will of the polis: "Each standing was like a catharsis for us. I remember very clearly that at the beginning of the vigil I was in a certain state of mind, and after an hour of standing I would find myself somewhere else." Camaraderie and endurance outside the ordained matrix of appearing and belonging was not only an occasion of social alienation, but also one of resistant and transformative ek-stasis. The vulnerabilities and the joys of collective agonism account for the possibility of persisting together, within operations of power which condition us as ecstatic subjects—dispossessed yet relational. The traumas and the ecstasies implicit in reappearing as reclaiming a space for admitting the inadmissible denote, in WiB activism, the possibility of opening to a new partaking. In Derrida's words: "What is thus remarked is its *departure*, that to which it no doubt belongs but from which it departs in order to address itself to the other: a certain (im)parting [*partage*]."[32] Departure, partition, and partaking, in all their multilayered assemblages and intensities, are at stake in the appearance of the liminal figures that haunt and threaten the body politic from within and from without.

Nonpassive and Passionate:
The Political Performativity of Vulnerability

In opposition to considerations of vulnerability through moral universalism and the governmentality of self-management, at the heart of my argument lies an exploration of ways in which vulnerability might work to open the space for a nonsovereign vision of political subjectivity. Such a stance, it should be noted, entails an alternative to the apparatuses of the self-contained, self-regulating moral subject and a radical critique of the moralizing implications of current neoliberal biopolitics of producing and managing "vulnerable populations." Hence, the perspective on vulnerability suggested here is not a call for a return to a phenomenology of bodily facticity and does not make an appeal to a prediscursive, totalizing ontology of human essence (be it vulnerable, resilient, or both). Addressing finitude or vulnerability is not to address a universal fact of nature, one that would compel transubstantiation from vulnerability to safety. This is to suggest that a shared condition of vulnerability is thought not as a foundational condition preexisting subjection and prefiguring the political, but instead as political at the outset: in other words, it is inflected and afflicted from the start by the historically authorized power relations that differentially invoke it as a naturalizing marker of those disenfranchised by racial, gendered, or economic regulatory violence.[33] Put differently, there is no shared condition of vulnerability, human and nonhuman, which is not always already fraught with the historicity of such losses, interpellations, modalities of power, and differences of location. And further, there is no shared condition of vulnerability which is not marked by the historicity of critical, resistant, and oppositional responses to those injuries.

As I am working on a political performativity that could be mobilized to disrupt prevailing schemes of biopolitics and liberal humanism, my perspective remains skeptical of the binary positivity-negativity that often permeates certain stripes of current critical discourse on vulnerability. In describing her own work on contemporary ethics in an essay suggestively titled "Affirmation versus Vulnerability," Rosi Braidotti writes: "This is an affirmative project that stresses positivity and not mourning."[34] Why, however, does "affirmation" need to be affirmed at the expense of "mourning"? Why should one accord one term a priority over the other? Why does mourning have to be rendered in terms of reactive negativity and why does "negativity" have to be cast as reactive and in pure opposition to "positivity"? I think a work of radical and creative redefinition (not only of words but also of imaginaries, affects, and political practices) would be necessary here in order to move beyond the schema of affirmation versus vulnerability. Although I support the broad thrust of Braidotti's thought on postunitary corporeality and affectivity, I have sought in this text to displace the resolute certainty of the unilateral opposition positivity/negativity, and, instead, explore their mutual contamination, without bracketing the one over the other and without reducing the one to the other. My hope has been to problematize the contention that the aporias of political performativity occasion a crisis of "agency."

In my reflection of WiB activism, their performativity of mourning is not about quietism, resentment, vengeance, destruction, or self-destruction but rather about refashioning relationality (which differs significantly from liberal interest-pluralism) through a displacement of the destructive terms that demarcate memorability-as-belonging. As I noted earlier, this is about a catachrestic modality of mourning, which breaks through conventional loyalties of gender and nation. This not-being-at-home-with-itself of mourning poses a challenge to the ordinances of affirmation versus mourning understood as a structural opposition. Rather than being subjected to the epistemological separation of affirmation and negativity, the WiB poetics and politics of mourning inhabit a zone of indetermination where this dividing (and indivisible) line becomes, effectively, elusive. Nevertheless, as much as their stance is about tracing the incalculable political possibilities of mourning, it is also, significantly, about acknowledging the interminably unattainable possibilities of mourning. This enduring practice of remembrance implies the awareness that an adequate restitution is impossible: those obliterated by public memory are not appropriable by our technologies of representation, recuperation, and recollection. As Derrida had made explicit, the affirmation of mourning affirms the impossible.[35] This is the aporetic structure on which mourning relies: the condition of its possibility is inextricably linked to the condition of its impossibility. Indeed, aporia denotes an affirmative experience of the impossible as indeterminate becoming-possible. It has to do with the mutual constitution of nonpassage and passage; less with passing or surpassing than with nonpassive endurance and passionate work on limits.[36]

This provides a way of understanding WiB's work of mourning not as reactive but rather as an event of contestation that *reactivates*, albeit without guarantees, the terms of mourning itself. This work of mourning, in its critical connections to national and gender politics, is not to be reduced to the canonical logic of dutiful or successful mourning, which would require or establish a fixed and identifiable other, and would render reconciliation and closure possible. By contrast, it is always becoming-possible—instead of possible as a purely opposite of the impossible.[37] To invoke again the discussion of the "affirmation versus vulnerability" register, then: WiB political anamnesis, in *affirming* the enduring commemoration of those obliterated by public memory, affirms also the im/possibility of mourning, not as a reconcilable contradiction but as an interminable event: one which marks a structure of temporality that involves calling the normalizing forces of the past and the present into question.

Here we are therefore in a time and space where the notion of the impossible is not to be conceived as negative or impossible *tout court* vis-à-vis the possible, and the possible is not to be conceived as purely positive. Questioning the normative frames that regulate what kinds of losses are authenticated to interpellate witnessing, as WiB does, does not necessitate reiterating an uncritical account of witnessing as transparent truth-telling; nor is it reduced to making concessions to the protocols of state-sponsored memorialization.[38] It is the very breakdown of witnessing that marks massive traumatic events, and also the acknowledgment of this breakdown, that can produce a different archive—an archive open to new possibilities for change. Furthermore, in order to be able to tell a different story and create another domain of memorability, those who have been previously injured, occluded, or jettisoned by established regimes of memory need to transform not only the terms that made possible the inflicted violence but also the terms of remembering and witnessing. In other words, we are enjoined here to think how political activism provides ways of responding to the experience of vulnerability without the certainty and purity of affirmation versus vulnerability.

How might a politics of mourning draw its possibility from that which renders it impossible? How can this aporia be affirmed and lived, then, and how does it raise the question of a persistent and resistant politics of remembering otherwise? Such questions hail us to address the political implications and, more specifically, the destabilizing powers, of avowing vulnerability in the sense of collectively responding to the traumas of subjection that determine "why certain forms of grief become nationally recognized and amplified, whereas other losses become unthinkable and ungrievable."[39] Thus, the contested terrain of public mourning becomes a site of normalization, but also an occasion whereby the subjectivity of memory is performatively constituted through the relationality to others, including, crucially, lost others. Butler's concern is with the logic of foreclosure and exclusion through which mourning, as a way of attending to the vulnerability of others, is *made* impossible, and yet is activated as a resource for transformation—not in the sense of overcoming vulnerability, but rather in the sense of working with/in it, challenging its inherent injustices, and inventing new collective forms of relating to it.

Pointing to the affirmative aspects of, and responses to, vulnerability has significant effects for our understanding and avowing of vulnerability at the heart of political performativity. In further complicating Michel Foucault's theorization of resistance as part of the strategic relations of power, Butler's work on performative agency has importantly provided an account of the possibility for a resignification that may deplete the sign of its historically authorized degradations, and reappropriate it in affirmative modes. Butler makes clear that by "affirmative" she means "opening up the possibility of agency,"[40] whereby agency is linked with a spectral plurality of performative enactments without clear origin and guaranteed outcome, and without the sovereignty of an originating subject. The expropriation—or, performative vulnerability—of dominant norms and discourses offers a site for disrupting the historically sedimented power effects of such norms. It is, at the same time, a site of performative fallibility and vulnerability: performativity is "that which produces events . . . but it is also that which neutralizes the event."[41] This is about a vulnerability that indicates the originary contamination of the sign and thus is already implied in any performative event. This rendition of the performative potential to derive an affirmation from degradation[42] offers, I think, a convincing response to a particular routine criticism according to which the theory of agency intimated by deconstructive performativity promotes a "negative" model of action instead of providing illustrations for "affirmative" political configurations. I would suggest that these charges are premised upon reductive assumptions that seem to position the vulnerabilities of performativity as inherently at odds with political agency.

Quite to the contrary, the conditions of possibility as conditions of impossibility make performativity political, and crucial for resistant and subversive collective action. In this spirit, then, to displace the "affirmation versus vulnerability" schema, which often marks particular conceptualizations of political agency, requires a twofold work of critical reconsideration. First, to acknowledge that vulnerability is inextricable from the domain of agency (as a domain necessarily implicated in power), to the surprise of the conceits of impassable, autarchic, and self-contained subjectivity as the self-evident ground of politics, according to which agency is what heroically exceeds (or liberates from) vulnerability. And secondly, rather than agency being understood in terms of impermeable plenitude and sovereignty of selfhood, to shift toward an understanding of agency premised on a suspension of the humanist tenets of the sovereign "I" and to imply a mode of being, becoming, and resisting always already traversed by the norms, traumas, and passions of vulnerability. Thinking vulnerability (as both susceptibility to power relations and disposition to others) together with performative affirmation would prompt us to trouble the calculative, individualistic accounts that posit subjectivity in terms of sovereign free will which masters an array of possibilities in order to confound vulnerability.

We might say in this regard that WiB agonistic mourning, as it performatively attends to the call of the unmournable other, affirms what escapes affirmation and activates what escapes activation. Instead of seeking to transcend or forestall vulnerability, these activists affirm vulnerability as an enabling condition for what Yael Navaro-Yashin has called "sensing the political"[43] through being with others and being affected by others. This politics of vulnerability calls for politicizing (as opposed to policing) interrelation to others within and against the operations of power ranking what and who can "appear" in the political space. This is about the political agonism of being moved by/with others as moving towards what is made impossible to present itself in the common, and yet decidedly uncommon, space of the polis—notably, injuries unrecognized, desires disavowed, and injustices unaddressed. Through their embodied emergence as spacing the dominant matrices of appearance, these activists wield public space as a register of the emergent—open and responsive to the contingencies of finitude and agonistic contention.

Notes

This essay is a condensed and reworked version of a lengthier text to appear in the author's forthcoming book entitled *Agonistic Mourning: Counter-Memory and Feminist Political Subjectivity in Post-Yugoslavia*.

1   Deutscher, "Mourning the Other," 159.
2   Ronell, *Finitude's Score*, 2.

3 Nancy refers to the "infinite birth of finitude," *The Inoperative Community*, 27. The question of how Nancy invokes the metaphor of birth, thus resonating with Arendt's "natality," would deserve a separate treatment.

4 Nancy, *Being Singular Plural*.

5 Nancy, *Being Singular Plural*, 95.

6 See Cockburn, *From Where We Stand*; Zajović, "Feminist Ethics, Women in Black Resistance."

7 Butler, *Antigone's Claim*.

8 The bronze monument of Knez Mihailo at Belgrade's Republic Square was erected in 1882 in honor of the Serbian hero, who in 1867 had liberated the remaining seven Serbian towns which were still under Ottoman rule. The names of the liberated towns, as well as heroic scenes from Serbian history, are engraved on the statue's pedestal. The statue of Prince Michael has even lost its "proper name," as in recent years it has become known simply and anonymously as *kod konja* (by the horse).

9 Arendt, *The Human Condition*, 198.

10 Butler, "Bodies in Alliance."

11 Arendt, *The Human Condition*, 198.

12 Arendt, *The Human Condition*, 200, emphasis added.

13 Arendt, *The Human Condition*, 199.

14 Butler, "Bodies in Alliance."

15 Butler, "Bodies in Alliance."

16 Although "agonistic" is the more typical Arendtian term, I muster also the word "agonal" here in order to convey that, devoid of the element of agony, the analytics of agonism risks reiterating the register of biopolitical sovereignty. See also Barder and Debrix, "Agonal Sovereignty."

17 Butler has importantly alerted us against accounts of disaggregation or effacement from the plural that take the excluded and the destitute to be "simply unreal, or [to] have no being at all." Butler, "Bodies in Alliance."

18 Derrida, "Et Cetera," 301.

19 Butler and Athanasiou, *Dispossession*, 194.

20 Butler, "Bodies in Alliance."

21 Honig, "Antigone's Two Laws," 26.

22 Honig, "Antigone's Two Laws," 9.

23 In reading Arendt's political thought along with the Occupy Gezi movement in Turkey, and in slightly modifying Bonnie Honig's reading of agonism in Arendt, Zeynep Gambetti (in this volume) addresses the aporetic nature of *agon* in ways that are relevant and valuable to my perspective. Much as *agon* might appear to conflate agency and fatality, it is precisely because of this reason, Gambetti argues, that it enables a critical rethinking of the very binary logic that defines "vulnerability and power as incommensurate terms."

24 Derrida writes: "In speaking of an ontotheology of sovereignty, I am referring here, under the name of God, this One and Only God, to the determination of a sovereign, and thus indivisible, omnipotence." Derrida, *Rogues*, 157.

25 Arendt, *The Human Condition*, 234.

26 However, Arendt's approach to sovereignty is not absolutely and homogeneously dismissive. At certain moments of her oeuvre, which bespeak a rather ambiguous and ambivalent attitude towards sovereignty, she seems to concede that sovereignty is rather inevitable in modern political life. (See, for example, *On Revolution*, 1963.)

27 Derrida, *Specters of Marx*.

28 Derrida, *Specters of Marx*.

29 Derrida, *The Beast and the Sovereign*, 115. Derrida's ambivalence with regard to sovereignty is consonant with his reservations about the term "democracy" as well. His hesitation has to do with the figuration of democracy in the tradition of Western modernity through the notion of "fraternity," which is saturated with the monotheistic tradition of women's subjugation. For an excellent discussion of the gender underpinnings of Derrida's democracy-to-come and his critique of fraternal democracy, see Pulkkinen, "Tradition, Gender and Democracy to Come."

30 Honig, *Political Theory and the Displacement of Politics*, 110.

31 Loraux, *The Divided City*.

32 Derrida, "As If It Were Possible," 13.

33 See Butler, *Precarious Life*.

34 Braidotti, "Affirmation versus Vulnerability."

35 Derrida, *Mémoires*, 32.

36 Derrida, *Aporias*, 14–15.

37 Derrida, "As If It Were Possible," 91.

38 See Feldman, "Memory Theaters."

39 Butler, *Precarious Life*, xiv.

40 Butler, *Excitable Speech*, 15.

41 Derrida, "Performative Powerlessness," 467.

42 Derrida, "Performative Powerlessness," 468.

43 Navaro-Yashin, " 'Life Is Dead Here.' "

CHAPTER 13

Permeable Bodies

Vulnerability, Affective Powers, Hegemony

LETICIA SABSAY

In recent years, increasing importance has been given to vulnerability as a critical concept for reconsidering the ethics and politics of our neoliberal times.[1] In rethinking the value of vulnerability as it has been mobilized in contemporary politics and as a theoretical concept, the embodied character of the subject has been central to this work. At the same time, the body has reemerged as pivotal in contemporary debates about current political dynamics as they have been paying special attention to the affective dimension of our political lives.[2] This renewed interest in vulnerability, affects, and bodies might be indicative of the political challenges posed by our historical present, especially in light of current global governmental logics, heightened processes of precarization, militarized securitization, political disenchantment with traditional party politics, and subsequent new forms of resistance. Among other issues, the various meanings, predicaments, and potential of democracy vis-à-vis the hegemony of neoliberalism are at stake. In this context, I would like to ask: How do discourses of vulnerability and the embodied and affective character of political dynamics figure in relation to an account of hegemony? By addressing this question, I will also try to assess whether vulnerability can operate in ways that either support or go against a radical democratic view.

One premise of this project is that we need to consider bodies and vulnerability in a way that questions the negation of politics by means of moralization, as happens, for instance, in the case of many humanitarian practices. However, it might be the case that this critical insight into vulnerability goes only part of the way. In my view, it is most important to regard these vulnerable, affective, material, and relational bodies in a way that does not amount to views of affect and embodiment that neglect the role of hegemony and articulation in politics. By these views, I refer to those responses to neoliberal biopolitical governmentality that hold that the truly effective resistance is in our bodies; that representation and counterhegemonic politics have become ineffective or irrelevant; that now is the time for developing affirmative (mostly micro) politics that find in the energies of bodies a counterforce to outmoded political subjects and obsolete state-oriented political aims.[3]

My intention in posing this caveat is not to override the crucial role of affect and vulnerability in political dynamics. Rather, the question is: How can embodied vulnerability and the affective dimension of politics bolster a radical democratic perspective that at the same time accounts for hegemony? I tackle this question following Judith Butler's conceptualization of vulnerability, which is central to her ethical-political framework.[4] Broadly speaking, this relational perspective is based on the subject's radical dependency and capacity to affect and be affected, which, in turn, indicates the vulnerable and embodied character of subjectivity.[5] I understand this relational affective dimension to be indicative of the permeable character of embodied political subjectivities. The way, then, in which we conceptualize these permeable embodied political subjects is central to our understanding of radical democratic practices. Following Ernesto Laclau and Chantal Mouffe's theorization of hegemony and radical democracy, key for my understanding of radical democratic practices is the constitutively antagonistic character of society. In their view, the representation of society as a totality is the effect of a hegemonic articulation and depends on an exclusion that figures as its constitutive outside; hence the necessarily open-ended struggle for hegemony, and the key role of contingent political articulations.[6]

The approach to the politics of vulnerability that I try to formulate, linking it with hegemony and radical democracy, is not only at odds with that of immanent approaches to affect and politics. These approaches tend to rely on the conviction that current political dynamics are mainly played out in unmediated ways (i.e., avoiding articulation). Further, it might also be dissonant with those agonistic takes on the politics of vulnerability that are significantly influenced by Hannah Arendt's model. At this point, I hope to incorporate into the politics of vulnerability and the public assembly of a plurality of bodies acting in concert—two topics extensively theorized by Butler—the antagonistic dimension of the political.[7] In this way, I hope to shed light on another aspect of vulnerability's political potential, while critically considering how radical democratic practices may look when the political dimension of embodiment is taken into account.

Embodied Vulnerabilities, Biopolitics, Resistance

In contesting the devastating effects of both coloniality and neoliberalism, which subject whole populations and sectors of populations to dreadful conditions, condemning some to social death while literally murdering others, humanitarian enterprises refer to vulnerable populations as a mechanism for presenting a moral or ethical call to appeal to the public to "help the victims," and in so doing they reaffirm rather than question the borders of assigned injurability.[8] What these humanitarian views cannot address is how we are all involved in the production of this vulnerability, as can be seen, for instance, with the effects of coloniality.[9] The effect of this approach is to depoliticize the situations that led to such extremes forms of deprivation—for example, by framing the potentially demandable situations of injustice and further claims for rights or egalitarian principles as human needs that require charitable gestures and benefactors. These different evocations of vulnerability constitute a renewed theoretical attention given to affects and bodies. As Lilie Chouliaraki points out, the media's showcasing of the suffering of distant others is key to humanitarian practices.[10] According to Chouliaraki, this suffering imposes an ethical demand on the audiences to feel and act in solidarity with those who suffer by means of a sustained appeal to their sensibility or even their moral sentiments. Similarly, Didier Fassin shows us how the portrayal of the recipients of humanitarian action as vulnerable— which is key to the whole humanitarian machine—depicts these subjects almost exclusively as the carriers of bodies subjected to naked violence.[11] The construction of "the suffering other" as a mute and helplessly un-nurtured, violated, or deprived body demands affective responses willing to commit to humanitarian enterprises, thereby moralizing otherwise potentially political claims.

By ignoring the role we all play in the differential distribution of vulnerability and its political character, humanitarianism does not really question the causes that produce this inequality. Instead, it attempts to mitigate some of their most painful effects. But these moral appeals to human sensibilities actually obscure the biopolitical dimension of global governmentality, that is, the regulation of human-life processes under a governmental rationality that takes as its object targeted populations.[12] Arguably, humanitarian evocations of an abstract and purely decontextualized human condition demanding a moral response tend to cover up the murderous governmental logics of coloniality and neoliberal securitarian and austerity policies.[13] Humanitarian pleas for aid, after all, seem to compensate for the deprivation and violence to which certain populations are subjected, either in war zones, refugee camps, or shantytowns, while in fact it is indirectly contributing to the perpetuation of a vicious circle.

Further, humanitarianism may participate in the expansion of the bio-power exercised over those populations declared in need of protection or humanitarian help, insofar as the very vulnerability of those populations becomes the ground of their regulation and control.[14] The way the question of violence against women has been mobilized in human rights campaigns and developmental projects, as well as being central to campaigns against sex work, is a case in point.[15] In these cases, the bodies of the victims are presented to us for the most part in isolation from their complex social contexts. These calls avoid any serious engagement with questions of poverty, exclusion, discrimination, or axes of inequality more generally. The reframing of sex work within the paradigm of trafficking and the campaigns for the criminalization of clients following the so-called Nordic model in Europe show that the advancement of the criminalization of sex work altogether is animated by the understanding of commercial sex as a form of sexual violence exercised upon women's bodies per se, rather than by a focus on violence against *sex workers*. So much so that, as sex workers' organizations have systematically pointed out, abolitionist impulses tend to serve the prosecution and control of sex workers, worsening their work conditions and increasing the likelihood of them becoming targets of violence, and not the other way around.

Likewise, the tendency of international women's human rights agendas is to concentrate primarily on the violence against women's "bare" bodies. However, this is in stark contrast to their selective focus, mostly centered on racialized gender-based violence, rape (mostly as a weapon of war), and female genital cutting, for which they tend to respond in decontextualized ways, by adopting negative cultural stereotypes, "rescuing women," and promoting individualist forms of empowerment.[16] As has been amply documented, by not addressing the geopolitical context in which these dynamics operate, when violence against women becomes an international object of feminist concern, it tends to serve civilizational crusades and the production of the racialized cultural other.[17]

The centrality of "vulnerable bodies" and affective appeals within humanitarianism is, in fact, part of a broader and far more complex scenario where the biopolitical power that organizes bodies and affects has taken center stage. Notably, precarization is at the heart of this problem. As Ilaria Vanni and Marcello Tari point out, precarization is not just about the expansion of a form of organization of labor that parallels the decline of the Fordist model;

rather, it is the norm through which the government of life is enacted.[18] Of course, this norm does not affect everybody in uniform terms as it works across stratified populations, and certainly does not operate in the same way in the global North as in the global South, or within different regions. What unifies it as a biopolitical tool of neoliberal governance is the way it signals the social, political, economic, but, most of all, affective and subjective conditions of current global capitalism. The precarization of jobs (doing away with the ideal of secure and stable employment), the blurring of the borders between work and life, and the centrality of affective and immaterial labor actually aimed at the production of new subjectivities are some of its crucial traits.[19]

In light of this panorama, it has been argued that as neoliberal biopolitics functions through the direct government of bodies and affectivities, it is at this level that we may find effective forms of resistance to it. This is the claim of Michael Hardt and Antonio Negri, who argue for an affective resistance, the formation of other biopowers from below.[20] Further, inspired to a great extent by Hardt and Negri, thinkers such as Jon Beasley-Murray argue that we live in posthegemonic times.[21] According to this view, the concept of hegemony is not useful for explaining contemporary political logics, as "ideology no longer plays a significant role" in the way we are governed, which occurs instead by and through "every pore of society as the distinction between the political and the social is eroded."[22] Given, then, that we are primarily governed through nonconscious affective means rather than through persuasive discourse, the argument goes, the current political moment requires forms of resistance that operate beyond the politics of representation and subsequent counterhegemonic strategies. Such effective forms of resistance would mobilize new forms of affect, and political formations that, like the multitude, escape the logics of representation.[23] Based on nonrepresentational theories, the argument could be understood as asserting that current biopolitical forms of subjectivation overdetermine any ideological position and any discursive formation. To counter such overdetermination, the primary modality of resistance should be played out at the level of bodies and affects; new subjectivities outside the grips of neoliberal norms of subjectivation should be forged.

In "Chantal Mouffe's Agonistic Project: Passions and Participation," Yannis Stavrakakis criticizes the posthegemony thesis not only for not being able to recognize the mutual entanglement of discourse and affect, but also for not taking into account that the theory of hegemony of Laclau and Mouffe does consider the affective dimension of politics.[24] And I could not agree more with Stavrakakis. For my part, while I do concur with those accounts that claim that we need to counter the biopolitical dimension of neoliberal governmentality, in line with Stavrakakis, I cannot accept an idea of biopolitical power that implies a neat distinction between body and discourse (understood in a broad sense as processes of signification or meaning making). Contrary to Foucault's basic tenet about the coconstitutive entanglement between discursive practices and bodies,[25] Beasley-Murray writes: "Posthegemony signifies the shift from a rhetoric of persuasion to a regime in which what counts are the effects produced and orchestrated by affective investment in the social, if by affect we mean the order of bodies rather than the order of signification."[26] The presumption here is that biopolitics is opposed to hegemony, but this opposition only makes sense to the extent that we accept the premise, wrong in my view, that biopolitical forms of power are disconnected from discursive formations and that such formations have no operation in the field of affect.

Neither posthegemonic nor post-Operaist visions are divorced from social processes, though.[27] There are clear synergies between them and forms of activism that are indifferent to, if not skeptical of, the possibility of pushing social changes through the politics of liberal representative democracy. Movements inspired by different versions of autonomism, commons activism, and anarchism, or the forms of organization in direct popular assembly among others, propose instead to generate alternative sites to both parliamentary and governmental logics of state apparatuses. And when democratic states have been hijacked by the dictates of finance capital, other forms of manifesting a democratic claim (or a claim to democracy) inevitably had to emerge.[28]

While precarization places the question of affect and bodies at the center of debates, the politicization of the vulnerability of bodies as a form of resistance has acquired a new significance in the light of the changing neoliberal politics of recent years. The intensification of precarization after the 2008 financial crisis—affecting vast sectors of populations from the global North, including many who were not expecting to belong to the disenfranchised (the new poor) and particularly the young population—together with longer processes of pauperization across the globe, have triggered public manifestations of social discontent in many parts of the world. This has led a number of authors, Judith Butler among them, to pay special attention to the so-called politics of the street, engaging in an extensive reflection on forms of resistance that have recently challenged the limits of representative democracy for not being democratic or representative enough, such as the Occupy movement or the Outraged People in Mediterranean Europe. The criminalization of social protest and the subsequent intensification of securitarian policies via the militarization of security forces, particularly after 9/11 and increasingly so after the 2008 financial crisis, have only heightened the role of bodily vulnerability in these forms of resistance.

In this context, Judith Butler has reflected positively on the politics of the street as a form of public assembly, an enactment of the popular will, a demand for self-determination and popular sovereignty, all of which are essential values for a democratic view of politics.[29] Throughout these timely interventions, she highlighted, rightly in my view, key aspects that amount to the political potential of these public demonstrations. The performative dimension of the gathering of bodies occupying (or rather claiming) public spaces is central to her argument about how the popular will is brought about.[30] It is through the acting in concert of the bodies gathered in different forms of public assembly, and not necessarily through their explicitly verbalized demands, Butler argues, that a plural popular will might be performed. Importantly, Butler also finds in these public demonstrations an instance that locates vulnerability at the core of resistance. Vulnerability is not opposed to agency here, but entangled with it.

This central role granted to the plurality of *the bodies acting in concert* as well as her focus on the political mobilization of vulnerability in practices of resistance, however, is at a distance from posthegemonic views. In the following sections I show how Butler's theorization of public assemblies suggests the possibility of moving toward articulation and counterhegemonic politics by looking into Butler's theorization of vulnerability vis-à-vis its differences from liberal-humanist as well as immanent and vitalist approaches to embodiment that belong to some of the new discourses on affect. In so doing, I aim to argue for an approach to vulnerability and radical democratic practices that take hegemony and antagonism into account.

Vulnerability/Permeability

Butler's theorization of the bodily politics of assembly and vulnerability seems to share with other approaches to vulnerability and posthegemony theoretical-political visions a preoccupation with the corporeal life of the subject. However, her approach clearly differs from them in significant ways. To a large extent, the difference between them is indebted to the distinctive conceptualization of bodies and affects in the relational ethics of vulnerability that Butler offers, which rejects both sovereign ideas of agency and either an immanent or a vitalist consideration of embodiment. This conception involves, first, an understanding of vulnerability that is based on the social (and therefore mediated) configuration of bodies. And second, it presupposes a reading of Foucault that diverges from those interpretations of biopolitics that presume it is possible to separate affects from discourse. To unpack these arguments, let us start by considering Butler's approach to bodily vulnerability.

One of the usual meanings of vulnerability implies the idea of unwanted permeability, or a kind of permeability that renders the permeable entity (be it an object, matter, the environment, or an individual or collective subject) weak or exposed to injury. Etymologically, vulnerability comes from late Latin *vulnerābilis,* from Latin *vulnerāre*: "to wound," from *vulnus,* "a wound." According to *Oxford Dictionaries*, to be vulnerable is to be "exposed to the possibility of being attacked or harmed, either physically or emotionally; [or] (of a person) in need of special care, support, or protection because of age, disability, or risk of abuse or neglect."[31]

This conventional definition, the one that circulates in contemporary imperial forms of global exploitation and liberal human rights frameworks, tends to equate vulnerability with injurability and refers to the possibility of being exposed to injury or attack, and therefore the need for either defense or protection.[32] However, as Butler points out, vulnerability cannot be reduced to injurability.[33] While injury results from the "exploitation of that vulnerability,"[34] vulnerability emerges from subjects' relationality, and it is constitutive of our capacity for action. Butler highlights two aspects of vulnerability in association with relationality: on the one hand, its link with dependency— the idea that we are radically dependent on others, and on the material and social world in which we come into being, and which might sustain us or fail to sustain us.[35] On the other hand, to be vulnerable implies the capacity to affect and be affected. This aspect of vulnerability involves a constitutive openness in the subject, regardless of whether it is wanted or not. This openness could be interpreted as a reminder that we are socially formed subjects whose shape and agency is actually coconstitutive with an outside that necessarily impinges on us. Following Butler, however, the inescapable capacity to be affected, which amounts to our responsiveness, is in fact inextricably enmeshed with our capacity to "act."[36] This intertwining is at the basis of her critique of the dichotomy between activity and passivity, or, in other terms, between agency and vulnerability. There is neither an opposition nor a necessary causal or sequential logic between them.

This chiasmic structure of agency and vulnerability recalls for me the dialogic theory of Mikhail Bakhtin, who insists on the permeable character of "our acts," "our voices," and ultimately ourselves. Following Bakhtin's dialogic approach to subject constitution, I understand permeability as a transindividual way of being in the world.[37] Given the transindividual character of subjectivity, permeability becomes a marker through which to highlight the idea that the subject is always decentered by the primacy of the other in its own being.[38] According to Bakhtin, we live in dialogue and can only come to know ourselves through the perspectives of others. At the same time, our uniqueness requires us to be responsive, as "our own acts" and crucially our "own voice" are, from the start, always already answers both constituted by and responding to other acts and voices; the world is addressing us.[39]

For Bakhtin, this dialogical character of subjectivity situates us in the realm of answerability from the start and therefore grounds our ethical relation to the world. As all our voices are mutually coconstitutive, the subject is conceived as a polyphonic palimpsest for which self and other can hardly be differentiated.[40] Understanding the metaphor of the "voice" in a phenomenological rather than a strictly discursive sense, permeability points more clearly to the idea that, being open (and therefore permeable) beings, we are all mutually affected by each other and the world around us, which in turn, is permeable as well. Permeability indicates the relational character of vulnerability in a way that highlights the impossibility of establishing a clear origin and destiny for the circulation of affect (both in spatial and temporal terms), and by this move it also reminds us of the unstable (and always in the process of being negotiated) boundaries of the vulnerable "I."

This focus on permeability may well be just a semantic nuance, but it is helpful for distinguishing two distinctive conceptual uses of vulnerability: (1) vulnerability as the capacity to be affected (which might be acknowledged or disavowed)—I call this permeability; and (2) vulnerability as a condition that is differentially distributed and might relate more straightforwardly with Butler's notion of precariousness.[41] While permeability seems to be a phenomenological, albeit socially structured condition, vulnerability emerges as an effect of that condition. I cannot manage my permeability, but given my subjective and objective position, this permeability can make me more or less vulnerable. Vulnerability may indicate an objective state: no matter how invulnerable I pretend to be or feel, my vulnerability will be there despite my will. But it can also describe a subjective state, as it might be something that one feels or is capable of acknowledging to a greater or a lesser extent, or fails to acknowledge at all (subject to "resistance" in the psychoanalytic sense). In either case, we can see that there are always some subjects who find themselves more vulnerable than others, while we could not say that some subjects are more permeable than others without compromising the relational paradigm altogether.

Permeability can be understood as one of the instantiations of relationality, and the body figures as an emblematic locus where reflections on relationality, injurability, and vulnerability have for the most part been staged.[42] However, while bodies may better expose this constitutive permeable character of the subject, bodies and affects have also served the reaffirmation of injurability and victimhood in ways that are contrary to the politics of vulnerability suggested here. For instance, this version of vulnerability clearly diverges from the humanitarian views described in the previous section. But how does our consideration of "affectability" and vulnerable bodies differ from how bodies and affects have been conceived within discourses on affect?

How do these differences give way to a different reading of biopolitical power, one that does not dismiss the relationship between affect, discourse, and power, and the role of hegemony in contemporary politics of resistance?

The Politics of Affect, Power, Hegemony

In this section, I hope to show the differences between a posthegemonic approach to affect and the politics of vulnerability discussed here. To do so, I follow Linda Zerilli's remarks on the shortfalls of the so-called affective turn, which, according to the author, are due not only to its immanent and vitalist characterization of affect, but also to the ontological status it is granted.[43] Following this discussion, I will consider how biopolitical power might be interpreted and resisted in light of a critical view that incorporates the insights of Foucault, Laclau, and Mouffe.

Zerilli is interested in assessing the reach and implications of the so-called affective turn as it has been increasingly influencing feminist and democratic political thinking. What is particularly problematic for Zerilli is how the ontological split between body/matter and mind/culture produced by these latter theories of affect forecloses the possibility of thinking seriously about the "judging subject." Zerilli argues for a postsovereign theory of judgment that challenges the dualism these theories of affect reiterate. My reading, however, is concerned less with the question of judgment than with the differences between those critiques of the sovereign subject that are based on "affect," and the critique of the liberal individual and sovereignty that a critical and relational approach to embodied vulnerability proposes.

Zerilli reminds us that many of the problems posited by the affective turn are not new. Indeed, the question of embodiment and materiality has been at the center of feminist concerns for decades—if not since its inception. Clare Hemmings has made this case well.[44] The other element that we need to take into account is its lack of conceptual unity. Zerilli rightly takes into account a first necessary distinction within the work on affect: On the one hand, there are those authors whose work is concerned "with the irreducible entanglement of feeling and thinking," such as Lauren Berlant and Sara Ahmed, among others.[45] On the other, there are those theorists who propose a new ontology, either in its vitalist or new materialist understanding of affect via Gilles Deleuze, particularly as read by Brian Massumi, replaying the old dualism between reason/mind, and affect/body, while pretending to overcome it. Zerilli's focus in this regard will be on the perspective developed by William Connolly, as an exemplary representative of this second trend.[46]

I am particularly interested in this ontological dimension insofar as it touches on a key element within current discussions on vulnerability, namely the body. In effect, this vitalist turn to affect presumes the materiality of the body—conceived as prior to the work of culture or signification. How to think about the link between corporeality and subjectivity is pivotal to the definition of this move as an ontological one. This point is important for my argument, as this question is at the center of what differentiates it from the relational considerations of vulnerability that we are dealing with, and with other approaches to feelings and emotions that do not deny the coconstitution of affects and the social (addressed later on).

Zerilli argues that this ontological turn to affect delinks affect from objects and any form of cognition or intentionality, radically detaches judgment from any affective or embodied basis, reinstalls a new sort of naive empiricism that believes in direct unmediated contact with and perception of the world, and therefore is not able to account for the normativity of experience. Significantly, according to Zerilli, this approach posits unbounded irrational affect as the ultimate determinant of subjects' conduct and beliefs and, finally, rehearses the same mistake that other critiques of rationalism have made, reproducing a strict split between conceptual thought and preconceptual experience or perception.

The insistence on the specificity of affect as that which is essentially prepersonal and presocial—in sum, prior to any labor of culture, concepts, or signification, and therefore not conditioned by any force other than itself—is aimed at underscoring its radical autonomy. Hence the conclusion that affect is the ultimate determinant of our conduct and beliefs and yet fully separated from them—a point that is central to Zerilli's critique. Zerilli rightly points out that such a view ultimately would not be able to give an account of resistance, as it is destined to conclude that anything we may think or do as political subjects is in the last instance the result of the manipulation of our affects, conceived as belonging to a fully different order than our thoughts.

This observation resonates with some criticisms made of Foucauldians for not leaving space for agency,[47] as well as those interpretations of biopolitical forms of power as purely affective to which I have referred earlier on. Foucauldian understandings of subjectivation in general, and regulative power in particular, point to the fact that power dynamics may well require the subjective affective investment of individuals to effectively operate, and even produce these investments. This is one of the central arguments of Judith Butler's *Psychic Life of Power*. Furthermore, according to this view resistance is never opposed to power, but rather is one of its forms and possible effects. However, this does not mean that resistance can only mirror and reproduce the power relations that it is resisting. Simply put, this means only that resistance can seek to transform some of the effects of a power field, but by no means will resistance ever put an end to it. In other words, we cannot think of freedom or justice outside of power (these very same ideals are implicated in it), nor can we aspire, through resistance, to achieve radical autonomy, self-transparency, or total social harmony.

Here I risk making a wild and bold association of sorts: with all the caveats that account for the huge differences between the two approaches, we can still find some resonances between Foucault's approach to power, the theory of hegemony of Ernesto Laclau and Chantal Mouffe, and the theory of agonistic politics developed by Mouffe.[48] My intention in suggesting this parallelism is not to dismiss the conceptual disparities between these perspectives. For instance, there is a radical epistemological dissonance between regulation and hegemony that I consider important, as it has implications for how we may understand the role of affective forces in relation to politics, a point I will address later on.

Let us consider this parallelism. Foucault's critical approach to power questioned Marxist views on ideology and the emancipatory ideals of the sexual liberation movement, concerned as they were with liberating their subjects from the grip of power. In this sense, one could read Foucault's observations on the mutual implication of regulation and resistance as a theory of the ineffably agonistic character of freedom. Laclau and Mouffe, at first together and later through different theoretical moves, have also criticized orthodox Marxism, drawing attention to the constitutive but at the same time indeterminate and contingent antagonistic character of society, which underlies the fact that there can be no ultimate truth, nor final accord, on ideals of justice and equality. The meaning of those signifiers is always already a matter of the content of hegemonic and counterhegemonic struggles.[49] According to Mouffe's model, it is precisely the unavoidability of this antagonism that structures ongoing agonism.[50]

Foucault's agonistic approach to power and resistance is one that, like Mouffe's, can never be foreclosed by definition. At an ontological level, power dynamics have no outside for Foucault; resistance is a never-ending struggle. In turn, both Laclau and Mouffe have argued that we can aim to transform social relations toward a more just organization of the social, but we will never definitively achieve a totally reconciled society. Antagonism and therefore hegemonic power relations are constitutive of the political, and there is no escape from this ontological limit.[51]

Foucauldian analysis points to those instances of power dynamics that may well not be yet politically articulated as an object of struggle (i.e., in the form of a claim) insofar as subjectivation, regulative power, and concomitant forms of biopolitical governmentality operate through discourses of truth (notably scientific ones) that present themselves as nonpolitical. Laclau and Mouffe, however, focus on precisely how subjects articulate political claims, or rather how political subjects are constituted through those articulations. Each of them highlights different aspects of politics: one is concerned with the biopolitical mode of government by which our bodies are regulated and we are subjectivated, the other with the constitution of political subjects in the specific field of the political struggle for hegemony. Arguably, the affective dimension of our social existence might work differently in each of these instances. But this only confirms that affective forces are present in both of them. We need to take into account that, after all, the theory of hegemony relies fundamentally on a psychoanalytic account of the human subject and its desires, and only within this framework can we pose the question of what motivates and mobilizes people. As Laclau points out, "Hegemonic totalization requires a radical investment . . . and engagement in signifying games that are very different from conceptual apprehension."[52] To the extent that it is precisely affective investment that will sustain a contingent articulation of arbitrary chains of equivalences among heterogeneous signifiers, it seems totally misleading to assert that the dynamics of affect are crucial to one realm (say biopower) but not the other (hegemony).

Going back to our discussion about those approaches to politics that privilege the biopolitical to the detriment of hegemony based on the assumption that affect is not implicated in hegemonic articulations as the advocates of the posthegemony thesis suggest, I therefore reject the conclusion that we necessarily have to radically oppose the two insights and to assume that we may find the truly politically relevant questions for our times (let alone their answers) exclusively in one or the other camp. I would also call into question the way the Foucauldian notion of biopolitics is used to indicate the futility of those political theories that concern questions of political articulation. In fact, I think both approaches to power and politics are necessary, for neither alone can give a full account of how politics works today—mainly because in order to effectively resist biopolitical neoliberal governmentality, the naturalization of the latter has to be challenged through a process of politicization; that is, it needs to be brought into the game of signifiers as an object of political discourse.

Psychic Investments, Body Languages

There is no reason to assume that the affective dimension of our lives absolutely determines social and political practices. This caveat does not imply a dismissal of affectivity, nor a stake in a cognitivist approach to politics or a claim to sovereign agency. The same idea of affectability at the core of Butler's notion of vulnerability relies on the understanding that our experience of the world is certainly traversed by affective currents that are not fully in our control. Further, it also suggests that affectivity is never fully autonomous, since its chiasmic structure makes it impossible to separate the affect from what affects it. Butler's approach to vulnerability, Laclau and Mouffe's approach to hegemony, and the discourses on affect considered here are wary of the all-too-powerful capacity accorded to sovereign agency. But unlike Butler and Laclau and Mouffe, the discourses on affect considered here are also reluctant to work with psychoanalytic insights into the limits of consciousness in order to understand what drives human action.

Psychoanalysis, however, offers one of the most powerful theories for explaining the tenacity of our attachment to what subjugates us, and the persistence of forms of oppression despite their widespread critique. If Freud has left an enduring lesson, it is that awareness does not itself lead to change.

And this is why hegemony is not merely about persuasion; rather, it is about cathectic investments in an articulation. Laclau writes, "It would be a mistake to think that by adding affect to . . . signification, I am putting together two different types of phenomena which would—at least analytically be separable. . . . Affect . . . constitutes itself only through the differential cathexes of a signifying chain. This is exactly what investment means."[53]

In effect, one could conjecture that what the turn to affect is trying to account for is in fact unconscious drives that are not under our control. From a psychoanalytically informed perspective, the source of this compulsive behavior would be located not at an ontological presocial and prepersonal level, but at the core of unconscious processes involved in the social formation of the subject. Even with all their differences, Butler, Laclau, and Mouffe all highlight the key role played by psychic investments and passionate attachments in political life. As Stavrakakis has remarked, both Laclau and Mouffe actually consider this affective dimension of politics a crucial element for the production of political identities and the works of hegemony and counterhegemonic strategies.[54]

Starting from the idea that psychic contents are socially formed, and that social discourses require the psychic investment of the subjects they interpellate in order to actually operate, it seems necessary to accept that some aspect of unconscious life remains opaque. This claim does not necessarily lead to the conclusion that unconscious affective currents are radically autonomous from social processes and are the last determinant of our political behavior. Rather, they just lead to the affirmation of the mediation of embodied affectability for thinking political identifications and articulations.

To claim that there is an area of experience and even knowledge that is embodied, nonintentional, and prereflexive may point to the critique of the sovereign subject, and the limits of transparency (of what can be disclosed). But that does not mean this experience is not mediated by signification (if only at an unconscious or prereflexive level).[55] Everything depends on how we conceive the process of social meaning making. This resonates with Butler's approach to embodied processes of signification, best exemplified by the performative dynamic of norms. Norms are not general rules articulated through mechanisms of representation, as if they were presented to us as objective prescriptive truths we are required to follow. Rather, they structure and inform bodily practices that enact psychic processes of identification by which we come into being. They are pre-predicative, not explicit, and learned in embodied practical ways, and they are certainly open to other movements of the body, other practices that might subvert them.

As Butler has stated on a number of occasions, if we are vulnerable sub-jects, one dimension of this vulnerability is undoubtedly our vulnerability to interpellation and to the name, where the name functions as a synecdoche for the normative social world that precedes us and marks the process of sub-ject constitution. Now, interpellation is not just about verbal speech acts; it is also about unintentional modes of touching, relating to, looking, and moving, hence the importance of affectability for understanding how bodily performa-tivity works. This also means that signification exceeds speech: the body com-municates unspeakable "messages" in languages that might not be translated into representational discourse, but this does not mean there is no significa-tion at all. When it comes to ethical relationality, Butler writes, "any sign of injurability counts as the 'face.'"[56] The uncomfortable place of vulnerability in between relationality and injurability shows the central role of the paradig-matic permeability of the embodied subject on which the ethical demand is made, but also suggests that this permeability is not devoid of processes of signification, as enigmatic as they might be.[57] Correspondingly, the somatic is never to be found outside fantasy, while fantasy, in turn, is never to be com-pletely asocial;[58] the circulation of affect, its attachment to an object, and its random transferability to another operate in tandem with communicative pro-cesses whether or not we can put them into words.

Both Stavrakakis and Zerilli rightly point out that, contrary to this idea of intertwined mediations among the social, the psyche, and the body, the affec-tive turn is part of a broader ontological turn in political theory, where affect and body figure as privileged tropes for mobilizing the fantasy of a material unmediated relation to how things really are. This sort of reconstituted em-piricism hinders the mediation of signification—and therefore the omnipres-ence of power and norms.

But I am tempted to read this ontological turn as a symptom. Given that the promise of a direct access to reality also elevates affect (outside the socially formed subject), matter, or objects to the new role of agents, one could argu-ably see it as a symptom that in some cases even works in favor of an evacu-ation of the political. My sense is that the celebration of material agency also has a stake in dismissing our subjective involvement in the political, some-times disguised as an appeal to the humility of the human, other times be-coming the occasion for disavowing our own political apathy, lack of hope, or sense of either deception or anticipated defeat. The impasse we are in, which according to Lauren Berlant drives forms of "cruel optimism," may also lead to different negotiations of the "desire for the political" in times of neoliberal systematic crisis.[59] And one could perhaps think of this hope professed for the autonomous agency of affect as one of them.

In a similar vein, it could also be seen as a symptom that mirrors the perverse transparency of power and the cynicism of our times. And so the question emerges: given the current cynical modality of power, according to which it is not so much the opacity of the operations of power that allow for their resilience, but their very transparency, their presence on the surface, it is clear that awareness and critical judgment might not be enough to counter it. This is a moment when it is not so much a neurotic-paranoid logic that we are haunted by and therefore supposed to unveil the insidious hidden operations of power that subject us, but rather one that perversely fetishizes the overt exercise of power. Despite, or perhaps even as a response to, massive criticism, we bear witnesses to the exhibition of violence in the most obscene ways. We are thus compelled to wonder: how does the investment in a democratic imaginary manage to shift despair, resignation, indifference, or condescending compassion into political solidarity, and collective, active resistance to this violence? Where might we find forms of counterhegemonic "affective articulation" that effectively challenge this logic and that might be understood to put at stake a reconsideration of this important dimension of hegemony?

Embodied Articulations and Radical Democratic Politics

As I have argued in previous sections, the focus on bodies and affectability might suggest that there are some resonances between the turn to affect and the ethical turn to vulnerability. The paradigmatic materiality, affectability, and permeability of bodies are pivotal to both the affective turn and the recuperation of vulnerability as a generative concept. Yet the focus on bodies and affectability can lead to very different political outcomes depending on how we understand them, and these differences do matter if we are to consider how to account for hegemony and move toward effective radical democratic politics. Can vulnerability and embodied forms of resistance be cast in ways that disregard neither the importance of affective investments, nor the importance of counterhegemonic articulations in politics?

One could understand Butler's claim that "when the body 'speaks' politically, it is not only in vocal or written language"[60] to suggest that, in certain circumstances, bodies could produce political articulations. When reflecting on public assembly, Butler points out that the plurality of bodies on the streets may, through concerted action, enact a right—for instance, performing the right to appear in the political field—or a demand—against precarity, or for the sustainability of those very same bodies.[61] Yet there is a difference between affirming the political signification of these instances and saying that the bodily performativity of the public assembly may articulate particular political "contents." Could we read these bodies acting in concert as the site of potential articulations?

According to Ernesto Laclau and Stuart Hall, what is central to an articulation is the contingent way by which two or more elements come together to produce certain meanings, subjects, or identities.[62] Articulation makes manifest that there is "no necessary or essential correspondence of anything with anything,"[63] and it is precisely the contingency of articulations that makes them the object of political dispute. But this also suggests that articulation can and actually may be performed in many different ways, including social practices, discourses, events, and surely forms of embodiment. Arguably, articulation should not be limited to representational discourse (that is, the equation of discourse to verbal speech), and, in this sense, what bodies *do* may well perform political articulations. However, the question remains, How are we to interpret what might be articulated in the embodied dimension of public assemblies, mostly when the legitimacy of a state regime or vision is challenged, when, by their very nature, public assemblies challenge the established meaning of democracy, and the whole space of politics? This question confronts us with two related problems: on the one hand, the temporality of what we may understand as a political articulation; on the other hand, what is articulated there beyond representational discourse or verbal speech.

Butler writes: "Perhaps these are anarchist moments or anarchist passages, when the legitimacy of a regime is called into question, but when no new regime has yet come to take its place. This time of the interval is the time of the popular will . . . characterized by an alliance with the performative power to lay claim to the public."[64] Certainly, one could read the alliances of bodies in this performance as a form of articulation. And, as Butler suggests, when considering the meaning of such articulation, temporality is important. If we limit our analysis to what has been said or enacted in that moment, we may not be able to consider the political space that the same articulation opens. These moments articulate something, the effects of which we cannot assess in the here and now of the political happening itself. They belong, in certain measure, to the contingency of political struggles and the unpredictability of what these moments might open up.

The gap between these manifestations of the popular will, whose task is precisely to disrupt the usual course of politics, and what comes next opens the space of hegemonic struggles. This gap, theorists of hegemony caution, should prevent us from celebrating too summarily the moment of disruption per se. In turn, Butler indicates that "there are many reasons to be suspicious of [these] idealized moments."[65] And this, regardless of whether or not that political moment leads to more conventional state-oriented counterhegemonic battles for government rule—this can happen or not, and many other things may happen too. Consider the aftermath of the so-called Arab Spring in Egypt, where soon after the electoral victory of Mohamed Morsi, the democratically elected government was removed in 2013, and the dreadful situation in the region, in contrast to the fate of the Indignados movement, the electoral success of Syriza in Greece, and the mixture of success and difficulty that followed, to some extent similar to the success and challenges that Podemos faces in Spain.[66] Even if we accept the contingency of hegemonic struggles, this is different from giving in to that contingency. Surely we cannot reduce the meaning of a political happening to its explicit demands, and it is clear that political articulations exceed the conscious intentionality of any particular actor. But we might want to be cautious not to definitely celebrate the affective force of the happening itself when such a celebration's focus on the affective dimension of experience serves to dismiss the necessary transience of such moments and to disavow the current difficulty for articulating effective and sustainable political alternatives to neoliberal policies.

At stake here is the task of counterhegemony and the articulation of the "we" who is assumed to belong to the political community, and the "other" it necessarily produces. While we may not always be able to perceive a clear intention, what these bodies assembling in public articulate is a "we" that in one way or another necessarily opposes an "other." At this point, the question of antagonism becomes key, as it signals the orientation of such articulation. Butler also suggests the inevitability of this antagonism.[67] It might be precisely in light of this antagonism that we may be able to determine whether or not the articulations at stake could be counterhegemonic.

Antagonism is pivotal to radical democratic politics. Such a politics points to the constitutively antagonistic character of the political.[68] According to Laclau and Mouffe, the political is defined by its undecidability and therefore its arbitrariness—there is no rationalist or deliberative response that could justify our political views.[69] The arbitrariness of the political points to its essential lack of foundation. It is precisely this foundational lack that, in turn, demands that any political position struggle hegemony—when any position credibly presents itself as common sense, a natural truth, or rational, that is, in fact, the sign of its hegemony. What this struggle for hegemony also produces is the "we" of the political community it claims to represent.

Antagonism is central to radical democratic politics, as any decision implies the exclusion of other political possibilities; but more crucially, because the hegemonic definition of the political community needs the demarcation of a "constitutive outside" to define itself as such, out of this border a constitutive exclusion remains.[70] A radical democratic politics involves the understanding that there is no ultimate political closure, and therefore accepts the ever-present existence of antagonist forces. It is a politics that conceives the boundaries of the polity as always open—perhaps vulnerable or permeable?—to the challenges of what has been excluded.

The "we" of the public assembly could be the 99 percent occupying streets and parks, the "outraged people" camping on central squares in protest against political classes that do not deliver "real democracy," or the self-perceived autochthonous Europeans marching against the migrants.[71] All these demonstrations articulate a different version of the body politic. If we think about this "we" across the differential distribution of vulnerability, we see that in some cases the exposure of vulnerability serves as a claim of the excluded and the redefinition of the political community. In other cases, it works as a demand for more exclusion—leading to an enhancement of the vulnerability of the other. Yet in some cases, the act of exposing vulnerability does question how vulnerability is extremely ill-distributed but without questioning the outer limits of the "we."

The permeability of bodies, in this sense, works as a metaphor for the permeability of the body politic, and the constant negotiation of its boundaries. According to Butler, this "we" performs a popular will that might be plural and heterogeneous. But if this is so, it is not because of the immediate performativity of the acting in concert. Rather, the "we" that these bodies perform articulates an antagonistic relationship with what they are resisting, and particularly with what they are also excluding. The question, then, is how affective investments and shared vulnerability produce articulations that agonistically reconfigure social antagonisms, calling into question the hegemonic borders of the body politic. This questioning has to endure toward an always-open horizon for further struggles to come. A radical vision of democracy, after all, seems to be less concerned with the realization of an ultimate ideal than with the ceaseless mobilization of permeable alliances that may question its own limits.

Notes

I am grateful to Judith Butler and Zeynep Gambetti for their insightful comments on earlier versions of this chapter and their thoughtful suggestions for improvement. My gratitude extends to all of the workshop participants for their inspiration.

1 On the increasing renewed interest in vulnerability, see Mackenzie, Rogers, and Dodds, *Vulnerability*; Drichel, "Vulnerability"; and a special issue of *Feminist Formations* to be coedited by Wendy Hesford and Rachel Lewis, titled "Mobilizing Vulnerability: New Directions in Transnational Feminist Studies and Human Rights" (http://www.feministformations.org/submit/cfp.html#sthash.Hvlkdw6S .K411ZzoH.dpbs). Likewise, this trend is clear in projects such as "Vulnerability and the Human Condition Interdisciplinary Initiative," hosted at Emory University; the Scholar & Feminist Conference, "Vulnerability: The Human and the Humanities," held at the Barnard Center for Research on Women (March 3, 2012); and the workshop "Risquer la Vulnérabilité: Risking Vulnerability," held at the Graduate Centre of the City University of New York (April 23, 2015).

2 For an account of the so-called turn to affect, see Hemmings, "Invoking Affect"; Clough, introduction to *The Affective Turn*, 1–33; Blackman and Venn, "Affect"; and Pedwell and Whitehead, *Affecting Feminism*.

3 There are a variety of positions that draw on the primacy of affective currents, and/ or the potential of life forces to argue for a new form of politics more suitable to respond to the challenges of our times. They might range from the "affirmative politics" proposed by Rosi Braidotti (on Braidotti's affirmative politics, posthuman nomadic ethics, and zoe-egalitarianism, see *The Posthuman*, 100–104, 190–195), to Jon Beasley-Murray's posthegemonic politics (see *Posthegemony*); from Michael Hardt and Antonio Negri's *Multitude*, to William Conolly's neuropolitics (on Conolly's use of neurosciences and Deleuzian approaches to affect to develop his perspective on pluralism, see *Neuropolitics*; on his recourse to the creativity of life-processes for thinking democratic practices, see *The Fragility of Things*).

4 Cf. Butler, *Precarious Life*; *Giving an Account of Oneself*; *Frames of War*; and *Parting Ways*.

5 On dependence and affectability, see Butler, *Giving an Account of Oneself*, 50–84; *Frames of War*, 33–54; and Butler, this volume.

6 Laclau and Mouffe, *Hegemony and Socialist Strategy*.

7 By "the political" I refer to the ontological/ontic distinction between the political and politics respectively, as it has been staged by Laclau and Mouffe according to Oliver Marchart (see Marchart, *Post-Foundational Political Thought*, 134–153). Here the ontological/political level indicates both the impossibility of society as a totality (or its impossible representation of the universal) and the necessary suture of society as a totality (or its necessary claim to be representing the universal). Antagonism emerges at the core of the political as it indicates, then, the ontological arbitrariness of a given totality and its ontological condition as an effect of

antagonistic struggles. Politics, by contrast, refer to the ontic materializations that suture society's fundamental lack of foundations. See Laclau, *Emancipation(s)*. Later Mouffe will equate the political to antagonism as inherent to human relations. See Mouffe, *On the Political*.

8 My observations are specifically directed to those instances where human rights frameworks have tended to take the path of "aid," rather than a more politicized interpretation of them. Actually, while human rights are systematically violated by the heightened precarization of populations (i.e., neoliberal global economics, and permanent production of war refugees), human rights–based claims are also used to contest precarization, and against neoliberalism, and could be far more radical in this sense. It is true that the formulation of human rights imposes limits on how we conceive equality, always qualified, as it refers to being equal to; or how we conceive freedom, already naturalized in liberal terms. Yet we need to distinguish the epistemic limits of human rights, as their formulation belongs to Western modernity and coloniality, from their political potential (and be attentive to how the epistemological critique sometimes obfuscates the political one). Human rights principles have been catachrestically appropriated in ways that, for instance, allowed for the defense of peoples against state violence in the context of dictatorial governments, and to some extent they continue to do so. The fact that human rights are systematically violated by legitimized forms of state violence from the global North (think of the criminalization of social protest, the murderous logic of neoliberalism after the 2008 financial crisis and neocolonial enterprises, and the legalization of torture, not to mention war dynamics), while at the same time being used to demonize specific cultures, especially Islamic ones, is not just an epistemic problem, but a political one. As critical legal scholarship has pointed out, this "culturalization" of human rights politics by which the focus of attention has been displaced from state violence more generally to the targeting of specific cultures as the main one responsible for human rights violations is a relatively recent process. Furthermore, there are different instances in which human rights frameworks work, from international courts to binding treaties, NGO activities, international forums, and aid industries, that need to be analyzed according to the logics they create for themselves. These instances depend on this epistemic framework, but exceed it.

9 Following Anibal Quijano, I use "coloniality" to indicate the pervasiveness of colonial relations after decolonization. See Quijano, "Coloniality of Power, Eurocentrism, and Latin America."

10 Chouliaraki, *The Spectatorship of Suffering*.

11 Fassin, *Humanitarian Reason*.

12 On biopolitics, international relations, and neoliberal governmentality see Foucault, *The Birth of Biopolitics*.

13 I thank Marsha Henry for pointing out to me the masking function of abstract human rights in relation to the murderous logic of imperial impulses and military interventions.

14 On an approach to vulnerability as a transformative ground able to challenge the biopolitical management of vulnerability, see Ziarek, "Feminist Reflections on Vulnerability."

15 See Grewal, "Women's Rights as Human Rights." On the connections between humanitarianism, migration policies, and sex work see Mai, "Between Embodied Cosmopolitism and Sexual Humanitarianism."

16 For a critical analysis of the use of vulnerability and the neoliberal reframing of empowerment within the field of gender and development, see Madhok and Rai, "Agency, Injury, and Transgressive Politics in Neoliberal Times."

17 Precise examples of this trend are pointedly analyzed in Narayan, "Cross-Cultural Connections, Border-Crossings, and 'Death by Culture'"; and Abu-Lughod, "Do Muslim Women Really Need Saving?"

18 Vanni and Tari, "On the Life and Deeds of San Precario."

19 On the relationship between immaterial labor, biopolitics, and the production of new subjectivities, see Hardt and Negri, *Empire*.

20 Hardt and Negri, *Multitude*.

21 Beasley-Murray, "On Posthegemony."

22 Beasley-Murray, "On Posthegemony," 118–119.

23 Beasley-Murray, *Posthegemony*.

24 Stavrakakis, "Chantal Mouffe's Agonistic Project."

25 Foucault, *History of Sexuality, Vol. I.*

26 Beasley-Murray, "On Posthegemony," 120.

27 By "post-Operaism" I refer to the Italian autonomist tradition, in this chapter represented by Negri.

28 We can understand many contemporary public demonstrations, social movements, and political manifestations along these lines, from those against evictions, precarious jobs, unemployment, austerity policies—especially those against cuts in public health and education—to migrants' organized resistance to violence at the borders.

29 Butler, *Notes toward a Performative Theory of Assembly*.

30 Butler, "Bodies in Alliance."

31 S.v. "vulnerability," and "vulnerable," *Oxford Dictionaries* (online), http://www .oxforddictionaries.com/us/definition/american_english/vulnerability, http:// www.oxforddictionaries.com/us/definition/american_english/vulnerable, accessed May 3, 2016.

32 See Butler, *Precarious Life*. As has been extensively noted, the othering of Islam as a threat to the West after 9/11 encouraged renewed imperial impulses presented as self-defense, while mobilizing civilizational enterprises allegedly aimed at "protecting the Other's victims."

33 Butler, *Frames of War*, 54–62.

34 Butler, *Frames of War*, 61.

35 Butler, *Frames of War*, 19–20.

36 Butler, *Giving an Account of Oneself*, 65–75, 84–90.

37 On the transindividual character of the speaking subject, see Bakhtin, *The Dialogical Imagination*.

38 Bakhtin, "The Problem of Speech Genres."

39 Bakhtin, *Toward a Philosophy of the Act*.

40 On the notion of polyphony in Bakhtin, see "The Problem of Speech Genres" and "Dostoevsky's Polyphonic Novel and Its Treatment in Critical Literature."

41 Butler, *Precarious Life*.

42 On the body as the emblematic locus of vulnerability, see, for example, Anne Phillips, *Our Bodies, Whose Property?*

43 Zerilli, "The Turn to Affect and the Problem of Judgment."

44 Hemmings, "Invoking Affect."

45 Cf. Berlant, *Cruel Optimism*; Ahmed, *The Cultural Politics of Emotion*.

46 Cf. note 2 above.

47 For an account of feminist critiques of Foucault's notion of power in relation to the project of feminism, see McLaren, *Feminism, Foucault, and Embodied Subjectivity*.

48 Cf. Laclau and Mouffe, *Hegemony and Socialist Strategy*, and Mouffe, *Agonistics*.

49 On the role of signifiers in hegemonic struggles, see Laclau, *Emancipation(s)*.

50 Mouffe, *Agonistics*.

51 On the postfoundational position of Laclau and Mouffe, see Marchart, *Post-Foundational Political Thought*, 134–153. Cf. note 7 above.

52 Laclau, *On Populist Reason*, 71.

53 Laclau, *On Populist Reason*, 110–111.

54 Stavrakakis, "Chantal Mouffe's Agonistic Project," and Laclau, "Glimpsing the Future," quoted in Stavrakakis, "Chantal Mouffe's Agonistic Project."

55 A number of social theorists have conceptualized this nonobjectified realm of experience in different ways, developing influential approaches, such as the lifeworld of Alfred Schultz (taken up, in turn, by Jürgen Habermas), the constituent imaginary of Cornelius Castoriadis, and the habitus of Pierre Bourdieu.

56 Butler, *Parting Ways*, 10.

57 See Butler's reading of Jean Laplanche's enigmatic signifiers in *Giving an Account of Oneself*, 71–73.

58 Butler, *Giving an Account of Oneself* and *Bodies That Matter*.

59 Berlant, *Cruel Optimism*.

60 Butler, "Bodies in Alliance."

61 Butler, *Notes toward a Performative Theory of Assembly*.

62 Hall and Grossberg, "On Postmodernism and Articulation," 139–143.

63 Hall, "Minimal Selves," 44.

64 Butler, "Bodies in Alliance."

65 Butler, "Bodies in Alliance."

66 The Indignados movement emerged in Spain after a massive anti-austerity demonstration held on May 15, 2011, in a number of cities across the country. This movement gathered (and propounded the articulation of) a series of activist

groups and ongoing assemblies and led to the formation of the platforms 15-M and Democracia Real Ya (Real Democracy Now) among others, giving way to a long-standing series of massive protests and permanent camps in emblematic places throughout Madrid, Barcelona, and other important cities. Podemos (We Can), the radical Left political movement that emerged in part as a result of these popular mobilizations, transfigured the political scene in Spain, making it first into the European Parliament, and then at local elections, amid the strong opposition presented by the two main parties and the media. Syriza, the coalition of the radical Left, won the national Greek elections in January 2015. However, the government entered a crisis in August of the same year vis-à-vis the refusal of the European Union to negotiate economic measures that would relieve Greece from an exacting austerity package, leading to a call for new elections to take place in September 2015.

67 See Butler, introduction to *Notes toward a Performative Theory of Assembly*.

68 See Mouffe, "Radical Democracy."

69 Laclau and Mouffe, *Hegemony and Socialist Strategy*. On the critique of rationalist understandings of liberalism and deliberative democracy, see Mouffe, *On the Political*.

70 On the development of the notion of constitutive outside, see Laclau, *New Reflections on the Revolution of Our Time*.

71 The series of demonstrations organized by the group Patriotic Europeans against the Islamization of the West (PEGIDA) in Dresden, Germany, between December 2014 and February 2015, followed by a smaller but still worrying demonstration in Newcastle, UK, on February 28, 2015, illustrate the point. Auspiciously, strong antiracist demonstrations against PEGIDA and its offshoot, BOGIDA, eclipsed or frustrated other demonstrations to be held in Edinburgh, Berlin, and Bonn.

Abrahams, Ray. *Vigilant Citizens: Vigilantism and the State*. Cambridge: Polity, 1998.

Abu-Lughod, Lila. "Do Muslim Women Really Need Saving? Anthropological Reflections on Cultural Relativism and Its Others." *American Anthropologist* 104, no. 3 (2002): 773–790.

Agamben, Giorgio. *Homo Sacer: Sovereign Power and Bare Life*. Stanford, CA: Stanford University Press, 1998.

———. *Nudités*. Paris: Rivages, 2009.

———. *Potentialities: Collected Essays in Philosophy*. Translated by Daniel Heller-Roazen. Stanford, CA: Stanford University Press, 2000.

———. *State of Exception*. Chicago: University of Chicago Press, 2005.

Ahıska, Meltem. "'Kadına Yönelik Şiddet'le Uğraşmak, Kadınlık Hallerine Nasıl Bir Ayna Tutuyor?" In *Şiddete Karşı Anlatılar: Ayakta Kalma ve Dayanışma Deneyimleri*, edited by Mort Çatı. Istanbul: Mor Çatı Yayınları, 2009.

———. "Occidentalism: The Historical Fantasy of the Modern." *South Atlantic Quarterly* 102, nos. 2/3 (2003): 351–379.

Ahmed, Sara. *The Cultural Politics of Emotion*. Edinburgh: Edinburgh University Press, 2004.

———. "Willfulness as a Style of Politics." In *Willful Subjects*. Durham, NC: Duke University Press, 2014.

Ahmed, Sara, Claudia Castaneda, Annie-Marie Fortier, and Mimi Sheller, eds. *Uprootings/Regroundings: Questions of Home and Migration*. Oxford: Berg, 2003.

Alcoff, Linda, and Laura Gray. "Survivor Discourse: Transgression or Recuperation?" *Signs: Journal of Women in Culture and Society* 18, no. 2 (Winter 1993): 260–290.

Alessandrini, Anthony, Nazan Üstündağ, and Emrah Yildiz. "'Resistance Everywhere': The Gezi Protests and Dissident Visions of Turkey." *JadMag* 1, no. 4 (Fall 2013).

Alkan, Mehmet Ö. "Taksim'in Siyasî Tarihine Mukaddime." *Birikim* (July–August 2013): 291–292.

Allison, Dorothy. "Survival Is the Least of My Desires." In *Skin: Talking about Sex, Class, and Literature*. Ithaca, NY: Firebrand Books, 1994.

Althusser, Louis. "Ideology and Ideological State Apparatuses (Notes Towards an Investigation)." In *Lenin and Philosophy and Other Essays*, translated by Ben Brewster. New York: Monthly Review Press, 1971.

Altunpolat, Remzi. "Gezi Vesilesiyle LGBT Hareketi ve Sosyalistler." *Kaos GL Dergi*, July 20, 2013.

Anders, Gunters. *Nous Fils d'Eichmann*. Paris: Payot, 1999. Originally published 1988.

Arat, Yeşim, and Ayşe Gül Altınay. *Violence against Women in Turkey: A Nationwide Survey*. Istanbul: Punto, 2009.

Arendt, Hannah. *Between Past and Future*. New York: Viking, 1961.

———. "Civil Disobedience." In *Crises of the Republic*. San Diego: Harcourt, Brace & Co., 1972.

———. *Eichmann in Jerusalem: A Report on the Banality of Evil*. New York: Penguin, 1994. Originally published 1963.

———. "The Great Tradition II: Ruling and Being Ruled." *Social Research* 74, no. 4 (2007): 941–954.

———. *The Human Condition*. Chicago: University of Chicago Press, 1998. Originally published 1958.

———. *The Jewish Writings*. Edited by J. Kohn and R. H. Feldman. New York: Schocken, 2007. Originally published 1943.

———. *On Revolution*. New York: Penguin, 1965.

———. *On Violence*. New York: Penguin, 1970.

———. *Les origines du totalitarisme, I, II, III*. Paris: Seuil, 2005. Originally published 1951.

———. *The Origins of Totalitarianism*. London: Andre Deutsch, 1986. Originally published 1951.

———. *Rahel Varnhagen: The Life of a Jewish Woman*. New York: Harcourt Brace Jovanovich, 1974. Originally published 1957.

———. "Some Questions on Moral Philosophy." In *Responsibility and Judgement*, edited by J. Kohn, 49–146. New York: Schocken Books, 2003. Originally published 1965–1966.

———. "Thinking and Moral Considerations." In *Responsibility and Judgement*, edited by J. Kohn, 159–189. New York: Schocken Books, 2003. Originally published 1971.

Ariès, Philippe, and Georges Duby. *Histoire de la vie privée en 5 volumes*. Paris: Seuil, 1985.

Aristotle. *Metaphysics: Books 1–9*. Translated by Hugh Tredennick. Cambridge, MA: Harvard University Press, 1933.

Aryen, Şafak. "Kurumlaşmış Egemenlik" ("Institutionalized Sovereignty"). *Makhmur Women's Charity* (2011).

Aslan, Özlem. "Politics of Motherhood and the Experience of Mothers of Peace in Turkey." MA thesis, Boğaziçi University, Department of Politics and International Relations, 2007.

Asper, Barbara, Hannelore Kempin, and Bettina Münchmeyer-Schöneberg. *Wiedersehen mit Nesthäkchen: Else Ury aus heutiger Sicht*. Berlin: Text Verlag, 2007.

Ataman, Hakan. "Less than Citizens: The Lesbian, Gay, Bisexual and Transgender Question in Turkey." In *Societal Peace and Ideal Citizenship for Turkey*, edited by Rasım Özgür Dönmez and Pınar Enneli, 125–158. Plymouth: Lexington Books, 2011.

Athanasiou, Athena. "Reflections on the Politics of Mourning: Feminist Ethics and Politics in the Age of Empire." *Historein: A Review of the Past and Other Stories* 5 (2005): 40–57.

Aubert, Nicole. *L'individu hypermoderne*. Paris: ERES, 2006.

Aubert, Nicole, and Claudine Haroche. *Les tyrannies de la visibilité*. Paris: ERES, 2011.

Azoulay, Ariella. *The Civil Contract of Photography*. Translated by Rela Mazali and Ruvik Danieli. New York: Zone, 2008.

———. *Civil Imagination: A Political Ontology of Photography*. London: Verso, 2012.

———. "Potential History: Thinking through Violence." *Critical Inquiry* 39, no. 3 (Spring 2013): 548–574.

Bachelard, Gaston. *Air and Dreams: An Essay on the Imagination of Movement*. Translated by Edith R. Farrel and C. Frederick Farrel. Dallas: Dallas Institute Publications, 2011. Originally published 1943.

———. *On Poetic Imagination and Reverie*. Translated by Colette Gaudin. Indianapolis: Bobbs-Merrill, 1971.

Bakhtin, Mikhail. *The Dialogical Imagination*. Austin: University of Texas Press, 1981.

———. "Dostoevsky's Polyphonic Novel and Its Treatment in Critical Literature." In *Problems of Dostoevsky's Poetics*, 5–46. Minneapolis: University of Minnesota Press, 1984.

———. "The Problem of Speech Genres." In *Speech Genres and Other Late Essays*, 60–102. Austin: University of Texas Press, 1986.

———. *Toward a Philosophy of the Act*. Austin: University of Texas Press, 1993.

Bal, Mieke. *Of What One Cannot Speak: Doris Salcedo's Political Art*. Chicago: University of Chicago Press, 2010.

Balibar, Étienne. "Historical Dilemmas of Democracy and Their Contemporary Relevance for Citizenship." *Rethinking Marxism* 20, no. 4 (2008): 522–538.

Barder, Alexander, and François Debrix. "Agonal Sovereignty: Rethinking War and Politics with Schmitt, Arendt and Foucault." *Philosophy and Social Criticism* 6, no. 2 (June 2011): 117–141.

Barthes, Roland. *Camera Lucida: Reflections on Photography*. Translated by Richard Howard. New York: Hill & Wang, 1981.

———. *Mythologies*. Translated by Annette Lavers. New York: Hill and Wang, 1972.

Baykan, Ayşegül, and Tali Hatuka. "Politics and Culture in the Making of Public Space: Taksim Square, 1 May 1977, Istanbul." *Planning Perspectives* 25, no. 1 (2010): 49–68.

Bayraktar, Sevi, and Esen Özdemir, eds. *Feminizm Tartışmaları 2012*. Istanbul: Amargi, 2012.

Bayram, Sidar. "Another Story of the Daily Circulation of *Özgür Gündem*: Affective Materiality." MA thesis, Boğaziçi University, Department of Sociology, 2011.

Baytok, Cemre. "Political Vigilance in Court Rooms: Feminist Interventions in the Field of Law." MA thesis, Boğaziçi University, 2012.

Beasley-Murray, Jon. "On Posthegemony." *Bulletin of Latin American Research* 22, no. 1 (2003): 117–125.

———. *Posthegemony: Political Theory and Latin America Poetics*. Minneapolis: University of Minnesota Press, 2010.

Beck, Ulrich. *Risk Society: Towards a New Modernity*. London: Sage, 1992.

Benhabib, Seyla. "Judgment and Moral Foundations of Politics in Arendt's Thought." *Political Theory* 16, no. 1 (1988): 29–51.

———. "Toward a Deliberative Model of Democratic Legitimacy." In *Democracy and Difference: Contesting the Boundaries of the Political*, edited by S. Benhabib, 67–94. Princeton, NJ: Princeton University Press, 1996.

Benjamin, Jessica. *The Bonds of Love: Psychoanalysis, Feminism, and the Problem of Domination*. New York: Pantheon, 1988.

Benjamin, Walter. *The Arcades Project*. Translated by Howard Eiland and Kevin McLaughlin. Cambridge, MA: Belknap Press of Harvard University Press, 2002.

———. "Theses on the Philosophy of History." In *Illuminations*, translated by Harry Zohn. New York: Schocken, 1969.

Bergner, Daniel. "What Do Women Want?" *New York Times*, January 22, 2009, http://www.nytimes.com/2009/01/25/magazine/25desiret.html?pagewanted=all&_r=0, accessed October 29, 2014.

Berlant, Lauren. *Cruel Optimism*. Durham, NC: Duke University Press, 2011.

Bernstein, Richard. *The New Constellation: The Ethical-Political Horizons of Modernity/Postmodernity*. Cambridge, MA: MIT Press, 1992.

Beşikçi, İsmail. *Devletlerarası Sömürge Kürdistan*. Istanbul: Alan Press, 1990.

Biehl, Janet. "Bookchin, Öcalan and the Dialectics of Democracy." Paper presented at the conference "Challenging Capitalist Modernity: Alternative Concepts and the Kurdish Question," Hamburg, Germany, February 3–5, 2012. http://www.networkaq.net/.

Birdal, Sinan. "Queering Conservative Democracy." *Turkish Policy Quarterly* 11, no. 4 (2011): 119–129.

Blackman, Lisa, and Couze Venn, eds. "Affect." Special issue, *Body and Society* 16, no. 1 (2010).

Bora, Tanıl. "Erkeklik ve Futbol: Beşlik yeme kaygısı." *Kaos GL Dergi*. June 5, 2009.

Bos, Dennis. "Building Barricades: The Political Transfer of a Contentious Roadblock." *European Review of History* 12, no. 2 (2005): 345–365.

Bouchard, Gérard. "Neoliberalism in Québec: The Response of a Small Nation under Pressure." *Social Resilience in the Neoliberal Age*, edited by Peter Hall and Michèle Lamont. Cambridge: Cambridge University Press, 2013.

Bowring, Finn. "Repressive Desublimation and Consumer Culture: Re-evaluating Herbert Marcuse." *New Formations* 75 (2012): 8–24.

Bracke, Sarah. "Subjects of Debate: Secular and Sexual Exceptionalism, and Muslim Women in the Netherlands." *Feminist Review* 98 (2011): 28–46.

Braidotti, Rosi. "Affirmation versus Vulnerability: On Contemporary Ethical Debates." *Symposium: Canadian Journal of Continental Philosophy* 10, no. 1 (Spring 2006): 235–254.

———. "Becoming Woman: Or Sexual Difference Revisited." *Theory Culture and Society* 20 (2003): 43–64.

———. "Embodiment, Sexual Difference, and the Nomadic Subject." *Hypatia* 8, no. 1 (1993): 1–13.

———. *Nomadic Subjects: Embodiment and Sexual Difference in Contemporary Feminist Theory.* New York: Columbia University Press, 2011.

———. *The Posthuman.* London: Polity, 2013.

———. *Transpositions. On Nomadic Ethics.* Cambridge: Polity, 2006.

Brennan, Andrew, and Jeff Malpas. "The Space of Appearance and the Space of Truth." In *Action and Appearance: Ethics and the Politics of Writing in Hannah Arendt,* edited by A. Yeatman, P. Hansen, M. Zolkos, and C. Barbour, 39–52. New York: Continuum, 2011.

Brezina, Corona, ed. *Sojourner Truth's "Ain't I a Woman?" Speech: A Primary Source Investigation.* New York: Rosen, 2005.

Brodsky, Marcelo. *Buena memoria / Good Memory.* Hanover: Sprengel Museum, 2003.

Brown, Wendy. "American Nightmare: Neoliberalism, Neoconservatism, and De-Democratization." *Political Theory* 34, no. 6 (2006): 690–714.

———. *Edgework: Critical Essays on Knowledge and Politics.* Princeton, NJ: Princeton University, 2005.

———. *Regulating Aversion: Tolerance in the Age of Identity and Empire.* Princeton, NJ: Princeton University Press, 2006.

———. "Resisting Left Melancholy." *boundary 2* 26, no. 3 (1999): 19–27.

———. *Undoing the Demos: Neo-liberalism's Stealth Revolution.* New York: Zone Books, 2014.

"Bülent Arınç: 'Kadın herkesin içinde kahkaha atmayacak.'" *CNNTürk,* July 28, 2014, http://www.cnnturk.com/haber/turkiye/bulent-arinc-kadin-herkesin-icinde-kahkaha—atmayacak, accessed October 27, 2014.

Burcu Baba, H. "The Construction of Heteropatriarchal Family and Dissident Sexualities in Turkey." *Fe Dergi* 3, no. 1 (2011): 56–64.

Butler, Judith. *Antigone's Claim: Kinship between Life and Death.* New York: Columbia University Press, 2000.

———. "Bodies in Alliance and the Politics of the Street." *Transversal,* October 2011. http://www.eipcp.net/transversal/1011/butler/en.

———. *Bodies That Matter: On the Discursive Limits of "Sex."* London: Routledge, 1993.

———. "Bodily Vulnerability, Coalitions and Street Politics." In *Differences in Common. Gender, Vulnerability and Community,* edited by Joana Sabadell-Nieto and Marta Segarra. Amsterdam: Rodopi, 2014.

———. *Excitable Speech: A Politics of the Performative*. New York: Routledge, 1997.

———. *Frames of War: When Is Life Grievable?* London: Verso, 2009.

———. *Gender Trouble: Feminism and the Subversion of Identity*. London: Routledge, 1990.

———. *Giving an Account of Oneself*. New York: Fordham University Press, 2005.

———. "How Can I Deny That These Hands and This Body Are Mine." In *Material Events: Paul De Man and the Afterlife of Theory*, edited by T. Cohen, B. Cohen, J. H. Millier, and A. Warminski, 254–273. Minneapolis: University of Minnesota Press, 2001.

———. *Notes toward a Performative Theory of Assembly*. Cambridge, MA: Harvard University Press, 2015.

———. *Parting Ways: Jewishness and Critique of Zionism*. New York: Columbia University Press, 2012.

———. *Precarious Life: The Powers of Mourning and Violence*. London: Verso, 2004.

———. "Precarious Life, Vulnerability and the Ethics of Cohabitation." *Journal of Speculative Philosophy* 26, no. 2 (2012): 134–151.

———. *The Psychic Life of Power: Theories in Subjection*. Stanford: Stanford University Press, 1997.

———. *Undoing Gender*. New York: Routledge, 2004.

Butler, Judith, and Athena Athanasiou. *Dispossession: The Performative in the Political*. Cambridge: Polity, 2013.

Çağlayan, Handan. "From Kawa the Blacksmith to Ishtar the Goddess: Gender Constructions in Ideological-Political Discourses of the Kurdish Movement in Post-1980 Turkey. Possibilities and Limits." *European Journal of Turkish Studies* 14 (2012): 2–23. http://ejts.revues.org/4657.

Caruth, Cathy, ed. *Trauma: Explorations in Memory*. Baltimore: Johns Hopkins University Press, 1995.

———. *Unclaimed Experience: Trauma, Narrative, and History*. Baltimore: Johns Hopkins University Press, 1996.

Cavarero, Adriana. *For More than One Voice: Toward a Philosophy of Vocal Expression*. Stanford, CA: Stanford University Press, 2005.

———. *Horrorism: Naming Contemporary Violence*. New York: Columbia University Press, 2008.

———. *Relating Narratives. Storytelling and Selfhood*. London: Routledge, 2000.

Celep, Ödül. "Can the Kurdish Left Contribute to Turkey's Democratization?" *Insight Turkey* 16, no. 3 (2014): 165–180.

Chamayou, Grégoire. *Théorie du drone* [Drone theory]. Paris: Fabrique, 2013.

Char, René. *Leaves of Hypnos*. Translated by Cid Corman. New York: Grossman, 1973.

Charusheela, S. "Social Analysis and the Capabilities Approach: A Limit to Martha Nussbaum's Universalist Ethics." *Cambridge Journal of Economics* 33 (2009): 1135–1152.

Chouder, Ismahene, Malike Latreche, and Pierre Tévanian. *Les Filles Voilées Parlent* [Veiled girls speak]. Paris: Fabrique, 2008.

Chouliaraki, Lilie. *The Spectatorship of Suffering*. London: Sage, 2006.

Çınar, Alev. *Modernity, Islam, and Secularism in Turkey: Bodies, Places, and Time.* Minneapolis: University of Minnesota Press, 2005.

Claassen, Rutger. "Capability Paternalism." *Economics and Philosophy* 30, no. 1 · (2014): 57–73.

Clastres, Pierre. *Society against the State*. New York: Zone Books, 1989.

Clough, Patricia. *The Affective Turn*. Durham, NC: Duke University Press, 2007.

Cockburn, Cynthia. *From Where We Stand: War, Women's Activism and Feminist Analysis*. London: Zed Books, 2007.

Çolak, Saliha. "Bekar Erkeğe Cinsel İhtiyaç Ödeneği Verilsin." *HaberTurk*, February 3, 2015, http://www.haberturk.com/gundem/haber/1038316-bekar-erkege-cinsel -ihtiyac--odenegi-verilsin, accessed February 5, 2015.

Coleman, Gabriella. "Hacker Politics and Publics." *Public Culture* 23, no. 3 (2011).

Conolly, William E. *The Fragility of Things: Self-Organizing Processes, Neoliberal Fantasies, and Democratic Activism*. Durham, NC: Duke University Press, 2013.

———. *Neuropolitics: Thinking, Culture, Speed*. Minneapolis: University of Minnesota Press, 2002.

Constantinou, Costas M., and Yiannis Papadakis. "The Cypriot State(s) In Situ: Cross-Ethnic Contact and the Discourse of Recognition." *Global Studies* 15, no. 2 (2001): 125–148.

Cornell, Drucilla. "Gender Hierarchy, Equality, and the Possibility of Democracy." *American Imago* 48, no. 2 (1991): 247–263.

Cornwall, Andrea, and Mamoru Fujita. "Ventriloquising 'the Poor'? Of Voices, Choices and the Politics of 'Participatory' Knowledge Production." *Third World Quarterly* 33, no. 9 (2012): 1751–1765.

Courtine, Jean-Jacques, and Claudine Haroche. *Histoire du visage*. Paris: Payot, 1994.

Coy, Patrick C. "The Privilege Problematic in International Nonviolent Accompaniment's Early Decades: Peace Brigades International Confronts the Use of Racism." *Journal of Religion, Conflict and Peace* 4, no. 2 (2011).

———. " 'We Use It but We Try Not to Abuse It': Nonviolent Accompaniment and the Use of Ethnicity and Privilege by Peace Brigades International." Paper presented at the American Sociological Association Annual Meeting, April 2000.

Craps, Stef. *Postcolonial Witnessing: Trauma Out of Bounds*. New York: Palgrave Macmillan, 2012.

Critchley, Simon. *Ethics-Politics-Subjectivity: Essays on Derrida, Levinas, and Contemporary French Thought*. London: Verso, 2009.

Culberson, William. *Vigilantism: Political History of Private Power in America*. New York: Greenwood, 1990.

Das, Veena. *Life and Words: Violence and the Descent into the Ordinary*. Berkeley and Los Angeles: University of California Press, 2007.

———. "Sexual Violence, Discursive Formations, and the State." *In States of Violence*, edited by Fernando Coronil and Julie Skurski, 393–424. Ann Arbor: University of Michigan Press, 2006.

Davis, Angela Y. *Abolition Democracy: Beyond Prisons, Empire and Torture.* New York: Seven Stories, 2005.

———. "Slavery, Civil Rights, and Abolitionist Perspectives toward Prison." In *Are Prisons Obsolete?* New York: Seven Stories, 2003.

Dayan, Colin. *The Law Is a White Dog: How Legal Rituals Make and Unmake.* Princeton, NJ: Princeton University Press, 2011.

D'Cruze, Shani, and Anupama Rao. "Violence and the Vulnerabilities of Gender." *Gender and History* 16, no. 3 (2004): 492–512.

De Lauretis, Teresa. *Technologies of Gender: Essays on Theory, Film, and Fiction.* Bloomington: Indiana University Press, 1987.

Deleuze, Gilles. *Pourparlers.* Paris: Minuit, 1990.

Derrida, Jacques. *Aporias.* Translated by Thomas Dutoit. Stanford: Stanford University Press, 1993.

———. "As If It Were Possible." In *Paper Machine.* Stanford: Stanford University Press, 2005.

———. *The Beast and the Sovereign.* Chicago: University of Chicago Press, 2011.

———. "Et Cetera." In *Deconstructions: A User's Guide,* edited by N. Royle. London: Palgrave, 2000.

———. *Mémoires: For Paul de Man,* Translated by Cecile Lindsay, Eduardo Cadava, Jonathan Culler, and Peggy Kamuf. New York: Columbia University Press, 1989.

———. *Monolingualism of the Other: or, The Prosthesis of Origin.* Translated by Patrick Mensah. Stanford: Stanford University Press, 1998.

———. "Performative Powerlessness: A Response to Simon Critchley." *Constellations* 7, no. 4 (2000): 466–468.

———. *Rogues: Two Essays on Reason.* Stanford: Stanford University Press, 2005.

———. *Specters of Marx: The State of the Debt, the Work of Mourning and the New International.* Translated by Peggy Kamuf. New York: Routledge, 1994.

———. *The Work of Mourning.* Chicago: University of Chicago Press, 2001.

Deutscher, Penelope. "Mourning the Other, Cultural Cannibalism, and the Politics of Friendship: Jacques Derrida and Luce Irigaray." *differences: A Journal of Feminist Cultural Sciences* 10, no. 3 (1998): 159–186.

Diner, Çağla, and Şule Toktaş. "Women's Shelters in Turkey: A Qualitative Study on Shortcomings of Policy Making and Implementation." *Violence against Women* 19, no. 3 (2013): 338–355.

Dorlin, Elsa. "Le grand striptease: Feminisme, nationalism et burqa en France." In *Ruptures post-coloniales,* edited by Mbembe Achille et al., 429–442. Paris: La Découverte, 2010.

———. *Sexe, race, classe: Pour une épistémologie de la domination.* Paris: Presses universitaires de France, 2009.

Douglas, Mary. *Purity and Danger: An Analysis of the Concept of Pollution and Taboo.* New York: Routledge Classics, 1996.

Douglas, Stacy. "Between Constitutional Mo(nu)ments: Memorializing Past, Present and Future at the District Six Museum and Constitution Hill." *Law and Critique* 22, no. 2 (2011): 171–187.

Drichel, Simone, ed. "Vulnerability." Special issue, *SubStance* 42, no. 3 (2013).

Dunne, J. "Beyond Sovereignty and Deconstruction: The Storied Self." In *Paul Ricoeur: The Hermeneutics of Action,* edited by R. Kearney. London: Sage, 1996.

Dutent, Nicolas. "Slavoj Žižek: The Eternal Marriage between Capitalism and Democracy Has Ended." *L'Humanité,* September 2, 2013, http://www.humaniteinenglish.com/spip.php?article2332.

Editör. "Hakikatin Arayışında Jineoloji." *Demokratik Modernite* 5 (April–May 2013): 4–5.

Elden, Asa, and Berna Ekal. " 'Amblem Vakalar' ve Erkek Şiddetinin Görünürlüğü." *Bianet,* July 26, 2013, http://bianet.org/biamag/kadin/145142-amblem-vakalar-ve-erkek-siddetinin--gorunurlugu, accessed February 18, 2015.

Elias, Norbert. *The Society of Individuals.* Edited by Michael Schroter. Translated by Edmund Jephcott. New York: Continuum, 2001. Originally published 1987.

Ellison, Ralph. *Invisible Man.* New York: Random House, 1952.

Elson, Diane, and Ruth Pearson. " 'Nimble Fingers Make Cheap Workers': An Analysis of Women's Employment in Third World Export Manufacturing." *Feminist Review* 7 (1981): 87–108.

"Erdoğan: Kadın-Erkek Eşitliği Fıtrata Ters." *BBC Türkçe,* November 24, 2014. Accessed February 15, 2015, http://www.bbc.co.uk/turkce/haberler/2014/11/141124_kadininfitrati_erdogan.

Erhart, Itır. "Ladies of Besiktas: A Dismantling of Male Hegemony at Inönü Stadium." *International Review for the Sociology of Sport* 48, no. 1 (2013): 83–98.

Evans, Brad, and Julian Reid. "Dangerously Exposed: The Life and Death of the Resilient Subject." *Resilience: International Policies, Practices and Discourses* 1, no. 2 (2013): 83–98.

Evans, Mary. "Feminism and the Implications of Austerity." *Feminist Review* 109 (2015): 146–155.

Eyüpoğlu, O. Meriç. "Şiddet Değil Erkek Şiddeti." *Feminist Politika* 5 (2010): 24–25.

Falk, Richard. *Unlocking the Middle East: The Writing of Richard Falk: An Anthology.* Edited by Jean Allain. New York: Olive Branch, 2003.

Fanon, Frantz. *The Wretched of the Earth.* Translated by Richard Philcox. New York: Grove, 2004.

Fassin, Didier. *Humanitarian Reason: A Moral History of the Present.* Berkeley: University of California Press, 2012.

Fassin, Didier, and Richard Rechtman. *The Empire of Trauma: An Inquiry into the Condition of Victimhood.* Translated by Rachel Gomme. Princeton, NJ: Princeton University Press, 2009.

Feige, Michael. "Jewish Settlement of Hebron: The Place and the Other." *GeoJournal* 53, no. 3 (2001): 323–333.

Feldman, Allen. "Memory Theaters, Virtual Witnessing and the Trauma-Aesthetic." *Biography* 27, no. 1 (Winter 2004): 163–202.

Felman, Shoshana, and Dori Laub. *Testimony: Crises of Witnessing in Literature, Psychoanalysis and History*. London: Routledge, 1992.

Fineman, Martha. "The Vulnerable Subject: Anchoring Equality in the Human Condition." *Yale Journal of Law and Feminism* 20, no. 1 (2008): 1–23.

Fineman, Martha, and Anna Grear, eds. *Vulnerability: Reflections on a New Ethical Foundation for Law and Politics*. Burlington: Ashgate, 2013.

Fırat, M. Efe. Interview by Berkant Çağlar, "LGBT'lerin Gözünden Gezi Direnişi." *Kaos GL Dergi*, June 26, 2013.

Folke, Carl. "Resilience: The Emergence of Perspective for Social-Ecological Systems Analysis." *Global Environmental Change* 16 (2006): 253–267.

Foucault, Michel. *The Birth of Biopolitics: Lectures at the Collège de France, 1978–1979*. London: Palgrave, 2010.

———. *The Care of the Self: The History of Sexuality, Vol. 3*. Translated by Robert Hurley. London: Fontana Press, 1998.

———. *Discipline and Punish: The Birth of the Prison*. New York: Random House, 1975.

———. *The History of Sexuality, Vol. 1: An Introduction*. Translated by Robert Hurley. New York: Vintage, 1990.

———. *The History of Sexuality, Vol. 2*. New York: Vintage, 1990.

———. "Sex, Power and the Politics of Identity." In *Essential Works of Foucault: Ethics, Subjectivity, Truth, Vol. 1*, edited by Paul Rabinow. New York: New Press, 1997.

———. *The Use of Pleasure*. New York: Vintage, 1990.

Foucault, Michel, and Ludwig Binswanger. *Dream and Existence*. Translated by Keith Hoeller. New Jersey: Humanities Press, 1994.

Fraser, Nancy. "Feminism, Capitalism and the Cunning of History." *New Left Review* 56 (2009): 97–117.

———. "Michel Foucault: A 'Young Conservative'?" *Ethics* 96, no. 1 (1985): 165–184.

———. "Rethinking the Public Sphere: A Contribution to the Critique of Actually Existing Democracy." *Social Text* 25/26 (1990): 56–80.

Freud, Sigmund. *The Interpretation of Dreams*. Translated by James Strachey. New York: Basic Books, 2012.

Gambetti, Zeynep. "The Agent Is the Void! From the Subjected Subject to the Subject of Action." *Rethinking Marxism* 17, no. 3 (2005): 425–437.

———. "The Conflictual (Trans)Formation of the Public Sphere in Urban Space: The Case of Diyarbakır." *New Perspectives on Turkey* 32 (Spring 2005): 43–71.

Gandhi, Mahatma. "Part I. Satyagraha: The Power of Nonviolence." In *Gandhi: Selected Political Writings*, edited by Dennis Dalton, 27–94. Indianapolis: Hackett, 1996.

Ghanim, Hunaida. "Bio-power and Thanato-politics: The Case of the Colonial Occupation in Palestine." In *Thinking Palestine*, edited by Ronit Lentin. London: Zed Books, 2008.

Gines, Kathryn T. *Hannah Arendt and the Negro Question*. Bloomington: Indiana University Press, 2014.

Goffman, Erving. *Interaction Ritual: Essays in Face-to-Face Behavior*. Garolen City, NY: Anchor/Doubleday, 1967.

Göker, Emrah. "Kadın Cinayetleri ve 'Veriye Dayalı' Siyaset." *Emrah Göker'in İöker GGker*. March 30, 2013. http://istifhanem.com/2013/03/30/kadincinayetleri/.

———. "Kadınlara Yönelik Şiddetin Azal(tıl)(a)mayışı." *Emrah Göker'in İstifhanesi*, February 9, 2015. http://istifhanem.com/2015/02/09/kadinasiddet/.

Goldman, Emma. "The Tragedy of the Political Exiles." *Emma Goldman Papers*, October 10, 1934, http://ucblibrary3.berkeley.edu/Goldman/Writings/Essays /exiles.html, accessed September 29, 2014.

Goulimari, Pelagia. "A Minoritarian Feminism? Things to Do with Deleuze and Guattari." *Hypatia* 14, no. 2 (1999): 97–120.

Grewal, Inderpal. "Women's Rights as Human Rights: The Transnational Production of the Global Feminist Subject." In *Transnational America: Feminisms, Diasporas, Neoliberalism*, 121–157. Durham, NC: Duke University Press, 2005.

Gül, Zeynel. "Gezi, Temsiliyet, Ütopya." *Bianet*, August 1, 2013.

Gumpert, Lynn. *Christian Boltanski*. Paris: Flammarion, 1993.

Güneş, Cengiz. *The Kurdish National Movement in Turkey: From Protest to Resistance*. London: Routledge, 2012.

Hacıvelioğlu, Fatoş. "Kadın Kurtuluş Hareketini Sınırlayan Bir Dinamik: 'Projecilik.'" *Feminist Politika* 1 (2009): 16–17.

Halavut, Hazal. "Gezi ya da Uzanıp Kendi Yanaklarından Öpmenin İhtimali." *5harfliler*, June 27, 2013, http://www.5harfliler.com/gezi-ya-da-uzanip-kendi -yanaklarindan-opmenin-ihtimali/.

———. "Gezi'nin Kalanı." *Amargi*, September 28, 2013, http://www.amargidergi .com/yeni/?p=245.

Hall, Peter, and Michèle Lamont, eds. *Social Resilience in the Neoliberal Age*. Cambridge: Cambridge University Press, 2013.

Hall, Stuart. "Minimal Selves." In *Identity: The Real Me*, edited by Homi Bhabha et al. London: Institute for Contemporary Arts, 1987.

———. "When Was 'the Post-colonial'? Thinking at the Limit." In *The Post-Colonial Question: Common Skies, Divided Horizons*, edited by Iain Chambers and Lidia Curti, 242–260. London: Routledge, 1996.

Hall, Stuart, and Lawrence Grossberg. "On Postmodernism and Articulation: An Interview with Stuart Hall." In *Stuart Hall: Critical Dialogues in Cultural Studies*, edited by David Morley and Kuan-Hsing Chen. London: Routledge, 1996.

Hancok, Claire. "Spatialities of the Secular: Geographies of the Veil in France and Turkey." *European Journal of Women's Studies* 15, no. 3 (2008): 165–179.

Haraway, Donna. *Modest_Witness@Second_Millennium: FemaleMan_Meets_Onco-Mouse*. New York: Routledge, 1997.

Hardt, Michael, and Antonio Negri. *Empire*. Cambridge, MA: Harvard University Press, 2000.

———. *Multitude: War and Democracy in the Age of Empire*. London: Penguin, 2005.

Haritaworn, Jin, Esra Erdem, and Tamsila Tauqir. "Gay Imperialism: The Role of Gender and Sexuality Discourses in the 'War on Terror.'" In *Out of Place: Silences in Queerness/Raciality,* edited by E. Miyake and A. Kuntsman, 9–33. York: Raw Nerve Books, 2008.

Haroche, Claudine. "L'Invisibilité interdite." In *Les Tyrannies de la Visibilité*, edited by Nicole Aubert and Claudine Haroche, 77–102. Paris: Eres, 2011.

Harvey, David. *A Brief History of Neoliberalism*. Oxford: Oxford University Press, 2007.

———. "Monument and Myth." *Annals of the Association of American Geographers* 69, no. 3 (1979): 362–381.

Hass, Amira. *Drinking the Sea at Gaza: Days and Nights in a Land under Siege*. New York: Henry Holt, 2000.

Hasso, Frances. "Discursive and Political Deployments by/of the 2002 Palestinian Women Suicide Bombers/Martyrs." *Politics of the Modern Arab World: Critical Issues in Modern Politics* 3 (2009): 535–566.

Hazan, Eric. *The Invention of Paris: A History in Footsteps*. Translated by David Fernbach. London: Verso, 2011.

Heer, Jeet, and Kent Worcester, eds. *A Comics Studies Reader*. Jackson: University Press of Mississippi, 2008.

Hemmings, Clare. "Invoking Affect: Cultural Theory and the Ontological Turn." *Cultural Studies* 19, no. 5 (2005): 548–567.

Henderson, Victoria. "Citizenship in the Line of Fire: Protective Accompaniment, Proxy Citizenship, and Pathways for Transnational Solidarity in Guatemala." *Annals of the Association of American Geographers* 99, no. 5 (2009): 969–976.

Hirsch, Marianne. "Connective Histories in Vulnerable Times." PMLA 129, no. 3 (2014): 330–348.

———. *Family Frames: Photography, Narrative, and Postmemory*. Cambridge, MA: Harvard University Press, 1997.

———. *The Generation of Postmemory: Writing and Visual Culture after the Holocaust*. New York: Columbia University Press, 2012.

Hirsch, Marianne, and Leo Spitzer. *Ghosts of Home: The Afterlife of Czernowitz in Jewish Memory*. Berkeley: University of California Press, 2010.

———. "Vulnerable Lives: Secrets, Noise and Dust." *Profession* (2011): 51–67.

Hobsbawm, Eric. *The Invention of Tradition*. Cambridge: Cambridge University Press, 1983.

Hoffmann, Eva. *Time*. London: Picador, 2009.

Honig, Bonnie. "Antigone's Two Laws: Greek Tragedy and the Politics of Humanism." *New Literary History* 41, no. 1 (Winter 2010): 1–33.

———. "The Arendtian Question in Feminism." In *Feminist Interpretations of Hannah Arendt*, edited by Honig. University Park: Pennsylvania State University Press, 1995.

———. *Political Theory and the Displacement of Politics*. Ithaca, NY: Cornell University Press, 1993.

———. "Toward an Agonistic Feminism: Hannah Arendt and the Politics of Identity." In *Feminist Interpretations of Hannah Arendt*, edited by Bonnie Honig. University Park: Pennsylvania State University Press, 1995.

———. "Toward an Agonistic Feminism: Hannah Arendt and the Politics of Identity." In *Feminists Theorise the Political*, edited by J. Butler and W. J. Scott. London: Routledge, 1992.

Honneth, Axel. *La lute pour la reconnaissance*. Paris: Folio, 2013. Originally published 1996.

———. "Recognition: Invisibility: On The Epistemology of 'Recognition.'" *Aristotelian Society Supplementary Volume* 75, no. 1 (July 2001): 111–126.

Huffer, Lynne. "Foucault's Ethical Ars Erotica." *SubStance* 120, no. 38, no. 3 (2009): 125–147.

Hussain, Nasser. "Hyperlegality." *New Criminal Law Review* 10, no. 4 (2007): 514–531.

Hyndman, Jennifer. "Feminist Geopolitics Revisited: Body Counts in Iraq." *Professional Geographer* 59, no. 1 (2007): 35–46.

"İki Eşini Öldüren Adam Seda Sayan'a Konuk Oldu," *Milliyet*, September 3, 2014, http://www.milliyet.com.tr/iki-esini-olduren-adam-seda-magazin-1934550/, accessed October 28, 2014.

Isaac, Jeffrey C. *Arendt, Camus and Modern Rebellion*. New Haven, CT: Yale University Press, 1992.

James, Robin. *Resilience and Melancholy: Pop Music, Feminism, Neoliberalism*. Alresford, UK: Zero Books, 2015.

Jawad, Rania. "Staging Resistance in Bil'in: The Performance of Violence in a Palestinian Village." *Drama Review* 55, no. 4 (Winter 2011): 128–142.

Johnson, Penny. "Violence, Gender-Based Violence and Protection: A Dangerous Decade." In *Dangerous Decade: The Second Gender Profile of the West Bank and Gaza 2000–2010*. Institute of Women's Studies, Birzeit University, http://sites.birzeit.edu/wsi/jupgrade/index.php/publications.

———. "'Violence All Around Us': Dilemmas of Global and Local Agendas Addressing Violence against Palestinian Women, an Initial Intervention." *Cultural Dynamics* 20, no. 2 (2008): 119–132.

"Kadın Cinayetleri 14 Kat Arttı." *Bianet*, September 15, 2011. Accessed February 18, 2015, http://bianet.org/bianet/kadin/132742-kadin-cinayetleri-14-kat-artti.

Kadına Yönelik Şiddetle Mücadele Ulusal Eylem Planı 2012–2015. Ankara: T. C. Aileve Sosyal Politikalar Bakanlığı Kadının Statüsü Genel Müdürlüğü, 2012.

"Kadına Yönelik Şiddet Kadın Örgütlerinin Bilgi ve Deneyimi Yok Sayılarak Son-
landdklarakao." Press release, *Sivil Toplum Geliim Gel Merkezi*, February 16,
2015. http://www.stgm.org.tr/tr/manset/detay/kadina-yonelik-siddet-kadin
-orgutlerinin--bilgi-ve-deneyimi-yok-sayilarak-sonlandirilamaz.

Kandok, Halil. "Spor eşcinsellerin varolmaları için bir fırsattır." *Kaos GL Dergi*,
August 25, 2014.

Kaplan, Morris. *Sexual Justice: Democratic Citizenship and the Politics of Desire.*
New York: Routledge, 1997.

Katrivanou, Vassiliki, and Bushra Azzouz. *Women of Cyprus.* 2009. https://www
.youtube.com/watch?v=cDHoob2s11g, accessed September 29, 2014.

Khanna, Ranjana. "Technologies of Belonging: *Sensus Communis*, Disidentification." In *Communities of Sense: Rethinking Aesthetics and Politics*, edited by
Beth Hinderliter et al., 111–132. Durham, NC: Duke University Press, 2010.

King, Martin Luther, Jr. "I Have a Dream." Speech delivered August 28, 1963.
American Rhetoric: 100 Speeches. http://www.americanrhetoric.com/speeches
/mlkihaveadream.htm, accessed September 29, 2014.

Klein, Naomi. *The Shock Doctrine: The Rise of Disaster Capitalism.* Toronto: Knopf
Canada, 2009.

Klockars, Carl B. "The Dirty Harry Problem." *Annals of the American Academy of
Political and Social Science* 452 (1980): 33–47.

Koğacıoğlu, Dicle. "The Tradition Effect: Framing Honor Crimes in Turkey." *differences: A Journal of Feminist Cultural Studies* 15, no. 2 (2004): 118–152.

Koopman, Sara. "Alter-geopolitics: Other Securities Are Happening." *Geoforum* 42,
no. 3 (2011): 274–284.

———. "Cutting through Topologies: Crossing Lines at the School of the Americas."
Antipode 40, no. 5 (2008): 825–847.

———. "'Mona, Mona, Mona!' Whiteness, Tropicality, and International Accompaniment in Colombia." Latin American Studies Working Paper. University of
British Columbia, Geography Department, 2012.

Koselleck, Reinhard. *Futures Past: On the Semantics of Historical Time.* Translated
by Keith Tribe. New York: Columbia University Press, 2004.

Kristeva, Julia. *Powers of Horror: An Essay on Abjection.* New York: Columbia University Press, 1982.

Küçük, Bülent. "Between Two Rationalities: The Possibility of an Alternative Politics in Turkey." *Jadaliyya*, May 23, 2014.

Kunst, Bojana. *Artist at Work: Proximity of Art and Capitalism.* Winchester, UK:
Zero Books, 2015.

Kuntsman, Adi, and Rebecca Stein. "Digital Suspicion, Politics and the Middle
East." *Critical Inquiry* (2011). http://criticalinquiry.uchicago.edu/digital
_suspicion_politics_and_the_middle_east/.

Laclau, Ernesto. *Emancipation(s).* London: Verso, 1996.

———. "Glimpsing the Future: A Reply." In *Laclau: A Critical Reader*, edited by
Simon Critchley and Oliver Marchart, 279–328. London: Routledge, 2004.

————. *New Reflections on the Revolution of Our Time*. London: Verso, 1990.

————. *On Populist Reason*. London: Verso, 2005.

Laclau, Ernesto, and Chantal Mouffe. *Hegemony and Socialist Strategy: Towards a Radical Democratic Politics*. London: Verso, 1985.

Lagerquist, Peter. "In the Labyrinth of Solitude: Time, Violence and the Eternal Frontier." *Middle East Report* 248, no. 24 (2008).

Lang, Amy, and Daniel Lang/Levitsky, eds. *Dreaming in Public: Building the Occupy Movement*. Oxford: New International Publications, 2012.

Layton, Lynne. "What Divides the Subject? Psychoanalytic Reflections on Subjectivity, Subjection and Resistance." *Subjectivity* 22 (2008): 60–72.

Le Blanc, Guillaume. *L'Invisibilité sociale*. Paris: Puf, 2009.

Lefebvre, Henri. *The Production of Space*. Translated by Donald Nicholson-Smith. Oxford: Blackwell, 1991.

Lefranc, Sandrine, and Sommier Lefranc. "Conclusion." In *Emotions . . . mobilisation!*, edited by Christophe Traïni. Paris: Presses de Sciences Po.

Lentzos, Filippa, and Nikolas Rose. "Governing Insecurity: Contingency Planning, Protection, Resilience." *Economy and Society* 38, no. 2 (2009): 230–254.

Lepore, Jill. *The Secret History of Wonder Woman*. New York: Knopf, 2014.

Le Roux, Wessel. "War Memorials, the Architecture of the Constitutional Court Building and Counter-Monumental Constitutionalism." In *Law, Memory and the Legacy of Apartheid: Ten Years after AZAPO v President of South Africa*, edited by Wessel le Roux and Karin van Marle, 65–90. Pretoria: Pretoria University Law Press, 2007.

Levinas, Emanuel. *Autrement qu'être ou Aud-delà de l'essence*. Paris: Livre de Poche, 2004.

————. *Entre Nous*. Paris: Livre de Poche, 1993.

Libal, Kathryn. "Staging Turkish Women's Emancipation: Istanbul, 1935." *Journal of Middle East Women's Studies* 4, no. 1 (2008): 31–52.

Lifton, Robert J. *Death in Life: Survivors of Hiroshima*. Chapel Hill: North Carolina University Press, 1991.

Loizidou, Elena. "Disobedience Subjectively Speaking." In *Disobedience: Concept and Practice*, edited by E. Loizidou, 108–124. New York: Routledge, 2013.

————. "Dreams of Flying-Flying Bodies." *The Funambulist*, March 8, 2014. http://thefunambulist.net/2014/03/08/the-funambulist-papers-50-dreams-of-flying-flying-bodies-by-elena-loizidou/.

————. *Judith Butler: Ethics, Law, Politics*. London: Routledge-Cavendish, 2007.

Loraux, Nicole. *The Divided City: On Memory and Forgetting in Ancient Athens*. Translated by Corinne Pache with Jeff Fort. New York: Zone Books, 2002.

Lozano-Hemmer, Rafael. "Alien Relationships from Public Space." In *Transurbanism*, edited by Arjen Mulder, 138–159. Rotterdam: V2/NAI, 2002.

Mackenzie, Catriona, Wendy Rogers, and Susan Dodds, eds. *Vulnerability: New Essays in Ethics and Feminist Philosophy*. Oxford: Oxford University Press, 2014.

Madhok, Sumi, and Shirin Rai. "Agency, Injury, and Transgressive Politics in Neo-liberal Times." *Signs: Journal of Women in Culture and Society* 37, no. 3 (2012): 645–669.

Mahmood, Saba. *The Politics of Piety: The Islamic Revival and the Feminist Subject.* Princeton: Princeton University Press, 2012. Originally published 2005.

Mahoney, Liam, and Louis Eguren. *Unarmed Bodyguards: International Accompaniment for the Protection of Human Rights.* West Hartford, CT: Kumarian, 1997.

Mai, Nicola. "Between Embodied Cosmopolitism and Sexual Humanitarianism." In *Borders, Mobilities and Migrations, Perspectives from the Mediterranean in the 21st Century*, edited by V. Baby-Collins, and L. Anteby. Brussels: Peter Lang, forthcoming.

Mansoor, Jaleh. "A Spectral Universality: Mona Hatoum's Biopolitics of Abstraction." *October* 133 (2010): 49–74.

Marchart, Oliver. *Post-Foundational Political Thought: Political Difference in Nancy, Lefort, Badiou and Laclau.* Edinburgh: Edinburgh University Press, 2007.

Marcuse, Herbert. *Eros and Civilization: A Philosophical Inquiry into Freud.* New York: Vintage Books, 1955.

Matonti, Frederike. "Le capital militant." *Actes de le Recherche en Sciences Sociales* 157/158 (2004/2005).

Mattelart, Armand, and André Vitalis. *Le Profilage des populations.* Paris: Le Découverte, 2014.

Mbembe, Achille. "Necropolitics." *Public Culture* 15, no. 1 (2003): 11–40.

———. *On the Postcolony.* Berkeley: University of California Press, 2001.

McAslan, Alastair. *Community Resilience: Understanding the Concept and Its Application.* Adelaide: Torrens Resilience Institute, 2010.

McLaren, Margaret. *Feminism, Foucault, and Embodied Subjectivity.* New York: State University of New York Press, 2002.

McLuhan, Marshall. *The Gutenberg Galaxy: The Making of Typographic Man.* Toronto: University of Toronto Press, 1962.

Meiselas, Susan. *In History.* Edited by Kristen Lubben. New York: International Center of Photography; Göttingen: Steidl, 2008.

———. *Nicaragua.* Edited by Claire Rosenberg. New York: Aperture, 1979.

———. "Return to Nicaragua: The Aftermath of Hope." In *Rites of Return: Diaspora Poetics and the Politics of Memory*, edited by Marianne Hirsch and Nancy K. Miller. New York: Columbia University Press, 2011.

Merleau-Ponty, Maurice. *Le visible et l'invisible.* Paris: Gallimard, 1964.

Miller, Tyrus. "From City-Dreams to the Dreaming Collective: Walter Benjamin's Political Dream Interpretation." *Philosophy and Social Criticism* 22, no. 6 (1996): 87–111.

Minow, Martha. *Between Vengeance and Forgiveness: Facing History after Genocide and Mass Violence.* Boston: Beacon, 1999.

———. "Surviving Victim Talk." *UCLA Law Review* 40 (1992–1993).

Mohanty, Chandra Talpade. "Under Western Eyes." In *Feminism without Borders: Decolonizing Theory, Practicing Solidarity*. Durham, NC: Duke University Press, 2003.

Mor Çatı. *Şiddete Karşı Anlatılar: Ayakta Kalma ve Dayanışma Deneyimleri*. Istanbul: Mor Çatı Yayınları, 2009.

Morris, Rosalind. "Introduction." In *Can the Subaltern Speak? Reflections on the History of an Idea*, edited by Rosalind Morris, 1–18. New York: Columbia University Press, 2010.

Mouffe, Chantal. *Agonistics: Thinking the World Politically*. London: Verso, 2013.

———. "Deliberative Democracy or Agonistic Pluralism?" *Social Research* 66, no. 3 (1999): 745–758.

———. *Democratic Paradox*. London: Verso, 2000.

———. "For a Politics of Nomadic Identity." In *Travellers' Tales: Narratives of Home and Displacement*, edited by George Robertson, et al. London: Routledge, 1994.

———. *On the Political*. London: Routledge, 2005.

———. "Radical Democracy: Modern or Postmodern?" In *The Return of the Political*. London: Verso, 1993.

Nancy, Jean-Luc. *Being Singular Plural*. Stanford, CA: Stanford University Press, 2000.

———. *Corpus*. New York: Fordham University Press, 2008.

———. *The Inoperative Community*. Minneapolis: University of Minnesota Press, 1991.

Narayan, Uma. "Cross-Cultural Connections, Border-Crossings, and 'Death by Culture': Thinking about Dowry-Murders in India and Domestic-Violence Murders in the United States." In *Dislocating Cultures: Identities, Traditions, and Third-World Feminism*, 81–117. London: Routledge, 1997.

Navaro-Yashin, Yael. *Faces of the State: Secularism and Public Life in Turkey*. Princeton, NJ: Princeton University Press, 2002.

———. "'Life Is Dead Here': Sensing the Political in 'No Man's Land.'" *Anthropological Theory* 3, no. 1 (March 2003): 107–125.

———. *The Make-Believe Space: Affective Geography in a Postwar Polity*. Durham, NC: Duke University Press, 2012.

Neocleous, Mark. "Resisting Resilience." *Radical Philosophy* 178 (2013).

———. "Resisting Resilience." In *Social Resilience in the Neoliberal Age*, edited by Peter A. Hall and Michèle Lamont. Cambridge: Cambridge University Press, 2013.

Nixon, Rob. *Slow Violence and the Environmentalism of the Poor*. Cambridge, MA: Harvard University Press, 2011.

Nora, Pierre. "Between Memory and History: Les Lieux de Mémoire." *Representations* 26 (Spring 1989): 7–25.

Ohl, Jessy, and Aaron Duncan. "Taking Aim at Sexual Harassment: Feminized Performances of Hegemonic Masculinity in the First-Person-Shooter Hey Baby."

In Guns, Grenades, and Grunts: First-Person Shooter Games, edited by Gerald Voorhies, Josh Call, and Katie Whitlock. New York: Continuum, 2012.

Okin, Susan Moller. *Justice, Gender and the Family*. New York: Basic Books, 1991.

Öktem, Kerem. "Another Struggle: Sexual Identity Politics in Unsettled Turkey." *Middle East Report*, September 15, 2008.

Özenen, Ferhan. "That Obscure Object of Desire." Paper presented at Homosexualities COWAP Conference, Istanbul, May 31–June 1, 2013.

Özsoy, Hişyar. "Between Gift and Taboo: Death and the Negotiation of National Identity in the Kurdish Conflict in Turkey." PhD diss., University of Texas at Austin, 2010.

Parks, Rosa. "Rosa Parks Interview" (1956). http://www.youtube.com/watch?v=NoOd51tjj8g, accessed April 10, 2013.

Pedwell, Carolyn, and Anne Whitehead, eds. "Affecting Feminism: Questions of Feeling in Feminist Theory." Special issue, *Feminist Theory* 13, no. 2 (2012).

Peteet, Julie. "Male Gender and Rituals of Resistance in the Palestinian Intifada: A Cultural Politics of Violence." *American Ethnologist* 21, no. 1 (1994): 31–49.

Phillips, Adam. *Side Effects*. London: Penguin, 2006.

Phillips, Anne. *Our Bodies, Whose Property?* Princeton, NJ: Princeton University Press, 2013.

Pithouse, Richard. "Producing the Poor: The World Bank's New Discourse of Domination." *African Sociological Review* 7, no. 2 (2003): 118–148.

Pitkin, Hannah. "Justice: On Relating Public and Private." *Political Theory* 9, no. 3 (1981): 327–352.

Poe, Edgar Allan. "A Dream within a Dream." 1849. http://www.poetryfoundation.org/poem/237388, accessed September 30, 2014.

PRIO Cyprus Centre. "'From Solea to Morphou,' Internal Displacement in Cyprus: Mapping the Consequences of Civil and Military Strife." 2011. http://www.prio-cyprus-displacement.net/default.asp?id=781, accessed September 28, 2014.

———. "'Petra,' Internal Displacement in Cyprus: Mapping the Consequences of Civil and Military Strife." 2011. http://wwwe.prio-cyprus-displacement.net/default.asp?id=349, accessed September 28, 2014.

Puig de la Bellacasa, María. "Flexible Girls: A Position Paper on Academic Genderational Politics." In *Gender Studies in Europe*, edited by L. Passerini, D. Lyon, and L. Borghi. Florence: European University Institute and Robert Schuman Centre for Advanced Studies, 2002.

Pulkkinen, Tuija. "Tradition, Gender and Democracy to Come: Derrida on Fraternity." *Redescriptions: Yearbook of Political Thought, Conceptual Change and Feminist Theory* 13 (2009): 103–124.

Quijano, Aníbal. "Coloniality of Power, Eurocentrism, and Latin America." *Nepantla: Views from South* 1, no. 3 (2000): 533–580.

Rancière, Jacques. *Dis-agreement: Politics and Philosophy*. Minneapolis: University of Minnesota Press, 1999.

El Rashidi, Yasmine. "Cairo, City in Waiting." In *Writing Revolution: The Voices from Tunis to Damascus*, edited by Layla Al-Zubaidi, Matthew Cassel, and Nemonie Craven Roderick. London: I. B. Tauris, 2013.

Rawls, John. *A Theory of Justice*. Cambridge: Harvard University Press, 1971.

Reddy, Vasu. "Troubling Genders, Subverting Identities: Interview with Judith Butler." *Agenda: Empowering Women for Gender Equity* 62, African Feminisms 2, no. 1, Sexuality in Africa (2004): 115–123.

Reissner, Larissa. "Hamburg at the Barricades." In *Hamburg at the Barricades and Other Writings on Weimar Germany*, translated by Richard Chappell. London: Pluto, 1977.

Renault, Emmanuel. *Le mépris social*. Paris: Le Passant, 2001.

Rich, Adrienne. *On Lies, Secrets and Silence: Selected Prose 1966–1978*. New York: Norton, 1979.

Richie, Beth E. *Arrested Justice: Black Women, Violence, and America's Prison Nation*. New York: New York University Press, 2012.

Risk Steering Committee. *DHS Risk Lexicon*. Washington, DC: Department of Homeland Security, 2010.

Riuz, Pollyanna. *Articulating Dissent in the Public Sphere*. New York: Pluto, 2014.

Robbins, Trina. *The Great Women Superheroes*. Northampton, UK: Kitchen Sink, 1996.

Rodin, Judith. *The Resilience Dividend: Being Strong in a World Where Things Go Wrong*. New York: Public Affairs, 2014.

Roei, Noa. "Molding Resistance: Aesthetics and Politics in the Struggle of Bil'in against the Wall." *Thamyris/Intersecting* 23 (2011): 239–256.

Ronell, Avital. *Finitude's Score: Essays for the End of the Millennium*. Lincoln: University of Nebraska Press, 1994.

Rose, Jacqueline. *The Last Resistance*. London: Verso, 2007.

Rose, Nikolas. *Inventing Our Selves: Psychology, Power, and Personhood*. Cambridge: Cambridge University Press, 1998.

Ross, Kristin. *The Emergence of Social Space: Rimbaud and the Paris Commune*. Minneapolis: University of Minnesota Press, 1988.

Rothberg, Michael. *Multidirectional Memory: Remembering the Holocaust in the Age of Decolonization*. Palo Alto, CA: Stanford University Press, 2009.

Said, Edward. *The Politics of Dispossession: The Struggle for Palestinian Self-Determination, 1969–1994*. New York: Vintage, 1995.

———. *Reflections on Exile and Other Essays*. Cambridge, MA: Harvard University Press, 2002.

Sakr, Rita. *Monumental Space in the Post-Imperial Novel*. New York: Continuum, 2012.

Salmon, Christian. *Storytelling*. Paris: La Découverte, 2007.

Schiebinger, Londa. *The Mind Has No Sex?* Cambridge, MA: Harvard University Press, 1993.

Scott, Joan W. *The Politics of the Veil*. Princeton, NJ: Princeton University Press, 2010.

Sedgwick, Eve Kosofsky. "Around the Performative." In *Touching, Feeling: Affect, Pedagogy, Performativity*. Durham, NC: Duke University Press, 2002.

Sezer, Sennur. "Antigone Bu Topraklarda Yaşıyor, Her ölünün mezar hakkını savunmak." *Evrensel*, July 30, 2011.

Shalhoub-Kevorkian, Nadera. "Palestinian Women and the Politics of Invisibility: Towards a Feminist Methodology." *Peace Prints: South Asian Journal of Peacebuilding* 3, no. 1 (2010).

Simpson, Audra. *Mohawk Interruptus: Political Life across States*. Durham, NC: Duke University Press, 2014.

Şirin, Mine. "Gezi'de Kürt Olmak." *Bianet*, June 25, 2013.

Sirman, Nükhet. "Kinship, Politics, and Love: Honour in Post-Colonial Contexts—The Case of Turkey." In *Violence in the Name of Honour: Theoretical and Political Challenges*, edited by Shahrzad Mojab and Nahla Abdo, 39–56. Istanbul: Bilgi University Press, 2004.

Smith, Andrea. *Conquest: Sexual Violence and American Indian Genocide*. Boston: South End, 2005.

Smith, Hilda L. "'Cry Up Liberty': The Political Context for Mary Astell's Feminism." In *Mary Astell: Reason, Gender, Faith*, edited by William Kolbrener and Michael Michelson. Surrey: Ashgate, 2007.

Sohrabi, Nader. *Revolution and Constitutionalism in the Ottoman Empire and Iran*. Cambridge: Cambridge University Press, 2011.

Sontag, Susan. *On Photography*. New York: Penguin, 2003.

———. *Regarding the Pain of Others*. New York: Farrar, Straus and Giroux, 2007.

Spaulding, Norman W. "Constitution as Countermonument: Federalism, Reconstruction, and the Problem of Collective Memory." *Columbia Law Review* 103, no. 8 (2003): 1992–2051.

Stamatopoulou-Robbins, Sophia. "The Joys and Dangers of Solidarity in Palestine: Prosthetic Engagement in an Age of Reparations." *CR: The New Centennial Review* 8, no. 2 (2008): 111–160.

Stavrakakis, Yannis. "Chantal Mouffe's Agonistic Project: Passions and Participation." *Parallax* 20, no. 2 (2014): 14–30.

Stein, Rebecca. "Viral Occupation Cameras and Networked Human Rights in the West Bank." *Middle East Research and Information Project*. March 20, 2013. http://www.merip.org/mero/mero032013.

Steinem, Gloria. *Wonder Woman*. New York: Outlet, 1977.

Suleiman, Susan. *Risking Who One Is: Encounters with Contemporary Art and Literature*. Cambridge, MA: Harvard University Press, 1994.

———. "Susan Suleiman Responds to Judith Herman." *WSQ: Women's Studies Quarterly* 36, nos. 1–2 (Spring/Summer 2008): 285–286.

Synman, Johannes. "Interpretation and the Politics of Memory." *Acta Juridica* (1998): 312–337.

Tarhan, Mehmet. "Barikatın LGBT Tarafı." *Kaos GL Dergi*. August 14, 2013.

Tassin, Etienne. "La question de l'apparence." In *Politique et Pensée*, edited by Miguel Abensour, et al., 67–91. Paris: Payot, 1996.

Taylor, Diana. *Disappearing Acts: Spectacles of Gender and Nationalism in Argentina's "Dirty War."* Durham, NC: Duke University Press, 1997.

Tekay, Cihan, and Zeyno Ustun. "A Short History of Feminism in Turkey and Feminist Resistance in Gezi." *Jadaliyya*, November 11, 2013.

Tévanian, Pierre. *Le Voile médiatique. Un faux débat: "l'affaire du foulard Islamique."* Paris: Raisons d'agir éditions, 2005.

Tonstad, Linn Marie. "Touching across Time: Performance as Queer Prophetic Practice." Paper presented at the *Religion, Gender, and Body Politics* conference, Utrecht. February 12–14, 2015.

Torpey, John. *The Invention of the Passport: Surveillance, Citizenship and the State.* Cambridge: Cambridge University Press, 2000.

Traugott, Mark. *The Insurgent Barricade.* Berkeley: University of California Press, 2010.

Tronto, Joan C. *Moral Boundaries: A Political Argument for an Ethic of Care.* London: Routledge, 1994.

Uluğ, Özden Melis, and Yasemin Gülsüm Acar. *Bir Olmadan Biz Olmak: Farklı Gruplardan Aktivistlerin Gözüyle Gezi Direnişi.* Ankara: Dipnot, 2014.

UN OCHA (United Nations Office of the Coordinator for Humanitarian Affairs). "Area C Humanitarian Response Fact Sheet." July 2011. http://www.ochaopt.org /documents/ocha_opt_area_c_fact_sheet_july_2011.pdf.

———. "Displacement and Insecurity in Area C of the West Bank." August 2011. http://www.ochaopt.org/documents/ocha_opt_area_c_report_august_2011 _english.pdf.

———. "Life in a 'Firing Zone': The Massafer Yatta Communities." May 2013. http://www.ochaopt.org/documents ocha_opt_massafer_yatta_case_ study_2013_05_23_english.pdf.

———. "Restricting Space: The Planning Regime Applied by Israel in Area C." December 2009. http://www.ochaopt.org/documents/ocha_opt_fact_ sheet_5_3_2014_en_.pdf.

Van Marle, Karin. "The Spectacle of Post-Apartheid Constitutionalism." *Griffith Law Review* 16, no. 2 (2007): 411–429.

Vanni, Ilaria, and Marcello Tari. "On the Life and Deeds of San Precario, Patron Saint of Precarious Workers and Lives." *Fibreculture Journal* 5 (May 2015). http://five.fibreculturejournal.org/fcj-023-on-the-life-and-deeds-of-san -precario-patron-saint-of-precarious-workers-and-lives/print/.

Varikas, Eleni. *Les rebuts du monde: Figures du Pariah.* Paris: Stock, 2007.

Villa, Dana. *Arendt and Heidegger: The Fate of the Political.* Princeton, NJ: Princeton University Press, 1996.

Virilio, Paul. *L'Accident original.* Paris: Galilée, 2005.

Vlahou, S. "ονειρο . . . ον + ειρω', τα ονειρα." March 9, 2009. http://oneirokritis .blogspot.co.uk/2009/03/blog-post_09.html, accessed August 23, 2013.

Weeks, Kathi. *The Problem with Work: Feminism, Marxism, Anti-work Politics, and Postwork Imaginaries.* Durham, NC: Duke University Press, 2011.

Weizman, Eyal. *Hollow Land: Israel's Architecture of Occupation.* London: Verso, 2006.

Wenzel, Jennifer. *Bulletproof: Afterlives of Anticolonial Prophecy in South Africa and Beyond.* Chicago: University of Chicago Press, 2009.

White, Hayden. "Writing in the Middle Voice." In *The Fiction of Narrative.* Baltimore: Johns Hopkins University Press, 2010.

Williams, Linda. *Hard Core: Power, Pleasure and the Frenzy of the Visible.* Berkeley: University of California Press, 1989.

Williams, Raymond. *Keywords: A Vocabulary of Culture and Society.* Oxford: Oxford University Press, 1985.

Wolfe, Patrick. "Settler Colonialism and the Elimination of the Native." *Journal of Genocide Research* 8, no. 4 (2006): 387–409.

Women for Peace Initiative. *Report on the Process of Resolution: January–December 2013.* Istanbul: WPFI, 2014.

Yalçın-Heckman, Lale. "Kurdish Tribal Organisation and Local Political Processes." In *Turkish State, Turkish Society,* edited by Andrew Finkel and Nükhet Sirman, 289–312. London: Routledge, 1990.

Yazıcı, Göksun. "Velev ki ibneyiz, alışın her yerdeyiz." *Express* 136 (June–July 2013).

Yetkin, Murat. "Occupy Taksim." *Hürriyet Daily News.* June 1, 2013.

Yıldırım, Umut, and Yael Navaro-Yashin, eds. "An Impromptu Uprising: Ethnographic Reflections on the Gezi Park Protests in Turkey." Fieldsights—Hot Spots, *Cultural Anthropology Online.* October 31, 2013. http://culanth.org /fieldsights/391-an-impromptu-uprising-ethnographic-reflections-on-the-gezi -park-protests-in-turkey.

Young, James E. "The Counter-Monument: Memory against Itself in Germany Today." *Critical Inquiry* 18, no. 2 (1992): 267–296.

Young-Bruehl, Elisabeth. *Hannah Arendt: For the Love of the World.* New Haven, CT: Yale University Press, 1982.

Zagajewski, Adam, and Clare Cavanagh. "Try to Praise the Mutilated World." In *Without End: New and Selected Poems.* New York: Farrar, Straus and Giroux, 2002.

Zajović, Stasa. "Feminist Ethics, Women in Black Resistance: Always Disobedient." In *Women for Peace,* 14–36. Belgrade: Women in Black, 2013.

Zerilli, Linda. "The Turn to Affect and the Problem of Judgement." *New Literary History,* forthcoming.

Ziarek, Ewa Plonowska. *Feminist Aesthetics and the Politics of Modernism.* New York: Columbia University Press, 2012.

———. "Feminist Reflections on Vulnerability: Disrespect, Obligation, Action." *SubStance* 42, no. 3 (2013): 67–84.

....

MELTEM AHISKA is Professor of Sociology at Boğaziçi University in Istanbul. She has written and edited a number of books; the most recent is *Occidentalism in Turkey: Questions of Modernity and National Identity in Turkish Radio Broadcasting* (2010). Her articles and essays on Occidentalism, nationalism, social memory, and gender have appeared in various journals and edited volumes. She is currently working on a book project on monumentalization and countermonumentalization.

ATHENA ATHANASIOU teaches social anthropology and gender theory at Panteion University of Social and Political Sciences in Athens. Her publications include *Life at the Limit: Essays on Gender, Body and Biopolitics* (2007); *Rewriting Difference: Luce Irigaray and "the Greeks"* (coedited, 2010); *Crisis as a "State of Exception": Critiques and Resistances* (2012); and *Dispossession: The Performative in the Political* (2013), coauthored with Judith Butler.

SARAH BRACKE is Associate Professor in Sociology at Ghent University and Senior Researcher at RHEA, Center for Gender, Diversity, and Intersectionality, at the Free University of Brussels, Belgium. She has written extensively about gender, religion, secularism, and multiculturalism in Europe.

JUDITH BUTLER is Maxine Elliot Professor in the Department of Comparative Literature and the Program of Critical Theory at the University of California, Berkeley. She is the author of several books, including *Gender Trouble, Bodies That Matter, Undoing Gender, Precarious Life,* and *Frames of War.* Her most recent books are *Parting Ways: Jewishness and the Critique of Zionism* (2012); *Dispossessions: The Performative in the Political* (2013), coauthored with Athena Athanasiou; and *Notes toward a Performative Theory of Assembly* (2015).

ELSA DORLIN is Professor of Social and Political Philosophy in the Department of Political Science at Vincennes-Saint-Denis University (University of Paris VIII) in France. She is the author of several books and articles in French, including *La matrice de la race: Généalogie sexuelle et coloniale de la nation française* (2006) and *Sexe, genre et sexualité,* (2008), and the editor of *Black Feminism: Anthologie du féminisme africain américain 1975–2000* (2007) and *Sexe, race, classe: Pour une épistémologie de la domination* (2009).

BAŞAK ERTÜR is a Lecturer at the School of Law at Birkbeck College, University of London. Her current research focuses on trials, performativity, political violence, and memory. She is the editor of *Manual for Conspiracy* (2011), and the coeditor of *Waiting for the Barbarians: A Tribute to Edward Said* (2008).

ZEYNEP GAMBETTI is Associate Professor of Political Theory at Boğazici University. Her work focuses on collective agency, ethics, and public space. She has carried out extensive research on the transformation of the conflict between the Turkish state and the Kurdish movement, with particular emphasis on space as a vector of relationality. She has also published theoretical articles and book chapters on Hannah Arendt's political thought and subjectivity. She is the coeditor of *Rhetorics of Insecurity: Belonging and Violence in the Neoliberal Era* (2013), and of *The Kurdish Issue in Turkey: A Spatial Perspective* (2015).

REMA HAMMAMI is Associate Professor of Anthropology at the Institute of Women's Studies, Birzeit University. Her most recent publication, "On (Not) Suffering at the Checkpoint: Palestinian Narrative Strategies of Surviving Israel's Carceral Geography," was published in *Borderlands Journal* 14, no. 1 (2015). She serves on the editorial boards of *Arab Studies Journal, Jerusalem Quarterly, Middle East Reports, Development and Change,* and *American Ethnologist.*

MARIANNE HIRSCH is the William Peterfield Trent Professor of English and Comparative Literature at Columbia University and Director of the Institute for Research on Women, Gender, and Sexuality. She is one of the founders of Columbia's Center for the Study of Social Difference. Hirsch writes about the transmission of memories of violence across generations. Her recent books include *The Generation of Postmemory: Writing and Visual Culture after the Holocaust* and *Ghosts of Home: The Afterlife of Czernowitz in Jewish Memory,* coauthored with Leo Spitzer.

ELENA LOIZIDOU is Reader in Law and Political Theory at the School of Law, Birkbeck College. She is the author of *Judith Butler: Ethics, Law, Politics* (2007) and the editor of an essay collection titled *Disobedience: Concept and Practice* (2013). She is on the editorial board of the journal *Law and Critique* and publishes regularly on the blog *Critical Legal Thinking.*

LETICIA SABSAY is Assistant Professor of Gender and Contemporary Culture at the Gender Institute of the London School of Economics and Political Science. She is author of *Las normas del deseo: Imaginario sexual y comunicación* (2009), and *Fronteras sexuales: Espacio urbano, cuerpos y ciudadanía* (2011), and is completing her forthcoming book, *The Political Imaginary of Sexual Freedom: Subjectivity and Power in the New Sexual Democratic Turn.*

NÜKHET SIRMAN is Professor of Anthropology at Boğaziçi University, Istanbul, Turkey. She is the editor (with Andrew Finkel) of *Turkish State, Turkish Society* (1990) and has written numerous articles on gender and nationalism, honor crimes, and forced migration. She is also active in the Women's Initiative for Peace in Istanbul.

ELENA TZELEPIS teaches Philosophy at the University of Athens. She is currently a fellow at the Birkbeck Institute for the Humanities at the University of London. Her publications include *Rewriting Difference: Luce Irigaray and "the Greeks"* (coedited, 2010) and *Antigone's Antinomies: Critical Readings of the Political* (edited, 2014, in Greek).

Note: Italic pages indicate figures.

barricades: Gezi, 98–102, *99–101*, *102–3*; memory of, 112–18; permeability of, 101; resistance and, 97–98

Barthes, Roland, 87, 242

Baytok, Cemre, 217

BDP. *See* Peace and Democracy Party

Beasley-Murray, Jon, 282, 283

Beck, Ulrich, 57

belonging: in Hatoum's art, 146, 148, 153–54, 158; intimate, 259; loss of, 63, 164n1; personhood and, 238–39; precarious, 260–61, 270; in public space, 262; vulnerable, 9, 30; Zionist imaginary of, 189n32

Ben Ami, Amitai, 179

Benhabib, Seyla, 29–30

Benjamin, Jessica, 228

Benjamin, Walter, 112–13

Berlant, Lauren, 62, 64, 288, 293

Bertillon, Alphonse, 239

Beşikçi, İsmail, 194

biopolitics, 11n4, 56, 170, 257, 282–83, 285, 289, 291

bisexuality. *See* LGBTQ activism

blindness, 241–43, 247

Boltanski, Christian, *83*

Bookchin, Murray, 201

Bos, Dennis, 114, 115

Bosnian Muslim civilians, ethnic cleansing of, 261

Bouchard, Gérard, 55

Bowring, Finn, 226

Braidotti, Rosi, 29, 30, 37, 46, 227, 271–72

Brodsky, Marcelo, 84–88, *87*

Brown, Wendy, 62, 137–38, 141, 225

B'tselem, 179

Buena memoria (Brodsky photograph), *87*, 87–88, *88*

Butler, Judith: on accounts of oneself, 140; on Descartes's meditation, 136; on grief, 58, 171, 259; on injurability, 285, 293; on matter, 151; on normative power, 213; on performative agency, 154; on performativity, 297; on politics of the street, 284; on precarity and dependency, 172; on precarity vs. precariousness, 36; on relationality and dependency, 285; on thinking/action, 130–31; on vulnerability and dependency, 58, 279; on vulnerability and resilience, 68–69

Çağlayan, Handan, 199

care, 3, 25, 81, 172–73, 259

Cavarero, Adriana, 20, 152–53, 157, 163

Chang, Candy, *71*

Char, René, 97, 116–17

Charlie Hebdo attack, 245–46

Chong, Albert, *85*

Chouliaraki, Lilie, 280

civil disobedience, 133–36. *See also* resistance

Class Photo, The (Brodksy photo), 87, 87–88

Cluseret, Gustave-Paul, 114

collective resistance. *See* resistance

Connolly, William, 288

Corps étranger (Hatoum video installation), 158–61, *159–60*

counterhegemony, 296

countermemory, 263–65

countermonumentalization, 109–12, 116

Courtine, Jean-Jacques, 236

Critchley, Simon, 125

Cyprus, 122–23

Das, Veena, 36, 218

Davis, Angela, 20

Dayan, Colin, 141

death penalty, 20

Delany, Samuel R., 248

Deleuze, Gilles, 37, 288

Democratic Free Women's Movement (DFWM), 201, 203

Department of Homeland Security, U.S. (DHS), 52

53, 55, 60, 62–63, 68; poster resisting, 70–72, *71*; power of, 52–53; as raw material, 60–61; resistance and, 69–72, 93; security and, 56–59, 65, 70; social, 52, 55–56; subaltern, 60; survival and, 60; temporality and, 63
resistance, 1–2, 3; affective, 282, 283; agonism and, 289–90; belonging and, 148, 151–52; civil disobedience, 133–36; contemporary movements, 249–50; ecstasis of, 116–18; embodied, 146, 171–72, 279, 283–84; exposure and, 26; feminist approach, 3, 20; meanings of, 25–26, 70; monumentalization of, 115–16; nonviolent, 20, 26, 183–84; performativity of, 154; power relations in, 289–90; precarity and, 9; radical democratic politics, 294–97; regulation and, 289–90; resilience and, 69–72, 93; self-defeat in, 174; veils and, 243; violence against, 12; vocabularies of, 97, 164; vulnerability and, 1–2, 6–10, 12–15, 22, 24–27, 53, 116, 155–58, 205, 261, 284. *See also* activism; specific movements
risk management strategy, 52, 57, 59
Rose, Deborah Bird, 172
Rose, Nikolas, 53

Said, Edward, 155
Sandinista insurrection (Nicaragua), 90
Sarkozy, Nicolas, 242
science of women. See *jineoloji*
security: homeland, 52; Oslo Accords on, 168; resilience and, 56–59, 65, 70; risk and, 53, 57; vulnerability in, 81
Sedgwick, Eve, 16–18
September 11, 2001, terrorist attacks, 52, 57–59, 92
Serbia, 256, 260–61, 263–64. *See also* Women in Black movement
settler colonialism, 169–71

sexuality vs. Eros, 225–29. *See also* female desire
sex work, 281
Sezer, Sennur, 196–98
Shulman, David, 169, 178, 184, 186
Sisters, The (Chong photograph), *85*
social resilience, 52, 55–56
Socrates, 129
Somoza regime (Nicaragua), 90
Sontag, Susan, 84
sovereignty, 24, 26, 58, 170, 200, 267–69
spectrality, 264–65
stasis/ek-stasis, 269–71
state violence, 7–8
Stavrakakis, Yannis, 282–83, 292
Stein, Rebecca, 179
Stojanovic, Slavica, 270
Strauss-Kahn, Dominique, 246
subjectivity: dialogical character of, 286; dreams and, 125–32; ethical, 46, 62–63; nomadic, 154–58; permeability and, 10; Wonder Woman and, 249
suffering, 151, 280

Taksim Square (Istanbul, Turkey), 103–9. *See also* Occupy Gezi protests (2013)
Tarhan, Mehmet, 38
Tari, Marcello, 281–82
Taylor, Diana, 88
temporality, 63, 64, 80, 87, 89, 273, 295
Todd, Amanda, 250
transgenderism. *See* LGBTQ activism
transgression: acts of in Turkey, 193–95; gender and, 196–97; vulnerability and, 191–92, 199, 205
Traugott, Mark, 98–99, 113–15
trauma, concept of, 79–80
Truth, Sojourner, 16
Turkey, 7–8, 98, 103–9. *See also* Kurdish movement; Occupy Gezi protests; "Violence against Women" (campaign in Turkey)